Hugh Jackson Lawlor, Church Catholic

The Rosslyn Missal

An Irish Manuscript in the Advocates' Library Edinburgh

Hugh Jackson Lawlor, Church Catholic

The Rosslyn Missal
An Irish Manuscript in the Advocates' Library Edinburgh

ISBN/EAN: 9783744685139

Printed in Europe, USA, Canada, Australia, Japan

Cover: Foto ©ninafisch / pixelio.de

More available books at **www.hansebooks.com**

HENRY BRADSHAW SOCIETY

Founded in the Year of Our Lord 1890

for the editing of Rare Liturgical Texts.

VOL. XV.

ISSUED TO MEMBERS FOR THE YEAR 1898,

AND

PRINTED FOR THE SOCIETY

BY

HARRISON AND SONS, ST. MARTIN'S LANE,

PRINTERS IN ORDINARY TO HER MAJESTY.

THE

ROSSLYN MISSAL

AN IRISH MANUSCRIPT IN THE ADVOCATES' LIBRARY
EDINBURGH.

EDITED BY

HUGH JACKSON LAWLOR, D.D.,

*Professor of Ecclesiastical History in the University of Dublin, and Examining
Chaplain to the Bishop of Edinburgh.*

London.

1899.

LONDON:

HARRISON AND SONS, PRINTERS IN ORDINARY TO HER MAJESTY,

ST. MARTIN'S LANE.

CONTENTS.

PLATES.

ROSSLYN MISSAL, FOL. 64

INTRODUCTION.

THE mass book, which is now printed for the first time, was named by the late Bishop A. P. Forbes,[1] 'in the absence of any more suitable appellation,' the ROSSLYN MISSAL. The title can scarcely be regarded as happily chosen. It suggests a connexion, which did not exist, with the fifteenth century Collegiate Church of St. Matthew, widely known as 'Rosslyn Chapel,' or with its predecessor, the ruins of which remain hard by: and the only claim of our missal to bear it is the fact that it once rested in the library of the Sinclairs at Rosslyn Castle. It might perhaps have been considered, that it was for probably at least an equal period in the Balfour collection at Denmyln, and that since then it has been for a very much longer time in the Advocates' Library, Edinburgh. But though exception may be taken to the name, it has been so generally accepted by recent scholars that confusion would result from the adoption of a new one in its place, and accordingly it appears (under protest) on our title-page.

Still less apt was the name by which the book was known in the seventeenth and eighteenth centuries to the few scholars who were aware of its existence, *Missale* or *Liturgia Sancti Columbani Abbatis*. This designation, I have little doubt, was due to Sir James Balfour, by whose direction it was inscribed on a fly-leaf of the manuscript about the year 1630. As to its meaning, it may perhaps suffice to say that, the names Columbanus and Columba being interchangeable,[2] the former was frequently used in Balfour's day for the Irish Apostle of the

---

[1] *Liber Ecclesie Beati Terrenani de Arbuthnott*, Burntisland, 1864, p. xxxvii.

[2] Reeves' *Adamnan's Life of St. Columba* (Irish Archæological and Celtic Society), Dublin, 1857, p. 6, note h. Olden, *Church of Ireland*, p. 76.

Picts.[1]   His contemporary, fellow-countryman and perhaps
friend, Thomas Dempster,[2] went so far as to transfer to St.
Columbanus the founder of Bobbio what Notker had written
of St. Columba the founder of Iona, and is duly castigated
by Ussher therefor.[3]   With this dual personage, Columba or
Columbanus of Iona and Bobbio, Balfour probably intended to
connect our missal when he named it ' Liturgia S^{ti} Columbani
Abatis (*sic*).'   Very possibly he had nothing to warrant him
in doing so beyond the fact that it is written in an Irish hand.

Description.

The Rosslyn Missal (Advocates' Library, Edinburgh, MS.
18. 5. 19 : formerly A. 6. 12) is a small quarto manuscript
written on vellum in an Irish hand which may be assigned, with
the hesitation usual in such cases,[4] to the end of the thirteenth
or to the fourteenth century.   It consists of fourteen gatherings,
unsigned : the succession of the sheets of each gathering being
indicated by the letters *a*, *b*, *c*, etc., written primâ manu in the
upper or lower corners of the rectos of the first few leaves (see
Plate II).[5]   Most of these letters have, however, disappeared,
having probably been cut away by the binder.   The pages at
present measure 18 centimetres by 13 centimetres, but they
were originally considerably larger.

The punctuation marks most frequently used by the scribe

---

[1] Ussher, *Antiquitates*, cap. xv (*Works*, vi. 229).   So we have ' the feest of saynt
Colûbane ' under June 9 in the *Martiloge in Englysshe* (Ed. Procter and Dewick, 1893,
p. 91).

[2] His *Historia Ecclesiastica Gentis Scotorum* was published in 19 books in 1627,
and reprinted for the Bannatyne Club in 1829.

[3] Ussher, *ubi sup.*

[4] Thompson, *Greek and Latin Palæography*, London, 1893, p. 236 *sq.*

[5] These letters still remain on the following leaves : ff. 4 (*d*), 14 (*d*), 15 (*e*), 22 (*b*),
23 (*c*), 24 (*d*), 25 (*e*—these four in rubric), 43 (*a*), 44 (*b*), 45 (*c*), 47 (*e*), 54 (*b*), 55 (*c*),
56 (*d*), 63 (*a*), 64 (*b*), 65 (*c*), 73 (*a*), 74 (*b*), 81 (*e*), 93 (*e*) : to which we may perhaps
add f. 103 (*c*) but the existence of the letter is here doubtful.   These instances are
sufficiently numerous to determine the purpose of the letters.   The letters *a*, *b*, *c*,
d, *e*, *f* are similarly used to number the sheets of a gathering (xii : see below p. 157,
note), in the C.C.C.O. Missal (Warren's edition, p. 139.)

will be found on the facsimile plates. They are employed very capriciously. A sign resembling an inverted semi-colon (Plate I. l. 7 from end) is usually nearly equivalent to a comma. Another, having some likeness to our semi-colon (Plate II. l. 6 from end), has the value of a full stop or colon. It is often placed after words which introduce a quotation in the oratio recta. The single point is found in place of either of the foregoing, but sometimes it is inserted where there is no break in the sense and where it therefore appears to be quite unmeaning. At other times it is used merely as a sign of abbreviation. A question is indicated by a mark (see Plate I. l. 11) placed over its first word, or at the end, or in both places. Another mark, not always readily distinguished from the last, is frequently found in the epistles (Plate I. ll. 1, 5; Plate II. l. 7 from end) and now and then in the gospels. Without venturing upon a theory as to its meaning we may in future references to it call it an 'inflection mark.' Once or twice in the Canon, another punctuation mark is found, consisting of a point followed by a comma (.,). The hyphen is freely used (*e.g.* Plate II. ll. 4, 5 from end). Such words as *et*, *ut*, and the prepositions are frequently written as if they were part of the following words (Plate I. l. 6, ' desabaa ').

The arrangement of the gatherings may be indicated as follows, the letters denoting the gatherings, the superscribed figures the number of leaves in each.

    I. TEMPORALE (+ *Missa de Inuentione S. Crucis* and *Praefationes*): $a\ b\ c^{10}\ d^{12}\ e\ f\ g^{10}\ h^4$.

    II. SANCTORALE: $i\ j\ k^{12}$.

    III. CANON: l^5 (*l* 1 without conjugate).

    IV. MISSAE VOTIVAE: $m^{10}\ n^8$.

It will be observed that the book is divided into four distinct parts, much on the same principle as the *Liber Eveshamensis*.[1]

---

[1] *Officium Ecclesiasticum Abbatum secundum usum Eveshamensis Monasterii*, ed. H. A. Wilson (Henry Bradshaw Society, vol. vi). London, 1893, p. x. *sq.*

The number of lines of writing in each page is in the first part 22, with the exception of f. 31, which has but 21, and ff. 43–51, which have 23. In the second part gatherings *i k* have 24 (except f. 112, which has 23), gathering *j* 23. The third part has 20 throughout. The fourth part has 21 in f. 118, 20 in ff. 119–127, 22 in ff. 128–132r., 23 in ff. 132v.–135. The portion of the pages occupied by the writing measures about 14 or 14·5 cent. × 8·5 cent. in the first and second parts. In the third and fourth parts the measurement is somewhat greater—15·5 (except gathering *m* : 14·5) × 10.

There is evidently a lacuna at the beginning of the Temporale, probably of one gathering,[1] and apparently also at the end of the volume.[2] But the loss through mutilation seems to be greater than is evident at first sight. The manuscript appears at one time to have contained a pretty full Commune Sanctorum, witness to the existence of which still remains in a large number of places in the Sanctorale in which only the cues of the choral parts and lessons are given,[3] and in two of which there are explicit directions that the full text was to be sought elsewhere,[4] though it does not now appear in the manuscript. The Commune Sanctorum seems to have preceded the Sanctorale.

It must here be mentioned, as somewhat militating against the soundness of this conclusion, that our missal is a mere excerpt from a larger book. This is evident from the fact that the masses for the Vigils of St. Andrew and St. Matthew, and apparently also the services for the Vigil of Whitsunday and the Benedictio Cerei and Benedictio Fontis on Easter Even are implied by rubrics and titles in various places,[5] though these offices do not, and never did, form part of the missal.

---

[1] See note on p. 3, l. 3. [2] See note on p. 95, l. 11.

[3] P. 46, ll. 3, 12, 18; p. 47, ll. 17, 32, 38; p. 52, l. 30 *sq.*; p. 53, l. 18; p. 57, ll. 8, 14; p. 61, l. 13; p. 62, l. 5; p. 68, l. 25; p. 71, ll. 2, 33. See the notes on these passages.

[4] See p. 47, l. 38; p. 53, l. 18, and notes.

[5] See notes on p. 33, l. 10; p. 34, l. 34; p. 41, l. 2; p. 46, l. 2; p. 68, l. 14.

It may perhaps be thought likely that among the parts of his exemplar omitted by our scribe was the Common of Saints. But on the other hand the number of implied references to the Common is so great, that it is scarcely credible that this could have been the case. And it may perhaps be added, that with so meagre a Proper a Common would have been almost a necessity, if the book were to be of practical service.

The present arrangement of the volume is probably in part[1] due to the binder: and it is apparently different from that which the scribe intended. It seems to be the habit of the copyist to represent by cues only such portions of the masses as had been written in full in a *previous* part of the missal. Now in the Missae Votivae the complete text of the introits, grails, commons and lessons is always given. But in more than one instance we have in the Sanctorale, and once apparently in the Temporale, only the first words of forms of which the remainder is to be sought in what is now the fourth part of the missal.[2] The present fourth part would therefore seem originally to have preceded the present first part. This inference is borne out by an inspection of the manuscript. As we pass from the Sanctorale to the Canon we are conscious of a considerable difference in the character of the script—not sufficient, indeed, to point to a change of hand, but enough to suggest want of continuity of work. There is no such contrast between the writing of the latter part of the Canon and the Votive Masses. And again, the last pages of the Masses for the Dead agree more closely in script with those of the earliest remaining pages of the Temporale than do the last of the Sanctorale and the first of the Canon (ff. 112, 113) with each other. For these reasons we conclude that the original order of the parts of the manuscript may have been: I. Canon (gathering *l*). II. Votive Masses (*m n*). [III. Common of Saints]. IV.

---

[1] Only in part, for the recto of fo. 1 has unmistakable marks of having been an outside page before binding.

[2] See p. 33, l. 8; p. 63, ll. 3, 5, 18, 25; p. 66, l. 22; p. 67, l. 4, with notes.

Proper of Time (*a b c d e f g h*). V. Proper of Saints (*i j k*). This, it will be seen, agrees with the arrangement of the Corpus Christi College Oxford Missal, except as to the position of the Common of Saints.

This appears to be the proper place to mention that in the exemplar, or at least in an ancestor, of our manuscript the Canon appears to have been combined with the Mass of the Holy Trinity,[1] the proper Prefaces to have been given with the masses to which they severally belonged,[2] and the Votive Masses differently arranged.[3]

Place of Writing.

Evidence as to the provenance of the manuscript is disappointingly meagre. But such as it is it must now be laid before the reader. We are obliged to take as our starting-point a hypothesis, which cannot be regarded as certainly correct, but which reasons to be given hereafter may show to be at least fairly probable—that the Church for which the Rosslyn Missal was written claimed to be the burial place of St. Patrick.[4] Unfortunately, however, the place of the Saint's burial has been for many centuries, and still is, a matter of controversy. Armagh, Downpatrick and Saul—not to speak of Glastonbury—have claimed the honour. Bishop Reeves[5] argued with much learning for Downpatrick, Dr. Olden,[6] apparently with more reason, and in the light of evidence unknown to the former writer, for Armagh. Happily we need not enter the lists. Our task is not to decide where St. Patrick was buried, but to determine what Church, at the time at which our manuscript was written, was likely to have made the claim for itself; and if this prove to be the case with more than one, to notice the phenomena of the missal which may serve to indicate

---

[1] See notes on p. 73, l. 16; p. 78, ll. 2, 23. [2] See note on p. 44, l. 18.
[3] See note on p. 81, l. 32; p. 82, l. 15. [4] Note on p. 84, ll. 9, 12.
[5] *Antiquities of Down, Connor, and Dromore*, p. 223 *sqq.*
[6] *Proceedings of the Royal Irish Academy*, 3rd ser. vol. ii. p. 655 *sqq.*

to which of the rivals it belonged. We may confine ourselves to Armagh, Downpatrick and its near neighbour Saul.

And first as to Armagh. It is certain that as late as the first half of the twelfth century a claim was made on its behalf. St. Bernard[1] tells us that Armagh was 'sedes illa in qua et uiuens praefuit et mortuus requiescit.' The testimony of Bernard of course reduces itself to that of his friend St. Malachy, who ruled the diocese of Armagh from 1134 till 1136. But after this date there seems to be no evidence that any of the ecclesiastical authorities of Armagh professed that St. Patrick was buried in their city. William of Newbridge indeed says fifty years later[2] : 'Ardmachia ubi esse dicitur prima sedes Hiberniae, propter honorem beati Patricii atque aliorum indigenarum sanctorum, quorum ibidem sacrae reliquiae requiescunt.' The sentence is not perhaps altogether free from ambiguity.[3] But in any case William speaks as an outsider. On the other hand Jocelin, whose *Life of St. Patrick* was published about the year 1183,[4] is most emphatic that Down was the resting place of the Saint,[5] writing, as we may suspect, not without reference to assertions that had been made on behalf of the metropolitan see. Now Jocelin's *Life*, it should be carefully noted, was written by the command of Thomas Archbishop of Armagh (*i.e.* Thomas O'Conor,[7] the sixth successor of Malachy O'Morgair) and Malachy[8] Bishop of Down.[9] And a century later (as the Irish

---

[1] *Vita S. Malachiae*, cap. 10 (Migne *P.L.* clxxxii. 1086.)   See also cap. 29 (col. 1111.)

[2] *De rebus Angliae*, iii. 9.

[3] ' Propter honorem S. Patricii' may mean merely 'on account of the honour due to St. Patrick (its first bishop),' the antecedent of 'quorum' being 'aliorum,' etc.

[4] Ussher, *Britannicarum Eccl. Antiquitates*, cap. xvii (*Works*, vi. p. 372); Reeves, *Antiquities*, p. 228.

[5] See his *Vita Patricii*, 164, 171 (*AA. SS. Boll.*, Mart. t. ii. pp. 578 F, 580 B.)

[7] Tomaltach (Toirdhelbhach) O'Concobhair was Archbishop A.D. 1181–1201 (*Annals of Loch Cé*, Rolls Edition, 1871, vol. i. pp. 163, 219.)

[8] This Malachy (to be distinguished from his more eminent predecessor just mentioned, who was Archbishop of Armagh, A.D. 1134-1136, and Bishop of Down, A.D. 1136-1148) was Bishop A.D. 1176-1201.

[9] *Vita S. Patricii*, Prologus, p. 540 D.

Annalists[1] significantly inform us under the year 1293), probably within a few years of the date of our missal, Nicholas Mac
Maelisa, Archbishop of Armagh, 'the most godly and devout
ecclesiastic of his time in Ireland' discovered, disinterred, and
enshrined the remains of St. Patrick, along with those of St.
Columba and St. Brigid, not at Armagh, but at Saul.[2] We
might call a later witness,[3] but it is needless. When such things
as these happened we are surely warranted in the inference that
if not by Thomas O'Conor, at least by Nicholas Mac Maelisa,
the pretence that the Primates of Armagh were the guardians
of the body of the Apostle of Ireland was given up.

But indeed that our missal did not belong to Armagh seems
clear enough from internal evidence. The manuscript supplies
two masses both of which are headed *Pro episcopo*.[4] It would be
surprising, in a missal which is but an excerpt from a larger book,
if these two masses were mere alternatives.[5] And in fact they
are not. The second is really a mass for an archbishop. There
is thus a mass *pro archiepiscopo* in addition to that *pro episcopo*.
This suits the case of Downpatrick or Saul, both of them in the
diocese of Down, which formed part of the Province of Armagh ;
but it is scarcely conceivable at Armagh, the archiepiscopal city.

Armagh being excluded, we have therefore to decide between
Saul and Downpatrick.

External evidence does not help us much. But it is worth
while to consider—for whatever it may count—the comparative
unlikelihood that we have in our hands a service-book from the
poor and struggling house at Saul rather than from its important

---

[1] *Four Masters, Annals of Loch Cé, Annals of Ulster.*
[2] Mr. O'Laverty, indeed, is disposed to identify this Saul with the Sabhall at
Armagh (see Reeves, *Antiquities*, p. 220 *sq.*), and thinks that the reference is to stray
relics, not to the bodies of the saints. *Dioceses of Down and Connor*, vol. i. p. 235.
This, however, is but a convenient way out of a difficulty, and is opposed to the
evidence. The Saul in question was near the sea. See the Book of Armagh,
f. 15b.2. (Stokes, *Tripartite Life*, vol. ii. p. 332.)
[3] Primate Mey (A.D. 1451) : *Reg. Mey* iii. p. 357, quoted by Reeves, *Antiquities*
p. 229.
[4] Page 84 *sq.*   [5] Compare note on p. 89, l. 16.

and wealthy neighbour and rival. The monastery at Saul, if I read the records correctly,[1] would seem to have had a precarious existence from 1170 till 1293; and, though the invention of the Three Patrons in the latter year seems to some extent to have revived it, the house was never again affluent or powerful.[2]

We stand perhaps on firmer ground when we turn once more to internal evidence. But in order to make its import clear, it is necessary to relate in some detail the history of Down Cathedral for some eight or ten years. In the third quarter of the twelfth century this Church was presided over by a chapter of secular canons, its dedication was to the Holy Trinity, and an image of the Trinity stood over its high altar.[3] In 1177 John de Courcey invaded Ulster, and in the same year captured the city of Down, as it was then called. Henceforth it was his head-quarters. Immediately afterwards he made extensive ecclesiastical changes in the district of which it was the centre,[4] and a few years later he turned his attention to the Cathedral Church. The old tradition that this Church was the last resting place of St. Patrick (which had no doubt slumbered during the episcopate of Malachy O'Morgair, 1136–1148) was revived. The Cathedral received a fresh dedication to St. Patrick; Jocelin was employed to write a life of the saint, in which it was set forth that he was buried at Down; and the image of the Holy Trinity was dis-

---

[1] In 1170 the Abbat and convent were driven out and deprived of all their property (*Four Masters, Ann. Ult.*) We hear nothing of Saul from the Annalists between this date and the invention mentioned in the text, which may well have been an attempt to recover its former fame and fortune. The only recorded events in its history between 1170 and 1293 will be mentioned below (p. xxii. note [2]).

[2] In 1296 the Abbat and monks inform the King that their property had been alienated ' in diminucionem elemosinarum et dispersionem canonicorum. (Prynne, *Records*, iii. p. 688, quoted by Reeves, *Antiquities*, p. 40). In 1306 it is not thought worthy of mention among the Religious Houses in the Taxation of Down, Connor, and Dromore (Reeves *loc. cit.*).

[3] The documents on which the statements in this and some of the following sentences are founded have been collected by Reeves, *Antiquities of Down, Connor, and Dromore*, pp. 174 *sq.*, 229.

[4] As, for instance, at Neddrum in 1178 (Reeves, *Antiquities*, p. 190 *sqq.*)

placed in favour of one of the new patron of the Church. After an interval of some three years (1183)[1] the bishop, Malachy, saw a vision in which the grave, hitherto unknown, of St. Patrick, St. Brigid and St. Columba was pointed out to him. The three bodies were duly discovered lying side by side, and were translated with great pomp into a more suitable part of the edifice. From that time onwards the unvarying Anglo-Norman tradition, which has since become the popular belief, was that St. Patrick rested in Down Cathedral. And from the same period dates the modern name of the city—Downpatrick. But this was not all. In 1183 the secular canons were dismissed and a convent of Benedictine monks was brought from St. Werburgh's, Chester, to take their place. These were to form the chapter of the Cathedral, presided over by the Bishop as *ex officio* Abbat, and the Dean as *ex officio* Prior, the constitution being modelled on those of Winchester and Coventry.[2]

The main purpose of the revival of the cultus of St. Patrick at Down appears to have been to gain favour with the native Irish. De Courcey posed as 'Sancti Patricii specialissimus dilector et venerator.'[3] But however successful this policy may have been as a whole, in one respect it failed. De Courcey was accused of sacrilege[4] for having removed the image of the Trinity. Now an easy way to rebut this charge would have been to institute frequent devotions to the Holy Trinity.[5] And the Rosslyn Missal exhibits phenomena which are not inconsistent with— which perhaps point towards—the inference that it belonged to

---

[1] The date is given by Giraldus Cambrensis, *Topographia Hiberniae*, iii. 18 (*Works*, Rolls edition, vol. v. p. 164).

[2] See the instrument of Malachy, given by Reeves, *Antiquities*, p. 163; and, for the constitution of Winchester and Coventry, Dugdale, *Monasticon*, edd. 1817-1830, 1846, vol. i. pp. 194, 200, vol. iii. p. 178.

[3] Jocelin, *Vita S. Patricii*, Prologus, p. 540D.

[4] Pembridge's *Annals, sub. ann.* 1204 (*Chartularies of S. Mary's Abbey, Dublin*, etc., ed. J. T. Gilbert, Rolls Series, vol. ii. p. 309).

[5] It is perhaps not fanciful to suppose that it is with some such object in view that Jocelin in the *Vita S. Patricii* so frequently alludes to the saint as pre-eminently a preacher of the doctrine of the Holy Trinity. See, for example, §§ 1, 11, 14, 65.

a Church where the Missa de S. Trinitate, or at least the Trinity Preface, was in constant use.[1]

Again, with nothing to guide us but the internal evidence of our missal we might have hesitated to determine whether it was intended for monastic or secular use.[2] But if it is a monastic book it can scarcely be supposed to have been written for such a monastery as that of Saul. The Abbat is not once mentioned in its pages. The Bishop everywhere takes the part in the services which the Abbat might have been expected to assume : in his absence his place is taken, in one case at least, by the Dean.[3] There is no Missa pro abbate, though Missae pro episcopo and pro archiepiscopo are provided : and, so far as we can judge, neither was there a Missa pro abbate defuncto, though the necessary collects for a deceased bishop and a deceased priest are found. All this may easily be explained in the case of a Down missal, for at Down the Bishop was Abbat and the Dean Prior : but Saul had an Abbat distinct from the Bishop.[4]

As the result of this argument we may perhaps give a somewhat hesitating assent—the more hesitating on account of the doubt which envelopes the assumption on which the reasoning of this section is based—to the theory that our missal was written for the Cathedral Church of St. Patrick at Down : the theory receives support from further evidence which must be reserved for the next section.

Origin.

I propose in this section to determine, as far as this is possible, the ancestry of the Rosslyn Missal. I begin by quoting two documents, one of which has been very generally misunderstood, the other as generally overlooked. The first of these

---

[1] See note on p. 73, l. 16.
[2] The mention of ‘fratres,’ p. 48, l. 24 is not decisive : see notes.
[3] Page 48, l. 27.
[4] See, for example, *Annals of Four Masters*, sub. ann. 1170.

is a portion of the seventh canon of the Synod of Cashel (1172). It runs as follows[1] :—

'Septimo, quia cum bona confessione decedentibus, et missarum et vigiliarum exhibitione, et in more sepeliendi, obsequium debitum persolvatur. Itaque omnia divina, ad instar sacrosanctae ecclesiae, juxta quod Anglicana observat ecclesia, in omnibus partibus ecclesiae amodo tractentur.'

It will be observed that nothing is said or implied about the Sarum or any other special use of the Church of England.[2] The terms of the canon would be fully satisfied by the introduction into Ireland of English service-books of any use, or from any place : the one essential was that the existing Irish books should be superseded, and superseded, we may add, not by Roman or continental books, as they might have been earlier in the century by Gillebert of Limerick[3] or Malachy of Armagh, but by the books then in use in the English Church.

This enactment received but scanty attention throughout Ireland, especially in the north, but it was faithfully obeyed by De Courcey ; both which facts are proved sufficiently for our purpose by a passage in Jocelin's *Vita S. Patricii.* Commenting on a vision of St. Patrick, in which, after a period of darkness, he saw Ireland overspread by a light which rose from the north, he says[4] :—

'Lucem uero prius ex aquilonari parte exorientem . . . Hibernigenae [S. Celestinum Machinensem archipraesulem totiusque

---

[1] Giraldus Cambrensis, *Expugnatio Hiberniae*, i. 34 (*Works*, Rolls Series, vol. v, p. 283); Wilkins, *Concilia*, I. 473.

[2] The contrary has been often assumed. See, e.g., G. T. Stokes, *Ireland and the Anglo-Norman Church*, London, 1889, p. 197 ; Olden, *The Church of Ireland*, 2nd ed., London, 1895, p. 248. It may be doubted whether the Sarum was the predominant use in England at this time :. H. B. Swete, *Church Services and Service-Books before the Reformation*, London, 1896, p. 13 *sqq.* Cf. W. H. Frere, *The Use of Sarum*, I. *The Sarum Customs as set forth in the Consuetudinary and Custumary*, 1898, p. xxxvii.

[3] Gillebert's aim was ' ut diuersi et schismatici illi ordines, quibus Hibernia pene tota delusa est, uni Catholico *et Romano* cedant officio.' Ussher, *Veterum Epistolarum Hibernicarum Sylloge*, Ep. 30 (*Works* iv. 500).

[4] *Vita S. Patricii*, 154 (*AA. SS. Boll.* Mart. vol. ii. p. 575F).

Hiberniae primatem asserunt, . . . seu]¹ S. Malachiam,² qui prius in Dunensi ecclesia postmodum in Ardmachana metropoli praefuit et Hiberniam ad Christianae legis statum reduxit. E contra Anglici lucem illam arbitrantur ascribendam suo aduentui, eo quod tunc ecclesia uidebatur suo iudicio in meliorem statum prouehi ; religio plantari ac propagari, atque *sacramenta ecclesiastica et Christianae legis instituta ritu competentiori obseruari.'*

De Courcey, it is plain, introduced new service-books into Down. Whence were they derived? In the very year, it would seem, in which these words were penned the Benedictine colony from Chester took possession of the Cathedral. What more natural than to suppose that they brought with them their books? Two centuries previously Benedictine monks from Abingdon under their Abbat-Bishop Ethelwold, displaced the secular canons of Winchester : and their new Church received from them the Abingdon Troper.³ It is likely enough that the Benedictines of St. Werburgh's, under their Abbat-Bishop Malachy, introduced into Down a St. Werburgh's missal. It is, in fact, difficult to imagine what else could have happened. New service-books were certainly introduced. That they were English books the decree of the Synod of Cashel leaves no room for doubt. The words of Jocelin make it equally certain that such books were in use in the neighbourhood of Down only in those Churches, such as Neddrum and possibly Inch, which had since 1178 come under English influence. Now if the Benedictines of St. Werburgh's brought a missal with them, it is natural to assume that our missal is its descendant.

And this hypothesis is confirmed by an examination of the contents of the missal itself. Let us turn first to the service

---

¹ The words enclosed in brackets are found in Ussher's quotation of the passage, *Antiquitates*, cap. xvii (*Works* vi. 480).

² The ordinary text adds here ' asserunt.'

³ W. H. Frere, *The Winchester Troper* (Henry Bradshaw Society, vol. viii.), London, 1894, p. xxix.

for the Blessing of the Candles on February 2. Here we find a service used widely in the Province of Canterbury in the twelfth century,[1] with some slight alterations, evidently made with the view of adapting it to local use—one of them being the addition of a rubric which is found *totidem verbis* in a Besançon Pontifical of the eleventh or twelfth century. The custom which this rubric sanctions—of blessing the candles at the Lady Altar—seems to have been both comparatively early and largely confined to the Benedictine order. It is clear that at least this part of our book is derived from an English source, and is contemporary with John de Courcey. This one fact is almost sufficient, if not to decide in favour of Downpatrick as the place where the Rosslyn Missal was written, at least to exclude Saul. If the latter monastery had anything more than a nominal existence in the last quarter of the twelfth century, we have every reason to believe that it was bitterly opposed to the English innovations, and was not in the least degree likely to have adopted English forms of service.[2]

---

[1] See notes on p. 48 *sqq.* It will be remembered that Chester was in the twelfth century in the Province of Canterbury. It lay within the limits of a diocese the see of which was sometimes at Lichfield, sometimes at Coventry, and sometimes at Chester (Dugdale, *Monasticon Anglicanum*, ed. 1846, vol. ii. p. 370). Among the suffragans of Canterbury addressed in a letter from Pope Alexander III. (Wilkins, *Concilia*, vol. i. p. 459) is the Bishop of Chester, and in a council held at Winchester in 1072, and confirmed at Windsor in the same year, the Province of York was defined as extending 'a terminis Lichifeldensis episcopi et Humbrae magni fluvii usque ad extremos Scotiae fines.' *Ib.* p. 325. In fact the city of Chester was not transferred to York until the year 1542 : Dugdale, *Monasticon*, vol. ii. p. 397.

[2] For more than one hundred and twenty years after it was plundered in 1170 Saul is not mentioned by the chroniclers. And during the same period there are, so far as I know, but two notices of it in contemporary documents. On both occasions its Abbat appears as acting in opposition to the English and their principal religious establishment at Down. In 1266 the Abbat of Saul, with others, disputed the validity of the election of a bishop, on the ground that the choice did not rest with the Benedictine convent of St. Patrick's, Down. (Theiner, *Vetera Monumenta*, No. 250, p. 100.) In 1273, the abbacy being vacant, the canons elected thereto, without royal licence, Molys (an Irishman if we may judge from his name) prior of Bangor, Co. Down. He was ejected, and in his room the Bishop of Down, having obtained licence from the secular power, appointed Galfrid de Stoks, Canon of Caerleon.

But this is not the only part of the missal which is as old as the twelfth century. The Antiphonale Missarum, from which the choral portions of the masses in the temporale were derived, was evidently of early date. In six cases[1] we find complete sets of offertory verses agreeing almost exactly with those in the Gregorian Antiphonary. Single verses are indeed occasionally found with the offertory in later English books, such as those of Westminster and Salisbury : but I am not aware that, except in our missal, an offertory survives with its verses complete after the twelfth century.[2]

Again, the collect for St. Patrick's Day, which seems to be based on an earlier composition, was apparently reduced to its present form not later than the twelfth century, possibly by Jocelin.[3] The mass for January 1 had in the exemplar, or an ancestor, of our missal its earlier title, which has been clumsily altered.[4] The form *Suscipe sancta trinitas* omits the name of St. John Baptist, which is usually found in later books.[5] And one preface is preserved which is not among those sanctioned by the Council of Westminster in 1175.[6] To these indications of early date we may perhaps add the fact that in several places mention is made of the Roman stations.[7] The stations

---

(Prynne, *Records*, iii. p. 130 *sq.*) The only known patron of the monastery in the thirteenth century was Nicholas Mac Maelisa (see above p. xvi), ' one of the greatest opposers of the English,' says O'Donovan (*Annals of Four Masters*, Dublin, 1848, vol. i. p. 458), ' that ever governed the see of Armagh '—' the most godly and devout ecclesiastic of his time in Ireland,' say the Annalists (*sub. ann.* 1299 *al.* 1303), who with one consent ignore Downpatrick from the moment it came into English hands. See further, R. King, *A Primer of the History of the Holy Catholic Church in Ireland*, Dublin, vol. ii. (4th ed. 1868) p. 627 *sq.*, vol. iii. (3rd ed. 1851) pp. 1109, 1114 *sq.*

[1] Christmas Day, Easter Day, Low Sunday, Vigil of Ascension, Ascension Day, Whitsunday, and we may perhaps add (though only one verse remains here) the first Sunday in Lent. See notes on p. 3, l. 6; p. 19, l. 29; p. 37, l. 13; p. 38, l. 13; p. 39, l. 12; p. 40, l. 19; p. 42, l. 31.

[2] Even the very early cues in the margin of the Leofric Missal have the verses of the offertory only for Easter Day and Advent Sunday. (Warren's ed. pp. 99, 126.)

[3] See note on p. 55, l. 11.　　　　　[4] Page 7, l. 14, with note.

[5] See p. 78, l. 6, and note.　　　　　[6] Page 80, l. 22.

[7] See p. 6, l. 14; p. 14, l. 10; p. 15, l. 16, with notes.

are frequently recorded in the tenth century Missal of Leofric, but in the early part of the twelfth century they are but seldom noticed in the Missal of Robert of Jumièges, and I have not observed them in any of the later English books which have been printed.[1]

But we may call in palæography to our assistance. The Rosslyn Missal, though evidently of English origin,[2] was transcribed from an Irish exemplar which was probably in existence for a considerable time before it was copied by our scribe, and which we may assume to have belonged to the Church in which he wrote. The former fact is evident from the character of many of the errors of which he has been guilty, while the age of the copy upon which he worked gives a simple reason for the extraordinary number of his blunders. We cite here but one instance, the common but peculiarly Irish symbol for *autem* (ƕ)[3] has several times been mistaken for h̄ (*haec*) or ħ (*hoc*) or for the somewhat similar symbol for *enim*.[4] This indicates that the exemplar was in an Irish hand. And it seems also to show that the interval between the writing of the exemplar and the date of the Rosslyn Missal was sufficient to allow of the symbol having almost passed out of use. Our scribe himself uses it but once, and on that one occasion he may perhaps be supposed to have simply reproduced it from the manuscript which lay before him. If the Irish missal upon which the scribe worked was already so antiquated in the fourteenth century, the English manuscript from which it was in its turn copied may well have been written in the days of John de Courcey.

But a discussion which has been necessarily lengthy may now be brought to an end. Its result has perhaps been to make

---

[1] For another mark of early date, see note on p. 43, l. 12.

[2] The only mass which has any trace of Irish origin gives an indication that its source was different from that of the rest of the book. See note on p. 65, l. 6.

[3] This symbol is not confined to Irish manuscripts, though very rare elsewhere.

[4] Page 3, l. 10; p. 28, l. 12, and, in the Appendix, Exod. xii. 5; (Joh. vi. 40); 1 Cor. ix. 25. Still more frequent is the converse error: Luc. xviii. 36; Joh. iii. 9, xviii. 13; Rom. x. 16; 1 Cor. x. 1; Eph. v. 5.

the conclusion probable that the missal here printed is descended from one which belonged to the Benedictine house of St. Werburgh, Chester, in the twelfth century, and that it preserves some of its characteristic features.

Later History.

It appears that our missal was but little, if at all, used at the altar. For proof of this statement we have recourse, not so much to the many errors which the carelessness and ignorance of the scribe, together with the probable difficulty of deciphering his exemplar, have produced, as to the fact that some of them must have been corrected at a very early date if the book was to serve any practical purpose. In two masses one or more of the collects have been omitted[1]; the Proper Prefaces are arranged in such a way as to be most perplexing to anyone using the book, and are without titles[2]; and in one case *Qui pridie* is immediately connected with the clause *Hanc igitur* of the Canon,[3] without any indication of the intervening *Quam oblationem*. None of these errors have been corrected by later hands. As negative evidence it may be mentioned that there is no mark of the Canon having been read more frequently than other parts of the book. And finally one gathering of the manuscript has been left unfinished.[4]

The conjecture[5] seems not an unreasonable one that shortly after the manuscript was written it was carried off from Downpatrick by one of the followers of Edward Bruce in 1316, and that it subsequently found its way into Scotland with the

---

[1] Pages 11, 78.   [2] See note to p. 44, l. 18.

[3] Page 27, l. 23.

[4] Ff. 73–76: see note on p. 42, l. 26. It may be added that some of the fourteenth century scribblings enumerated below, p. xxxi *sq.*, would hardly have been placed in the margin while the book was in use.

[5] Reference may here be made to a paper entitled *Notes on the History of the Library of the Sinclairs of Rosslyn*, published in the *Proceedings of the Society of Antiquaries of Scotland*, vol. xxxii. p. 90 *sqq.*, in which the evidence for the statements made in this paragraph is given in detail.

remnant of his army. There it was probably deposited in some monastic library. It may have owed its preservation during the troubles of the sixteenth century to the action of Henry Sinclair, Bishop of Ross, or of his nephew, Sir William Sinclair, Justiciar of Laudone, and in any case was probably added to the library collected by the latter at Rosslyn Castle, Midlothian, in 1560 or a few years later. It was certainly at Rosslyn Castle between 1582 and 1612, as it has been signed by the Sir William Sinclair, son of the last named, who held the estates during that period. About 1630 the Rosslyn Library was for the most part dispersed, and our missal, already mutilated, passed, with other books, into the hands of the well-known collector Sir James Balfour, and was placed in his library at Denmyln, Fifeshire. It then received its present binding, and the title ' Liturgia S^{ti} Columbani Abatis (*sic*)' which is inscribed on a fly-leaf. The Denmyln collection was sold by auction in 1699, the greater part of it being acquired by the Faculty of Advocates : among the rest our missal, which was purchased for the not very extravagant sum of three shillings. In the Advocates' Library the book has remained ever since.

Some time before 1729 the manuscript was examined by Thomas Innes, who noticed the similarity of the script to that of the Drummond Missal, regarding both manuscripts as of the eleventh century.[1] Subsequently some other antiquaries appear to have inspected the missal and to have assigned it to the tenth century, but I am not aware that their researches have been published. In 1864, Bishop A. P. Forbes again drew attention to the book, in the introduction to his edition of the *Arbuthnott Missal*, in which he printed a list of the services contained in it, and the Collect for St. Patrick's Day.[2] He believed it to be 'perhaps not so old as the fourteenth century.' Mr. David Laing somewhat later studied the volume, but did not publish

---

[1] *A Critical Essay on the Ancient Inhabitants of the Northern parts of Britain or Scotland*, by Thomas Innes, London, 1729, vol. ii. p. 565. Historical MSS. Commission, *First Report*, p. 118.

[2] *Liber Ecclesie Beati Terrenani de Arbuthnott*, Burntisland, 1864, pp. xxxvi-xl.

his results. Mr. F. E. Warren, in his edition of the Irish Missal at Corpus Christi College, Oxford (1879), gave a collation of the Canon,[1] and subsequently (1881) printed the masses for St. Brigid and St. Patrick in his *Liturgy and Ritual of the Celtic Church*.[2] And finally Dr. J. Wickham Legg collated the Temporale and Sanctorale in the notes to his edition of the *Westminster Missal* (1897, Henry Bradshaw Society, vol. xii.)

Relation between the Drummond, Corpus Christi College, Oxford, and Rosslyn Irish Missals.

The notes will serve to some extent to show the very close connexion which exists between the Rosslyn and Corpus Missals, and the somewhat less intimate relationship between them and the Drummond manuscript. Some of the results may perhaps with advantage be stated here. The matter may be regarded from three standpoints: with reference to (1) the text of the mass-collects and Canon; (2) the rubrics; (3) the choral portions of the masses. Let us examine these in their order.

1. The collects and Canon.[3] We begin with the Sanctorale, where the various authorities cited in our collations form themselves into groups much more clearly and satisfactorily than in the Temporale; and we restrict ourselves to those collects which are found in all the authorities save DGLΣ. The first fact which emerges is the close resemblance between the text of H and Y. In the collects just referred to there are 91 places in which one or more variants are recorded (exclusive of the endings of prayers). In no single one of these does H differ from Y. After this we notice a group of three which bear a striking resemblance to one another, though by no means so closely related as the two just mentioned: CEW. Of the 91 places referred to, E coincides with C in 83, and with W in 78; while C agrees

---

[1] Page 3 *sqq.*   [2] Page 269 *sqq.*

[3] In this paragraph the use of symbols is unavoidable. The meaning of those employed is stated below, p. 113.

with W 82 times. When we bear in mind the countless scribal errors in both C and E this result is sufficiently remarkable. A third group is ΓΛP. ΓΛ coincide 81 times, ΓP also 81 times, ΛP 78 times. With this group may be associated M, which agrees frequently with Γ (79 times) and P (78 times), but differs considerably from Λ (18 times). Turning now to that part of the Canon found in all the manuscripts, we discover the first two of these groups reappearing, with a slight modification. S joins HY—HY agreeing 71 times out of 78, HS 69 times, and SY no less than 72 times. CEW form a group as before, CE occurring 67 times, EW 71 times, CW 66 times. D, with which it is now possible to deal for the first time, is found to be more akin to E than to any other text, though it coincides less frequently with it than do CW. It differs from E 12 times, from C 17 times, and from W 16 times. In the Temporale H and Y are more frequently in agreement than any other pair of authorities, being found together 121 times out of 127. Γ is now associated rather with J and M than with Λ and P. ΓJ and ΓM appear each 117 times and JM 116. The group CEW disappears. Proceeding to examine the collects of the votive masses common to CDEHSWY, our previous results are confirmed. We have to remark, however, that there is here greater variety among the different texts than before, and that the group CEW is somewhat disturbed, apparently through the influence of the Sarum upon the Westminster text. C agrees with E and W oftener than with any of the remaining books: CE being found 90 times, CW 92 times, CS only 76 times: EW 79 times, but ES nearly as often,—75 times. W in fact, though it coincides more frequently here with C than with any other text, agrees rather more closely with S (84) than with E (79). D is again an associate of the group CEW. It agrees 75 times with C, 76 times with E, 67 times with W, only 57 times with S, 50 times with H, and 46 times with Y. In consequence possibly of the Sarum influence on W alluded to above, we find D further from W than is any one of the remaining manuscripts.   HY as before are close companions. They agree 115 times out of 128.

For our present purpose the main fact to be noted is that the Rosslyn and C.C.C.O. Missals are in the verbal text of their collects closely related, except in the Temporale, the Westminster Missal being their most constant English ally : while D follows in their wake, but at some little distance.

2. The Rubrics.   Where they can be compared the resemblance of the rubrics in the Corpus and Rosslyn Missals is so close as to suggest a common source not very far removed from either.[1]   Comparison with the Drummond Missal is here impossible.

3. The Antiphonale Missarum from which the choral parts of the masses of the Sanctorale in the Corpus and Rosslyn Missals have been derived, may very well have been the same book, the few variations between them being easily accounted for by a difference of choice among alternatives allowed in the Antiphonal.   Here are the facts as gleaned from our notes. There are altogether sixteen masses common to the two books in the Proprium.   For these they differ not once in the offices, and twice are together against the majority of authorities.[2] In the office psalms they differ but once,[3] and are in agreement against the majority eight times.[4]   In the grails (including the verses) they differ once[5]—or twice if we include a case in which the Rosslyn manuscript stands alone in one verse, while in the next it is with the Corpus manuscript against all others[6]— in ten cases they coincide absolutely against the bulk of authorities,[7] and in one instance our missal has an alternative lesson and grail peculiar to itself.[8]   In two tracts[9] they are in company against most others, and are never apart.   In the offer-

---

[1] See notes on p. 32, l. 4 *sqq.* ; p. 48, l. 24.
[2] See pp. 65, 67.   [3] Page 56.
[4] Pages 47, 57, 58, 59, 65, 66, 67, 70.   [5] Page 43, in the verse only.
[6] Page 52.
[7] Pages 43 (not in the verse), 47, 54, 58, 60, 64, 65, 66, 67, 71.
[8] Page 52.   [9] Pages 53, 54.

tories they differ once only,[1] and five times agree against the majority.[2] And in the commons they only once disagree,[3] and eight times are together with support from only a few English books,[4] or from none at all.[5] The Drummond Missal can be compared with the other two in only one mass (St. Michael), and in this it differs from them both, and from the majority of books, in one of the verses of the grail, and in the offertory.[6] Whether the resemblance between the choral portions of the Corpus and Rosslyn Missals extends to the Temporale we have scarcely evidence to decide, on account of the comparatively small amount of variation among the different books in the common masses in that part of the missal. Both of them agree much more closely with the Gregorian Antiphonary in the Temporale than in the Sanctorale. In the Votive Masses and the Mass for the Dead, evidence is again scanty: but it is not suggestive of a close affinity between the two missals. Both in its three Masses de tempore and in the Votive Masses the Drummond Missal differs considerably from both.[7]

Scribblings.

The vacant spaces in the margins of our manuscript have often been made the receptacle of notes of various kinds and written at various times. Only the very few which are liturgical in character have been recorded in the footnotes to the text. The remainder, so far as they can be transcribed, are gathered together here. They are for the most part not easy to read, and I have to thank Dr. Thomas Dickson for help in deciphering and dating them.

---

[1] Page 44. [2] Pages 47, 64, 65, 66, 71.

[3] Page 44. The coincidence between C and E in the Sanctorale is even more marked if the mass De Inuentione S. Cruce is left out of account. See note on p. 43, l. 13.

[4] Pages 59, 60, 64, 66, 67, 68, 71. [5] Page 63.

[6] See notes on p. 69, l. 29; p. 70, l. 2.

[7] See notes on p. 39, l. 34; p. 40, l. 11 *sqq.* ; p. 42, ll. 11, 23; p. 77, ll. 20, 22; p. 79, l. 5; p. 80, ll. 6, 28; p. 93, l. 39 *sqq.*

f. 9r. (*upper marg.*)
    m[1] Viuamus corde

f. 20v. (*lower marg.*)
    tres sorores fuerunt | tres

f. 28v. (*lower marg.*)
    qui scripsit scriptum apud
                       Fourteenth century or later.[2]

f. 31r. (*lower marg., upside down*)
    . . dn d dñī

ff. 37v., 38v., 41v. *bis* (*lower marg.*)
    Si quis amat x̅ mūdum nō diligit istum
These four apparently in same hand—fourteenth century.

f. 39v., 40r. (*lower marg.*) *obliterated.*

f. 55v. (*lower marg., upside down*)
    James Henrie.

f. 56r. (*right and lower marg., written at right angles to the rulings of the text*).
    Maister James | S | Sym(on)[3] | chalmer(s) | with my h(and) | . . . . . J . . . . | . . . . . | James | chalm(ers)
                       Late sixteenth century.[4]

f. 62v. (*lower marg., upside down, partly erased*)
    Symond Chalmer . ... | Henr(ie) . . . ot[5] | . . . .
                       Late sixteenth century.

---

[1] This mark may perhaps be read *in* : or it may be merely a flourish. It is written inside the loop of the following *V*. The scribbling is in the same hand as that on f. 85r. *q.v.*

[2] See above p. xxv note [4].

[3] The letters enclosed in round brackets here and lower down have been cut away by the binder.

[4] Our missal was not bound till it came into Sir James Balfour's hands in or about 1630. This fact, and the number of sixteenth century scribblings executed by the Chalmers and others, prove that it was badly cared for at Rosslyn. To this circumstance may be due its present mutilated condition.

[5] This letter may be *c* or *e* (?).

f. 63r. (*lower marg., upside down*)

[.]¹ of Leswaid² and De . d D . yles | buik yat trublis all our kyn

Sixteenth century.

f. 63v. (*lower marg., erased*) *illegible.*

f. 70r. (*lower marg., upside down*)

(. . . .)ane elphe . . . . | . . . . of nature Denyit | thow (?) flait³ with thy . . .

Late sixteenth or early seventeenth century.

f. 84v. (*left marg.*) (. . .) at | (. . .) sio.

f. 85r. (*lower marg., upside down*)

Dum sumus in mūdo viuamus corde iocundo

Fifteenth century.

f. 92r. (*lower marg., upside down, erased*). *Four illegible lines.*

f. 104v. (*lower marg.*)

est mea meus mota parte speciosa megota

*Fourteenth century.*⁴

f. 111v. (*left marg., at right angles to ruling of text*) *bis.*

Ad te leuaui animam deus meus.

Fourteenth century.

f. 112v.   ᴅSINCLAIR OF ROISLING.⁵

f. 132r. (*lower marg.*)

Si sapiens fore vis sex serua que mando | Quid loqueris de quo cui quomodo quando.

Sixteenth century.

---

¹ An initial.

² Now Lasswade, a village five miles from Edinburgh, 2½ miles from Rosslyn. Rosslyn is in the parish of Lasswade.

³ Past participle of Scots *flyte*, to scold.

⁴ See above p. xxv, note 4.

⁵ See above p. xxvi. A facsimile of this signature may be seen in the *Proceedings of the Society of Antiquaries of Scotland*, vol. xxxii, p. 96.

Abbreviations.

In the following list of the *compendia scribendi* of our manuscript mere contractions, occurring only once or twice, and plainly used without fixed rule, are omitted. They are found for the most part in the grails, &c., and rubrics. They consist of the first few letters of a word surmounted by a horizontal stroke to indicate the remainder.

Symbols used both in lessons (or collects) and grails are unmarked. Those marked *ˡ* are found only in lessons or collects, those marked *ᵍ* only in grails, &c., those marked *ʳ* only in rubric. Those marked *ˡʳ* occur in lessons or collects and rubricated portions, but not elsewhere. Abbreviations peculiar to the Canon are marked *ᶜ*. In the case of less frequently used abbreviations references are given.

7   = et (see Plate II. last line but one).

Ð   = eius (see Plate I. l. 2).

ɔ *or* ꝫ   = est (Plate II. ll. 7, 17).

⧾   = enim (Plate I. l. 12).

ᴐ   = con.

ˡ ᴋ   = autem, f. 65r.

⁊̄   = etiam, ff. 19r, 64r (Plate II. l. 12).

ꝫ *after any consonant except q* = us (Plate I. ll. 13, 14).

ꝫ *after q* = ue (Plate II. l. 6 from end).

; *after b, ˡl, m, ˡn, ˡr* (f. 95v) = us (Plate II. l. 2).

⁓ *over ˡm* (ff. 44r, 127r), *ᵍs* (f. 10r), *t* (ff. 30r, *ᵍ*80v, *ᶜ*116r) = ur.

＊ over c, ˡf, g, ˡp, t = ra; *or, over f,* = r (*ᵍ*f. 21r) (see Pl. II. l. 2).

ᴖ   = um ; *or* = m.

‾, ᴐ   = n (*exceptional instances are* ˡmağa f. 42r, ˡnō f. 27r, ˡūt f. 23v, *ʳ*euāgel f. 3v) ; *or, over m,* = en ; *or, over b, ˡc, ˡd, ˡg, ᵍn* (muñe f. 11r) *t, u,* er ; *or, after b, ˡʳl,* = is ; *or, over c (in the* =

words hunc, nunc, tunc), *t* = un ; *or, after* 'd, *n*, = em.

The simple horizontal stroke is also used as a general mark of abbreviation, as the following examples will show.

ʳā, ʳañphā (f. 83r), ʳantī, ᶠantħa (f. 82v) = antiphona.

āīa   = anima.

all⸍, ᶠallā = alleluia.

aħ   = ante ; *or* = anti.

angls̄, &c. = angelus, &c.

ap̄   = apud.

apls̄, &c. = apostolus, &c.

aū   = autem.

ƀ   = bene : *see also above* (˘).

c̓   = cri.

c̊   = cre.

ᶜc̣   = cri (f. 114r).

ᶦcaīnẹ = catenẹ (f. 94v).

clm̄, &c. = celum, &c.

ʳcō (*twice* ʳcom̄, ff. 16r, 25v) = communio (*in full,* ᶠ f. 63v).

cp̄   = caput.

ᶜc̄s̄   = cuius (f. 117r).

ʳd̊   = duo (f. 56r).

ᶦdcñs, ᶦdc̄r̄ē (f. 81r, v), ᶦd̄r̄ē (f. 5v) = dicens, dicere.

dc̄s̄, &c. = dictus, &c. (ff. 6r, 83r, 87r).

ᶦd̄d̄   = dauid (f. 61r).

ᶦdesc̄ñdet = descendet (f. 133r).

ᶦdis̄   = discipulis.

ᶦdisciplī = discipuli (ff. 35r, 71v).

dñs̄, &c. = dominus, &c.

ᶜdr̵   = dicitur.

ds̄, &c. = deus, &c.

ᶦʳdⱦ   = dicit.

dx̄   = dixit.

ᶦdx̄erunt (dx̄er̄t) = dixerunt.

ecclīa,&c. = ecclesia, &c.

ēē, ēēt, &c. = esse, esset, &c.

epō   = episcopo (ᶠ f. 8ov, ᶦ f. 125v).

ᶜetī   = etiam (f. 120v).

ᶜexclᶺ   = excelsis (f. 113r).

f̄   = for (ff. 28r, 112r).

ᶦf̰   = fra (f. 97v).

ᶦf̣   = fri.

fc̄r̄e   = facere.

ᶦfc̄s, &c. = factus, &c.

ᶜflīō   = filio (f. 113v). ·

fls̄, &c.   = filius, &c.

ᶦfō   = foro (f. 15r).

fr̄, &c.   = frater, &c.

ḡ   = gre ; *or* = ᶦge (f. 44v) ; *or* = ᶦger.

g̈   = gra.

g̗   = igitur (ff. 40r, 63v, 71r) ; *or* = gri (f. 55r).

g̊   = ergo.

ʳg̃d, ʳg̃ (ff. 6v, 95r) = gradale (Plate I. l. 5 ; Plate II. l. 3
                from end).

ᶜglīā   = gloria (f. 113r).

gloā, &c. = gloria, &c.

ᶜglosȩ̄   = gloriosę (f. 114r).

gr̄ā, &c.   = gratia, &c. ; *or* = ᶦgenera, &c.

ḡs   = gentes (ff. 67r, 97v).

h̄   = hoc.

h̵   = hec.

ᶦh̵   = hic (f. 107v).

ᶦhōēm   = hominem (f. 87v).

ᶦhōïem, hōīum = hominem (ff. 49v, 87v), hominum (f. 77v).

ᶦhs̄   = huius.

h̄t, h̄nt, &c. = habet, habent, &c.

ɨ   = inter (ff. 18r, 67r).

ᶦi̦   = idest (f. 47v).

'idō   = ideo.

ihs̄, &c.   = ihesus, &c.

'ihūs   = ihesus (f. 93v).

ill〉   = illis *or* = 'illo.

ʳiohīs   = iohannis.

'iohs̄   = iohannis (f. 1r).

ipē, &c.   = ipse, &c.

isrl〉   = israhel.

ʳkl〉   = kalendae (*or* kallaind).

'kmē, 'km̄ī = karissime (f. 8v), karissimi (f. 27v).

ł   = uel ; *or* = ʳlectio.

'm⁹   = mus (f. 68r).

m̂   = michi (ᶠf. 32v, 'f. 117v).

m̊, &c.   = mea, &c.

'm̓   = michi.

m̊   = 'meo (f. 86r) ; *or* = 'modo (f. 115r), *cf.* f. 37v
             (Matt. xxvi. 53), f. 60r (Is. iv. 2).

'misǣ, misam = misericordiæ (ff. 53v, 54v), misericordiam
             (f. 21r).

'misc̄diam = misericordiam (f. 92r).

m̄m̄   = meum.

m̄r, mr̄is, &c. = mater, matris, &c.

ms̄   = meus.

n̄   = non.

'n̓   = nisi (ff. 17r, 65r).

ncē̄   = nocte.

nł   = nichil.

nō, nōī, &c. = nomen, nomini, &c.

'nōcē   = nocte (f. 74r).

'nōīē   = nomine (f. 120r).

nr̄, nr̄i, &c. = noster, nostri, &c.

'nūs   = numerus (f. 132r).

ocls̄, &c. = oculus, &c.

ʳof̄, of̄f   = offerenda (*in full* ᶠf. 63v).

oīā, oēm, &c. = omnia, omnem, &c.

omnipṥ, 'omnipoṥ (f. 131v), 'omp̄s (f. 61v) = omnipotens.

om̄s   = omnes.

oῤ   = 'oremus (*in full* ff. 9v, 19r, 46v, &c.) ; *or* = 'ora (f. 62r).

orā   = 'oratio (f. 70r); *or* = ᵉorationem (f. 132v).

.p   = pro (*see* Pl. II. l. 13).

p̄   = pre.

'p̣   = pri (*see* Pl. I. l. 3 from end).

'p'   = per (f. 116r).

p̣   = per (*see* Pl. II. l. 3).

'ᶦp   = pri.

'p'   = propri (f. 1r).

p̊   = post.

ᴵʳp̣   = post.

plṥ, &c.   = populus, &c.

'pōtatem = potestatem (f. 123v).

pp̄   = propter.

pῤ, &c.   = pater, &c.

prā   = presta (*in full* 'f. 117v).

'prē   = petre (f. 62r) ; *or* = patre.

prophā (.pphā), profā, &c. = propheta, profeta, &c.

pῑ   = potest ; *or* = post (ᶠf. 45v, 'f. 62r ? See note on p. 34, l. 34.)

q̄   = que ; *or* = 'quo (f. 3r).

q̃   = quem ; *or* = 'qua (f. 19r).

q̣   = quia.

q̣   = quam.

'q̣   = quod.

'q̣   = qua.

q   = qui.

q̊   = quo.

q̄d   = quod.

qm̄   = quoniam.

ˡqm̄o = quomodo.
ˡqm̄s = quesumus.
ˡqn̄ = quando.
ˡqn̄do, qn̄ta, ˡqn̄to = quando (f. 96r), quanta (f. 79r), quanto (ff. 32r, 87v).
ˡq̄p̄ = quippe (f. 64v).
q̄q̄ = quoque.
qr̄ē = quare (ff. 16r, 32v).
qs̄ī, qs̄s̄ī = quasi, quassi.
ˡqt̄ = quot (ff. 1r, 67r).
ˢr̄ = responsorium.
ˢrł = reliqua.
ʳ·s· = secreta (*in full* f. 91r).
s̄ = sed ; *or* = ˡ*final* us.
ʳS, ꝭ = secundum.
sᵃ = sicut.
ˡsᵃ = sua (f. 99r).
sᶜ = sic.
sᵗ = sunt.
ʳꝭa = secunda (f. 88r).
ˢʳsc̄dum = secundum.
ˡꝭdam = secundam (f. 95r).
s̄c̄lm, &c. = seculum, &c.
sc̄s̄, &c. = sanctus, &c.
ʳsē, sēc = secreta (*in full* f. 91r).
s̄ī̄c̄ = sicut.
sm̄r̄ = semper.
sn̄ = sine.
ˢsp̄em = speciem (f. 100v).
sps̄, &c. = spiritus, &c.
s̄r̄ = super.
ˡsrᵃ = supra (f. 72r).
sr̄ā = supra.
ꝭs = suis.

ꞌsū	= siue.
t'	= tur (Pl. I, l. 9).
ꞏt̂	= tibi (ff. 115r, v).
ꞏt̲̅	= ter (f. 115r.)
t̂, &c.	= tua, &c. ; *or* = tra (ff. 48r, 51v).
ț	= tibi ; *or* = tri.
ꞌt̥	= tro (f. 86r) ; *or* = tuo.
ʳt̂c̄ (f. 14v), ʳt̂c̄t̄ = tractus.	
ꞌtm̄	= tantum (f. 97v).
ꞌtñ	= tamen (ff. 36v, 89r).
ʳv̄	= uersus.
u̦	= ꞌubi (f. 64v) ; *or* = ꞏuir.
ů	= uero (ff. ʳ62r, ꞌ77r, ꞏ 82v).
ꞏul⁻	= uel (f. 114r).
ꞌuñ	= unde (ff. 29r, 76v).
ꞌūr, &c.	= uester, &c.
ūs	= usque.
ꞌutrq₃	= utrumque (f. 47v).
x̣, ꞈx̣, ꞌx̥ (f. 26v), ꞏx̄ (f. 117v) = christus, -ti, -to, -tum.	
ꞌxpm	= christum (f. 55v).
ꞌxp̄s, &c.	= christus, &c.

Orthography.

It is hoped that the subjoined list of the irregular spellings of our scribe may be found fairly complete, but in such a table it is often a matter of some difficulty to decide what should be included and what omitted. When a noun appears in an oblique case it may be assumed that it occurs with the spelling recorded only in that case, and usually only once. When a word is followed by *&c.* it is to be understood that the anomalous orthography is found in the cognate words. The note (*passim*) indicates that the word which it follows occurs frequently, and in most cases with the anomalous spelling here given.

a *omitted*	...	caiphas (-fas), ebrice.
a *for* ae	...	*very common in gen. sing. and nom. pl. of first decl.*
a *for* e	...	alaxandrinorum, catacuminis, conciliat, eripias, faciam, fiat, habitant, offerant, operiat, regat, repellandas, sancta (*for* -te), saraphim, septam, sequabatur, ueniat.
a *for* i...	...	pharasei.
a *for* o	...	abodiens, abumbrasti, carbonan (Matt. xxvii. 6), colasenses, golgatha, hierusalima, lithostratos, nostrarum, patrocinia, tarcular.
a *for* u	...	aperibus (= uberibus), arabam, exaltauit, hostiam, nostram, plorabant.
aa *for* a	... ...	sabaa.
æ *or* ę *for* a	...	*Common in nom. sing.* 1*st decl.*, æius, æclesia.
æ *for* e	... ...	coetæ, gloriosæ, tæ.
b *omitted before* r	...	gariel.
b *for* bb	... ...	barabas, gabatha.
b *for* p	... ...	ambutare, obprobrium, obtatę, subplantare.
b *for* u	... ...	*common in perfects in* -ui, *also* debitare, octabæ.
c *omitted*	...	plantu.
c *for* cc	... ...	acipio, æclesia, cocineam, sucesserat.
c *for* ch	...	carissime, caritas, catacuminis, cerubin, crisogoni, pascalia, patriarcarum, pulcer *&c.*, scismaticis.
c *for* qu	...	inciris, scamæ, trancillam.
c *for* t	...	condicio, natalicia.
cc *for* c	...	acceto, occuli.
ch *for* c	...	chohors, chorintheos, holochausta, hyppochritæ, sadoch.
ch *for* h	...	michi (*passim*), nichil (*passim*), uechimenter.
d *for* dd	...	redat.
d *for* t	...	codidie, eundem, *cf.* rud.
e *inserted*	...	ı tueri, tuere.
e *for* a	...	*common in verb endings* 3 *sing.* 1 & 3 *pl.* ebreice, ecclesie, elimento, sancte (*for* -ta).
e *for* ae	...	*very common in gen. sing. and nom. pl.* 1*st decl. and common in proper nouns and adjectives in* -aeus, cedis, celum *&c.* (*passim*), cesaria, cessar,

cessus, coetaneos, demonium, edifico, egiptus
(-tius), egrotantibus, egrotos, emulatur, enig-
mate, equum, ereas (-ris), erumpna, estimator,
estus, etate, eternus &c. (*passim*), grece, hec
(*passim*), hedum, heretici &c., letari &c., mes-
tus, pena, penitentia &c., pre-, premia, preter,
pretorio, que (*passim*), quero (*passim*), quesso,
seculum, sepe, seuissimus.

e *for* ee ... ... belzebub, bethlem, deorum (= de eorum), dest,
redificat.

e *for* i ... ... *somewhat common in terminations of 3rd conj.
pres.*, assteterunt, compremis, corintheos, decepit, decet, defusa, degitum, deiudicaremus,
demittere, denumerare, desoluat, desputans,
effesseos, excedit, fareseorum, hec, hordeiceus,
impone, iteneribus, natale, necodemus, omnes,
perfideam, perheberet, precedet, propitiationes,
regenerationes, requerebant, sempeternam,
senistris, sustenete, transetus, trigenta, uidet,
uigenti.

e *for* oe ... ... obediens &c.

e *for* y ... ... azemi, prespeteris.

ę *for* a ... ... *See above*, ae *for* a.

ę *for* e ... ... benignissimę, ęquum, sanctę, uidę, uirguinę.

ę *for* eae ... ... galilę, rędificare.

ę *for* oe ... ... obędiens.

ea *for* e ... ... fereabatur (-antur), impleatum, posteam, processi-
seant.

f *for* d *before* f ... afferre, affirmare, affligeret, afflues.

f *for* ff ... ... defusa.

f *for* ph ... ... caifas, epifania, fantasma, fanuel, farisei, fiolas,
frigiam, profeta (*passim*), stefanus (*passim*).

ff *for* f ... ... defferre, indefficiens.

ff *for* ph ... ... effa, effessus &c., effraim.

g *for* ch ... ... dragmas.

g *for* gg ... ... agregentur.

gg *for* g ... ... introggressus.

h (*initial*) *inserted* ... habundare &c., helamite, horans, hostium &c., cf. perhennis &c.

h (*initial*) *omitted* ... abere, arundo, ebdomadario, ebrei &c. (*passim*), ieremias, ierosolima, ierusalem, ordeicios, ortus, ossanna, ymnus, cf. peribeo.

i *inserted* ... ... abiel, citharias, custodies, elimoisinam, induitus, inuestigiabiles, iozias, ominem, pariens, trans-imigratione.

i *omitted* ... ... accipetis, archepiscopum, audeis (*for* a iudaeis), egredetur, eicens, heremiam, hericho, tiberadis, tinnens, ozam, peor.

i *for* a ... ... hordeiceus, octoginti, paginis, quadraginti, sede-bit, testimenta.

i *for* e ... ... accipit &c., alligoriam, apariat, aperiitur, calcia-menta &c., califacere, catacuminis, cesaria, concipiretur, contristari, conuertit, discendere, distruere, dromidarii, elimentis, eliuatus, extrin-sicus, fecirim, |finistram, flagillatum, fratri, genitrix (*passim*), heritica, herodis, intelligere, interficit, intigra, iohannis, locuplitantes, merie-mur (= mereamur), miseriatur, necodimus, paraclitus, parasciue, passioni, peluim, penti-costes, perhibit, perigrinantibus, predistina-tionis, primia, priori, proficiret, prosiliti, quin-quagissima, redimisti, sepilire, septuagissima, sid, spiculator, terrimotus, transiat, uechi-menter, uegitari, uidiamus, uiditis, uincenti, uinissent, uixillum.

i *for* ee ... ... elimoisinam.

i *for* ii ... ... brachi, diudicans, essurit, gaudis, hostiaris, ieiunis, letanis, misteris, obsequis, patrocinis, pissimo, preui.

i *for* u ... ... mirra, monimenta.

i *for* y ... ... acolitis, apocalipsis, azimus, babilonis, bithinia, bu-tirum, cimbalum, cipriani, cirine &c., clamide, crisogoni, didimus, egiptius &c., elimoisinam, frigiam, hierusolima, hisopo, kirrieleison, libie, martires *&c.* (*passim*), misterium (*passim*), misticis, pampiliam, prespiter, prosiliti, siluester, simeon, sinagoga (*passim*), tirii.

ii *for* i ...	...	filii, hii, hiis, laurentii, reficiis, sacriis, tirii, uincentii.
k *for* ch ...	...	karismata, karissimi(-e).
l *for* ll ...	...	querela, tranquilitate.
ll *for* l ...	...	camellorum, sillua.
m *for* mm ...	...	consumabuntur, emanuel.
mm *for* m ..	...	confitemmini.
n *for* d *before* n	...	annuntiare.
n *for* m *before* n	...	sollennis *&c.* (*passim*).
before p	...	conpunctione.
before q	...	cunque (*passim*), nanque, utrunque.
nn *for* n ...	...	annanias, channanea, mannases.
o *for* a ..	...	apocolipsis, capodociam, cognotus, colophizet, fiolas, lxº, oblato (*for* ablato), oblutio, obsoluat *&c.*, obsorueat, porco, sumendo, tesolonicenses, uniuersorum.
o *for* u ...	...	fulgor, incolomem, insolae, seruator, tonica.
oe *for* ae ...	..	coetæ, foenum.
p *inserted between* m *and* n	columpna, condempnationem, contempnitis, dampnare *&c.*, erumpna, sompnus.	
p *omitted* ...	...	presumtio.
p *for* b ...	...	aperibus, optinet, prespiter, puplicani, sup.
p *for* ph ...	...	pampiliam, pilipenses *&c.*
p *for* pp ...	...	apariat, apellauit, apretiauerunt, capadocia, oportunus *&c.*, philipenses.
pp *for* p ...	...	appostoli *&c.*, hyppochritæ, opportet.
q *for* c ...	...	persequti.
qu *for* c ...	...	liquet, postquat (*for* poscat).
qu *for* g ...	...	quinquaquinta.
r *for* rr ...	...	coripimur, offere, scurilitas.
rr *for* r ...	...	kirrieleison.
s *omitted after* preposition ex *in composition.*	Passim.	

s *for* ss	... ...	*Very common in perf. part. in* -ssus *and in pluperf. inf. and subj.*, abysi, colasenses, desoluat (*for* diss-), imposibile, iusit (-isti), iusu, mannases, misa (*passim*), naason, pasio (*passim*), posidentes, promisionem, remisio (*passim*), repromisionem, tesolonicenses.
s *for* st	... ...	sephane.
ss *for* s	... ...	accussationem, asser, assia, assinaria, assteterunt &c., basses, cessar, cessus, circumcissio, confussa, diuissit, diuissus, effessus &c., essum, essurit, extassi, fesstinantes, fusstibus, gauissus, gloriossus, heresses, impossuisset, inaquossa, infussio, innotessceris, misissti, missiset, missit, occissus, ossanna, possitus, possuit, pretiossior, pussillus, quadragessimalis, quassi, quesso &c. quinquagissima, religiossi, rossæ, septuagissima, speciossam, transseat.
st *for* s	... ...	postuerunt.
st *for* z	... ...	astimi, citharistantium, nastareth &c., stacharias, stebedei.
t *for* c	... ...	quantotius.
t *for* d	... ...	confitentem, mentacium &c.
t *for* dt	... ...	ate.
t *for* s	... ...	cirinentium.
t *for* th	... ...	acolitis, corinti, nazaret, neptalim, ortodoxis, taddei, talamo, tarsis, teophile, tesaurizabit, tesolonicenses, tomas, tronus.
t *for* tt	... ...	quatuor.
t *for* z	... ...	thesauritate.
th *for* d	... ...	obeth.
th *for* t	... ...	arethae, galathas, iosaphath, lintheum, tharsensem, theloneo.
th *for* tth	... ...	matheus (*passim*), mathia.
tt *for* t	... ...	uttriusque.
u *inserted after* g	...	eguerunt, longue, uirguinitas &c.
u *omitted after* g	...	extingere, linga (*passim*), sangis (*passim*).

u *for* a	...	... audiendum, oblutionem, sanctum, stabunt, ues-perum, *cf.* unōcē *p.* 60, *l.* 16.
u *for* b	...	... *common in fut. ind.*, obsorueat.
u *for* o	...	... baiolans, hierusolima, huc, idula, parabula, penti-custes.
u *for* uu	...	... fluctum.
uu *for* u	...	... manuum.
y *for* i	...	... cynamomum, hely, helyam, ymmolatus.
z *for* s	...	... elizabeth, zaphnai (= sabacthani).
z *for* st	...	... baptiza (*passim*), euangeliza (*passim*).
zt for z	...	... boozt.

The Present Edition.

In printing the text the manuscript has been followed closely, italics representing rubrics, and smaller type being used for grails, &c., for which the scribe has reserved a smaller script. As to punctuation : the inverted semi-colon has been reproduced as nearly as this could be accomplished with modern type (⁏), the mark resembling a semi-colon is indicated by a point on the line (.), and the single point, by a point above the line (·). Contractions have been expanded. Where the scribe has accidentally omitted letters or words, these have been supplied within *square* brackets. Clerical errors which could not be dealt with in this way have been marked with an obelus (†), and this symbol has also been occasionally inserted after words which probably do not fall under the category of errors, as an indication that they have been exactly copied from the manuscript, when without some such mark they might have been regarded as mis-prints. Words or letters which from any cause have become illegible are conjecturally restored and enclosed in *round* brackets.

Deviations from the rule of exactly following the manuscript occur in the following cases. Titles of masses are printed in small capitals instead of italics ; other headings begin with a capital letter ; a full stop is placed at the end of all titles, and all collects, grails, verses, &c., without regard to the punctuation mark (if any) used in the manuscript, and in numerals V is used, though the MS. has U.

In the notes the text of the canon, the collects, and such other portions of the services as are not mere quotations from the Scriptures, are collated with seventeen other missals and sacramentaries. The method of notation employed in these collations may be most easily explained by taking an example.

Thus in the notes on p. 44, l. 6 *sqq.* the following statements are made:—The same collect occurs as secret of the corresponding mass in ACG, &c. (indicated by printing these symbols after the word *Secret*); in Γ it is the secret of the 'missa in tempore belli.' In l. 6 HY add the word 'nostrum' after 'sacrificium'; in l. 7 *all* the authorities named read 'bellorum' instead of 'bellatorum'; in l. 8 all except AΓRS read 'potestatis' for 'potestates,' and of these four R omits the word, while AΓS agree with E.

The index of forms has been so constructed as to serve for the Corpus, Drummond and Stowe Missals. It includes all forms printed in the side-notes to the printed editions of these MSS. or referred to in the notes to the present work.

A record of the words in the epistles and gospels over which 'inflection marks' are placed in the manuscript is also kept in the notes.

The lessons are not printed in full in the text, but in the appendix they are collated with Vercellone's edition of the Vulgate.

To the Bishop of Edinburgh is due the first suggestion that it would be convenient for students to have in their hands a printed edition of the Rosslyn Missal. Its preparation for the press has been made by him the occasion of many kindnesses to the editor, not the least of which has been the permission to make use of his valuable collection of liturgical books. Mr. H. A. Wilson, Mr. E. S. Dewick, and Dr. J. Wickham

Legg have been good enough to read the proofs of this work. How useful their criticisms and suggestions have been to the editor the members of the Henry Bradshaw Society will not need to be told ; but how frequent and troublesome have been his demands upon their learning and their time, and with what unfailing kindness they have answered questions, and consulted printed books and manuscripts on his behalf, is known only to himself. The editor is also much indebted to Miss C. M. Mackenzie for help in preparing the Index of Forms.

TRINITY COLLEGE,
    DUBLIN, *St. Patrick's Day*, 1899.

THE ROSSLYN MISSAL.

ROSSLYN.

[TEMPORALE].

[IN NATIUITATE DOMINI].

*   *   *   *   *

/et tenebræ eam non comprehenderunt. fuit . . .   [fo. 1r.
.   a patre plenum ;/ gratia† et ueritatis.¹

5   *Offerenda.*

Tui sunt celi et tua est terra orbem terrarum et (ple)nitudinem eius
tu fundasti.

    [*V.*] Iustitiam† /et iudicium preparatio sedis tuæ.   [fo. 1v.
    V.   Magnus et metuendus super omnes qui in circuitu eius sunt.
10   *V.*   Tu dominaris potestatis † maris motum hoc † fluctu[u]m eius
tu mitigas.
    V.   Tu humiliasti sicut uulneratum superbum et in brachio
uirtutis tuæ dispersisti inimicos tuos.
    V.   Firmetur manus tua et exaltetur dextera tua domine.²

15   *Secreta.*

Oblata domine munera noua unigeniti tui natiuitate
sanctifica nosque a peccatorum nostrorum maculis emunda
per.

Communicantes et diem ut supra.

20   *Communio.*

Uiderunt omnes fines terre salutare dei⸱ n.³

           Post communionem.

Presta quesumus omnipotens deus ;/ ut natus hodie saluator
mundi⸱ sicut diuinæ nobis generationis est auctor ;/ ita et im-
25 mortalitatis sit ipse largitor qui tecum uiuis†.

          Alia ad horas diei.

Respice nos misericors deus et mentibus clementer humanis
nascente christo summæ ueritatis lumen ostende ;/ per dominum.

---

¹ Joh. i. 5–14.   ² Ps. lxxxviii. 12, 15 a, 8 b, 10, 11, 14 b.
³ Ps. xcvii. 3 b.

·VII· KL′ ENAIR NATALE STEPHANI ET † MARTIRIS.

/Etenim sederunt principes et aduersum [me] loquebantur [fo. 2r.
et iniqui persequti sunt me adiuua me domine deus meus quia
seruus tuus exercebatur in iustificationibus tuis.[1]
5   *Ps.* Beati.[2]

Oremus.

Omnipotens sempiterne deus qui primitias martirum in
beati· et† leuitæ stephani sanguine dedicasti· tribue quesumus·
ut pro nobis intercessor existat qui [pro] suis etiam persecutori-
10 bus exorauit ⸴ dominum· n.

Lectio actuum apostolorum.

In diebus illis ⸴ stefanus plenus gratia et fortitudine ⸴ .
/ . . et cum hoc dixisset ⸴ obdormiuit in domino.[3] [fo. 2v.

Gradale.

15 Sederunt principes et aduersum me· l· et in[i]qui persecuti sunt
me.
   V. Adiuua me domine deus meus saluum me fac propter misericordiam tuam alleluia·
   [*V.*] Uideo celos apertos et ihesum stantem a dextris uirtutis dei.[4]

20   ### Secundum matheum.

/In illo tempore ⸴ dicebat ihesus turbis iudeorum· et [fo. 3r.
principibus sacerdotum. ecce ego mitto . . . . benedictus
qui uenit ⸴ in nomine domini.[5]

Offerenda.

25 Elegerunt apostoli stefanum leuitam plenum fide et spiritu
sancto /quem lapidauerunt iudei orantem et dicentem domine [fo. 3v.
accipe spiritum meum·[6] alleluia.

Secreta.

Suscipe domine munera pro comme[mo]ratione protomartiris
30 stefani· ut sicut illum pasio gloriosa effecit innocentem sic nos
deuotio reddat inoculost ⸴ per.

Communio.

Uideo celos apertos et ihesum stantem a dextris uirtutis dei.
   [*V.*] Domine ihesu accipe spiritum meum· et ne statuas illis·
35 hoc peccatum quia nesciunt· q· f.[7]

---

l. 24. The letters ōf, representing ' offerenda,' originally written before
' Elegerunt,' are erased. They have been re-written (*p.m.*) in the margin.
[1] Ps. cxviii. 23 a, 86 b, cviii. 26 a, cxviii. 23 b.   [2] Ps. cxviii. 1.
[3] Act. vi. 8–10, vii. 54–60 a.
[4] Ps. cxviii. 23 a, 86 b, cviii. 26; Act. vii. 56.
[5] Matt. xxiii. 34–39.   [6] Act. vi. 5, vii. 59.
[7] Act. vii. 56, 59 b, 60 a ; Luc. xxiii. 34 a.

Post communionem.

Auxilientur nobis domine sumpta misteria· et intercedente beato stefano protomartire tuo sempiterna nos protectione confirment ː' per dominum.

5   [*Alia. Oremus.*]

Da nobis quesumus domine imitari quod colimus ut discamus et inimicos diligere quia natalicia eius celebramus ː' qui nouit etiam pro suis persecutoribus exorare ː' perł dominum.

VI· KL' ENAIR NATIUITAS S· IOHANNIS· EUANGELIZÆ.

10   In medio ecclesie aperuit os eum ł et impleuit eum dominus spiritu sapientiæ et intellectus stolam gloriæ induit eum.[1]
[*Ps.*]   Bonum est confiteri.[2]

[Oremus].

·· Ecclesiam tuam domine benignus illustra /ut beati [fo. 4r.
15 iohannis euangelizæ illuminata doctrinis· ad dona perueniat sempiterna ː' per dominum.

Lectio libri sapientiæ s(alomonis).

Qui timet dominum ː' faciet bona et qui . . . . hereditabit illum ː' dominus deus noster.[3]

2)   *Gradale.*

Exiit sermo inter fratres quod di[s]cipulus ille non moritur.
[℣.]   Sed sic ·eum uolo manere donec ueniam tu me sequere alleluia.
℣. hic est discipulus ille qui testimonium perhibet et ł de his et
25 scimus quia uerum est testimonium estł.[4]

         |*Secundum iohannem.*   [fo. 4v.

In illo tempore ː' dixit ihesus petro. sequere me. . . . . et scimus quia uerum est testimonium eius.[5]

*Communio*ł.

30   Iustus ut palma florebit sicut cedrus libani multiplicabitur.[6]

         .*Secreta.*

Suscipe domine munera nostra que in eius tibi sollenniaate͚ł deferimus cuius nos confidimus patrocinia·ł liberari ː' per dominum.

[1] Sir. xv. 5.   [2] Ps. xci. 2.   [3] Sir. xv. 1–6.
[4] Joh. xxi. 23, 24.   [5] Joh. xxi. 19 b–24.   [6] Ps. xci. 13.

Communio.

Exiit sermo inter fratres quod discipulus ille non moritur· et
non dixit ihesus non moritur sed sic eum uolo manere donec
ueniam.[1]

5 ### Post communionem.

Refecti cibo potuque celesti deus noster te suppliciter de-
/precamur ;ʹ ut in cuius hec commemoratione percepimus [fo. 5r.
eius muniamur et precibus.

Alia. Oremus.

10   Beati iohannis apostoli tui et euangelistæ domine supplicatione placatus et ueniam nobis tribuat† et remedia sempiterna
concede ;ʹ per.

·V· KL' FNAIR NATALE INNOCENTIUM MARTIRUM.

Ap̄ paul'.

15   Ex ore infantium et lactentium deus perfecisti laudem propter
inimicos tuos ei†.[2]
Ps. Domine dominus noster.[3]

Oremus.

Deus cuius hodierna die preconium innocentes martires non
20 loquendo sed moriendo confessi sunt ;ʹ omnia in nobis uitiorum
mala mortifica· ut fidem tuam quam lingua nostra loquitur
etiam moribus uita fateatur ;ʹ per.

Lectio libri· a[pocalipsis]· iohannis apostoli.

In diebus illis ;ʹ uidi super montem sion agnum stantem et
25 cum eo . . / . . est mentacium sine macula sunt ;ʹ [fo. 5v.
ante tronum dei.[4]

Gradale.

Anima nostra sicut passer erepta est de laqueo uenantium.
   V̸. Laqueus contritus est et nos liberati sumus.
30   *V̸.* Adiutorium nostrum in nomine domini qui fecit celum et
terram.
   V̸. Fulgebunt iusti et tanquam scintillæ in arundineto discurrent
in ęternum.[5]

Secundum matheum.

35   In illo tempore ;ʹ angelus domini apparuit [in] sompnis
ioseph ;ʹ . . / . . rachel plorans filios suos. et noluit [fo. 6r.
consolari quia non sunt.[6]

---

[1] Joh. xxi. 23.   [2] Ps. viii. 3.   [3] Ps. viii. 10.
[4] Apoc. xiv. 1–5.   [5] Ps. cxxiii. 7, 8 ; Sap. iii. 7.   [6] Matt. ii. 13–18.

Offerenda.

Anima nostra sicut passer erepta est de laqueo uenantium.[1]

Secreta.

Sanctorum tuorum nobis domine pia non desit oratio· que
5 et munera /nostra conciliat†· et tuam nobis indulgentiam [fo. 6v.
semper obtineat per dominum.

Communio.

Uox in rama audita est ploratus et ululatus rachel plorans filios
suos noluit consolari quia non sunt.[2]

10 ### *Post* [*communionem*].

Uotiua domine dona percepimus ꞉' que sanctorum innocentium nobis et† precibus et presentis uitæ pariter et eternę quesumus tribue conferre subsidium ꞉' per dominum.

OCTABÆ NATALIS DOMINI KL' IANUARII IN CIRCUM-
15 ### CISSIONE.

Puer natus est nobis et filius datus est nobis cuius imperium
super humerum eius et uocabitur nomen eius magni consilii
angelus.[3]
Ps. Cantate domino· n· quoniam.[4]

20 ### *Oremus.*

Deus qui nobis nati saluatoris diem celebrare concedis
octauum fac nos quesumus eius perpetua diuinitate muniri ꞉'
cuius sumus carnali commericio † separasti†· qui tecum.

Epistola.

25 Carissime apparuit gratia dei saluatoris.[5]

Gradale.

Uiderunt omnes.
V. Notum fecit.[6]
[*V.*] Dies sanctificatus.

30 ### *Secundum lucam.*

In illo tempore ꞉' postquam consummati sunt dies   .   .
/   .   . priusquam in utero conciperetur†.[7]   [fo. 7r.

Offerenda.

Tui sunt celi ut supra.[8]

---

[1] Ps. cxxiii. 7 a.
[2] Matt. ii. 18.
[3] Isai. ix. 6.
[4] Ps. xcvii. 1.
[5] Tit. ii. 11 sqq.
[6] Ps. xcvii. 3 b, 2.
[7] Luc. ii. 21.
[8] Ps. lxxxviii. 12 etc.

Secreta.

Muneribus nostris quesumus domine precibusque susceptis·
et celestibus nos munda misteris et clementer exaudi ꞉ per
dominum.

5
Communio.

Uiderunt omnes termini terre salutare dei.[1]

Post communionem.

Presta quesumus domine· ut quod saluatoris nostri iterata
sollennitate percepimus perpetuæ nobis redemptionis conferat
10 medicinam ꞉ per eundem.

Alia.

Hec nos communio domine purget a crimine et intercedente
beata maria semper uirguinis † celestis remedii faciat esse
consortes ꞉ per.

15
DOMINICA Iᵃ POST NATALE DOMINI.

Dum medium silentium tenerent omnia et nox in suo cursu
medium iter haberet omnipotens sermo tuus domine de celis a
regalibus sedibus uenit.[2]
Ps. Dominus regnabit decorem induitus † est.[3]

20
Oremus.

Omnipotens sempiterne deus ꞉ dirige actus nostros in bene-
placito tuo ut in nomine· dilecti filii tui meriemur † bonis
operibus /habundare qui tecum.　　　　　　　　　[fo. 7v.

Ad galatas.

25 Fratres ꞉ quanto tempore heres paruulus est .　　.　.
quod si filius et heres per deum.[4]

Gradale.

Speciosus forma pre filiis hominum diffusa est gratia in labiis
tuis.
30 *Ꝟ.* Eructauit cor meum usque· regi· linga mea calamus· usque
scribentis alleluia.
Ps. † Dominus regnabit decorem induitus † induitus†· d· pre.[5]

Secundum lucam.

In illo tempore ꞉ erat ioseph /et maria mater .　. 　[fo. 8r.
35 / .　. et confortabatur in spiritu plenus sapientia.[6] 　[fo. 8v.

---

[1] Ps. xcvii. 3 b. 　　　[2] Sap. xviii. 14, 15a. 　　　[3] Ps. xcii. 1.
[4] Gal. iv. 1–7. 　　　[5] Ps. xliv. 3 a, 2, xcii. 1. 　　　[6] Luc. ii. 33–40 a.

Offerenda.

Dominus enim firmabit orbem· t.
ut † deum † r.[1]

Secreta.

5 Concede quesumus domine ut oculis tuæ maiestatis munus
oblatum et gratia † in† nobis deuotionis obtineat et effectum
beatæ perhennitatis adquirat.

Communio.

Tollite† puerum et matrem eius et uade in terram iudam defuncti
10 enim sunt qui querebant animam· pueri.[2]

Post [communionem].

Sumpto sacrificio domine tua generaliter exultet ecclesia·
quo infirmitates eius sunt absumptæ· ut diuinæ particeps fieret
ipsa substantiæ ꞉ per.

15 NON ENAIR UIGILIA EPIŠ † DOMINI.

Lux fulgebit hodie super nos.[3]

Oremus.

Corda nostra quesumus domine uenturę festiuitatis splendor
illustret quo mundi huius tenebris carere ualeamus· et per-
20 ueniamus ad patriam claritatis ęt[er]nę· per.

Epistola.

Ka[r]i[ssim]e ꞉ apparuit benignitas.[4]

Secundum matheum.

In illo tempore꞉ defuncto herode꞉ ecce /apparuit . [fo. 9r.
25 . . . per prophetas ꞉ quoniam nastareus uocatur.[5]

Secreta.

Tribue quesumus domine ut deum† immolemus presentibus
sacrificiis et sumamus quem uenturæ festiuitatis pia munera
preloquuntur dominum· n.

30 *Post communionem.*

Illumina quesumus domine populum tuum et splendor[e]
gratiæ tuæ cor eius semper accende ꞉ ut saluatoris mundi stella
famulante manifestata natiuitas /mentibus eorum et [fo. 9v.
reueletur semper et crescat.

l. 23. At the top left hand corner of fo. 9r. is written the letter x (*p. m. ut uid.*).
[1] Ps. xcii. 1 b, 1 a (?).   [2] Matt. ii. 20.
[3] The officium so beginning in the Sarum Missal is from Is. ix. 6, 7 a.
[4] Tit. iii. 4, sqq.   [5] Matt. ii. 19-23.

VIII. IDUS IANUARII EPIFANIA DOMINI. IN DIE AD MISAM.

Ecce adueniet dominator dominus et regnum in manu eius et
potesttas † et imperium.[1]
5 *Ps.* Deus iudicium regi da et· t· f.[2]

Oremus.

Deus qui hodierna die unigenitum tuum gentibus stella
duce reuelasti· concede propitius ·/ ut qui iam te ex fide cog-
nouimus· usque ad contemplandam speciem tuæ celsitudinis
10 perducamur per eundem.

Lectio isaię profetæ.

Surge illuminare hierusalem quia uenit . . / . . [fo. 10r.
et tus differentes ·/ et laudem domino ·/ annuntiantes.[3]

Gradale.

15 Omnes de sabaa uenient aurum et tús defferentes· et laudem
domino annuntiantes.
    V. Surge et illuminare ierusalem quia gloria domini super te orta
est alleluia.
    V. Uidimus stellam eius in oriente et uenimus cum muneribus
20 adorare eum.[4]

Secundum matheum.

In illo tempore ·/ cum natus esset ihesus in bethlem . .
/ . . ad herodem ·/ per aliam uiam ·/ [reuersi] [ff. 10v., 11r.
sunt in regionem suam.[5]

25   #### *Offerenda.*

Reges tarsis et insolæ munera offerant† reges arabam† et sabaa
dona ad^{d}ucent.
[*V.*] Et adorabunt eum omnes reges· usque ei.[6]

Secreta.

30 Ecclesie tuæ quesumus domine dona propitius intuere
quibus non iam aurum· tús et mirra profertur· sed quod
eiusdem † muneribus declaratur immoletur† · et sumitur ihesus
christum † qui tecum uiuit.

Communicantes et diem sacratissimum celebrantes· quo
35 unigenitus tuus in tua tecum gloria coeternus· in ueritate carnis
nostræ uisibiliter corporalis apparuit et memoriam.

---

[1] Cf. Mal. iii. 1.   [2] Ps. lxxi. 2 a.   [3] Is. lx. 1-6.
[4] Is. lx. 6 b, 1 ; Matt. ii. 2 b.   [5] Matt. ii. 1-12.   [6] Ps. lxxi. 10, 11.

Communio.

Uidimus stellam in oriente et uenimus cum munere adorare· d.[1]

Post communionem.

Presta quesumus domine deus noster ; ut que sollenni cele-
5 bramus officio purificatæ mentis intelligentia consequamur ;
per.

OCTABÆ EPIFANIA†.

Ecce aduenit dominator dominus.[2]

/Oremus. [fo. 11v.

10 Deus cuius unigenitus in substantia nostræ carnis apparuit
presta quesumus ; ut per eum [quem] similem nobis foris
agnouimus intus reformari mereamur ; per.

Lectio isaię profetæ.

Domine deus meus honorificabo te laudem tribuam nomini
15 tuo ; qui facis mirabiles res consilium tuum antiquum uerum
fiat.[3] domine excelsum est brachium tuum ;[4] deus sabaoth
corona spei que ornata est gloria.[5] exultet desertum ; et
exulte[n]t solitudines iordanis.[6] et populus meus uidebit alti-
tudinem domini ; et maiestatem dei[7] et erit congregatus et
20 redemptus per deum. et ueniet in sion cum lætitia †; et lætitia
sempiterna super caput eius laus et exultatio.[8] et aperiam in
montibus flumina ; in mediis campis fontes dirumpam.[9] et terram
sitientem sine aqua confundam. ecce puer meus exaltabitur et
eleuabitur et sublimis erit ualde[10] hauri[e]tis aquas in gaudio de
25 fontibus saluatoris et dicens † in illa die /confitemini [fo. 12r.
domino et inuocate nomen eius. notas facite in populis
adinuentiones eius ; cantate domino quia mirabilia fecit
annuntiate hec ; uniuersa terra.[11] dicit ; dominus omnipotens.

Gradale.

30 Omnes de sabaa.
V. Surge et lluminare†.
V. Uidimus.[12]

Secundum matheum.

In illo tempore ; uenit ihesus a galilea in iordanes . . .
35 . filius meus dilectus in quo michi complacuit.[13]

---

[1] Matt. ii. 2 b. [2] Cf. Mal. iii. 1. [3] Isai. xxv. 1.
[4] Ps. lxxxviii. 14. [5] Cf. Isai. xxviii. 5. [6] Isai. xxxv. 1.
[7] Isai. xxxv. 2 b. [8] Isai. xxxv. 10 (li. 11). [9] Isai. xli. 18 a.
[10] Isai. lii. 13. [11] Isai. xii. 3-5. [12] Isai. lx. 6 b, 1 ; Matt. ii. 2 b.
[13] Matt. iii. 13-17.

DOMINICA PRIMA EPIFANIA †.

In excelso throno uidi sedere uirum quem adorat multitudo
angelorum psallentes /in unum ecce cuius imperium nomen [fo. 12v.
est in eternum.

5   *Ps.* Iubilate deo omnis terra psalmum.[1]

Oremus.

Uotiua † quesumus domine supplicantis populi celesti pietate
prosequere ut et que agenda sunt uideant et ad implenda que
uiderint conualescant· per.

10   *Ad romanos.*

Fratres obsecro uos per misericordiam dei . . . .
/alter alterius membra. in christo ihesu domino [fo. 13r.
nostro.[2]

Gradale.

15   Benedictus dominus deus israhel qui facis· m· m· solus a seculo.
𝒱. Suscipiant montes p· usque iustitiam alleluia.
Ps.† Iubilate deo omnis terra.[3]

Secundum lucam.

In illo tempore :/ cum factus esset ihesus annorum xii :/ . .
20 / . . et etate et gratia apud deum et homines.[4]   [fo. 13v.

Offerenda.

Iubilate deo omnis terra seruite domino in letitia introite in
conspectu eius in exultatione quia dominus ipse deus est.[5]

Secreta.

25   Oblatum tibi domine sacrificium :/ uiuificet nos semper· et
muniat :/ per.

Communio.

Filii quid fecisti nobis sic ego et pater tuus dolentes quereba-
mus te et quid est quod me querebatis· nesciebatis quia in his que
30 patris mei sunt oportet me esse.[6]

Post [*communionem*].

Tua domine sancta libantes et perfectæ capiamus purgationis effectum· et continuum diuinæ defensionis auxilium :/ per
dominum.

---

[1] Ps. lxv. 1, 2.   [2] Rom. xii. 1–5.   [3] Ps. lxxi. 18, 3, xcix. 2 a (lxv. 1).
[4] Luc. ii. 42–52.   [5] Ps. xcix. 2, 3 a.   [6] Luc. ii. 48 b, 49.

/DOMINICA IN SEPTUAGISSIMA. [fo. 14r.

. Circundederunt me gemitus mortis dolores inferni circundederunt
me et in tribulatione mea inuocaui dominum· et exaudiuit de templo
sancto suo uocem meam.¹
5 *V*.† Diligam te domine fortitudo mea.²

Oremus.

Preces populi tui quesumus domine clementer exaudi ꝰ ut
qui iuste pro peccatis nostris affligimur pro tui nominis gloria
misericorditer liberemur· per.

10 ### *Ad chorintheos.*

Fratres ꝰ nescitis quod hí qui in stadio . . / . [fo. 14v.
. consequente eos petra. petra autem erat christus.³

Gradale.

Adiutor in oportunitatibus in tribulatione· sperent in te qui
15 nouerunt te quoniam non derelinquis querentes te domine.
V. Quoniam · non in finem obliuio erit pauperis patientia
pauperum non peribit in finem exurge domine non preualeat
homo.⁴

Tractus.

20 De profundis clamaui ad te domine domine exaudi uocem meam.
V. Fiant aures tuae intendentes in orationem serui t[ui].
V. Si iniquitates obseruaberis domine domine quis sustinebit.
V. Quia apud te propitiatio est et propter legem tuam sustinuit †
te domine.⁵

25 ### *Secundum lucamatheum.*

In illo tempore ꝰ dixit dominus ihesus discipulis suis. para-
bolam hanc. simile est regnum . . / . . [fo. 15r. *et* v.
nouissimi. multi enim sunt uocati ꝰ pauci uero electi.⁶

Offerenda.

30 Bonum est confiteri domino et psallere nomini tuo altissime.⁷

Secreta.

Muneribus quesumus domine precibusque susceptis· et
celestibus nos munda misteriis· et clementer exaudi ꝰ per.

---

l. 25. The letters 'luca' are partially erased.

¹ Ps. xvii. 5 a, 6 a, 7 b.   ² Ps. xvii. 2.   ³ 1 Cor. ix. 24–27, x. 1–4.
⁴ Ps. ix. 10 b, 11, 19, 20 a.   ⁵ Ps. cxxix. 1–4 a.   ⁶ Matt. xx. 1–16.
Ps. xci. 2.

Communio.

Illumina faciem tuam super seruum tuum· et saluum me fac in tua· misericordia domine non confundar /quoniam [fo. 16r. inuocaui te.[1]

5 ### Post communionem.

Fideles tui deus per tua dona firmentur· ut eadem et percipiendo requirant· et querendo sine fine percipiant ꝛ́ per dominum.

DOMINICA IN LX°†.

10 ### Statio· ad sanctum· paulum.

Exurge quare obdormis domine exurge et ne repellas in finem· Quare faciem tuam auertis obliuisceris tribulationem nostram adhęsit in terra uenter noster Exurge domine adiuua nos et libera nos usque tuum.[2]

15 *Ps.* Deus auribus.[3]

Oremus.

Deus qui conspicis quia ex nulla nostra actione confidimus concede propitius· ut contra aduersa omnia doctoris genti[um] protectione muniamur. per.

20 ### Ad corintheos.

Fratres ꝛ́ libenter suffertis insipientes ꝛ́ . . / [ff. 16v., 17r. *et* v. . . meis ꝛ́ ut inhabitet in me ꝛ́ uirtus christi.[4]

Gradale.

Sciant gentes quoniam nomen tibi deus tu solus altissimus super 25 omnem terram.

Ⅴ. Deus meus pone illos ut rotam et sicut stipulam ante faciem uenti.[5]

Tractus.

Commouisti domine terram et conturbasti eam.
30 *Ⅴ.* Sana contritiones eius quia commota est.
Ⅴ. Ut fugiant· a· arcus ut liberentur electi tui.[6]

Secundum lucam.

In illo tempore ꝛ́ cum turba plurima conueniret . . / . . retinent. et fructum afferunt in patien- [fo. 18r. *et* v. 35 tia.[7]

---

[1] Ps. xxx. 17, 18 a. [2] Ps. xliii. 23, 24, 25 b, 26. [3] Ps. xliii. 2.
[4] 2 Cor. xi. 19-33, xii. 1-9. [5] Ps. lxxxii. 19, 14.
[6] Ps. lix. 4, 6 b. [7] Luc. viii. 4-15.

Offerenda.

Perfice gressus meos in semitis tuis· domine non mouentur uestigia mea· inclina aurem tuam et exaudi uerba me[a]· mirifica misericordias tuas qui saluos facis sperantes in te domine.[1]

5
Secreta.

Oblatum tibi domine sacrificium· uiuificet nos semper et muniat ꝰ per.

Communio.

Introibo ad altare dei mei et ad deum qui letificat iuuentutem
10 meam.[2]

Post communionem.

Supplices te rogamus omnipotens deus ꝰ ut quos tuis reficiſs †
sac[ra]mentis /tibi etiam placitis moribus dignanter [fo. 19r.
deseruire concedas ꝰ per dominum.

15
DOMINICA IN QUINQUAGISSIMA.

Statio [ad sanctum petrum].

Esto michi [in deum] protectorem et in locum refugii ut saluum me facias Quoniam firmamentum meum et refugium meum es tu· et propter nomen tuum dux michi eris et enutries me.[3]
20 *Ps.* In te domine speraui.[4]

Oremus.

Preces nostras quesumus domine clementer exaudi ꝰ atque a peccatorum uinculis absolutos ab omni nos aduersitate custodi ꝰ per dominum.

25
Ad corintheos.

Fratres ꝰ si linguis hominum loquar et angelorum . .
/ . . fides· spes caritas ꝰ tria hec. maior autem ꝰ [ff. 19v., 20r.
his est caritas.[5]

Gradale.

30 Tu es deus qui facis mirabilia solus notam fecisti in gentibus uirtutem tuam.
V. Liberasti in brachio tuo populum tuum filios iacob et ioseph.[6]

Tractus.

35 Iubilate deo omnis· t· seruite domino in letitia.
V. Intrate in conspectu eius in exultatione.

---

[1] Ps. xvi. 5, 6 b, 7. [2] Ps. xlii. 4 a. [3] Ps. xxx. 3 b, 4.
[4] Ps. xxx. 2. [5] r Cor. xiii.ꝰ [6] Ps. lxxvi. 15, 16.

[℣.] Scitote quia dominus ipse est deus ipse fecit nos Nos autem populus tuus et oues pascue tuę.[1]

Secundum (. . . .)m Secundum lucam.

In illo tempore ꞏ/ assumpsit ihesus ꞏxiiꞏ discipulos . .
5 / . . et omnis plebs ut uidit ꞏ/ dedit laudem deo.[2] [fo. 20v.

Offerenda.

Benedictus es domine doce me iustificationes tuas.
[℣.] In labiis meis pronuntiaui omnia iudicia oris tui.[3]

Secreta.

10 Hec hostia domine quesumus emundet /nostra [fo. 21r. delicta· et sacrificium celebrandum subditorum tibi corpora mentesque sanctificet ꞏ/ per dominum.

Communio.

Manducauerunt et saturati sunt nimis et desiderium eorum
15 attulit eis dominus non sunt fraudati a desiderio suo.[4]

Post communionem.

Quesumus omnipotens deus ꞏ/ ut qui celestia alimenta percepimus per hec contra omnia aduersa muniamur ꞏ/ per.

BENEDICTIO CINERUM.

20 Omnipotens sempiterne deus qui misereris omnium et nichil odisti eorum que fecisti dissimulans peccata hominum propter penitentiam qui etiam subuenis in necessitate laborantibus bene✠dicere et sanctificare hós cineres dignare [quos] causa humilitatis et sanctę religionis ad emundanda delicta nostra
25 super capita nostra ferre constituisti more inuitarum†· et da per inuocationem tui nominis· ut eos qui omnes ad deprecandam misericordiam tuam super capita sua ·tulerint a té mereantur omnium delictorum /suorum ueniam [fo. 21v accipere· et hodie sic ieiunia inchoare sancta· ut in die resur-
30 rectionis purificatis mentibus ad sanctum mereantur accedere pascha et in futuro perpetuam accipere gloriam.

Alia oratio· oremus.

Deus qui in † mortem sed penitentiam desideras peccatorum ꞏ/ fragilitatem conditionis humanæ benignissimę respice et hos
35 cineres quos causa perferendæ humilitatis atque promerendę

---

l. 3. The words 'Secundum (. . .)m' have been erased.

[1] Ps. xcix. 2, 3.   [2] Luc. xviii. 31–43.
[3] Ps. cxviii. 12, 13.   [4] Ps. lxxvii. 29, 30 a.

[ueniæ] capitibus nostris impone† decernimus· benedi✠cere
pro tua pietate digneris· ut qui nos. cinerem et ob prauitatis
nostre meritum in puluerem reuers[ur]os cognouimus peccatorum ueniam et premia penitentibus repromisa misericorditer
5 consequi mereamur per.

Dum ponitur cinis in capita.

Memento homo quia cinis es ⸴ et in cinerem reuerteris· puluis es
et in puluerem reuerteris.[1]

Interim canitur

10 Exaudi nos domine quoniam benigna est misericordia tua
secundum multitudinem /miserationum tuarum respice nos [fo. 22r.
domine.[2]

Ps. Saluum me fac deus.[3]
Gloria seculorum amen.

15 *Ant.* Iuxta uestibulum et altare plorabant† sacerdotes et leuitas†
ministri domini et dicent parce domine parce populo tuo·[4] et ne
dissipes ora clamantium ate † domine.

Ps. Beati immaculati.[5]

Ant. Immutemur habitu in cinere et cilicio ieiunemus et plore-
20 mus ante dominum·͵ quia multum misericors est dimittere peccata
nostra deus noster.

Ps. Deus misereatur.[6]

Oremus.

Presta domine fidelibus tuis· ut ieiuniorum ueneranda
25 sollennia et congrua pietate suscipiant· et secura deuotione
percurrant.

AD MISAM.

Misereris omnium domine et nichil odisti eorum que fecisti
dissimulans peccata hominum propter penitentiam et parcens illis
30 quia tu es dominus deus noster.[7]

Ps. Miserere mei deus miserere mei quoniam· in [te] confidit.[8]

Oremus.

Concede nobis domine presidia militiæ christiane sanctis
inchoare ieiuniis ⸴ ut contra spirituales nequitias pugnaturi·
35 continentie muniamur /auxiliis ⸴ per dominum.   [fo. 22v.

Lectio iohelis profetæ.

Hæc dicit dominus deus. conuertimini ad me   .   .
/   .   . ultra opprobrium in gentibus. dicit dominus ⸴ [fo. 23r.
omnipotens.[9]

[1] Gen. iii. 19 b.   [2] Ps. lxviii. 17.   [3] Ps. lxviii. 2.
[4] Joel. ii. 17 a.   [5] Ps. cxviii. 1.   [6] Ps. lxvi. 2.
[7] Sap. xi. 24, 25 a, 27 a.   [8] Ps. lvi. 2.   [9] Joel. ii. 12-19.

ROSSLYN.   C

Gradale.

Miserere mei deus· miserere mei quoniam in te confidit animam †
meam †.

℣. Misit de celo et liberauit me dedit in obproprium conculcantes
5 me.[1]

Tractus.

Domine non secundum peccata nostra facias nobis neque
secundum iniquitates nostras retribuas nobis.

℣. Domine ne memineris iniquitatum nostrarum antiquarum·
10 cito anticipent nos nos † misericordiæ tuæ quia pauperes facti
sumus nimis.

℣. Adiuua nos deus salutaris noster et propter gloriam nominis
tui domine· libera nos· et propitius esto peccatis nostris propter
nomen· t.[2]

15   ### Secundum matheum.

In illo tempore ⫶ dixit dominus ihesus discipulis suis. cum
ieiunatis ⫶ . . / . . ubi enim est thesaurus tuus [fo. 23v.
ibi est et cor tuum.[3]

Offerenda.

20 Exaltabo te domine quoniam suscepisti me nec dilectasti
inimicos meos super me· domine clamaui ad te et sanasti me.[4]

Secreta.

Fac nos quesumus domine his muneribus offerendis con-
uenienter aptari quibus uenerab[il]is ieiunii celebramus exor-
25 dium ⫶ per dominum.

Communio.

Qui meditabitur in lege domini die ac nocte dabit /fruc- [fo. 24r.
tum suum· in tempore suo.[5]

Post communionem.

30 Percepta no[bi]s domine prebeant sacramenta subsidium· ut
et tibi grata sint nostra ieiunia· et nobis proficiant ad me[de]-
lam per.

Super populum.

Inclinantes se domine maiestati tuę propitiatus intende ⫶ ut
qui diuino munere sunt refecti· celestibus semper nutriantur
auxiliis ⫶ per dominum.

---

[1] Ps. lvi. 2 a, 4 a.   [2] Ps. cii. 10, lxxviii. 8, 9.   [3] Matt. vi. 16–21.
[4] Ps. xxix. 2, 3.   [5] Ps. i. 2 b, 3 b.

DOMINICA IN XLMA.

Inuocauit me et ego exaudiam eum et eripiam eum et glorificabo eum longitudinem † dierum adimplebo.[1]
Ps. Qui habitat in adiutorio altissimi.[2]

5
Oremus.

Deus qui ecclesiam tuam annua quadragessimali obseruatione purificas· presta familiæ tuæ ut quod a te obtinere abstinendo nititur hoc bonis operibus exequatur ⫽ per.

Ad chorintheos.

10 Fratres ⫽ hortamur uos ne in uacuum . . / . . [fo. 24v. tanquam nichil habentes ⫽ et omnia posidentes.[3]

Gradale.

Angelis suis mandauit de te ut custodiant te in omnibus uiís tuis.
15 /℣. In manibus portabunt te ne nunquam † offendas [fo. 25r. ad lapidem.[4]

Tractus.

Qui habitat in adiutorio altissimi [usque] commorabitur.
℣. Dicet domino susceptor meus es· et refugium meum deus
20 meus sperabo in eum.
℣. Quoniam ipse liberauit· me de laqueo uenantium.[5]

Secundum matheum.

In illo tempore ⫽ ductus est ihesus in desertum . . / . . et ecce angeli accesserunt ⫽ et ministrabant [fo. 25v.
25 ei.[6]

Offerenda.

Scapulis suis obumbrauit tibi dominus et sub pennis eius sperabis.
℣. Scuto circundabit te ueritas eius non timebis a timore
30 nocturno.[7]

Secreta.

Sacrificium quadragessimalis initií sollenniter immolamus te domine deprecantes· ut cum epularum restrictione carnalium a noxiis quoque uoluptatibus temperemus.

35
Communio.

Scapulis suis obumbrauit tibi domine † et sub pennis eius sperabis scuto circundabit te ueritas eius.[8]

---

[1] Ps. xc. 15, 16 a.   [2] Ps. xc. I.   [3] 2 Cor. vi. I–10.
[4] Ps. xc. II, 12.   [5] Ps. xc. I, 2, 3.   [6] Matt. iv. I–II.
[7] Ps. xc. 4, 5.   [8] Ps. xc. 4, 5 a.

C 2

Post communionem.

Tui nos domine sacramenti libatio /sancta restauret· [fo. 26r.
et a uetustate purgatos in inisterii † salutaris faciat transire
consortium ꞉ per dominum.

DOMINICUS † SECUNDUS †.

Reminiscere miserationum tuarum domine et misericordię tuæ·
quę a seculo sunt ne nunquam † dominentur· nobis inimici nostri
libera nos deus israhel ex omnibus angustíís nostris.[1]
Ps. Ad te domine leuaui animam meam deus meus in te
10 confido non erubescam.[2]

Oremus.

Deus qui conspicis omni nos uirtute destitui ꞉ misterius †
exteriusque custodi ut et ab omnibus aduersitatibus muniamur
in corpore· et a prauis cogitationibus mundemur in mente ꞉
15 per.

Ad tesolonicenses.

Fratres ꞉ rogamus uos et obsecramus . . / . . [fo. 26v.
sed in sanctificationem ꞉[3] in christo ihesu ꞉ domino nostro.

Tractus.

20 De necessitatibus meis eripe me domine uide humilitatem meam
et laborem meam † et dimitte omnia peccata mea.
Ꝟ. Ad te domine leuaui animam meam deus meus in te confido
non erubescam· neque irrideant me inimici mei etenim uniuersi
qui te expectant non confundentur confundantur omnes facientes
25 uana.[4]

Secundum matheum.

In illo tempore ꞉ egressus dominus ihesus secessit . .
/ . . fiat tibi sicut uis. et sanata est filia eius ꞉ ex [fo. 27r.
illa hora.[5]

30 ### Offerenda.

Meditabor in mandatis tuis que dilexi ualde leuabo manus meas
ad mandata tua que dilexi.[6]

Secreta.

Ecclesia † tua † domine munera placatus assume· que et
35 misericors offerenda /tribuisti· et in nostræ salutis [fo. 27v.
potenter efficis transire misterium per dominum.

---

[1] Ps. xxiv. 6, 3 a (?), 22.   [2] Ps. xxiv. 1, 2.   [3] 1 Thess. iv. 1-7.
[4] Ps. xxiv. 17 b, 18, 1-4 a.   [5] Matt. xv. 21-28.   [6] Ps. cxviii. 47, 48 a.

Communio.

Intellige clamorem meum intende uoci orationis meę rex meus et deus meus· quoniam adorabo.[1]

Post communionem.

5 ˙ Corporis et sanginis sacrosancti domine quesumus gratia nos sumpta uiuificet· et quod misticis actionibus pollicetur eternis effectibus largiatur ;́ per dominum.

DOMINICA TERTIA.

Occuli mei semper ad dominum quia ipse euellet de laqueo
10 pedes meos.[2]
Ps. Respice in me et miserere mei quoniam unicus et pauper sum ego.[3]
Ps. Ad te domine l· a· meam.[4]

Oremus.

15 Quesumus omnipotens deus· uota humilium respice atque ad defensionem nostram dexteram tuæ maiestatis extende ;́ per.

Ad effesseos.

Fratres estote imitatores dei sicut filii karissimi ;́ . .
20 / . . est in omni bonitate ;́ et iustitia et ueritate.[5] [fo. 28r.

Gradale.

Exurge domine non preualeat homo· iudicentur gentes in conspectu tuo.
℣. In conuer[t]endo inimicum m[eu]m retrorsum infirmabuntur
25 et peribunt a facie tua.[6]

Tractus.

Ad te leuaui oculos meos qui habitas in celo.
℣. Ecce sicut oculi seruorum in manibus dominorum suorum.
℣. Et sicut oculi ancillæ in manibus /dominę suæ ita [fo. 28v.
30 oculi nostri· usque nostri.
℣. Miserere nobis domine miserere nobis.[7]

Secundum lucam.

In illo tempore ;́ erat dominus ihesus eic[i]ens demonium
. . / . . beati qui audiunt uerbum dei ;́ et custo- [fo. 29r.
35 diunt. illud.[8]

---

l. 35.́ The punctuation mark after ' custodiunt' has been erased.

[1] Ps. v. 2 b, 3, 4 a. [2] Ps. xxiv. 15. [3] Ps. xxiv. 16.
[4] Ps. xxiv. 1. [5] Eph. v. 1–9. [6] Ps. ix. 20.
[7] Ps. cxxii. 1–3 a. [8] Luc. xi. 14–28.

Offerenda.

Iustitię domini rectæ lętificantes corda· et dulciora super mel et fauum.

[*V.*] Nam et seruus tuus custodit ea.[1]

5 |*Secreta.*   [fo. 29v.

Suscipe quesumus domine deuotorum munera famulorum et tua diuinis purifica seruientes pietate misteríís· quibus etiam iustificas ignorantes :' per.

Communio.

10 Passer inuenit sibi domum et turtur indum † ubi ponat pullos suos· Altaria tua domine uirtutum rex meus et deus meus beati qui habitant in domu tua in seculum seculi laudabunt te.[2]

Post communionem.

A cunctis nos domine reatibus et periculis dignanter
15 propitius absolue· quos tanti misterii tribuis esse participes :' per.

DOMINICA QUARTA.

Lętare ierusalem et conuentum facite omnes qui diligitis eam· gaudete cum lętitia qui in tristitia fuistis· ut exultetis et satiemini
20 ab aperibus † consolationis nostræ.[3]
  V. Lætatus sum.[4]

Oremus.

Concede quesumus omnipotens deus· ut qui ex merito nostre actionis affligimur· tue gratiæ consolatione respiremus :'
25 per dominum.

Ad galathas.

Fratres :' scriptum est :' quoniam abraham . . / [fo. 30r.
. . /itaque fratres :' non sumus ancillæ filii sed liberę. [fo. 30v.
qua libertate christus nos liberauit.[5]

30   *Gradale.*

Lætatus sum in his que dicta sunt michi in domum domini ibimus.
  V. Fiat pax in uirtute tua et abundantia in turribus tuis.[6]

Tractus.

35 Qui confidit in domino sicut mons sion non commouebitur in ęternum qui habitat in ierusalem.

---

[1] Ps. xviii. 9 a, 11 b, 12 a.   [2] Ps. lxxxiii. 4, 5.   [3] Isai. lxvi. 10, 11 a.
[4] Ps. cxxi. 1.   [5] Gal. iv. 22-31.   [6] Ps. cxxi. 1, 7.

Ɲ. Montes in circuitu eius et dominus in circuitu populi sui ex hoc nunc et usque· in.[1]

Secundum iohannem.

In illo tempore ʒ· abíít ihesus trans mare galileę . . / [fo. 31r.
5 . . /signum ʒ· dicebant quia hic est uere propheta ʒ· [fo. 31v. qui uenturus est in mundum.[2]

Offerenda.

Laudate dominum quia benignus est psallite nomini eius quoniam suauis est omnia quecumque uoluit in celo fecit et in
10 terra.[3]

Secreta.

Annue nobis quesumus domine· ut et diu[i]nis semper sollennitatibus occupemur· et misteriis sacris mente pariter congruamus et corpore ʒ· per dominum.

15 ### *Communio.*

Ierusalem que ędificatur ut ciuitas cuius participatio eius in idipsum· illuc enim ascenderunt tribus tribus domini ad confitendum nomini tuo domine.[4]

Post communionem.

20 Da nobis quesumus misericors deus ʒ· ut sancta tua quibus incessabiliter explemur· sincéris tractemus obsequis. et fideli semper mente sumamus ʒ· per dominum.

DOMINICA· Vᵃ· IN PASSIONE DOMINI.

(I)udica me deus· et discerne causam meam de gente non sancta
25 ab homine iniquo et doloso eripe me quia tu es deus meus et fortitudo mea.[5]
[*Ps.*] Quare fremuerunt gentes.[6]

(O)*remus. Ad eb(reos)* †.

Quesumus omnipotens deus familiam tuam /pro- [fo. 32r.
30 pitius respice ʒ· ut te largiente regatur in corpore· et te seruante custodiatur in mente ʒ· per.

Ad ebreos.

Fratres ʒ· christus assistens pontifex futurorum . . . .

---

l. 24. The large ornamental initial has been cut away with a knife.
l. 28. The title *A ebreos* is erased. *Oʳ* (= *oremus*) was written in the place which ought to have been occupied by the *Ps.* of the previous line, the letter *o* having disappeared with the initial referred to in the last note.

[1] Ps. cxxiv. 1, 2.   [2] Joh. vi. 1–14.   [3] Ps. cxxxiv. 3, 6 a.
[4] Ps. cxxi. 3, 4.   [5] Ps. xlii. 1, 2 a.   [6] Ps. ii. 1.

qui uocati sunt ęternę hereditatis[1] /in christo ihesu ꞏ/ [fo. 32v.
domino nostro.

Gradale.

Eripe me domine de inimicis meis doce me facere uoluntatem
5 tuam.
   Ⱳ. liberator meus domine de gentibus iracundis ab insur-
gentibus in me exaltabis me a uiro iniquo eripias † me.[2]

Tractus.

Sepe expugnauerunt me a iuuentute· usque· israhel.
10   *Ⱳ.* Sepe expugnauerunt me· usque michi.
   Ⱳ. Supria † dorsum meum· usque· iniquitatem sibi.
   Ⱳ. Dominus iustus concidet· ceruices· p.[3]

Secundum iohannem.

In illo tempore ꞏ/ dicebat dominus ihesus turbis iudeorum ꞏ/
15 et principibus sacerdotum· quis ex uobis arguit me· de
peccato? . . / . . ihesus autem abscondit [fo. 33r. *et* v.
se ꞏ/ et exiuit de templo.[4]

Offerenda.

Confitebor tibi· d· in toto corde meo.
20   [*Ⱳ.*] Retribue seruo tuo [ut] uiuam et custodiam sermones tuos.
   Ⱳ. Uiuifica me secundum uerbum tuum domine.[5]

Secreta.

Hostias fidelium tuorum deus omnipotens propitius intuere
et concede ne catena seculi captiuos teneat quos passione
25 filii tui in omnibus liberos esse uoluisti ꞏ/ per dominum.

Communio.

Hoc corpus quod pro uobis tradetur· hic calix noui testamenti
est in meo sanguine· dicit dominus· hoc facite quotiescunque
sumitis in meam commemorationem.[6]

30   ### *Post communionem.*

Adesto nobis domine deus noster et quos tuis misteriis
recreasti perpetuis defende presidiis ꞏ/ per dominum.

---

l. 16. At the top left hand corner of fo. 33r. are the letters xБ.
[1] Heb. ix. 11–15.   [2] Ps. cxlii. 9 a, 10 a, xvii. 48 b, 49.
[3] Ps. cxxviii. 1–4.   [4] Joh. viii. 46–59.
[5] Ps. ix. 2 a (cx. I a, cxxxvii. I a, lxxxv. 12 a), cxviii. 17, 25 b.
[6] I Cor. xi. 24 b, 25 b.

DOMINICA PALMARUM.[1]

Domine ne longue facias auxilium tuum a me ad defensionem meam aspice· libera me domine de ore leonis et a cornibus /unicorniorum † humilitatem meam.[1]   [fo. 34r.

5   *Ps.* Deus deus meus respice in me quare.[2]

Oremus.

Omnipotens sempiterne deus· qui humano generi ad imitandum humilitatis exemplum· saluatorem nostrum carnem sumere et crucem subire fecisti concede propitius ꝰ ut et
10 patientiæ ipsius habere documenta· et resurrectionis eius consortia mereamur ꝰ per eundem.

Ad philipenses.

Fratres ꝰ hoc sentite in uobis· quod et   .   .   .   .
/dominus ihesus christus ꝰ in gloria est dei patris.[3]   [fo. 34v.

15   ### Gradale.

Tenuisti manuum † meam dexteram in uoluntatem † tua deduxisti me et cum gloria suscepisti me.
Ⅴ. Quam bonus israhel deus rectis corde mei autem pene moti sunt pedes pene effusi sunt gressus mei.
20   *Ⅴ.* Quia zelaui in peccatoribus pacem peccatorum uideas †.
Ⅴ. Deus deus meus respice in me quare· usque[4]

Passio domini nostri ihesu christi secundum matheum.

In illo tempore ꝰ dixit ihesus discipulis suis ᶠscitis quia post biduum pascha fiat † et filius hominis tradetur ut crucifigatur.
25 ᶜtunc congregati sunt principes sacerdotum et seniores populi in atrium principis sacerdotum qui dicebatur caiphas et consilium fecerunt ut ihesum dolo tenerent ut occiderent· dicebant autem ᶠnon in die . . / . . [fo. 35r. *usque ad* fo. 36r.
Et ᶜymno dicto exierunt in montem oliueti· tunc dixit
30 illis ihesus ᶠomnes . . . / . . . [fo. 36v. *usque ad* fo. 42v.
Altera autem die quę est post parasceuen . . / [fo. 43r.
. . sepulcrum signantes lapidem cum custodibus.[5]

l. 16.   The first letter of 'meam' has been corrected from t before the remainder of the word was written.
l. 23.   The letters *t* (denoting the words of Christ), *s* (those of the Jews and others), and *c* (the narrative) are added in vermilion throughout this Passion, apparently by the hand of a different scribe, who has also made a few corrections of the text and punctuation.
l. 31.   fo. 43r. has the letters xb in its top left corner.

[1] Ps. xxi. 20, 22.   [2] Ps. xxi. 2.   [3] Phil. ii. 5-11.
[4] Ps. lxxii. 24, 1-x, xxi. 2.   [5] Matt. xxvi. xxvii.

Offerenda.

Improperium expectauit cor meum et miseriam et sustinui qui
simul contristaretur et non fuit consolantem me quesiui et non
inueni et dederunt in escam meam fel et in siti mea potauerunt me
5 aceto.[1]

Secreta.

Concede quesumus domine ut oculis tuæ maiestatis oblatum
munus et gratiam nobis deuotionis obtineat et effectum
perhennitatis adquirat ꝛ́ per dominum.

10   ## Communio.

Pater si non potest hic calix transire nisi bibam illum fiat
uoluntas tua.[2]

Post communionem.

Per huius domine operationem misterium † et uitia nostra
15 purgentur et iusta desideria complea[n]tur· per dominum.

MISA ·V· FERIA†.

Nos autem gloriari oportet in cruce domini nostri ihesu christi
in quo est salus uita et resurrectionis † nostra per quem saluati et
liberati sumus.[3]
20   ꝟ.† Deus miseriatur.[4]

Oremus.

Deus a quo et iudas proditor reatus /penam et [fo. 43v.
confessionis suæ latro premium sumpsit concede nobis pro-
piti[ati]onis effectum ut sicut in pasione suæ † ihesus christus
25 dominus noster diuersa intulit uttrisque † stipend[i]a meri-
torum ita nobis oblato † uetustatis errore resurrectionis suæ
gratiam largiatur· qui· t.

Lectio e· b· p· a· ad corintheos.

Fratres ꝛ́ conuenientibus uobis in unum ꝛ́ . . / [fo. 44r.
30 . . coripimur ꝛ́ ut non cum hoc mundo dampnemur.[5]

Gradale.

Christus factus est abodiens † patri pro nobis /usque ad [fo. 44v.
mortem mortem autem crucis.

l. 24.   A letter is erased after s in 'pasione.'
l. 25.   'Uttrisque' is written over an erasure.

[1] Ps. lxviii. 21 b, 22.   [2] Matt. xxvi. 42.
[3] Cf. Gal. vi. 14.   [4] Ps. lxvi. 2.
[5] 1 Cor. xi. 20-32.

ut † propter quod deus illum exaltauit et donauit illi nomen super omne nomen.[1]

Secundum iohannem.

In illo tempore ; ante diem festum paschæ sciens ihesus
5 . . . / . . ego feci uobis ; ita uos faciatis.[2]   [fo. 45r.

Of[ferenda].

Dextera domini fecit uirtutem dextera domini exaltauit [me] dextera domini· f· usque opera domini.[3]

Secreta.

10   Ipse tibi quesumus domine sancte pater omnipotens eterne deus sacrificium nostrum re[d]dat acceptum qui discipulis /suis in sui commemoratione hec fieri hodierna [fo. 45v. traditione monstrauit ihesus christus dominus noster qui tecum.

15   Communicantes et diem sacratissimum celebrantes in quo lauit pedes discipulorum suorum et immolauit corpus suum et sanguinem in misterium redemptionis nostrę sed et memoriam.

     Hanc igitur oblationem seruitutis nostræ sed ut † cuncta †
20 familia † tuæ quam tibi offerimus ob diem in qua dominus noster ihesus christus tradidit discipulis suis corporis et sanguinis sui misteria celebranda quesumus domine· ut placatus accipias·

     qui pridie quia † pro nostræ † omniumque salute pateretur·
25 hodie accepit panem in sanctas.

Communio.

Dominus ihesus postquam cenauit cum discipulis suis lauit pedes eorum et ait illis scitis que fecirim uobis ego dominus et magister exemplum enim dedi uobis ut et uos ita faciatis.[4]

30   ### *Post communionem.*

     Refecti uitalibus alimentis quesumus domine deus noster ut quod tempere † nostre /mortalitatis ex[se]quimur [fo. 46r. immortalitatis tuæ munere consequamur ; per dominum.

Ad uesperas.

35 *Ant.*   Calicem salutaris accipiam nomen domini et reliqua.[5]
     Ps.   Credidi propter quod.[6]

---

[1] Phil. ii. 8, 9.   [2] Joh. xiii. 1-15.   [3] Ps. cxvii. 16, 17.
[4] Cf. Joh. xiii. 4, 5, 12-14.   [5] Ps. cxv. 13.   [6] Ps. cxv. 10.

Ant. Cum his qui oderunt· p· eram· p· cum loquebar illis
impugnabant me gratis.[1]
      Ps. Ad dominum.[2]
      Ant. Ab omnibus† iniquis libera me domine.[3]
5   *Ps.* Eripe me.[4]
      Ant. Custodi me a laqueo quem statuerunt me † et ab scandalis
[operantium] iniquitatem.[5]
      Ps. Domine clamaui· a.[6]
      Ant. Considerabam ad dexteram et uidebam et non erat qui
10 cognosceret me.[7]
      [*Ps.*] Uoce mea.[8]
      euangelium† cenantibus hec† accepit ihesus panem benedixit
ac· fregit dedit discipulis suis.[9]

Post communionem.

15   Refecti uitalibus alimentis ut supra.

FERIA· VI[ae] †· IN PARASCIUEN†.

Oremus.

Deus a quo et iudas ut supra.

Lectio isaię † profetæ.

20   Hæc dicit dominus deus. in tribulatione . . | [fo. 46v.
. . et scientiam :' plus quam holochausta.[10]

Gradale.

Domine audiui auditum tuum et timui consideraui opera tuę †
et expaui.
25   ℣. In medio duum animalium innotessceris dum approprin-
quauerunt † anni cognosceris dum aduenerit tempus ostenderis.
      sed † in eo dum conturbata fuerit anima mea in ira misericordię
memor eris.
      sed †· deus a libano ueniet et sanctus de monte umbroso et
30 condenso.
      sed † aperuit† celos maiestas eius et laude eius plena est terra.[11]

Oremus.

Deus qui peccati ueteris hereditariam mortem in qua
posteritatis genus omne su[c]cesserat christi filii tui domini

---

l. 16. This title (with the exception of the last six letters, which are in red)
is in the small character used for grails, &c.

[1] Ps. cxix. 7.	[2] Ps. cxix. 1.	[3] Ps. cxxxix. 5 b.
[4] Ps. cxxxix. 2.	[5] Ps. cxl. 9.	[6] Ps. cxl. 1.
[7] Ps. cxli. 5 a.	[8] Ps. cxli. 2.	[9] Matt. xxvi. 26 a.
[10] Osee vi. 1–6.	[11] Hab. iii. 2, 3.	

[nostri] /passionis † uoluisti † da [ut] conformes eiusdem[fo.47r.
facti sicut imaginem terreni natura † necessitate po[r]taui-
mus ita imaginem celestis gratiæ sanctificatione portem[us]
ihesu christi domini nostri qui tecum.

5   *Lectio libri exodi.*

In diebus illis ⁊ dixit dominus ad moysen et aaron . .
/ . . phase ⁊ id est transetus domini.¹   [fo. 47v.

                        Gradale.

Eripe me domine ab homine malo a uiro iniquo eripe me.
10   ℣. Qui cogitauerunt malitias in corde tota die constituebant
prelia.
     ℣. Acuerunt lingas suas sicut serpentes uenenum aspidum sub
labiis eorum.
     ℣. Custodi [me] domine de manu peccatoris ab hominibus ·ii· †
15 libera.
     /℣. Qui cogitauerunt subplantare gressus meos et reliqua.[fo.48r.
     ℣. Et funes extenderunt.
     ℣. Dixi domino deus meus es tu exaudi domine uocem
orationis· mea†.
20   ℣. Domine domine uirtus salutis· mea†· abumbrasti† super
caput meum· d· b.
     ℣. Non † tradas domine usque exaltentur.
     ℣. Caput circuitus eorum.
     ℣. Uerumtamen iusti confitebuntur nomini tuo habitabunt recti
25 cum uultu tuo.²

       Pasio domini nostri· i· christi· secundum iohannem.

In illo tempore ⁊ egressus est ihesus cum discipulis suis .
     · \/ . . . . [fo. 48v. *usque ad* fo. 53r.
/fuerat. ibi ergo propter parasciuen iudeorum ⁊ quam † [fo. 53v.
30 iuxta erat monumentum possuerunt ihesum.³

                 Orationes in parasciue.

Oremus dilectissime † nobis pro ecclesia sancta dei· ut eam
deus et dominus noster pacificare et custodire dignetur· toto
orbe terrarum subieciens ei principatus et potestates· detque
35 nobis quietam et trancillam uitam degentibus glorificare deum
patrem omnipotentem.
     Oremus flectamus genua prosternitur leuate.

Omnipotens sempiterne deus qui gloriam tuam omnibus in
christo gentibus reuelasti ⁊ custodi opera misericordiæ tuæ ut

---

l. 28.   The outer margin of fo. 49 has been cut away.
¹ Exod. xii. 1-11.   ² Ps. cxxxix. 2-10, 14.   ³ Joh. xviii. xix.

ecclesia tua toto orbe defusa stabili fide in confessione tui
nominis perseueret ꝫ per dominum.

Oremus et pro beatissimo papa nostro ·n· ut deus et
dominus noster qui elegit eum in ordinem episcopatus saluum
5 atque incolomem custodiat ecclesiæ suæ· sanctæ ad regen-
dum populum sanctum dei.

/*Oremus flectamus g l.*   [fo. 54r.

Omnipotens sempiterne deus cuius iudicio uniuersa fundan-
tur respice propitius ad preces nostras et electum nobis
10 antistitem tua pietate conserua· ut christiana plebs que tali
gubernatur auctore sub tanto pontifice credulitatis suæ meritis
augeatur per.

Oremus pro omnibus episcopis prespeteris † diacionibus †
subdiaconibus acolitis exorcistis lectoribus hostiaris con-
15 fessioribus † uirginibus uiduis· et pro omni populo sancto dei.

Oremus· flectamus g le.

Omnipotens sempiterne deus· cuius spiritu totum corpus
ecclesie sanctificetur † et regitur· exaudi nos pro uniuersis
ordinibus supplicantes ut gratiæ tuæ munere ab omnibus
20 gradibus tibi fideliter seruator † ꝫ per.

Oremus et pro christiano imperatore nostro ·n· ut deus et
dominus noster subditas faciat omnes barbaras nationes ad
nostram perpetuam pacem.

Oremus flectamus g l.

25 /Omnipotens sempiterne deus in cuius manu sunt [fo. 54v.
omnium potesttates† · et omnia iura regnorum respice ad
christianorum benignus imperium ut gentes que in sua uirtute
confidunt potentiæ tuæ dextra comprimantur· per dominum.

Oremus et pro catacuminis nostris· ut deus ac dominus
30 noster adaperiat aures precordiorum ipsorum ianuamque
misericordiæ· ut per lauacrum regenerationis accepta re-
misione omnium peccatorum et ipsi inuenientur † in christo
ihesu domino nostro· per.

Oremus flectamus· g leuate.

35 Omnipotens sempiterne deus qui ecclesiam tuam noua
semper prole fecundas auge fidem et intellectum catacuminis

nostris· ut renati fonte baptismatis adoptionis tuæ filiis a[g]-
gregentur :' per dominum.

Oremus dilectissimi nobis deum patrem omnipotentem
mundum· ut cunctis deus pater omnipotens purget erroribus
5 morbos auferat· famem depellat /aperiat carceres [fo. 55r.
uincula desoluat perigrinantibus reditum infirmantibus sanitatem nauigantibus portum· salutis indulgeat :' per.
                    Flec· g· le.

Omnipotens sempiterne deus· mestorum consolatio labor-
10 antium fortitudo :' peruentant ad te preces de quacunque tribulatione clamantium ut omnes sibi in necessitatibus suis
misericordiam tuam gaudeant affuisse :' per.

Oremus et pro hereticis et scismaticis ut deus et dominus
noster ihesus christus eruat eos ab erroribus uniuersis et ad
15 sanctam matrem ecclesiam catholicam et apostolicam reuocare
dignetur :' per.
                    Oremus flectamus· g· leuate.

Omnipotens sempiterne deus qui saluas omnes et neminem
uis perire· ad animas respice diabolicaticat† fr[a]ude deceptas
20 ut omni heritica prauitate deposita errantium corda resipiscant
et ad ueritatis tuæ redeant unitatem per.

/Oremus et pro perfidis iudeis : ut deus et dominus [fo. 55v.
noster auferat uelamen de cordibus eorum ut et ipsi agnos-
cant ihesum christum dominum nostrum.
25   *Oremus híc non flectuntur· g.*

Omnipotens sempiterne deus· qui qui † etiam iudaicam perfideam [a] tua misericordia non repellis· exaudi preces nostras
quas pro illius populi obcecatione defferimus ut agnita ueritatis tuæ luce que christus est a suis tenebris eruantur :' per.

30   Oremus et pro paginist† ut deus omnipotens auferat iniquitatem de cordibus eorum· ut relictis idulis suis conuertantur
ad deum uerum et unicum filium eius ihesum christum dominum nostrum cum quo uiuit et regnat cum spiritu sancto
deus per omnia secula seculorum amen.
35   *Oremus flectamus g.*

Omnipotens sempiterne deus qui non uis mortem peccatorum sed uitam semper inciris· suscipe propitius orationem

l. 25. The second ' qui ' is erased.

nostram· et libera eos ab idulorum /cultura et aggrega [fo. 56r.
ecclesiamꝉ tuamꝉ sanctamꝉ ad laudem et gloriam nominis tui·
per· d.

His expletis preparatur crux et ponitur uelata iuxta altare et
5 sustineatur hinc et inde a duobus acolitis cantantibus hos uersus.
Hic induit episcopus se capa.

Ant. Popule meus quid feci tibi aut in quo contristaui te re-
sponde michi qui[a] eduxi te de terra egipti parasti crucem
saluatori tuo.

10 *Alia † duo parati ita respondent*

Agios otheos agios ysciros agios atanathos eleisonẏmas.

flexis genibus deinde subsequatur chorus et dicit †·
Sanctus deus sanctus fortis sanctus et immortalis miserere nobis.

Item ii· tenentes crucem dicunt Antiphonam.

15 Quia eduxi te per desertum ·xl· annos uestimenta tua et calcia-
menta uetustate non sunt atrita manna quoque cibaui te et introduxi in terram satis optimam[1] parasti crucem saluatori tuo.
Preui dicunt· Agios· Sanctus.

Deinde duo primi dicunt

20 Qui[d] ultra debui facere tibi et non feci. ego quid[em] pla[n]taui
te uineam meam fructu decoram[2] et tu facta es michi satis amara
aceto nanque mixto cum felle /sitim meam potastisꝉ[3] et [fo. 56v.
lancea perforasti latus[4] saluatoris tui.
Agios.

25 *Ymnus.*

Crux fidelis inter omnes arbor una nobilis nulla silluaꝉ talem
profert fronde flore germine dulce lignum dulce[s] clauos dulce
pondus sustinet.
Pange lingua gloriosi prelium certaminis et super crucis tropheo
30 dic triumphum nobile[m]· qualiter redemptor orbis immolatus
uicerit.

[Oremus.]

Preceptis salutari[bu]s· pater libera nos.
Refecti uitalibus.

35 *Antiphona.* Calicem salutaris accipiam.[5]
Ps. Credidi.[6]
Ps. Ad dominum cum.[7]

[1] Cf. Deut. viii. 2–4, 7, xxix. 5.   [2] Isai. v. 4 a, 2 a.
[3] Cf. Ps. lxviii. 22 ; Matt. xxvii. 34 a.   [4] Cf. Joh. xix. 34 a.
[5] Ps. cxv. 13.   [6] Ps. cxv. 10.   [7] Ps. cxix. 1.

Ps. Eripe.[1]
Ps. Domine clamaui.[2]
Ps. Uoce mea ad dominum.[3]
Ant. Mulieres sedentes ad monumentum lamentabantur flentes
5 dominum.[4]
[*Ps.*] Magnificat.[5]

Oremus.

Deus qui unigeniti filii tui domini· n· i· christi· et reliqua.

[UIGILIA PASCHÆ.]

10   *Lectio libri genesis hic induit se casula.*

In principio creauit deus celum et terram ·/ · ·
/ · · et requieuit die septimo [fo. 57r. *usque ad* fo. 58v.
ab omni opere [quod] patrarat.[6]

        /*Oremus.*   [fo. 59r.

15 Deus qui mirabiliter creasti hominem et mirabilibus †
redimisti· da nobis contra oblectamenta peccasti† mentis
ratione persistere ut mereamur ad gaudia eterna peruenire
per.

        Lectio libri exodi.

20 In diebus illis ·/ factum est in uigilia matutina· et ecce · ·
/ · · et filii israhel carmen hoc domino dixerunt.[7] [fo. 59v.

        Gradale.

Cantemus domino gloriosæ enim honorificatus est ęquum et
ascensorem proiecit in mare adiutor et protector factus est in
25 salutem.
  V. Hic deus meus· honorabo eum deus patris mei et exaltabo
eum.
  V. Dominus conterens bella dominus nomen est illi.[8]

        Oremus.

30 Deus cuius antiqua miracula etiam [nostris seculis corus-
care] sentimus dum quod uim † populo a persecutione egiptia
liberando dextra † /tuæ potentia contulisti id in salu- [fo. 60r.
tem gentium per aqua[m] regenerationes† operaris ·/ presta.
ut in abrahę filios et in israheliticam dignitate[m] totius
35 mundi transeat plenitudo ·/ per.

---

[1] Ps. cxxxix. 2.   [2] Ps. cxl. 1.   [3] Ps. cxli. 2.
[4] Cf. Joh. xx. 11 a.   [5] Luc. i. 46–55.   [6] Gen. i, ii. 1, 2.
[7] Exod. xiv. 24–31, xv. 1 a.   [8] Exod. xv. 1 b, 2 b, 3.

Lectio isaię profetæ.

In diebus illis apprehendit † septem mulieres . . / [fo. 60v.
. . et absconsionem a turbidine et a pluuia.[1]

Gradale.

5   Uinia facta est dilectu † in cornu in loco uberi.
ut † et maceriam circundedit et circundedit † et plantauit uineam
edificauit turrim in medio.
   V. Et tarcular † fodit in ea uineam † enim domini sabaoth
domus israhel.[2]

10   *Oremus.*

Deus [qui] nos ad celebrandum paschale sacramentum
uttriusque † testamenti paginis imbuisti ꞉ da nobis intelligere
imisericordias † tuas ut ex perceptione presentium munerum
firma sit expectatio futurorum· per dominum.

15   *Lectio isaię profetæ.*

Hæc est hereditas seruorum . . / . . [fo. 61r. *et* v.
uerbum meum quod egred[i]etur de ore meo [dicit] dominus
omnipotens.[3]

               Oremus.

20   Deus qui ecclesiam tuam semper gentium uocatione multi-
plicas· concede propitius ut quos aqua baptismatis abluis·
continua protectione tu[e]aris ꞉ per dominum.

               Gradale.

Sicut ceruus desiderat ad fontes aquarum ita desiderat anima mea
25 ate † deus.
   V. Sitiuit anima mea ad deum uiuum quando ueniam et
apparebo ante faciam † dei mei.
   V. Fuerunt michi lacrimæ meæ panes die ac nocte dum dicitur
michi /per singulos dies ubi est deus tuus.[4]   [fo. 62r.

30   *[Oremus].*

Concede quesumus omnipotens deus· ut qui festa paschalia
agimus celestibus desideriis accensi fonte[m] uitæ sitiamus ꞉
per dominum.
    Post est † sacerdote red[e]unte in uestiar[i]um. hic procedat ad
35 *fontes cum lętanis prolixis· red[e]untes uero a fonte decantent*
subiectam letaniam choris alternatim respondentibus.
Christe audi nos· Sancta maria ora pro nobis.
Sancta diei † genitrix ora pro nobis.

l. 13. The first i is expuncted.
[1] Isai. iv.   [2] Isai. v. 1 b, 2 a, 7 a.   [3] Isai. liv. 17 b, lv. 1–11 a.
[4] Ps. xli. 2–4.

Sancta uirgo uirginum· o· Sancte michel or[a] pro.
Sancte gabriel ora pro [pro· Sancte rapael· Sancte
iohannes ora pro nobis Sancte petre· Sancte pau-
Sancta † andrea Sancte sephane† le or[a] pro
5 Sancte laurentii Sancte uincentii
Sancte siluester ora pro Sancte griori† o· pro
S· benedicte· o· pro Sancta petronilla· o· pro
Sancta agatha o[ra] pro Sancte † margareta· or· pro
Omnes sancti orate pro Propitius esto parce nobis· d·
10 Propitius esto libera nos domine
Per crucem tuam libera nos domine
Per sanctam resurrectionem tuam libera· n· d·
/Peccatores te rogamus audi nos   [fo. 62v.
Ut pacem nobis dones te rogamus audi· n·
15 Ut pluuiam nobis dones· t· r· audi nos
Ut fructum terre nobis dones· t· r· a· n·
Ut nos exaudire digneris· t· r· a· n·
Filii dei te rogamus audi nos

Hic breuiter siliant et duo cantores dicant· ter· accendite accen-
20 dite· accendite· Sequatur deinde festiuum· Cirileison quod dum
inceperunt sollenni processione ingrediatur sacerdos· et facta
oratione adoleat incensum· Cirileison· iii· christe[leison]· iii· Cirie-
leison· iii· Gloria in excelsis deo plurentur†.

Oremus.

25 Deus qui hanc sacratissimam noctem gloria dominica† resurrectionis illustras conserua in noua familiæ tuæ progenie
adoptionis spiritum quem dedisti ut corpore et mente reno-
uasti † puram tuam exhibeant seruitutem in unitate eiusdem
per†.
30 ### *Lectio ad colasenses†.*

Fratres qui ;' consurrexistis cum christo· quæ . . / [fo. 63r.
. . tunc et uos apparebitis cum ipso in gloria·[1] alleluia.

Ps.† Confitemini domino quoniam bonus quoniam in seculum·
misericordia eius.[2]
35 ### *Tractus.*

Laudate dominum omnes· g.[3]

Secundum matheum.

Uespere autem sabbati quę lucescit in prima . . [fo. 63v.
/ . . ibi eum uidebitis sicut predixit uobis.[4]

[1] Col. iii. 1-4.   [2] Ps. cxvii. 1.
[3] Ps. cxvi. 1.   [4] Matt. xxviii. 1-7.

Ipsa die non canitur offerenda nec agnus dei nec communio neque pax accipitur.

Secreta.

Suscipe domine quesumus preces populi tui cum oblationi-
5 bus hostiarum ut paschalibus initiatæ misertus † ad eternitatis nobis medelam te operante percipiaht † ꞌ per dominum.

Et te quidem omni tempore ꞌ sed in hanc†.

Communicantes et noctem sacratissimam celebrantes resurrectionis domini nostri ihesu christi secundum carnem· sed et
10 memoriam uenerantes inprimis glori[os]ę semper uirginis marię genetricis eiusdem domini et dei nostri christi sed [et] beatorum.

Hanc igitur oblationem seruitutis nostræ sed et cunctæ familiæ tuæ quia † tibi offerimus pro his quoque quos regene-
15 rare dignatus es ex aqua et spiritu sancto tribuens eis remis-
sionem omnium peccatorum ꞌ quesumus domine ut placatus.

|*Post communionem.*   [fo. 64r.

Spiritum nobis domine tuæ caritatis infunde [ut quos] sacramentis paschalibus satiasti tua facias pietate concordes
20 per in unitatem † eiusdem.

IN DIE SANCTA† PASCHA†.

Antiphona.

Resurrexi et adhuc tecum sum alleluia possuisti super me manum tuam alleluia alleluia mirabilis facta est scientia tua alleluia
25 alleluia alleluia.[1]
Ps. Domine probasti me et cognouisti me[2] gloria.

Oremus.

Deus qui hodierna die per unigenitum tuum ęternitatis nobis aditum deuicta morte reserasti ꞌ uota nostra que pre-
30 ueniendo aspiras· etiam adiuuando prosequere per eundem.

Ad corintheos.

Fratres ꞌ expurgate uetus fermentum ꞌ ut sitis . . . . et nequitiæ ꞌ sed in azimis sinceritatis ꞌ et ueritatis.[3]

---

[1] Ps. cxxxviii. 18 b, 5 b, 6 a.   [2] Ps. cxxxviii. 1.   [3] 1 Cor. v. 7, 8.

Gradale.

Hec est dies quam fecit dominus exultemus et lætemur in ea.
V. Confitemini domino quoniam bonus quoniam /in [fo. 64v. seculum misericordia eius· Alleluia.
5 *V.* Pascha nostrum immolatus est christus.
V. Epulemur in astimis sinceritatis et ueritatis.[1]

Secundum marcum.

In illo tempore :/ maria magdalenæ et maria iacobi . . .
. precedet uos in galileam. ibi eum uidebitis sicut dixit
10 uobis.[2]

Offerenda.

Terra tremuit et quieuit dum resurg[er]et in iudicio deus· alleluia· notus in iudea deus· usque eius· et factus est in pace locus eius· usque· in sion· ibi confregit potentias· usque· eternis.[3]

15   /*Secreta.*   [fo. 65r.

Suscipe p[ro]pitius domine munera famulorum tuorum ut in confessione tui nominis et baptismate renouati sempiternam beatitudinem consequantur per.

Communio.

20 Pascha nostrum immolatus est christus alleluia· itaque epulemur in azemis † sinceritatis et ueritatis[4] alleluia alleluia.

Post communionem.

Spiritum nobis domine tuæ caritatis [infunde ut quos] sacramentis paschalibus satiasti tua facias pietate concordes·
25 per in unitate eiusdem.

DOMINICA IN ALBIS.

Quasi modo geniti infantes· alleluia· rationabile sine dolo lac concupiscite[5] alleluia alleluia alleluia.
Ps. Exultate deo· usque· iacob.[6]

30   · *Oremus.*

Presta quesumus omnipotens deus :/ ut qui pascalia festa peregimus· hec te largiente moribus et uita teneamus per.

---

l. 16. The rubricator has added the mark indicating 'ro' in the first syllable of 'propitius.'

[1] Ps. cxvii. 24, 1 ; I Cor. v. 7 b, 8 a, c.
[2] Marc. xvi. 1-7.   [3] Ps. lxxv. 9 b, 10 a, 2-5.   [4] I Cor. v. 7 b, 8 a,c.
[5] I Pet. ii. 2 a.   [6] Ps. lxxx. 2.

Lectio epistolæ b· iohannis· a·

Karissimi ·/ omne quod natum est ex deo ·/ . . | [fo. 65v.
. . qui credit in filium dei ·/ habet testimonium dei in se.[1]
Alleluia.

5   *Ν.* dominus regnauit decorem induitus†· usque seruitute†· alleluia alleluia.

[*Ν.*] Iubilate deo omnis· usque in lætitia.[2]

Secundum iohannem.

In illo tempore ·/ tomas autem unus de xii· qui . .
10 | . . ut credentes uitam habeatis ·/ in nomine meo.[3] [fo. 66r.

Offerenda.

Angelus domini discendit de celo et dixit mulieribus quem
queritis surrexit sicut dixit alleluia alleluia euntes dicite discipulis
eius· ecce precedet uos in galileam ibi eum uidebitis sicut dixit
15 dixit alleluia ihesus sicut dixit stetit in medio eorum et dixit eis
pax uobis uidete quia ego ipse sum.[4]

Secreta.

Suscipe munera quesumus domine exultantis ecclesie· et cui
causam tanti gaudií prestetisti· perpetuum /fructum [fo. 66v.
20 concede letitiæ.

Communio.

Mitte manuum † tuam et cognosce loca clauorum alleluia· et
noli e[ss]e [in]credulus sed fidelis.[5]

Post communionem.

25   Quesumus domine deus noster ut sacrosancta misteria que
pro prearationis † nostre munimine contulisti· et presens
nobis remedium esse facias et futurum ·/ per.

UIGILIA ASCENSIONIS.

Omnes gentes plaudite manibus· usque exultationis.[6]
30   [*Ps.*] subiecit populos nobis· usque nostris.[7]

Oremus.

Presta quesumus omnipotens deus· ut nostre mentis
intentio· quo sollennitatis hodiernę gloriossus auctor ingressus
est semper intendat et quo fide pergit conuersatione perueniat
35 per eundem.

---

l. 19. The second e of 'prestetisti' is altered from i.

[1] 1 Joh. v. 4–10 a.   [2] Ps. xcii. 1 a, xcix. 2 a.   [3] Joh. xx. 24–31.
[4] Matt. xxviii. 2 b, (5), 6 a, 7 ; Luc. xxiv. 36, 39 a.   [5] Cf. Joh. xx. 27.
[6] Ps. xlvi. 2.   [7] Ps. xlvi. 4.

Lectio actuum apostolorum.

In diebus illis ⸭ multitudinis credentium erat . . / [fo. 67r.
   . . diuidebantur autem singulis prout cunque † opus erat.[1]
Alleluia.
5   *V.* confitemini domino et inuocate nomen eius annuntiate inter
gentes· o· eius.[2]

Secundum iohannem.

In illo tempore ⸭ subleuatis dominus oculis in celum ⸭ ihesus
dixit. . . / . . non sum in mundo et híí in [fo. 67v.
10   mundo sunt ⸭ et ego ad te uenio.[3]

Offerenda.

Uiri galilei quid admiramini aspicientes in celum hic ihesus qui
assumptus est a uobis in celum sic ueniet quemadmodum uidistis
eum ascendentem in celum alleluia cunque intuerentur in celum
15   euntem illum duo· uiri assteterunt iuxta illos in uestibus albis.[4]

Secreta.

Sacrificium domine pro filii tui supplices uenerabili quam
preuenimus ascensione deferimus· presta quesumus ut et nos
per ipsum hiis commerciis sacrosanctis ad celestia /con- [fo. 68r.
20   surgamus· per.

Communio.

Pater cum essem cum eis ego seruabam eos quos dedisti michi
alleluia· nunc autem ad te uenio non rogo ut tollas eos de mundo·
sed ut serues eos a malo·[5] a· a.

25   *Post* [*communionem*].

Tribue quesumus domine· ut per hec sacramenta que
sumpsimus illuc tendat nostræ deuotionis affectus quo tecum
est nostra substantia· ihesus christus dominus noster· qui
tecum.

30   IN DIE AD MISAM.

Viri galilei quid admiramini aspicientes in celum alleluia
quemadmodum uidistis eum ascendentem in celum ita ueniet
alleluia alleluia.[6]
Ps. Omnes gentes plaudite· usque exultationis.[7]

l. 31. The initial of ' Viri' is here V not as usually elsewhere U.
[1] Acts iv. 32-35.   [2] Ps. civ. 1.   [3] Joh. xvii. 1-11 a.
[4] Act. i. 11, 10.   [5] Joh. xvii. 12 a, 13 a, 15.   [6] Act. i. 11 a, c.
[7] Ps. xlvi. 2.

Oremus.

Concede quesumus omnipotens deus :′ ut qui hodierna die
unigenitum tuum redemptorem nostrum ad celos ascendisse
credimus ipsi quoque mente in celestibus habitemus :′ per
5 dominum.

Lectio actuum apostolorum.

Primum quidem sermonem feci de omnibus . .
/ , . sic ueniat † quemadmodum uidistis eum [ff. 68v., 69r.
eundem † in celum.[1]
10 Alleluia.
  ℣. Ascendit deus in iubilatione dominus in uoce tubæ· alleluia
dominus in sina in sancto ascendens in altum captiuam duxit cap-
tiuitatem[2] alleluia.

Secundum marcum.

15 In illo tempore :′ recumbentibus illis· xi· discipulis :′ . .
/ . , et sermonem confirmante :′ sequentibus signis.[3] [fo. 69v.

Offerenda.

Ascendit deus in iubilatione dominus in uoce tubę alleluia.
  [℣.] Omnes gentes plaudite· usque exultationis quoniam
20 dominus summus terribilis rex magnus super omnem terram
alleluia subiecit populos nobis· usque nobis alleluia.[4]

Secreta.

Suscipe domine munera que pro filii tui gloriossa ascensione
deferimus· et concede propitius (. .) ut a presentibus
25 periculis liberemur et ad uitam perueniamus ęternam per.

Communicantes et diem sacratissimum celebrantes quo
dominus ihesus christus noster unigenitus tuus filius unitam
sibi fragilitatis nostræ substantiam· in gloriæ tuæ dextera
/collocauit· et memoriam uenerantes inprimis [fo. 70r.
30 gloriossę semper uirginis.

Communio.

Psallite domino qui ascendit super celos celorum ad orientem.[5]

Post (communionem).

Presta nobis quesumus omnipotens et misericors deus· ut
35 quę uisibilibus misteriis sumendo † percepimus· inuisibili
consequamur effectu· per dominum.

l. 15. The word 'illis' is erased.
l. 24. A word, following 'propitius' and connected by a hyphen with 'ut,' is
erased.
l. 33. The outer margin of fo. 70 has been cut away, and with it the last
letters of the titles *post communionem, ad misam.*
[1] Act. i. 1–11.   [2] Ps. xlvi. 6, lxvii. 18 b, 19 a (Eph. iv. 8 a).
[3] Marc. xvi. 14–20.   [4] Ps. xlvi. 6, 2–4.   [5] Ps. lxvii. 33 b, 34 a.

[UIGILIA PENTECOSTES.]

Ad mi(sam) oratio.

Kyrrieleison † ter christe eleison· ter kyrrieleison †· ter dominus uobiscum.

5 *Oremus.*

Presta quesumus omnipotens deus ut claritatis tuæ super nos splendor effulgeat· et lux tua † lucis corda eorum qui per gratiam tuam renati sunt et† sancti spiritus illustratione confirmet· per in unitate eiusdem.

10 *Lectio actuum apostolorum.*

In diebus illis ·/ factum est cum appollo esset corinti· . . / . . menses ·/ desputans et suadens de regno [fo. 70v. dei.[1]

Alleluia.
15 *V.·* Confitemini domino usque eius laudate dominum omnes gentes· usque in ęternum.[2]

Secundum iohannem.

In illo tempore ·/ dixit ihesus discipulis suis. si diligeritis me . . / ·. ·/ et ego· diligam eum ·/ et manifestabo ei [fo. 71r.
20 me ipsum.[3]

Offerenda.

Emitte spiritum tuum et creabuntur et renouabis faciem terrę sit gloria domini in secula·[4] alleluia.

Sec[reta].

25 Munera domine quesumus oblata sanctifica et corda nostra sancti spiritus illustratione emunda· per in.

Communicantes et noctem sacratissimam penticustes celebrantes quo spiritus sanctus apostolis innumeris lingis apparuit sed et memoriam uenerantes inprimis gloriossę.

30 Hanc igitur oblationem seruitutis nostre sed et cunctæ familie tuæ quam tibi offerimus p[ro] his quoque quos regenerare /dignatus es ex aqua et spiritu sancto [fo. 71v. trib[u]ens eis remisionem omnium peccatorum quesumus domine ut placatus accipias.

l. 2. See note on p. 40, l. 33.
[1] Act. xix. 1–8. [2] Ps. cxvii. 1 ; cxvi. [3] Joh. xiv. 15-21.
[4] Ps. ciii. 30, 31 a.

Communio.

Ultimo festiuitatis die dicebat ihesus qui in me credit flumina de
uentre eius fluent aquę uiuę hoc autem dixit de spiritu sancto
quem accepturi erant credentes in eum[1] alleluia alleluia.

5   ### Post [communionem].

Sancti spiritus domine corda nostra mundet infussio et sui
roris intima a[s]persione fecundet per.

DOMINICA PENTICOSTES.

Spiritus domini repleuit orbem terrarum alleluia et hoc quod
10 continet omnia scientiam habet uocis[2] alleluia alleluia alleluia.
Ps. Exurgat deus et dissipentur· usque eius confirma deus hoc
quod· usque nobis.[3]

Oremus.

Deus qui hodierna die corda fidelium spiritus sancti illus-
15 tratione docuisti ꝫ da nobis in eodem spiritu recta sapere et de
eius semper consolatione gaudere per in unitate eiusdem.

Lectio actuum apostolorum.

In diebus illis ꝫ cum complerentur dies penticustes ꝫ . .
/ . . audiuimus eos loquentes nostris linguis ꝫ [fo. 72r. *et* v.
20 magnalia dei.[4]
Alleluia.
V. Emitte spiritum tuum et creabuntur usque terre alleluia.
[*V.*] Spiritus domini replebit orbem terrarum usque habet.[5]

Secundum iohannem.

25 In illo tempore ꝫ dixit ihesus discipulis suis. si quis diligit
me . . / . . et sicut mandatum dedit michi [fo. 73r.
pater ꝫ sic facio.[6]

[Offerenda].

Confirma deus hoc quod operatus es nobis a templo tuo in
30 ierusalem· usque munera alleluia.
[*V.*] Cantate domino psalmum dicite nomini eius iter facite ei·
usque illi in ecclesiis benedicite dominum † deum † de fontibus
israhel· ibi beniamini· usque excessu regena † terra † cantate deo
psallite domino psallite deo qui ascendit· usque ad orientem.[7]

---

l. 26. The rubricator has entirely passed over ff. 73–76.

[1] Joh. vii. 37 a, 38, 39 a.   [2] Sap. i. 7.   [3] Ps. lxvii. 2, 29 b.
[4] Act. ii. 1–11.   [5] Ps. ciii. 30; Sap. i. 7.   [6] Joh. xiv. 23–31 a.
[7] Ps. lxvii. 29 b, 30, 5 a, 27, 28 a, 33, 34 a.

[Secreta].

Munera quesumus domine oblata sanctifica· et corda nostra sancti spiritus illiustratione † emunda per in· eiusdem.

Communicantes et diem· ut est in sabbato.

5   Hanc igitur oblationem ut est in sabbato.

/[*Communio*].   [fo. 73v.

Factus est repente de celo sonus tanquam aduenientis spiritus uehimentis ubi erant apostoli sedentes alleluia· et et † repleti sunt omnes spiritu sancto loquentes magnalia[1] alleluia.

10   *[Post communionem].*

Spiritus sancti domine corda nostra mundet infussio· et sui roris intima aspersione fecundet ꞉′ per in· e.

[DE INUENTIONE SANCTÆ CRUCIS].

Nos autem gloriari oportet in cruce domini nostri ihesu christi
15 in quo est salus et uita † resurrectio nostra per quem saluati et liberati sumus.[2]

[*Ps.*] Deus miseriatur nostri et benedicat· usque nostri.[3]

[Oremus].

Deus qui in preclara salutiferȩ crucis inuentione passionis
20 tuæ miracula suscitasti concede ut uitalis ligni pretio eterne uitæ susfragia † consequamur qui uiuis.

[Ad galatas].

Fratres ꞉′ confido de uobis in domino ꞉′ quod nichil . .
/ . . per quem michi mundus crucifixus est et ego [fo. 74r.
25 mundo.[4]

[Gradale].

Christus factus est pro nobis oboedens † patri usque ad mortem· mortem autem crucis· propter quod et d[eu]s exaltauit illum et dedit illi nomen quod est super omne nomen[5] alleluia.
30   [*V.*] Dulce lignum dulces clauos dulce † ferens pondera que sola fuisti digna sustinere regem celorum et dominum.

[Secundum iohannem].

In illo tempore ꞉′ erat homo ex fariseis necodemus . .
/ . . non pereat ꞉′ sed habeat uitam eternam.[6]   [ff. 74v., 75r.

---

l. 3. The second i of ' illiustratione ' is expuncted.
l. 34. The lower margin of fo. 75 has been cut away.

[1] Act ii. 2, 4 a, 11 b.   [2] Cf. Gal. vi. 14.   [3] Ps. lxvi. 2.
[4] Gal. v. 10-12, vi. 12-14.   [5] Phil. ii. 8, 9.   [6] Joh. iii. 1-15.

[*Offerenda*].

· Dextera domini fecit uirtutem dextera domini exaltauit me dextera domini fecit uirtutem.

[*N.*] Non moriar sed uiuam et narrabo opera domini.[1]

5 [*Secreta*].

Sacrificium domine quod immolamus. placatus intende ut ab omni :′ nos exuat bellatorum nequitia et per uixillum sanctę crucis filii tui ad conterendas potestates ereas et aduersariorum insidias nos in tuę protectionis securitate constituas :′ per.

10 /[*Communio*]. [fo. 75v.

Nos autem gloriari oportet in cruce domini nostri ihesu christi in quo est uita et resurrectio et reliqua.[2]

[*Post communionem*].

Repleti alimonia celesti et spirituali poculo recreasti †
15 quesumus omnipotens deus :′ ut nos ab hoste maligno defendas· quos per lignum sanctę crucis filii tui armis iustitiæ triumphare iusisti per· eundem.

[PREFATIONES].

[*In natiuitate domini*].

20 ℟ æterne deus. quia per incarnati uerbi misterium :′ noua mentis nostrę oculis lux tuæ claritatis infulsit. ut dum uisibiliter deum cognoscimus :′ per hunc inuisibilium amore rapiamur· et ideo cum angelis et archangelis cum tronis et dominationibus. cumque omni militia celestis exercitus :′
25 ymnum glorię tuę canimus· sine fine dicentes· s· s· s.

[*In epifania*].

℟ ęterne deus· quia cum unigenitus tuus in substantia nostrę mortalitatis apparuit :′ in nouam [nos] immortalitatis lucem reparauit. et ideo.

30 [*In feria· iv· in capite ieiunii*].

/℟ æterne deus· qui corporali ieiunio uitia com- [fo. 76r. premis :′ mentem ·eleuas :′ uirtutem largiris et premia :′ per christum dominum.

l. 19. The title is inserted by a modern hand : 'prefacio in die natiuitatis domini.'

l. 26. This Preface is wrongly inscribed, by the hand mentioned in the last note, 'de trinitate.'

.[1] Ps. cxvii. 16, 17. [2] Cf. Gal. vi. 14.

[In die paschæ].

℘ equum et salutare ⁒ te quidem omni tempore ⁒ sed in hac
potissimum die glorios[i]us predicare ⁒ cum pascha nostrum
ymmolatus est christus. ipse enim uerus est agnus ⁒ qui abstulit
5 peccata mundi· qui mortem nostram moriendo destruxit et
uitam resurgendo reparauit. et ideo cum.

[In festis sanctæ mariæ].

℘ ęterne deus. et te in purificatione uel annunti[ati]one ue.
assumptione· uel natiuitate beatę marię semper⸵ uirginis
10 exultantibus animis collaudare et predicare· quę et unigenitum
tuum sancti spiritus obumbratione concepit· et uirginitatis
gloria permanente huic mundo lumen et[er]num effudit ⁒
ihesum christum· d· n· per quem· m.

/[In festis sanctæ crucis].   [fo. 76v.

15 ℘ ęterne deus· qui salutem humani generis in ligno crucis
constituisti ⁒ et † unde mors oriebatur inde uita resurgeret· et
qui per lignum uincebat per lignum quoque uinceretur per
christum dominum.

[In dominica penticostes].

20 ℘ æterne deus per christum dominum nostrum· qui
ascen(. . .) super omnes celos· sedensque ad dexteram
tuam promisum spiritum sanctum hodierna die in filios
adoptionis effudit. quapropter profusis gaudiís totus in orbe
terrarum mundus exultat ⁒ sed et super[næ] uirtutes atque
25 angelice potestates ymnvm glorię tuæ concinunt sine fine
dicentes· s· s· s.

[In die ascensionis].

℘ æterne per christum dominum nostrum· qui post resurrectionem suam omnibus discipulis suis manifestus apparuit ⁒
30 et ipsis cernentibus est eleuatus in celum ⁒ ut nos diuinitatis
suæ tribueret esse participes. et ideo cum angelis.

---

ll. 14, 19.   Titles for these prefaces are supplied by the hand already mentioned,
viz.: 'de sancta cruce prefacio,' 'de spiritu sancto prefacio.'
l. 21.   The letters following 'ascen' have been partially erased.   They seem
to have been p̄ē.
l. 25.   In 'ymnvm' the scribe writes v for u.
l. 26.   The modern hand has added 'dominus dominus deus sababaoth†.'
l. 27.   The title 'de ascensione prefacio' has been supplied by the modern
hand.

[SANCTORALE].

/IN DIE [SANCTI ANDREÆ] AD MISAM. [fo. 77r.

Michi autem nimis honorati.[1]

Oremus.

5 Maiestatem tuam domine suppliciter exoramus ⫶ ut sicut
ecclesie tuę beatus andreas apostolus extitit predicator et
rector ita pro nobis apud te sit perpetuus intercessor ⫶ per
dominum.

Ad romanos.

10 Fratres ⫶ corde creditur ad iustitiam . . / . . [fo. 77v.
eorum ⫶ et in fines orbis terrę uerba eorum.[2]

℟. Constitues eos principes[3] alleluia.
℣. Dilexit andream dominus in odorem suauitatis.[4]

Secundum matheum.

15 In illo ⫶ ambulans ihesus iuxta mare galileę . . . . statim
relictis retibus et patre secuti sunt eum.[5]

Offerenda.

Constitues.[6]

Secreta.

20 Sacrificium nostrum tibi domine quesumus beati andreę
precatio sancta conciliet· ut cuius honore sollenniter exhibetur
meritis efficiatur acceptum ⫶ per.

Communio.

Dicit andreas simon[i] fratri suo inuenimus mess[i]am qui dicitur
25 christus· et adduxit eum ad ihesum.[7]

/Post [communionem]. [fo. 78r.

Sumpsimus domine diuina misteria beati andreę festiuitate
lętantes que sicut tuis sanctis ad gloriam uobis † quesumus ad
ueniam prodesse perficias ⫶ per.

---

[1] Ps. cxxxviii. 17. [2] Rom. x. 10-18. [3] Ps. xliv. 17 b.
[4] Cf. Sir. xxiv. 20. [5] Matt. iv. 18-22. [6] Ps. xliv. 17 b.
[7] Joh. i. 41 b, 42 a.

'VIII· KL' [FEBRUARII] CONUERSIO· S· PAULI APOSTOLI AD
FIDEM.

Letemur omnes in domino hodiernum diem sollenniter celebrantes quo beatus paulus conuersione sua presentem mundum
5 decorauit.
Ps. Prostratus est seuissimus persecutor et erectus est fidelis-
simus predicator.

Oremus.

Deus qui uniuersum mundum beati pauli apostoli prc-
10 dicatione docuisti· dá nobis quesumus ː ut qui eius hodierna †
die conuersionem colimus per eius ad te exempla gradiamur ː
per.

Lectio actuum apostolorum.

In diebus illis saulus adhuc spirans minarum et . .
15 / . . affirmans quoniam hic est [fo. 78v. *usque ad* fo. 79v.
christus.¹

R̸. Domine preuenisti.
V̸. Uitam petiit· alleluia.
[*V̸.*] Posui adiutorium super potentem et exaltaui electum de
20 plebe mea².

Tractus.

Tu es uæ † electionis sancte paule apostole uere digne es
glorificandus.
V̸. Predicator ueritatis et doctor gentium in fide et ueritate.
25 *V̸.* Per te omnes gentes cognouerunt gratiam dei.
V̸. Intercede pro nobis ad eum qui te elegit.

Secundum matheum.

In illo ː dixit simon petrus ad ihesum. ecce nos relinquimus
omnia ː . . . . . /centuplum accipiet ː et uitam [fo. 8or.
30 ęternam possidebit.³

Offerenda.

Posuisti.⁴

Secreta.

Apostoli tui pauli precibus domine plebis tuæ dona sancti-
35 fica· ut que ᵗⁱᵇⁱ grata tuo sunt instituto· gratiora fiant⸝ eius
patrocinio supplicantis per.⁸

Communio.

Amen dico uobis· ut supra.⁵

---

¹ Act ix. 1-22. ² Ps. xx. 4, 5, lxxxviii. 20 b.
³ Matt. xix. 27-29. ⁴ Ps. xx 4 b. ⁵ Matt. xix. 28 a, 29 b.

Post communionem.

. Salutari refecti misterio quesumus omnipotens deus· ut qui
hunc diem in beati pauli apostoli tui conuersione honorabilem
haberi uoluisti :' nos quoque conuersos a uitiis in tua facias
5 semper seruitute gratulari :' per.

MISA DE SANCTA BRIGITA KL' FEBRUARII.

[*Oremus.*]

Cęlorum atque terrarum conditor et gubernator omnipotens deus precanti populo succurre tua pietate et presta ut
10 qui in honore sancte brigite presentem d[i]ei huius gerimus
sollennitatem per ipsius suffragia perhenni misericordia tua
potiamur :' per.

Secreta.

Ecclesie tue quesumus domine preces et hostias beatę
15 brigitæ commendet oratio· ut qui pro illius meritis maiestatem
tuam indefessam atque exorabilem humiliter imploramus
/cuius† precibus adiuti misericordiam tuam· senti- [fo. 80v.
amus :' per.

Post [communionem].

20 Adiuuent nos quesumus domine hec misteria sancta quę
sumpsimus· et beatæ uirginis tuæ brigitæ intercessio ueneranda :' per.

[IN PURIFICATIONE SANCTÆ MARIÆ].

Incipit ordo in purificatione sancte marię postquam fratres exierint a capitulo pulsentur ter
25 signa sicut mos est et induant se sacris uestibus sicut soliti sunt facere in festiuis diebus
ueniendum [est] ante altare sancte marię ibique prosternantur tapetę' et desuper ponantur
candelę benedicanturq[ue] cum magna ueneratione ab episcopo uel diaconot uel ab ebdomadario
hoc modo.

Oremus.

30 Benedic domine ihesu christe hanc creaturam cerę supplicantibus nobis et infunde ei per uirtutem sancte crucis bene-✠
dictionem celestem· ut qui eam ad repellandas† tenebras
humano generi tribuisti· talem signaculo sancte ✠ crucis tuæ
fortitudinem et benedictionem accipiat· ut in quibuscunque
35 locis accensa siue [posita] fuerit· discedat diabolus et con-
tremescat· et fugiat pallidus cum omnibus ministris suis de
habitationibus illis nec presumat amplius inquietrare † seruientes tibi· qui cum deo patre et spiritu s[an]c[t]o uiuis et
regnas deus per omnia.

ll. 25, 31. Opposite the former of these lines, in right margin, are the letters
'In,' and opposite the latter 'Incipit' (?).
l. 35. In the right margin after 'siue,' in a later hand, 'possita.'
l. 37. The letters 'qui' in 'inquietrare' are erased. A few letters written in
the margin, also erased, are followed by 'qui' in a later hand (apparently not the
same as that mentioned in last note).

Oremus.

Domine sanctę pater omnipotens ęterne deus :' qui omnia
ex nichilo creasti· et iusu tuo per opera apium /hunc [fo. 81r.
liquorem ad perfectionem cerei euenire fecisti· et qui hodierna
5 die petitionem iusti simeonis implesti· te humiliter depreca-
mur· ut has candelas ad úsus hominum ᵉᵗ stantem † corporum
et animarum siue in terra siue in aquis per inuocationem
sanctissimi nominis tui et per intercessionem sanctę mariæ
semper uirginis cuius hodie [festa] deuota † celebrantur· et per
10 preces omnium sanctorum tuorum bene✠dicere et sancti-✠
ficare digneris· et huius plebis tuę que illas honorifice in
manibus desiderat portare· teque laudando exultare exaudias
uoces de celo sancto [tuo et de sede maiestatis tuę· et propitius sis omnibus clamantibus ad te quos redemisti pretioso
15 sanguine filíí tui· qui tecum uiuit et regnat in unitate.

Oremus.

Omnipotens sempiterne deus qui hodierna die unigenitum
tuum ulnis sancti simeonis in templo sancto tuo suscipiendum
presentasti tuam supplices deprecamur clementiam· ut has
20 candelas quas nos tui famuli in tui· /nominis magnifi- [fo. 81v.
centia suscipientes gestare cupimus luce accensas· bene✠di-
cere et sancti✠ficare digneris quatinus eas tibi domino deo
nostro offerendo digni· et sancto igne tuę dulcissimę caritatis
succensi· in templo sancto gloriæ tuæ representari mereamur
25 per.

Oremus.

Deus cuius unigenitus ·hodierna die cum substantia nostrę
carnis secundum legem cum hostiis debitis apparentibus † in
templo est oblatus et a iusto simeone in ulnis susceptus con-
30 cede quesumus ut sicut ille mortem non uidit quousque
uidere meruit christum domini :' ita et nobis tribue per intercessionem sanctę et intemeratę uirginis mariæ :' ut absque
contagione peccati in celesti templo túa mereamur uisione
perfrui· luminaria quoque que populus tuus in hóc sacro templo
35 tibi deuote offert tua bene✠dictione sanctifices· ut quicunque

---

l. 2.   In the upper margin of f. 81r. is written (*p.m. ut uid.*) a word, the upper
portions of the letters of which have been cut away by the binder : ' u(. . .)ce'.
    l. 6.   The word 'stantem' is partially deleted and 'et san(itntem)' (the last
letters cut away by the binder) written in a later hand in the margin.
    l. 9.   The hand mentioned in the last note has added 'festa' after 'hodie,'
and written 'e' in the left margin, apparently as a correction of the last letter of
'deuota.'

ROSSLYN.   E

ea gestauerint ƺ́ tam animæ quam corporis consequantur
/medelam ƺ́ per dominum nostrum.   [fo. 82r.

Oremus.

  Immensam maiestatis tuę misericordiam obsecramus omni-
5 potens deus ut qui uerum lumen dominum nostrum ihesum
christum hodierna die cum nostre carnis substantię † in
templo presentari· atque diu desideratum beatum † simeonis
brachíís amplecti uoluisti· mentis nostrę sensús dono tue
gratię illuminare digneris· quatinus hos cereos tua bene-✠
10 dictione sanctificatos ferentes· castitatis sinceritate tuique
amoris caritate illuminasti† ƺ́ nosmet ipsos hostiam uiuentem
sanctum†· tibique placentem exhibere ualeamus ƺ́ per.

  Tunc asperga[n]tur aqua benedicta et tuere † adoleantur et illuminentur et interim [canatur] a clero antiphona

15   Lumen ad reuelationem gentium et gloriam plebis tuę israhel.[1]
  [*Alia ant.*] Nunc dimittis seruum tuum domine secundum
uerbum tuum in pace quia uiderunt oculi mei salutare tuum.[2]

> Ante altare.

  Aue gratia plena dei genitrix uirgo· ex te enim ortus est sol
20 iustitiæ illuminans que in tenebris sunt lętare tu senior iuste
suscipiens in ulnans † liberatorem /animarum donantem [fo. 82v.
nobis et resurrectionem.

  Post hoc accipiatur † omnes singulos cereos de manu pontificis
uel editui et dicatur
25   *Oremus.*

  Omnipotens sempiterne deus qui unigenitum tuum ante
tempora de te genitum· sed temporaliter de maria uirguine
incarnatum lumen uerum et indefficiens ad depellendas
humani generis tenebras et ad incendendum lumen fidei et
30 ueritatis misissti in mundum· concede propitius· ut sicut
exterius corporali· ita etiam interius luce spirituali irradiari
mereamur ƺ́ per dominum.

> Hac oratione expleta circumeant in† ecclesiam cantando
> antiphonas ad diem pertinentes ad processionem.

l. 7. In the left margin is written a letter (? a), and opposite it, in the right margin, b.
l. 18. The line surrounding this title is in red.
l. 33. The line round this rubric is in red.

[1] Luc. ii. 32.   [2] Luc. ii. 29, 30.

[Antiphonæ].

Adorna thalamum tuum sion et suscipe regem christum amplec-
tere maria[m] que est celestis porta ipsa enim portat regem gloriæ
non † uero † lumine subsistit uirgo adducens in manibus filium ante
5 luciferum· quem accipiens simeon in ulnas suas predicauit pouulis
dominum eum esse uitę et·mortis et saluatorem mundi.
. Responsum accepit simeon a spiritu sancto non uisurum se
mortem nisi uideret christum domini· et cum inducerent puerum
in templo† ⁏ accepit eum /in ulnas suas· et benedixit deum [fo. 83r.
10 et dixit· Nunc dimittis domine seruum [tuum secundum] uerbum
tuum in pace.¹

Cum autem in chorum redierint dicta antiphona dicatur.

. Benedicta tu in mulieribus·² kirrieleison†· ter pater noster· et ne
nos inducas· post partum.
15 *Oremus.*

Erudi quesumus domine plebem tuam et que extrinsicus
annua tribuis deuotione uenerari· intercedente beata dei genitrice semper uirgine maria interius assequi gratiæ tuæ luce
concede⁏ per.

20 'IIII' NON FEBRUARII· PURIFICATIO SANCTĘ MARIĘ

Suscepimus deus misericordiam tuam in medio templi tui secundum nomen tuum ita deus et laus tua in fines terrę iustitia plena
tua dextera.³
[*Ps.*] Magnus dominus et laudabilis nimis.⁴

25 *Oremus.*

Omnipotens sempiterne deus maiestati † tuam supplices
exoramus⁏ ut sicut unigenitus filius tuus hodierna die cum
nostræ carnis substantia est in templo presentatus· ita nos
facias purificatis tibi mentibus presentari· per dominum.

30 *Lectio malachię pro[fetæ].*

Hec dicit dicit † dominus· ecce ego mitto angelum . .
/ . . et sicut anni antiqui⁵ dicit dominus⁏ [fo. 83v.
omnipotens.
Gradale.

35 Suscepimus deus misericordiam tuam in medio templi tui secundum nomen tuum domine ita et laus tua in fines terrę.

---

l. 31. The first ‘dicit’ is erased.
l. 34. In the margin are written some letters : (...)at | (...)e, most of which
have been cut away by the binder.

¹ Luc. ii. 26, 28, 29.   ² Luc. i. 28 b.   ³ Ps. xlvii. 10, 11.
⁴ Ps. xlvii. 2.   ⁵ Mal. iii. 1–4.

E 2

℣. Sicut audiuimus ita et uidimus in ciuitate dei nostri alleluia ecce uenit ad templum sanctum suum dominator dominus[1] uenite occurramus domino deo nostro·[2] Alleluia.

℣. Hodie oblatus est in templo uirginis filius cuius diuinitatem
5 omnis non capit orbis.

Tractus.

Gaude maria uirgo /cunctas heresses interemisti.   [fo. 84r.
℣. Que garielis † archangeli dictis credidisti.
℣. Dum uirgo deum et hominem genuisti et post partum uirgo
10 inuiolata permansisti· dei genitrix intercede· pro nobis.

Secundum lucam.

In illo ꝰ postquam impleti sunt dies purgationis marie . .
/ . . lumen ad reuelationem gentium et gloriam [fo. 84v.
plebis tuæ israhel.[3]

15 ### Offerenda.

Diffusa est gratia in labiis tuis propterea benedixit te deus in ęternum et in seculum seculi.[4]

Secreta.

Presta quesumus domine ut sicut hodierna munera uene-
20 randa filii tui oblatione consecrantur· ipsius gloriosæ genitricis precibus sempiterni luminis nobis caritatis† [conferatur].

Communio.

Responsum accepit simeon a spiritu sancto non uisurum se mortem nisi uideret christum domini.[5]

25 ### Post communionem.

Da nobis misericors deus eius presenti festiuitate uegi-
tari· cuius integra uirginitate suscepimus· auotorem † nostræ salutis· per.

VIII· KL' MARTA CATHEDRA SANCTA PETRI.

30 Statuit ei dominus.[6]
·*Ps.* Misericordias domini in ęternum.[7]

Oremus.

Deus qui beato petro apostolo tuo /collatis clauibus [fo. 85r.
regni celestis animas ligandi atque soluendi pontificum
35 tradidisti ꝰ conced(e) ut intercessionis eius auxilio ꝰ a peccatorum nostrorum nexibus liberemur· qui uiuis.

---

[1] Ps. xlvii. 10, 11 a, 9 a ; Mal. iii. 1 b.   [2] Cf. Jer. iii. 22.
[3] Luc. ii. 22-32.   [4] Ps. xliv. 3 b.   [5] Luc. ii. 26.
[6] Sir. xlv. 3c.   [7] Ps. lxxxviii. 2.

Lectio e· b· petri apostoli.

Petrus apostolus ihesu christi electis aduenis . . /[fo. 85v.
. . inueniatur in laudem et gratiam et honorem in reuelationem
ihesu christi domini nostri.[1]

5 [*Gradale*].

Exaltent eum in ecclesia plebis et in cathedra seniorum laudent
eum.

[*V.*] Confiteantur domino· misericordia eius et mirabilia filiis
hominum.[2]

10 [*Tractus*].

Tu es petrus et super hanc petram edificabo ecclesiam meam.
[*V.*] Et porte inferi non preualebunt aduersus eam et tibi dabo
claues regni celorum.
[*V.*] Quodcunque ligaueritis† super terram ؛ erit ligatum.
15 [*V.*] Et quodcumque solueris super terram erit solutum et in
celis.[3]

[*Secundum mathcum*].

In illo ؛ uenit ihesus in partes cessariæ.[4] Require

[*Offerenda*].

20 Tu es petrus et super hanc petram edificabo ecclesiam meam et
porte inferi non preualebunt aduersus eam· et tibi dabo claues regni
celorum.[5]

[*Secreta*].

Ecclesie tue preces domine quesumus· et munera beati
25 apostoli tui petri commendet oratio· ut quod pro illius gloria
celebramus· nobis prosit ad ueniam ؛ per dominum nostrum.

[*Communio*].

Tú es petrus et super hanc petram edificabo eam.[6]

[*Post communionem*].

30 Letificet nos domine munus oblatum /ut sicut in [fo. 86r.
apostolo tuo petro te mirabilem predicamus· sic per illum
sumamus tuæ indulgentiæ largitatem ؛ per dominum.

VIII KL' · APRILIS ANNUNTIATIO· S· M.

Rorate celi desuper et nubes pluant iustum aperiatur terra et ger-
35 minet saluatorem et iustitia oriatur† simul ego dominus creaui eum.

---

[1] 1 Pet. i. 1-7. [2] Ps. cvi. 32, 31. [3] Matt. xvi. 18, 19.
[4] Matt. xvi. 13 sqq. [5] Matt. xvi. 18, 19 a. [6] Matt. xvi. 18 a.
[7] Isai. xlv. 8.

Oremus.

. Deus qui de beatę mariæ uirguinis utero uerbum tuum
angelo nuntia[n]te carnem suscipere uoluisti :/ presta supplicibus tuis ut qui uere eam genitricem dei credimus eius apud
5 te intercessionibus adiuuemur per eundem.

Lectio isaie prophete.

In diebus illis est locutus est dominus ad achaz dicens. .
. / . . reprobare malum et eligere bonum.[1]　　[fo. 86v.

V.†

10 In sole posuit tabernaculum suum· et ipse tanquam sponsus
procedens de thalamo suo.
　V. A summo celo egressio eius et occurrust eius usque ad
summum eius.
　V. Aue maria gratia plena dominus tecum.
15 　V. Benedicta tu in mulieribus et benedictus fructus uentris tui.
　V. Ecce concipies et paries filium et uocabitur nomen emanuel.
　V. Quomodo iniquit † fiet istud quoniam uirum non cognosco·
et respondens angelus intulit ei.
　V. Spiritus sanctus superueniet in te et uirtus altissimi obum-
20 brauit tibi.
　V. Ideoque quod nascetur ex te sanctum uocabitur filius dei.[2]

Secundum lucam.

In illo :/ missus est angelus garielt a deo in ciuitatem . .
/ . . fiat michi secundum uerbum tuum.[3]　　[fo. 87r.

25 ### Oremust.

Aue maria gratia plena dominus tecum benedicta tu in mulieribus
et benedictus fructus uentris tui.[4]

/S[ecreta].　　[fo. 87v.

In mentibus nostris quesumus domine ueræ fidei sacramenta
30 confirma ut qui conceptum de uirgine deum uerum et hominem
confitemur· per eius salutifere resurrectionis potentiam ad
eternam peruenire mereamur lętitiam :/ per.

Communio.

Ecce uirgo concipiet et pariet filium et uocabitur nomen eius
35 emanuel.[5]

l. 7. The first ' est ' is erased.
l. 17. The second i of ' iniquit ' is erased. The letter V before this verse has
been twice written.
l. 28. S[ecreta] is a correction of Post [communionem] (erased).

[1] Is. vii. 10-15.
[2] Ps. xviii. 6 a, 7 a ; Luc. i. 28, 42, 31 (Matt. i. 23 a), 34 b, 35.
[3] Luc. i. 26-38 a.　　[4] Luc. i. 28, 42.　　[5] Isai. vii. 14 b.

Post [*communionem*].

Gratiam tuam quesumus domine mentibus nostris infunde·
ut qui angelo nuntiante christi filii tui incarnationem cognoui-
mus· per pasionem eius et crucem ad resurrectionis gloriam
5 perducamur ./ per dominum.

XIII· KL' APRILIS· IN NATALE† SANCTI PATRICÍÍ EPISCOPI
ET CONFESSORIS.

[*Oremus*].

Deus qui sanctum patricium scotorum apostolum tua pro-
10 uidentia elegisti· ut hibernenses gentes in tenebris et in errore
gentilitatis errantes· ad lumen uerum dei scientiæ reduceret·
et per lauacrum regenerationis filios excelsi dei efficeret tribue
nobis quesumus eius pÍÍs intercessionibus· ut ad ea que recta
sunt quantotius† festinemus ./ per dominum.

15 /*Secreta.* [fo. 88r.

Hostias tibi quas in honore sancti patricii offerimus deuotas
accipias· ut nos a timore iudicÍÍ liberemur.

Post communionem.

Omnipotentem deum uniuersitatis auctorem suppliciter
20 exoramus· ut qui spirituale sacrificium in honorem sancti
patricii offerimus· fiat nobis remedium sempiternum ./ per.

·MISA IN LETANIA MAIORE IN SECUNDA FERIA ET
TERTIA· FERIA.

Exaudiuit de templo sancto suo uocem meam alleluia et clamor
25 meus in conspectu æius introibit in aures eius[1] alleluia alleluia.
Ps. Diligam tè· d.[2]

Oremus.

Presta quesumus omnipotens deus ./ ut qui in afflictione
nostra de tua pietate confidimus contra omnia tua semper
30 protectione muniamur ./ per.

L· e· b· iacobi apostoli.

Karissimi ./ confitemini alterutrum peccata uestra ./ . .
/ . . et operit ./ multitudinem peccatorum.[3] [fo. 88v.
Alleluia.
35 *V.* Confitemini domino quoniam bonus quoniam in seculum
misericordia eius.[4]

[1] Ps. xvii. 7 b.   [2] Ps. xvii. 2.
[3] Jac. v. 16–20.   [4] Ps. cxvii. 1.

Secundum lucam.

In illo· tempore ː dixit dominus ihesus discipulis suis. quis
uestrum habebit . . / . . quanto magis pater [fo. 89r.
de celo dabit spiritum bonum ː' petentibus se.[1]

5   ### Offerenda.

Confitebor domino nimis in ore meo et in medio multorum laudabo
eum qui astitit adextram † pauperis ut saluum † faceret a persequen-
tibus animam meam[2] alleluia.

Secreta.

10   Hec munera quesumus domine et uincula nostræ paraui-
tatis † absoluant· et tuę misericordiæ dona concilient ː' per.

Communio.

Petite et accipietis querite et inuenietis pulsate et aperietur
uobis omnis enim qui petit accipit et qui querit inuenit pulsanti
15 aperiitur·[3] alleluia.

/Post [communionem].   [fo. 89v.

Uota nostra quesumus domine pio fauore prosequere· ut
dum dona tua in tribulatione percipimus de consolatione
nostra in tuo amore crescamus ː' per.

20   IX KL' IULÍ́· UIGILIA SANCTI IOHANNIS BAPTIZÆ.

Ne timeas zacharias † exaudita est oratio tua et elizafeth † uxor
tua pariet tibi filium (et u)ocabis nomen eius iohannem et erit
(ma)gnus coram domino et spiritu sancto replebitur adhuc ex utero
matris suæ et multi in natiuitate eius gaudebunt.[4]

25   *Ps.* Domine in uirtute tua letabitur rex· usque uechimenter.[5]

Oremus.

Presta quesumus omnipotens deus ut familia tua per uiam
salutis incendat †· et beati iohannis precursoris hortamenta
sectando ad eum quem predixit secura perueniat· per.

30   ### Lectio ieremię proph*ę*t.

In diebus illis ː' factum est uerbum domini ad me dicens.
. / . . et ędifices et plantes.[6] ait dominus [fo. 90r.
omnipotens.

l. 3. The lower margin of fo. 89 has been cut away with a knife.
l. 19. A letter has been erased between s and c in 'crescamus.'
ll. 22, 23. The following words have been erased, in whole or in part, to make
way for the large ornamental initial : 'tua' *pri.*, 'et uocabis,' 'magnus.'

[1] Luc. xi. 5-13.   [2] Ps. cviii. 30, 31.   [3] Luc. xi. 9, 10.
[4] Luc. i. 13, 15, 14 b.   [5] Ps. xx. 2.   [6] Jer. i. 4-10.

℟. Fuit homo misus a deo cui nomen erat iohannes hic uenit.

℣. Ut testimonium perhiberet de lumine parare domino plebem perfectam.[1]

I [*ni*]*tium s· e· secundum· lucam.*

5 Fuit in diebus herodis regis iudæ sacerdos . . / . . parare domino :' plebem perfe[c]tam.[2]   [ff. 90v. *et* 91r.

Of[*ferenda.*]

Gloria et honore coronasti.[3]

Secreta.

10 Munera domine oblata sanctifica :' et intercedente beato iohanne baptiza· nos post † hec a peccatorum nostrorum [maculis] emunda per.

Communio.

Magna est gloria eius.[4]

15 *Post* [*communionem*].

Beati iohannis baptizæ nos quesumus domine preclara comitetur oratio· et que[m] uenturum esse predixit· postquat † nobis fore placatum ihesum christum dominum nostrum· qui tecum uiuit.

20 IN ·DIE SANCTO † IOHANNIS.

De uentre matris meę uocauit me dominus nomine meo· et posuit os meum ut gladium acutum sub tegumento manus suæ protexit me posuit me quasi sagittam electam.[5]

Ps. Misit dominus manum suam et tetigit ós meum.[6]

25 *Or*[*emus*].

Deus qui presentem diem honorabilem in beati iohannis natiuitate fecisti :' da spiritualis† gratiam gaudiorum :' et omnium fidelium mentes /dirige in uiam salutis [fo. 91v. ęterne :' per.

30 *Lectio isaie profetæ.*

Audite insulæ :' et attendite populi . . . . et sanctum israhel qui elegit te.[7]

Gradale.

Priusquam te formarem in utero noui te et antequam exires de 35 uentre sanctificaui te.

℣. Misit dominus manum suam et tetigit ós meum [et dixit] michi alleluia.

---

[1] Joh. i. 6, 7 a ; Luc. i. 17 b.   [2] Luc. i. 5-17.   [3] Ps. viii. 6 b.
[4] Ps. xx. 6 a.   [5] Isai. xlix. 1 b, 2 a.   [6] Jer. i. 9 a.
[7] Isai. xlix. 1-3, 5 a, 6 b, 7 b.

℣. Inter natos mulierum non surrexit maior iohanne baptiza.
℣. Fuit homo misus a deo cui nomen erat iohannes erat†.[1]

Secundum lucam.

In illo ꞉' elizabeth /impletum [est] tempus . . . . [fo. 92r.
5 /deus israhel ꞉' quia uisitauit· et fecit redemptionem [fo. 92v.
plebis suæ.[2]

Offerenda.

Iustus ut palma florebit sicut cedrus que in libano est multi-
plicabitur.[3]

10   ### Secreta.

Tua domine muneribus altaria cumulamus illius natiuitatem
honore debito uenerantes· et opem nobis affore deprecantes ꞉'
qui saluatorem mundi et cecinit affuturum et adesse monstrauit ꞉' ihesum christum filium tuum dominum nostrum.

15   ### Communio.

Tu puer propheta altissimi uocaberis preibis enim ante faciem
domini parare uias eius.[4]

Post communionem.

Sumat ecclesie† tua deus beati iohannis baptizæ generatione
20 lẹtitiam per quem suæ regenerationis cognouit auctorem
dominum nostrum ihesum christum filium.

IIII· KL' IULII UIGILIA SANCTORUM APOSTOLORUM PETRI·
ET P[AULI].

(D)icit dominus petro cum esse[s] iunior cingebas te et ambulabas
25 ubi uolebas· cum autem senueris extendes manus tuas et alius
[te] cinget et ducet quọ tu non uis hoc autem dixit significans
qua morte clarificaturus esset deum.[5]

Ps. Si diligis me simon petre pasce oues meas.[6]

Oremus.

30   Deus qui nobis beatorum apostolorum /tuorum petri [fo. 93r.
et pauli gloriosa natalicia preuenire concedis· tribue quesumus·
eorum nos semper et preueniri beneficíís et orationibus
adiuuari· per dominum.

Lectio actuum apostolorum.

35   In diebus illis ꞉' petrus et iohannes ascendebant in templum :
. . / . . extassi in eo quod contigerat illi.[7]   [fo. 93v

---

l. 22. The large ornamental initial has been cut away with a knife.

[1] Jer. i. 5 a, 9 a ; Matt. xi. 11 a ; Joh. i. 6.   [2] Luc. i. 57–68.
[3] Ps. xci. 13.   [4] Luc. i. 76.   [5] Joh. xxi. 18, 19 a.
[6] Cf. Joh. xxi. 15–17.   [7] Act. iii. 1–10.

℞. In omnem terram exiuit sonus eorum et in fines orbis terra †
uerba eorum.

℣. Celi enarrant gloriam dei et opera manuum eius annuntiat
firmamentum.¹

5   *Secundum [iohannem].*

In illo ꞉ dixit simoni petro ihesus. simon iohannis   .   .
/   .   . significans qua morte clarificaturus esset [fo. 94r.
deum.²

                        Oremus †.

10   Michi autem nimis honorificati sunt amici tui deus nimis
confortatus est principatus eorum.³

                        Secreta.

Munus populi tui quesumus domine apostolica intercessione
sanctifica nosque a peccatorum nostrorum maculis emunda ꞉
15 per.

                        Communio.

Tu es petrus et super hanc petram edificabo ecclesiam meam.⁴

                    Post [communionem].

Quos celesti domine ab † elimento † satiasti ꞉ apostolicis
20 intercessionibus ab omni aduersitate custodi ꞉ per dominum.

NATALE ⁙S⁙ APOSTOLORUM PETRI⁙ ET P[AULI].

Nunc scio uere quia misit dominus angelum suum et eripuit me
de manu herodis⁙ et de omni expectatione plebis iudeorum.⁵
Ps. Et petrus ad se reuersus dixit.⁶

25   *Oremus.*

Deus qui hodiernam diem apostolorum tuorum petri et
pauli martirio consecrasti ꞉ da ecclesiæ tuæ eorum in omnibus
sequi preceptum⁙ per quos religionis sumpsit exordium per.

        /*Lectio actuum apostolorum.*   [fo. 94v.

30   In diebus illis ꞉ misit herodis rex manus ꞉   .   /. . [fo. 95r.
de omni expectatione ꞉ plebis iudeorum.⁷

                        Gradale.

Constitues eos p[ri]ncipes super omnem terram memores erunt
nominis tui domine.

35   ℣. Pro patribus tuis nati sunt tibi filii propterea populi confite-
buntur tibi alleluia.

---

¹ Ps. xviii. 5, 2.   ² Joh. xxi. 15–19 a.   ³ Ps. cxxxviii. 17.
⁴ Matt. xvi. 18 a.   ⁵ Act. xii. 11 b.   ⁶ Act. xii. 11a.
⁷ Act. xii. 1–11.

V. Tu es simon bariona caro et sanguis non reuelabit uerbum patris sed ipse pater [qui] in celis est.[1]

Secundum (. . .) matheum.

In illo tempore.' uenit ihesus in partes cesariæ   .   .
5 / . . solueris super terram.' erit solutum · et in [fo. 95v. celis.[2]

Offerenda.

Constitues eos principes super omnem terram memores erunt nominis tui domine in omni generatione et g[ene]ratione.[3] ·

10   ### Secreta.

Hostias domine quesumus quas nomini tuo sacrandas offerimus apostolica prosequatur oratio.' per quam nos et expiari tribuas et defendi.' per.

/Communio.   [fo. 96r.

15 Simon iohannis diligis me plus his domine tua † omnia nosti tu scis domine quia unōc̄e †.[4]

Post [communionem].

Quos celesti domine alimento satiasti.' appostolicis inter-cessionibus ab omni aduersitate custodi.' per.

20   II· KL' IULII NATALE SANCTI· P[AULI]· APPO[STOLI]

Scio cui credidi et certus sum quia potens est depositum meum seruare in illum.[5]
Ps. Bonum certamen certaui cursum consummaui fidem seruaui.[6]

25   ### Oremus.   ·   ·

Deus qui multitudinem gentium beati pauli apostoli predi-catione docuisti.' dá nobis quesumus.' ut cuius natalicia colimus eius apud te patrocinia sentiamus.

Ad galantas†.

30 Fratres.' notum facio uobis euangelium . . / [fo. 96v.
    . . ecce coram deo quia nomen† mentior.[7]

---

l. 3. The illegible letters have been erased.
l. 16. The first letter of 'unōc̄e' is perhaps corrected (!) from a.
l. 31. The final stroke of m in 'nomen,' and the two following letters, have been erased, the word being thus changed to 'non.'

[1] Ps. xliv. 17 b, 18 a, 17 a, 18 b; Matt. xvi. 17 b.   [2] Matt. xvi. 13-19.
[3] Ps. xliv. 17 b, 18 a.   [4] Joh. xxi. 15 a, 17 b.   [5] 2 Tim. i. 12 b.
[6] 2 Tim. iv. 7.   [7] Gal. i. 11-20.

℞. Qui operatus est petro in apostolatum circumcissionis operatus est et · michi inter gentes· et cognouerunt gratiam dei que data est michi.

℣. Gratia dei in me uacua non fuit[1] sed gratia eius semper in
5 me manet alleluia.

℣. Magnus sanctus paulus uas electionis ꞉ uere digne est glorificandus.

Secundum matheum.

In illo ꞉ dixit simon petrus ad ihesum ecce nos . .
10 / . . centuplum accipiet ꞉ et uitam ꞑternam possi- [fo. 97r. debit.[2]

Offerenda.

Michi autem nimis.[3]

Secreta.

15 Oblationem tibi domine uotiuam deferentes precamur· ut ad laudem tui nominis et apostolicæ reuerentiam dignitatis et ad nostram †.preueniat † sanctificata presidium per.

Communio.

Amen dico uobis quod uos qui reliquistis omnia et secuti estis
20 me centuplum accipietis et uitam ꞑternam possidebitis.[4]

[Post communionem].

Dá quesumus omnipotens deus ut ecclesia tua sacramentis refecta salutaribus· et beati pauli apostoli fulta supplicationibus sic presentia dona precipiat † ꞉ ut capere mereatur
25 eterna· p.

II· NON [I]ULII OCTAUAS † APOSTOLORUM P[ETRI]· ET P[AULI].

/Exclamauerunt ad te domine in tempore afflictionis suæ [fo. 97v. et tu de celo exaudisti eos[5] alleluia alleluia.   · ·
30   Ps. Exultate iusti in domino.[6]

Oremus.

Deus cuius dextera beatum petrum ambulantem in fluctibus ne mergeretur erexit· et coapostolum eius paulum tertio naufragantem de profundo pelagi liberauit exaudi nos
35 propitius ꞉ et concede ut amborum meritis eternitatis gloriam consequamur ꞉ per.

---

[1] Gal. ii. 8, 9 a ; 1 Cor. xv. 10 a.
[3] Ps. cxxxviii. 17.
[5] Cf. Ps. xxxiii. 18, cvi. 6.

[2] Matt. xix. 27–29.
[4] Matt. xix. 28 a, 29 b.
[6] Ps. xxxii. 1.

Ad galathas.

Fratres:' deus personam hominis non accipit. . . . .
sollicitus fui id ipsum facere.[1] in christo /ihesu [fo. 98r.
domino nostro.

5 *R̸.* Constitues eos pro patribus· alleluia.
N̸. Isti sunt duę oliuę et duo candelabra lucentia ante dominum
habent potestatem claudere celum[2] nubibus et aperire portas eius
quia lingę eorum claues celi factę sunt.

Secundum matheum.

10 In illo :' iussit ihesus discipulos suos ascendere in nauiculam :'
. . ./ . . uenerunt et adorauerunt eum dicentes. [fo. 98v.
uere :' filius dei es.[3]

Offerenda.

Constitues eos principes super omnem terram.[4]

15 ## Secreta.

Intende precamur altissime uota quæ reddimus tibique
placita fieri eorum precibus concede· pro quorum deferuntur
honore :' per.

Communio.

20 Ego uos elegi de mundo [ut] uen[ia]tis· et fructum afferatis et
fructus uester maneat.[5]

Post communionem.

Sumpta domine sacramenta beatis apostolis dep[re]cantibus
remedium nobis celeste concilient :' per dominum.

25 ## XIX· KL' SEPTEMBRIS UIGILIA ASSUMPTIO[NIS]· S· M.

Salue sancta pariens † enixa puerpera regem (qui celum) terramque
regit in secula seculorum.
Ps. Quę (. . .) seculorum.
Quę gaudium matris habens (cum) uirginitatis honorem † nec
30 primam similem uisa est† nec habere sequentem.[6]

Oremus.

Deus qui uirginalem aulæ † beatæ mariæ in qua habitares
eligere /dignatus es :' da quesumus· ut sua nos defen- [fo. 99r.

---

l. 8. A letter has been erased after u in ' claues.'
l. 26. The words of the Antiphon and Psalm enclosed in brackets have been
erased to make way for the ornamental initial.

[1] Gal. ii. 6 b-10.   [2] Ps. xliv. 17 b, a ; Apoc. xi. 4, 6 a.
[3] Matt. xiv. 22-33.   [4] Ps. xliv. 17 b.   [5] Joh. xv. 16 a.
[6] Sedulius *Carm. Pasch.* 63, 64, 66–68 (Migne xix. 599).

sione munitos iocundos faciat suæ interesse festiuitati·
qui tet.

(. . . .)· *n̄ cōm̄e c̄ resp̄o.*

Lectio libri sapientiæ.

5 Ab initio et ante secula.[1]

[*Lectio isaię profetæ.*]

Gaudens gaudeo in domino ꞉⸍ et exultauit . . . . gaudebit
super te [deus] tuus.[2] dicit dominus omnipotens.

℟. Specie tua et pulcritudine tua intende prospere procede et
10 regna.
[℣.] Propter ueritatem et mansuetudinem et iustitiam et
deducet te mirabiliter dextera tua.[3]

Secundum lucam.

In illo ꞉⸍ factum est cum loqueretur ihesus ad turbas ꞉⸍
15 extollens uocem quedam / . . audiunt uerbum dei ꞉⸍ [fo. 99v.
et custodiunt illud.[4]

Offerenda.

Felix nanque est sacra uirgo maria.

Secreta.

20 Munera nostra domine apud clementiam tuam dei genitricis
commendet oratio ꞉⸍ quam iccirco de presenti seculo trans-
tulisti· ut pro peccatis nostris apud te fiducialiter intercedat·
per· e.

Communio.

25 Benedicta.

Post communionem.

Concede misericors deus fragilitati nostrę presidium ꞉⸍ ut
qui sancte dei genitricis et uirguinis requiem celebramus·
intercessionis eius auxilio a nostris iniquitatibus resurgamus ꞉⸍
30 per eundem.

IN DIE AD MISAM.

Oremus †.

Gaudeamus omnes in domino diem festum celebrantes sub
honore sanctę marię uirginis de cuius assumptione gaudeant †
35 angeli et collaudant filium dei.

l. 3. Some words written in vermilion have been erased, of which the last
letter seems to have been *m*.
l. 26. The title is written twice, the second time in the abbreviated form
Post.

[1] Sir. xxiv. 14 sqq.   [2] Isai. lxi. 10, 11, lxii. 5.   [3] Ps. xliv. 5.
[4] Luc. xi. 27, 28.

Ps. Hodie maria uirgo celos ascendit gaudete quia cum christo regnat· gloria· p· et.

Oremus.

Ueneranda nobis domine huius diei festiuitas opem conferat
5 sempiternam in qua sancta dei genitrix /mortem [fo. 100r.
subíít temporalem ·/ nec mortis necibus † deprimi potuit quæ filium tuum dominum nostrum de se genuit incarnatum· qui· t.

Per octauas Oremus.

10 Concede quesumus omnipotens deus· ad beatæ mariæ semper uirguinis gaudia nos ęterna pertingere· de cuius ueneranda assumptione tribuás † annua sollennitate gaudere· per dominum.

Lectio libri sapientiæ.

15 In omnibus requiem quessiui ·/ et in hereditate . . .
/ . quasi mirra electa dedi sanitatem odoris.[1]   [fo. 100v.

℞. Propter ueritatem et mansuetudinem et iustitiam et deducet te mirabiliter dextera tua.

𝒱. Audi filia et uide et inclina aurem tuam quia concupiuit rex
20 speciem tuam·[2] alleluia.

𝒱. Hodie maria uirgo celos ascendit gaudete quia cum christo regnat in ęternum· alleluia.

𝒱. Assumpta est maria in celum gaudent angeli et collaudantes dominum benedicent†.

25 ### Secundum lucam.

In illo ·/ intrauit ihesus in quoddam castellum ·/ et . .
/ . . maria optimam partem elegit ·/ que non [fo. 101r.
auferetur ab ea.[3]

Offerenda.

30 Beata es uirgo maria que dominum portasti creatorem mundi genuisti· qui te fecit et in ęternum permanes uirgo.

Secreta.

Grata tibi domine munera nostra efficiat dei genetricis oratio· quam etsi pro condicione carnis migrasse cognoscimus ·/
35 in celesti gloria pro nobis apud te orare sentiamus per eundem.

Communio.

Beata uiscera mariæ uirguinis quę portauerunt ęterni patris filium.

---

l. 33. ' Genetricis ' is a correction from ' genitricis.'
[1] Sir. xxiv. 11b–13, 15–20.
[2] Ps. xliv. 5 b, 11 a, 12 a.   [3] Luc. x. 38–42.

Post [communionem].

Mense celestis participes effecti imploramus clementiam tuam domine deus noster ut qui festa dei genitricis colimus ꞊ a cunctis malis imminentibus eius intercessionibus liberemur·
5 per.

IIII KL' SEPTEMBRIS DECOLLATIO· S· IOHANNIS BAPTIZÆ.

Iohannes autem cum audisset in uinculis opera christi mittens duos de discipulos † suis ait illi· tu es qui uenturus es an alium expectamus.[1]
10 *Ps.* Respondens autem ihesus ait illis euntes renuntiate iohanni quę audistis et uidistis·[2] gloria.

Oremus.

Sancti iohannis baptizæ et martiris domine quesumus ueneranda festiuitas· salutaris auxilíí nobis prestet augmen-
15 tum ꞊ per.

Lectio sapientiæ.

Expectatio iustorum lętitia ꞊ spes /autem impiorum [fo. 101v.
. . . . in benedictione iustorum ꞊ exaltabitur ciuitas.[3]
℟. Herodes enim tenuit et ligauit iohannem· et posuit in
20 carcerem.
℣. Propter herodiadem quam tulerat fratri † suo uincenti † uxorem alleluia.
℣. Misso herodes speculatore precepit amputare caput iohannis in carcere.[4]

25   ### Secundum marcum.

In illo ꞊ misit herodes ac tenuit iohannem ꞊ . . / [fo. 102r. *et* v.
. corpus eius ꞊ et posuerunt illud in monumento.[5]

Offerenda.

Missit rex spiculatorem et precepit ambutare caput iohannis in
30 carcere· quo audito ꞊ discipuli eius uenerunt et sepilierunt eum·[6] alleluia.

Secreta.

Munera tibi domine pro sancti martiris tui iohannis baptizæ passioni † deferimus· quia dum finitur in terris· factus est
35 celesti sede perpetuus ꞊ quesumus ut eius obtentu nobis proficiant ad salutem ꞊ per.

---

[1] Matt. xi. 2, 3.
[3] Prov. x. 28–32, xi. 3, 6, 8–11 a.
[5] Marc. vi. 17–29.

[2] Matt. xi. 4.
[4] Marc. vi. 17, 27.
[6] Marc. vi. 27 a, 29 a.

Communio.

Ite dicite iohanni· ceci uident surdi audiunt mortui resurgunt·
et beatus est qui non fuit scandalizatus in me.[1]

Post [communionem].

5   Conferat nobis domine sancti iohannis baptizæ utrunque
sollennitas· ut et magnifica sacramenta quæ sumpsimus·
precibus nostris significata ueneremur· et in no[bi]s potius
edita gaudeamus :' per dominum.

VI· IDUS SEPTEMBRIS· NATIUITAS· S· MARIA †.

10   Gaudeamus omnes in domino diem festum celebrantes sub
honore· sanctę mariæ uirginis /de cuius natiuitate gaudent [fo. 103r.
angelum †· et collaudant filium dei.
Ps. Hodie nata est beata uirgo maria et † progenie deo †.

Oremus.

15   Supplicationem seruorum tuorum deus miseriator † exaudi
ut qui in natiuitate sanctæ dei genitricis· et uirguinis congre-
gamur· eius intercessionibus a te de instantibus periculis
eruamur :' per dominum.

Lectio libri sapientiæ.

20   Ego quasi uitis fructificaui suauitatem odoris :' . . .
et qui elucidant me :' uitam eternam habebunt.[2]
℞. Benedicta.
℣. Uirgo Alleluia.
℣. Natiuitas gloriosæ uirguinis /mariæ ex semine abræ [fo. 103v.
25 orta de tribu iuda clara ex stirpe dauid.

Gene[a]logia domini nostri· i· christi· s· matheum.

Liber generationis ihesu christi filii dauid :' filíí . .
/ . . de qua natus est ihesus :' qui uocatur christus.[3] [fo. 104r.

Offerenda.

30   Aue maria gratia plena dominus tecum.[4]

Secreta.

Unigeniti tui domine nobis succurrat humanitas· ut qui
natus de uirguine matris integritatem non minuit sed sacrauit·
in natiuita[ti]s eius sollenniis a nostris nos piaculis exuens·

l. 2. A letter is erased before 'ceci.'
[1] Matt. xi. 4 b, 5, 6.
[3] Matt. i. 1-16.
[2] Sir. xxiv. 23-31.
[4] Luc. i. 28 a.

oblationem nostram tibi faciat· acceptam· ihesus christus dominus noster· qui· t.

Communio.

Benedicta a filio tuo domina.

5   *Post* [*communionem*].

Sumpsimus domine celebritatis annue uotiua sacramenta· presta quesumus· ut intercedente beata maria /semper [fo. 104v. uirguine et temporalis uitę nobis remedia prebeant et ęterne per dominum.

10   XVIII· KL' OCTOBRIS EXULTATIO †· S· C[RUCIS].

In nomine domini omne genu flectatur celestivm terrestrium et infernorum quia dominus factus obediens usque ad mortem mortem autem crucis· ideo dominus ihesus christus in gloria est dei patris.[1]

Ps. Humiliauit semet ipsum factus obediens usque ad mortem.[2]

15   [*Oremus*].

Deus qui unigeniti filii tui domini nostri ihesu christi preti[o]so sanguine humanum genus redimere dignatus es· concede propitius ꞉/ ut qui [ad] adorandam uiuificam crucem aduenerunt a peccatorum suorum nexibus liberentur per· e.

20   *Ad pilipenses.*

Fratres hoc sentite in uobis quod et in christo ihesu. . . / . . . quia dominus ihesus christus ꞉/ in gloria est dei [fo. 105r. patris.[3]

℟.   Christus factus.

25   ℣.   Propter quod et deus Alleluia.

℣.   Michi autem absit gloriari nisi in cruce domini ihesu christi·[4] Alleluia.

℣.   Salua nos christe saluator per uirtutem sanctæ crucis qui saluasti petrum in mari miserere nobis.

30   *Secundum iohannem.*

In illo tempore ꞉/ dixit dominus ihesus turbis nunc iudicium est . . . . credite in lucem ꞉/ ut filíí lucis sitis.[5]

Offerenda.

Protege domine plebem /tuam per signum sanctę crucis [fo. 105v. 35 ab omnibus insidiis inimicorum omnium ut tibi gratam ex-hibeamus seruitutem et acceptabile tibi fiat sacrificium nostrum· alleluia.

l. 11. In the word 'celestivm' the scribe has written v for u. This letter seldom appears elsewhere except as the equivalent of the symbol ℣.

[1] Phil. ii. 10, 8, 11 b.   [2] Phil. ii. 8.   [3] Phil. ii. 5-11.
[4] Phil. ii. 8, 9; Gal. vi. 14 a.   [5] Joh. xii. 31-36 a.

Secreta.

Deuotas domine humilitatis nostrę preces et hostias misericordiæ tuæ precedat auxilium et salutem quam per adam in
paradiso ligni clauserat temerata presumtio ligni rursum fides
5 aperiat :′ per.

Communio.

Redemptor mundi signo crucis ab omni nos aduersi[tate] custodi
qui saluasti petrum in mari miserere nobis.

Post [communionem].

10   Ihesu christi domini nostri corpore et sanguine saginati per
quem crucis est sanctificatum uexillum quesumus domine
deus :′ ut sicut adorare meruimus ita perennitatis eius gloria
salutari potiamur effectu· per eundem.

IN DIE NATALI EIUSDEM [SANCTI MATHEI].

15   In medio ecclesie aperuit os eius et impleuit eum dominus
spiritu sapientię stola glorię induit eum.[1]
   Ps. Iocunditatem et exultationem thesaurizauit super eum.[2]

(. . .) Oremus.

Beati euangelizæ et apostoli tui mathei domine precibus
20 adiuuemur· ut quod possibilitas nostra non optinet· eius nobis
intercessione donetur :′ per.

|Epistolęt.   [fo. 106r.

Fratres :′ unicuique nostrum data est gratia :′ . . . . ′ in
mensuram ętatis plenitudinis christi.[3]
25   ℞. Beatus uir.
   ℣. Potens Alleluia.
   ℣. Primus ad sion dicet ecce adsum et ierusalem euangelizam
dabo.[4]

Secundum matheum.

30   In illo :′ cum transiret inde ihesus :′ uidit hominem . .
/ . . non enim ueni uocare iustos :′ sed pecca- [fo. 106v.
tores.[5]

Offerenda.

Iustus ut palma florebit sicut cedrus libani multiplicabitur
35 plantatus in domo domini in atriis domus dei nostri.[6]

---

l. 18.   The title has been erased and re-written (*p. m.*).
· l. 22.   The outer margin of fo. 106 has been cut away.

[1] Sir. xv. 5.   [2] Sir. xv. 6 a.   [3] Eph. iv. 7-13.
[4] Ps. cxi. 1, 2 ; Isai. xli. 27.   [5] Matt. ix. 9-13.   [6] Ps. xci. 13, 14.

[Secreta].

Supplicationibus apostol[ic]is beati mathei euangelizæ et apostoli tui quesumus domine [ecclesiæ] tuæ commendetur oblatio· cuius magnificis predicationibus eruditur.

5 *Communio.*

Amen dico uobis quod uos qui reliquistis omnia et secuti estis me centuplum accipietis et uitam ęternam possidebitis.[1]

(Post communionem).

Sumpsimus domine uenerabile sacramentum beati mathei
10 apostoli tui festiuitate lætantes· quesumus ut suis precibus gloriosis· et credendum nobis iugiter postulet et sequendum beatus euangeliza quod docuit ꝰ per christum.

·III· KL' OCTA† FESTIUITAS SANCTI· MICHAELIS
ARCHANGELI.

15 /Benedic[i]te dominum omnes angeli eius potentes [fo. 107r. uirtutes qui facitis uerbum eius ad audiendum † [uocem] sermonum eius.[2]
Ps. Benedic anima mea domino.[3]

Oremus.

20 Deus qui miro ordine angelorum ministeria hominumque dispensas· concede propitius ꝰ ut quibus tibi ministrantibus in celo semper assistitur ab his uita nostra muniatur ꝰ per.

Lectio libri apocalipsis iohannis· a.

In diebus illis ꝰ significauit deus quæ oportet . . . . et
25 lauit nos a peccatis nostris in sanguine suo.[4]

℞. Benedicite dominum omnes angeli eius potentes /uir-[fo. 107v. tutes qui facitis uerbum eius.
℣. Benedic anima mea domino et omnia interiora mea nomen sanctum eius· Alleluia.
30 ℣. In conspectu angelorum psallam tibi domine deus meus.[5]

Secundum matheum.

In illo tempore ꝰ accesserunt discipuli ad ihesum dicentes.
. . . / . . semper uident faciem patris mei ꝰ qui in [fo. 108r. celis est.[6]

l. 8. The title is almost entirely cut away: enough, however, remaining to show that it was not omitted by the rubricator.

[1] Matt. xix. 28 a, 29 b. [2] Ps. cii. 20. [3] Ps. cii. 1.
[4] Apoc. i. 1–5. [5] Ps. cii. 20 a, 1, cxxxvii. 1 b. [6] Matt. xviii. 1–10.

Offerenda.

Stetit angelus iuxta aram templi habens turibulum aureum in manu sua· et data sunt ei incensa multa et ascendit fumus aromatum in conspectu dei·[1] alleluia.

5 *Secreta.*

Munus populi tui quesumus domine dignanter assume· quod non nostris meritis sed sancti archangeli tui michaelis deprecatione tibi sit gratum ꝰ per dominum.

Communio.

10 Benedic[i]te omnes angeli eius domino ymnum dicite et super-exaltate eum in secula.[2]

Post communionem.

Beati archangeli tui michaelis intercessione suffultí· supplices te domine deprecamur ꝰ ut quod ore prosequamur† contin-
15 gamus et mente ꝰ per dominum.

·II· KL' NOUEMBRIS NAUI† UIGILIA OMNIUM SANCTORUM.

Timete dominum omnes sancti eius quesumus † nichil /dest † timentibus eum.[3]   [fo. 108v.
Ps. Diuites eguerunt et essurierunt inquirentes autem dominum
20 non deficient omni bono.[4]
Ps. Iusti epulentur exultent in conspectu dei delectentur in lętitia.[5]

Oremus.

Domine deus noster multiplica super nos gratiam tuam ꝰ et
25 quorum preuenimus gloriosa sollennia· tribue subsequi in sancta professione lętitiam ꝰ per.

Lectio libri· apocalipsis· iohannis· a.

Ego iohannes uidi in medio throni et quatuor   .   .
/ . . et gloriam et benedictionem ꝰ[6] in secula [fo. 109r.
30 seculorum.

℟. Exultabunt sancti in gloria lætabuntur in cubilibus suis.
℣. Cantate domino canticum nouum laus eius in ecclesia sanctorum.[7]

Secundum lucam †.

35 In illo ꝰ dixit dominus ihesus discipulis suis.   ego sum uitis
. . / . . et gaudium uestrum impleatur.[8]   [fo. 109v.

---

[1] Apoc. viii. 3 a, 4.   [2] Dan. iii. 58.   [3] Ps. xxxiii. 10.
[4] Ps. xxxiii. 11.   [5] Ps. lxvii. 4.   [6] Apoc. v. 6-12.
[7] Ps. cxlix. 5, 1.   [8] Joh. xv. 1-11.

Offerenda.

Exultabunt.[1]

Secreta.

Altare tuum domine deus muneribus cumulamus oblatis· da
5 quesumus ut ad salutem nostram omnium sanctorum tuorum
deprecatione proficiant· quorum sollennia uentura precurrimus·
per dominum.

Communio.

Ego uos elegi /de mundo ut eatis· et fructum afferatis [fo. 110r.
10 et fructus uester maneat.[2]

Post [communionem].

Sacramentis domine et gaudiis oblata† celebritate expletis·
quesumus ut eorum precibus adiuuemur· quorum recordation-
ibus exhibentur ꝶ per.

15 IN DIE AD MISAM.

Gaudeamus omnes in domino diem festum celebrantes sub
honore sanctorum omnium de quorum sollennitate gaudent angeli
et collaudant filium dei.
Ps. Exultate iusti in domino.[3]

20 *Oremus.*

Omnipotens sempiterne deus qui nos omnium sanctorum
merita sub una tribuisti celebritate uenerari ꝶ quesumus· ut
desideratam nobis tuæ propitiationes † abundantiam· multi-
plicatis intercessionibus largiaris ꝶ per.

25 *Lectio apocalipsis iohannis apostoli.*

Ego iohannes uidi quatuor angelos stantes super quatuor
. . / . . et fortitudo d[e]o nostro ꝶ in secula [ff. 110v. 111r.
seculorum.[4]

Gradale.

30 Timete dominum omnes sancti eius quoniam nichil deest
quoniam † timentibus eum.
℣. Inquirentes autem dominum non deficient omni bono.
[℣.] gloriosus deus· Alleluia.
℣. Iudicabunt sancti in † nationes· et dominabuntur populis
35 et regnabit illorum rex in eternum.[5]

---

[1] Ps. cxlix. 5.   [2] Joh. xv. 16 a.   [3] Ps. xxxii. 1.
[4] Apoc. vii. 1-12.   [5] Ps. xxxiii. 10, 11 b; Exod. xv. 11; Sap. iii. 8.

Secundum iohannem.

In illo tempore ꞉ respiciens ihesus in discipulos suos ꞉ dixit.
pater sancte ꞉ . . / . . ut dilectio qua [ff. 111v., 112r.
dilexisti me in ipsis sit et ego in ipsis.[1]

5   *Oremus* †.

Mirabilis deus in sanctis suis deus israhel ipse dabit uirtutem et
fortitudinem plebis † suæ benedictus deus.[2]

ᐧ *Secreta.*

Munera tibi domine nostræ deuotionis offerimus· que et
10 per † cunctorum tibi grata sint honore iustorum· et nobis
salutaria te miserante reddantur ꞉ per dominum.

Communio.

Gaudete iusti in domino alleluia rectos, decet collaudatio[3]
alleluia.

15   *Post* [*communionem*].

Dá quesumus domine fidelibus populis omnium sanctorum
tuorum semper ueneratione lætari· et eorum perpetua supplicatione muniri ꞉ per dominum.

IN· IIIª ET IN· VIª FERIA.

20   [*Oremus*].

Omnium sanctorum intercessionibus quesumus domine
gratia tua nos semper protegat et christianis fidelibus uiuentibus atque defunctis misericordiam tuam ubique pretende ꞉ ut
uiuentes ab omnibus impugnationibus defensi tua opitulatione
25 saluentur /et defuncti remissionem suorum omnium [fo. 112v.
mereantur accipere peccatorum ꞉ per.

[*Secreta*].

Oblationibus nostris quesumus domine propitiatus intende·
et ob tuorum omnium sanctorum honorem ueniam nobis
3⟩ nostrorum tribue delictorum ac christianis omnibus uiuentibus
atque defunctis· hec sancta presens libatio et uitæ presentis
commoda et futuri regni adquirat· per.

[*Post communionem*].

Hec sacrificia que sumpsimus domine meritis et inter-
35 cessione omnium sanctorum nobis proficiant ad salutem·
[et] uiuentibus atque defunctis omnibus christianis fidelibus te
fauente ęterna ac temporalia premia benigne adquirant ꞉ per
dominum.

---

[1] Joh. xvii. 11 b–26.   [2] Ps. lxvii. 36.   [3] Ps. xxxii. 1.

/[CANON].   [fo. 113r.

Per omnia secula seculorum· amen·
Dominus uobiscum· et cum spiritu tuo·
Sursum corda· habemus ad dominum
5   Gratias agamus domino deo nostro· dignum et iustum est·
Uere dignum et iustum est ęquum et salutare· nos tibi
semper et ubique gratias agere· domine sancte pater omnipotens eterne deus· per christum dominum nostrum· per quem
maiestatem tuam laudant angeli adorant dominationes· tre-
10   munt potestates· Celi celorumque uirtutes ac beata seraphin
socia exultatione concelebrant· Cum quibus et nostras uoces
ut admitti iubeas deprecamur supplici confessione dicentes·
Sanctus· sanctus· sanctus· dominus sabaoth· pleni sunt celi et
terra gloria tua [ossanna] in excelsis· benedictus qui uenit in
15   nomine domini ossanna in excelsis·
/⊕ ęterne deus· Qui cum unigenito filio tuo et spiritu [fo. 113v.
san[c]to ⁖ unus es deus· unus es dominus· non in unius singulari-
tate personę· sed in unius trinitate substantię. quod enim de
tua gloria reuelante te credimus· hoc de filio tuo· hoc de
20   spiritu sancto sine differentia † discretione sentimus. ut in
confessione uerae sempiternęque deitatis· et in personis pro-
prietas· et in essentia unitas et in maiestate adoretur æqualitas.
Quem laudant angeli atque archangeli· cerubin quoque ac
saraphin· qui non cessant iugiter clamare una uoce dicentes·
25   sanctus· s· s·
Et ideo cum angelis et archangelis· cum tronis et dominationibus ⁖ cumque omni militia celestis exercitus ⁖ ẏmnum
glorię tuę canimus sine fine dicentes· sanctus·
Te igitur clemententissime† pater per ihesum christum
30   filium tuum dominum nostrum supplices rogamus et
petimus uti accepta /habeas et benedicas· hec do✠na· [fo. 114r.
hec mu✠nera· hec sancta ✠ sacrificia illibata· inprimis que
tibi offerimus pro æclesia † tua sancta catholica quam pacificare·
custodire· adunare et regere digneris toto orbe terrarum· una
35   cum famulo tuo papa nostro· n· et antistitete † nostro· n· et
omnibus ortodoxis atque catholicę et apostolicę fidei cultoribus·
Memento domine famulorum famularumque tuarum· et

· l. 1. The recto of fo. 113 is written in a larger hand than that which is used
elsewhere. The scribe apparently intended to continue to use this character
throughout the Canon, but he gradually returns to the smaller hand.
l. 20. The final letter of ' discretione ' is erased.

omnium circumstantium quorum tibi fides cognita est et nota
deuotio pro quibus tibi offerimus uel qui tibi offerunt hoc
sacrificium laudis pro se suisque omnibus· pro redemptione
animarum suarum· pro spe salutis et incolumitatis suę tibi
5 reddunt uota sua æterno deo uiuo et uero.,

Communicantes et memoriam uenerantes inprimis gloriosę
semper uirginis marię genitricis dei et domini nostri ihesu
christi·

/S(ed) et beatorum apostolorum ac martirum [fo. 114v.
10 tuorum· petri· pauli· andreę· iacobi· iohannis· tomę· iacobi·
philippi· bartholomei· mathei· simonis· taddei· lini· cleti·
clementis· sixti· cornelíí· cipriani· laurentíí· crisogoni· iohan-
nis· et pauli· cosmę· et damiani· et omnium sanctorum tuorum
quorum meritis precibusque concedas· ut in omnibus protec-
15 tionis tuę muniamur· auxilio· per eundem christum dominum
nostrum.

Hanc igitur oblationem seruitutis nostrę sed et cunctę
familię tuę quesumus domine ut placatus accipias· diesque
nostros in tua pace disponas· atque ab eterna dampnatione
20 nos eripi· et in electorum tuorum iubeas grege numerari· per
christum dominum· n.,

Quam oblationem tu deus in omnibus quesumus· bene-
di✠ctam· ascri✠ptam· ra✠tam· rationabilem acceptabilemque
facere digneris· ut nobis co✠rpus et sa✠ngis fiat dilectissimi
25 filíí tui domini dei nostri ihesu christi.

/Qui pridie quam pateretur accepit panem in [fo. 115r.
sanctas ac uenerabiles manus suas· eleuatis occulis in celum
ad te deum patrem suum omnipotentem tibi gratias agens·
Bene✠dixit fregit dedit discipulis suis dicens· accipite et
30 manducate ex hoc omnes· hoc est enim corpus meum·

Simili modo posteaquam cenatum est accipiens et hunc
preclarum calicem in sanctas ac uenerabiles manus suas· item
tibi gratias agens· bene✠dixit dedit discipulis suis dicens·
Accipite et bibite ex eo omnes· hic est enim calix sanguinis
35 mei noui et eterni testamenti misterium fidei qui pro uobis et
pro multis effundetur in remisionem peccatorum· Hec quotiens-
cunque feceritis in mei memoriam faciatis†· Unde et memores
domine nos tui serui· sed et plebs tua sancta eiusdem christi
filíí tui domini dei nostri beatę passionis· necnon et ab inferis
40 resurrectiônis· sed et in celos gloriosę ascensionis offerimus
preclaræ maiestati tuę de tuis /donis ac datis· [fo. 115v.
hos✠tiam puram· hos✠tiam sanctam· hos✠tiam immacu-
latam· pan✠em sanctum uitę ęternę et cali✠cem salutis per-
petuę· supra que propitio ac sereno uultu respicere digneris·
45 et accepta habere sicuti accepta habere digneris † es munera

l. 45. The last four letters of ‘digneris’ have apparently been deleted.

pueri tui iusti abel· et sacrificium patriarchę nostri abrahę·
et·quod tibi obtulit summus sacerdos tuus melchisedech
sanctum sacrificium immaculatam hostiam· Supplices te
rogamus omnipotens deus· iube hec perferri per manus sancti
5 angeli tui in sublime altare tuum in conspectu diuinę maiestatis tuę· ut quotquot ex hác altaris participatione sacrosanctum filíí tui cor✠pus et sa✠nginem sumpserimus omni
benedic✠tione celesti et gratia repleamur· per eundem· chris-
tum· d· n·
10   Memento etiam domine famulorum famularumque tuarum·
n· qui nos precesserunt cum signo fidei· et dormiunt in sompno
pacis ipsis domine et omnibus in christo quiescentibus
/locum refrigeríí lucis et pacis ut indulgeas depreca- [fo. 116r.
mur· per christum dominum· n.,
15   Nobis quoque peccatoribus famulis tuis de multitudine
miserationum tuarum sperantibus partem aliquam et societatem donare digneris cum tuis sanctis apostolis et martiribus
cum iohanne· stefano· mathia· barnaba· ignatio· alexandro·
marcellino· petro· felicitate· perpetua· agatha· lucia· agne·
20 cecilia· anastasia·
    et cum omnibus sanctis tuis intra quorum nos consortium
non estimator meritis † sed uenię quesumus largitor admitte·
per christum dominum nostrum·
    Per quem hec omnia domine· semper bona creas· sanctifi-
25 ✠cas· uiui✠ficas· benedi✠cis et prestas nobis· per ip✠sum·
et cum ip✠so· et in ip✠so est tibi deo patri omnipotenti in
unitate spiritus sancti omnis honor et gloria·
    Per omnia secula seculorum· amen· oremus· Preceptis salu-
taribus moniti· et diuina institutione formati audemus dicere.,
30   Pater noster qui es in celis· sanctificetur nomen tuum·
/adueniat regnum tuum· fiat uoluntas tua sicut in [fo. 116v.
celo et in terra· panem nostrum cotidianum da nobis hodie· et
dimitte nobis debita nostra sicut et nos dimittimus debi-
toribus nostris· et ne nos inducas in temptationem· sed libera
35 nos a malo· amen·
    Libera nos quesumus domine ab omnibus malis preteritis
presentibus et futuris et intercedente beata et gloriosa semperque uirgine dei genitrice maria et beatis apostolis tuis
petro et paulo atque andrea cum omnibus sanctis·
40   Da propitius pacem in diebus nostris· ut ope misericordię
tuę adiuti et a peccato simus semper liberi et ab omni per-
turbatione securi· per dominum nostrum ihesum christum
filium tuum qui tecum uiuit· eiusdem†·
    Per omnia secula seculorum· amen·
45   ✠Pax domini sit semper uobiscum· et cum spiritu tuo·
Agnus dei qui tollis peccata mundi miserere nobis·

Agnus dei qui tollis· Agnus dei· dona nobis pacem·

Hec sacrosancta commixtio corporis et sanginis domini
nostri ihesu christi sit omnibus sumentibus salus mentis et
corporis et ad uitam eternam promerendam /pre- [fo. 117r.
5 paratio salut[ar]is·

Domine sancte pater omnipotens eterne deus da michi hoc
corpus et sanguinem domini nostri ihesu christi filii tui· ita
sumere· ut per hoc merear remissionem omnium peccatorum
meorum accipere et de tuo sancto spiritu repleri· quia tu es
10 deus et preter te non est alius cuius regnum et imperium
gloriosum permanet in secula seculorum· amen·

Percept[i]o corporis et sanguinis tui domine ihesu christe
quam ego indignus peccator sumere presumo non michi proueniat in iudicium et condempnationem· sed tua pietate prosit
15 michi ad purgationem peccatorum et ad tutamentum mentis
et corporis· qui cum deo·

Domine ihesu christe fili dei uiui qui ex uoluntate patris
cooperante spiritu sancto per mortem tuam mundum uiuifi-
casti· libera me per hoc sacrum corpus et sanguinem tuum a
20 cunctis iniquitatibus et uniuersis malis meis et fac me tuis
semper oboedire preceptis· et a te nunquam in perpetuum
separari· qui uiuis· ·

Placeat tibi domine deus sancta trinitas obsequium
/seruitutis meæ et presta ut sacrificium quod occulis [fo. 117v.
25 tuę maiestatis indignus obtuli tibi acceptabile michique et
omnibus pro quibus illud obtuli sit te miserante propitiabile·
qui uiuis· et regnas deus per omnia· secula seculorum· amen.

l. 7. In the MS. ' corpus et sanguinem ' is written in the vacant space at the
end of l. 5, preceded by the mark known by the name ' ceann fa eite ' (⟨þ).
l. 11. After ' amen ' is written in a later hand which imitates that of the text :
' hic dicitur· agnus.'
l. 18. The words ' cooperante spiritu ' are written at the end of l. 16, being
treated in a manner similar to ' corpus et sanguinem ' above, l. 7. These are the
only instances of this characteristically Irish method of writing found in the
manuscript.
l. 24. All but the first five lines of fo. 117v. is blank.

[MISSÆ UOTIUÆ].

/M· DE SANCTA TRINITATIS†. [fo. 118r.

Benedicta sit sancta trinitas indiuisa unitas confitebimur ei quia fecit nobiscum misericordiam suam.[1]

5   [*Ps.*] Benedicamus patrem et filium· cum.

Oremus.

Omnipotens sempiterne deus qui dedisti famulis tuis in confessione uere fidei (. .) eternę trinitatis gloriam agnoscere et in potentia maiestatis adorare unitatem unitatem † que-
10 sumus ꞉ ut eiusdem fidei firmitate ab omnibus semper munia-mur aduersis· qui uiuis· et regnas.

Ad corintheos.

Fratres ꞉ gratia domini nostri ihesu christi ꞉ et caritas dei. et communicatio sancti spiritus ꞉ sit semper cum omnibus uobis
15 in christo ihesu domino nostro.[2]

[*Ad romanos*].

Fratres ꞉ o altitudo diuitiarum . . . . /ipsi [fo. 118v. gloria ꞉ in secula seculorum· amen.[3]

[*Gradale*].

20   ℣. Benedicite dominum celi et coram omnibus uiuentibus con-fitemmini † ei alleluia.
  ℣. Benedicite † es domine deus patrum nostrorum et lauda-bilis.[4]
  [℣.] D†.

25

Secundum iohannem.

In illo tempore ꞉ dixit dominus ihesus discipulis suis· cum uenerit . . . . ut cum uenerit hora eorum ꞉ reminiscamini quia ego dixi uobis.[5]

Offerenda.

30   Benedictus deus pater unigenitusque dei filius sanctus quoque spiritus quia fecit nobiscum misericordiam suam[6] alleluia.

l. 8. Two or three letters (apparently ' et in ') are erased after ' fidei.'
l. 22. The second i and final e of ' Benedicite' appear to have been partially erased.

[1] Tob. xii. 6 b.   [2] 2 Cor. xiii. 13.   [3] Rom. xi. 33–36.
[4] Tob. xii. 6 a ; Dan. iii. 26 a.   [5] Joh. xv. 26, 27, xvi. 1–4.
[6] Tob. xii. 6 b.

Silenter

Suscipe sancta trinitas hanc oblationem quam tibi offero in
memoriam incarnationis /natiuitatis passionis resur- [fo. 119r.
rectionis atque ascensionis domini nostri ihesu christi· et in
5 honorem beatissimę uirginis marię genitricis eiusdem domini
nostri ihesu christi· et omnium sanctorum tuorum qui tibi
prolacuerunt † ab initio mundi· et † ut illis proficiat ad
honorem nobis autem omnibusque fidelibus christianis ad
salutem ut illi omnes pro nobis intercedere dignentur in celis
10 quorum memoriam facimus in terris qui in trinitate perfecta
uiuis et regnas deus per omnia· s· s· amen.

Deinde conuersus prespiter ad populum dicit

Orate fratres pro me miserrimo peccatore ut meum pariter
[ac] uestrum fiat acceptabile sacrificium in conspectu diuinę
15 maiestatis.

Et chorus respondet

Exaudiet te dominus in die usque confirmet.[1]

Secreta.

Sanctifica quesumus domine deus noster per unigeniti tui
20 uirtutem et per tui /nominis sancti inuocationem huius [fo. 119v.
oblationis hostiam et cooperante sancto spiritu per eam nosmet ipsos tibi perfice munus ęternum per eundem dominum
nostrum ihesum christum filium tuum qui.

FERIA VI· MISA DE SANCTA CRUCE.

25 Nos autem gloriari oportet in cruce domini nostri ihesu christi
in quo est salus uitę † et resurrectio nostra per quem et liberasti †
et saluasti † sumus.[2]

Ps. Deus misereatur.[3]

Oremus.

30 Deus qui unigeniti filii tui domini nostri ihesu christi pretioso sanguine uiuifice crucis uexillum sanctificare uoluisti
concede quesumus· eos qui eiusdem sancte crucis gaudent
honore tua quoque ubique protectione gaudere ꝰ per dominum
nostrum.

35 *Ad pilipenses.*

Fratres christus factus est pro nobis obediens . .
/ . . quia dominus noster christus ꝰ in gloria est [fo. 120r.
dei patris.[4]

---

ll. 26, 27. The superfluous letter s in each of the words ' liberasti ' and ' saluasti '
is erased.

[1] Ps. xix. 2–5.   [2] Cf. Gal. vi. 14.
[3] Ps. lxvi. 2.   [4] Phil. ii. 8–11.

℟. Christus factus est pro nobis obediens usque ad mortem mortem autem crucis.

℣. Propter quod et deus exaltauit illum et dedit illi nomen quod est super omne nomen·[1] alleluia.

5 ℣. Dulce lignum dulces clauos dulce † ferens pondera que sola fuisti digna portare regem celorum et dominum.

Secundum iohannem †.

In illo tempore ·: ascendens ihesus hierusolimam ·: . . . . et crucifigendum. et tertia die resurget.[2]

10 ### Offerenda.

Protege domine plebem tuam per signum sancte crucis ab omnibus insidiis inimicorum omnium ut tibi gratam /exhibeamus [fo. 120v. seruitutem et acceptabile tibi fiat sacrificiu(m) n(ost)r(u)m alleluia.

Secreta.

15 Hec oblatio domine quesumus ab omnibus nos mundet offensis quę in ara crucis· etiam totius mundi tulit offensam ·: per dominum.

Communio.

Per lignum serui facti sumus et per sanctam crucem liberati 20 fructus arboris seduxit nos filius dei redemit· alleluia alleluia.

Post [communionem].

Adesto nobis domine deus noster· et quos sancte cruci[s] lętari facis honore eius quoque perpetuis defende subsidiis.

IN SABBATO DE SANCTA M[ARIA]· AB OCTAUIS.

25 Salue sancta parens enixa paupera † regem qui celum terram[que] regit in secula seculorum.

℣. Que gaudium matris habens cum uirginitatis honore nec primam similem uisa es nec habere sequentem.[3]

Oremus.

30 Concede nos famulos tuos quesumus domine deus perpetua mentis et corporis salute gaudere· et gloriosa beatæ marię semper uirginis intercessione a presenti liberari tristitia et futura perfrui lętitia· per dominum.

Lectio libri sapientiæ.

35 Ab initio et ante secula creata sum ·: et usque /ad [fo. 121r. futurum . . . . et in plenitudine sanctorum detentio mea[4].

---

[1] Phil. ii. 8, 9.   [2] Matt. xx. 17–19.
[3] Sedulius *Carm. Pasch.* 63, 64, 66–68 (Migne xix. 599).
[4] Sir. xxiv. 14–16.

Gradale.

Benedicta et uenerabilis es uirgo maria que sine tactu pudoris inuenta es mater saluatoris.

N. Uirgo dei genitrix quem totus non capit orbis in tua se
5 clausit uiscera factus homo· alleluia.

N. Post partum uirgo inuiolata permansisti dei genitrix intercede pro nobis.

Secundum (. . .) lucam †.

In illo tempore ꞉' stabant iuxta crucem ihcsu mater eius et
10 . . . . ex illa hora ꞉' accepit eam discipulus in sua.[1]

Secundum lucam.

/In illo tempore ꞉' factum est cum loqueretur ihesus [fo. 121v. ad turbas ꞉' extollens . . . . qui audiunt uerbum dei [et] custodiunt illud.[2]

15 ### [*Offerenda*].

Felix es sacra uirgo maria et omni laude dignissima quia ex te ortus est sol iustitię christus deus noster.

[*Secreta*].

Tua domine propitiatione et beata † dei genitricis semper-
20 que uirginis marię intercessione ad perpetuam atque presentem hęc oblatio nobis proficiat prosperitatem.

♱ eterne deus· et maiestatem tuam pronis mentibus exorare· ut beatę semper et intemeratę uirginis mariæ supplicatione placatus et ueniam nobis ex omnibus nostris
25 tribuas criminibus [et] remedia sempiterna concedas per christum.

Communio.

Benedicta a filio suo † domino quia per te fructum uitæ communicauimus.

30 ### /Post [*communionem*].   [fo. 122r.

Sumptis domine salutis nostrę subsidiis· da quesumus beatę dei genitricis semperque uirginis marię patrocinis nos ubique protegi in cuius ueneratione hęc tuę obtulimus maiestati per dominum nostrum ihesum christum.

35 ### DE SANCTA MARIA IN ADUENTU DOMINI.

[*Oremus*].

Deus qui de beatę marię uirginis utero uerbum tuum angelo nuntiante carnem suscipere uoluisti· presta supplicibus tuis ut

l. 8. The illegible letters have been erased.
[1] Joh. xix. 25–27.   [2] Luc. xi. 27, 28.

qui uere eam genitricem dei credimus eius apud te intercessionibus adiuuemur per.

Secreta.

Intercessio quesumus domine beatę marię semper uirginis
5 munera nostra commendet nosque in eius ueneratione sancta
tuę maiestati reddat acceptos per.

Post [communionem].

Celesti munere satiati quesumus omnipotens deus tua nos
protectione custodi ꞓ et castimonię pacem mentibus nostris
10 atque corporibus intercedente sancta maria propitiatus in-
dulge· ut ueniente /sponso filio tuo unigenito accensis [fo. 122v.
lampadibus eius· digni prestulemur occursum· per dominum
nostrum ihesum christum.

DE SANCTA M[ARIA]· (IN N)ATIUITATI † DOMINI USQUE AD
15 PURIFICATIONEM.

Oremus.

Deus qui salutis eternę beatę mariæ uirginitate fecunda
humano generi primia † prestitisti tribue quesumus· ut ipsam
pro nobis intercedere sentiamus per quam meruimus auctorem
20 uite suscipere per dominum nostrum ihesum christum filium t.

Secreta.

Oblatis domine muneribus suppliciter deprecamur ut qui
ueram uerbi tui incarnationem fideliter ueneramur· ueram
eiusdem carnis ac sanguinis quam per spiritum sanctum uirgo
25 mater edidit substantiam in hoc presenti misterio salubriter
percipiamus ꞓ per dominum.

Post communionem.

Da quesumus misericors deus eius nos continua intercessione
uegetari cuius intigra uirguinitate suscepimus /auc- [fo. 123r.
30 toritatem † nostre salutis dominum nostrum ihesum christum
filium tuum.

(DE) S(ANCTA CRUC)E (IN) ᴰᴱRESURRECTIONE USQUE
ASCENSIONEM.

[Oremus].

35 Deus qui ad eternam uitam in christi resurrectione nos
reparas imple pietatis tuę ineffabile sacramentum ut cum in

l. 32. The four first words of the title are erased and *de* written above the
line (*p.m.*); but of the erased words the initial and horizontal stroke of *s̄c̄ū*
(= *sancta*) and the final letter of *cruce* are legible, and *ī* (= *in*) is almost
certain.

maiestate sua saluator nostra aduenerit quos fecisti baptismo
regenerari facias beata inmortalitate uestiri ⁊ per dominum.

ce in res[ur]rectione (. .) as (. .).

Secreta.

5   Deus qui pro salute mundi unigenitum tuum sacrificium
paschale fecisti propitiare supplicationibus nostris ut [in]ter-
pellans pro nobis pontifex summus nos per iest † quod
nostri est similis reconciliet per id quod tibi est ęqualis
absoluat· ihesus christus dominus noster qui· t· u.

10   *Post [communionem].*

Concede quesumus omnipotens deus ut ueterem cum suis
actionibus hominem deponentes illius conuersatione uiuamus
ad cuius nos substantiam /paschalibus remediis [fo. 123v.
transtulisti ihesu christi filii tui domini nostri· qui· t.

15   DE SA(N)C(TA) CRUCE IN RESURRECTIONE USQUE
ASCENSIONEM.

[Oremus].

Deus qui pro nobis filium tuum crucis patibulum subire
uoluisti ut inimici a nobis expelleres potestatem concede
20 nobis famulis tuis· ut resurrectionis gratiam consequamur⁊ per
dominum.

Secreta.

Purifica nos misericors deus ut ecclesie tuę preces que tibi
grata sunt pia munera deferentes fiant expiatis mentibus
25 gratiores ⁊ per dominum.

Post [communionem].

Largire·sensibus nostris omnipotens deus· ut per temporalem
filii tui mortem quam misteria ueneranda testantur· uitam
nobis dedise perpetuam confidamus ⁊ per.

30   DE SANCTA MARIA IN RESURRECTIONE USQUE
ASCENSIONEM· IOCT †.

[Oremus].

Deus qui coram matre agnus innocens mortem nostram
subire /dignatus es concede nos quesumus ipsius [fo. 124r.
35 uirginis precibus resurrectionis tue participes fieri· qui tecum †
uiuit †.

1. 3.   Over the first *c* is a mark which may perhaps represent *v*. There were
probably some letters now illegible, after *resurrectione*, and after *as* : but this is
somewhat doubtful.

Secreta.

In mentibus nostris domine uere fidei sacramenta confirma·
ut qui conceptum de uirgine deum uerum et hominem
confitemur· per eius salutiferę resurrectionis potentiam ad
5 ęternam [mereamur] peruenire lętitiam· per· eundem d·
nostrum.

Post [communionem].

Gratiam tuam quesumus domine [mentibus] nostram †
infunde ut qui angelo nuntiante christi filii tui incarnationem
10 cognouimus per pasionem eius et crucem ad resurrectionis
gloriam perducamur ·/ per.

DE OMNIBUS APOSTOLIS,

[Oremus].

Omnipotens et misericors deus qui beatos apostolos tuos
15 petrum et paulum atque andream omnesque apostolos celesti
corona decorare uoluisti presta quesumus· ut quemadmodum
deuotam /ipsorum frequentamus obsecrando memo- [fo. 124v.
riam ita eorum iugiter sublimia apud te sentiamus patrocinia·/
per [dominum] nostrum ihesum.

20 ## Secreta.

Hec hostia salutaris quesumus domine quam in sanctorum
apostolorum tuorum petri et pauli atque andrea † omniumque
apostolorum ueneranda commemorationc tuę maiestati suppliciter offerimus· et ligamina nostrę prauitatis suppliciter †
25 offerimus † [absoluat] et tuę nobis misericordię karismata
tribuat· per christum.

Post communionem.

Quesumus omnipotens et misericors deus ut quos in
sanctorum apostolorum tuorum petri et pauli atque andreę
30 omniumque apostolorum ueneranda memoria de tuis sacríís
donis satiasti per hec indulgentiam tuę propitiationis consequi
mereamur per dominum.

IN COMMEMORATIONE· S· A· P[ETRI]· ET P[AULI].

Oremus.

35 /Deus qui beatorum apostolorum tuorum pe*tri* [fo. 125r.
et pauli dignitatem ubique gloriosam tua gratia perfecisti·
quesumus ct ut doctrinis eorum semper muniamur et meritis:
per.

l. 35. The last four letters of 'petri' have been added by the rubricator.
There is perhaps a letter erased before this word.

Secreta.

Suscipe domine uota ut † apostoli † tui et apostolico
patrocinio confitentem † huius quam tibi offerimus hostia † participatione conserua.

5   *Post communionem.*

Protege domine plebem tuam et quam diuinis tribuis
participatione † sacramentis apostolica intercessione ab omnibus absolue peccatis? per dominum.

DE SANCTIS QUI ECCLESIE † REQUIESCUNT.

10   .   *[Oremus].*

Propitiare quesumus domine nobis famulis tuis per
sanctorum tuorum patricii· n· et eorum quorum reliquię
in hac continentur ecclesia merita gloriosa ut eorum pia
intercessione ab omnibus semper protegamur aduersis.

15   *Secreta.*

Suscipiat clementia tua quesumus /domine de [fo. 125v.
manibus nostris munus oblatum· et per beatorum confessorum
tuorum quorum corpora uel reliquię in presenti requiescunt
ecclesia orationes ab omnibus nos emundet peccatis? per
20 dominum nostrum.

Post communionem.

Diuina libantes misteria que per † sanctorum confessorum
tuorum· n· et n· quorum corpora uel reliquię in presenti
requiescunt ecclesia ueneratione tuę obtulimus maiestati?
25 presta quesumus domine· ut per ea ueniam mereamur peccatorum et celestis gratie donis reficiamur per.

MISA PRO EPISCO[PO].

Oremus.

Concede quesumus domine famulo tuo· n· episcopo nostro·
30 ut predicando et exercendo que recta sunt exemplo bonorum
operum animas suorum instruat subditorum et cternę remu-
nerationis mercedem a te pissimo† pastore percipiat? per.

/*Secreta.*   [fo. 126r.

Munera nostra quesumus domine suscipere † placatus et
35 famulum tuum episcopum nostrum· n· gregemque sibi com-
misum benignus semper et ubique misericorditer protege? per
dominum.

Post [*communionem*].

Hec nos communio domine purget a crimine et famulum tuum episcopum nostrum· n· commissumque sibi gregem benigna pietate conserua ꝰ per dominum.

5   PRO EPISCOPO.

[*Oremus*].

Deus omnium fidelium pa(stor et rector) famulum tuum archiepiscopum (quem pastorem) ecclesie tue preesse uoluisti propitius respice et da ei quesumus uerbo et exemplo quibus
10 preest proficere ut ad uitam una cum grege sibi commisso perueniat sempeternam ꝰ per.

Secreta.

Oblatis quesumus domine placare muneribus et famulum tuum arch[i]episcopum nostrum· n· quem ecclesie tuę pastorem
15 preesse uoluisti assidua protectione guberna.

Post [*communionem*].

Hec nos quesumus domine sacramenti perceptio protegat [et] famulum tuum /archiepiscopum nostrum· n· [fo. 126v. quem ecclesie tuę preesse uoluisti pastorem una cum grege
20 sibi commisso saluat † semper ac muniat.

                    (PRO REGE).

[*Oremus*].

Quesumus omnipotens deus ut famulus tuus rex noster· n· qui tua miseratione suscipit regni gubernacula uirtutum etiam
25 omnium percipiat incrementa ꝰ quibus docenter † ornatus et uitiorum uoraginem debitare et hostes superare et ate † qui uia u[er]itas et uita es gratiosus ualeat peruenire ꝰ per.

Secreta.

Suscipiat † domine preces et hostias ecclesie tui † pro salute
30 famuli tui· n· regis nostri te supplicantis et in protectione fidelium populorum antiqua brachi [tui] operare miracula ut superatis pacis inimicis secura tibi seruiat christiana libertas.

ll. 7, 8. The attempt has been made by a late hand to supply the illegible words. After ' fidelium pa ' this hand has restored the letters enclosed in brackets, and, after 'archiepiscopum,' has written 'nostrum' followed by two letters apparently deleted.

l. 21. Some traces remain of this title. It had, however, become illegible or been erased, and now appears re-written in a late hand.

Post [*communionem*].

Hæc domine salutaris sacramentis † perceptio famulum
tuum· n· ab omnibus tueatur aduersis quatinus et eccle-
siastice /pacis obtineat tranquilitate[m] et post istius [fo. 127r.
5 temporis decursum ad eternam perueniat hereditate[m]:· per
dominum.

PRO AMICIS CARNALIBUS.

[*Oremus*].

D[eu]s qui caritatis dona per gratiam in spiritus tuorum
10 fidelium infundis da famulis et famulabus tuis pro quibus
tuam deprecamur clementiam salutem mentis et corporis· ut
te tota uirtute diligant· et que tibi placita sunt tota dilectione
perficiant:· per dominum.

Secreta.

15 Miserere quesumus domine famulis et famulabus tuis [pro
quibus] hoc sacrificium laudis tue offerimus maiestati· ut per
hec sancta sacrificia superne benedictionis gratiam obtineant
et gloriam eterne felicitatis acquirant:· per.

Post [*communionem*].

20 Diuina libantes misteria quesumus domine ut hec sacramenta illis proficiant ad prosperitatem et pacem pro quorum
dilectione /hęc tuę obtulimus maiestati:· per.   [fo. 127v.

MISA QUAM P[RO] SEIPSO DICIT SACERDOS.

[*Oremus*].

25 Omnipotens sempiterne deus qui me peccatorem sacris
altaribus asstare uoluisti· et sancti nominis tui laudare
potentiam· concede quesso per huius sacramenti misterium
meorum ueniam peccatorum ut tue maiestati digne ministrare
merear:· per dominum.

30 *Secreta.*

Deus qui te precipis a peccatoribus exorari tibique sacrificium contriti cordis offerri· hoc sacrificium quod indignis
manibus meis offero acceptare dignare· et ut ipse tibi hostia
et sacrificium esse merear miseratus concede quo per
35 ministerii huius exhibitionem peccatorum omnium percipiam
remisionem:· per dominum.

Post communionem.

Aures tuę pietatis mitissime deus inclina precibus meis·
et per huius diuini sacramenti carnis et sanguinis domini

l. 2. The last letter of 'sacramentis' is scarcely legible. It has perhaps been
erased.
l. 39. The first 'et' appears to be written over s erased.

/nostri ihesu christi filii tui quod indignus sumpsi [fo. 128r. misterium gratia sancti spiritus illumina cor meum ut tuis misteriis digne ministrare teque ęterna caritate diligere et sempiterna gaudia percipere merear ʼ per.

5   MISA SANCTI SPIRITUS.

[Oremus].

Deus qui corda fidelium sancti spiritus illustratione docuisti da nobis in eodem spiritus † recta sapere et [de] eius semper consolatione gaudere· per.

10   *Secreta.*

Munera quesumus domine oblata sanctifica [et] corda nostra et† sancti spiritus illustratione emunda ʼ per dominum.

Post communionem.

Sancti spiritus domine corda nostra mundet infussio· et sui
15 roris intima aspersione fecundet ʼ per dominum.

           PRO EMUNDATIONE CARNIS.

[Oremus].

Deus cui omne cor patet· et omnis uoluntas loquitur et quem nullum latet secretum ʼ purifica per infussionem sancti
20 spiritus cogitationes cordis nostri ut perfecte [te] diligere et digne laudare [mereamur].

                       Secreta.

Hęc oblatio domine deus cordis nostri maculas emundet ut sancti spiritus digna efficiatur· habitatio ʼ per dominum.

25   */Post [communionem].*   [fo. 128v.

Sacrificium salutis nostre tibi offerimus † concede nobis domine deus purificatis mentibus sepius tuę pietatis celebrare misterium ʼ per.

                 PRO PACE

30   *[Oremus].*

Deus a quo sancta desideria recta consilia et iusta sunt opera· da seruis tuis illam quam mundus dare non potest pacem ut et corda nostra mandatis tuis dedita· et hostiam † sublata formidine tempora sint tua protectione tranquilla.

35   *Secreta.*

Deus qui credentes in te populos nullis sinis concuti

terroribus dignare preces et hostias dicata † plebis suscipere·
ut pax tua pietate concessa christianorum fines ab omni hoste
faciat esse securos.

Post [*communionem*].

5   Deus auctor pacis et amator quem nosse uiuere· cui seruire
regnare est protege ab omnibus impugnationibus supplicies †
tuos· ut qui in defensione tua confidimus nullius hostilitatis
arma timeamus ⸴ per dominum.

PRO PETITIONE LAC[RI]MARUM.

10   [*Oremus*].

Omnipotens mitissime deus· qui sitienti populo fontem
uiuentis atque † de petra produxisti /[educ de cordis] [fo. 129r.
nostri duritia conpunctionis lacrimas· ut peccata nostra
plangere ualeamus remisionemque te miserante mereamur
15 accipere.

Secreta.

Hanc oblationem tuam quam tibi domine deus pro peccatis
offerimus quesumus propitius respice· et perduc † de oculis
nostris lacrimarum flumina quibus debita flammarum incendia
20 ualeant † extingere ⸴ per dominum.

Post [*communionem*].

Gratiam sancti spiritus cordibus nostris domine deus
clementer infunde· que nos gemitibus lacrimarum efficiat
maculas nostrarum † diluere peccatorum atque obtatę nobis
25 indulgentiæ te largiente prestet effectum ⸴ per.

PRO TEMPTATIONE CARNIS.

[*Oremus*].

Ure igne sancti spiritus renes nostros et cor nostrum domine
ut tibi casto corpore seruiamus et mundo corde placeamus
30 per dominum.

Secreta.

Dirumpe domine uincula peccatorum nostrorum et ut sacrificia † tibi hostiam laudis obsoluti † libertate possimus retribue
que ante tribuisti et salua nos per indulgentiam quos dignatus
35 es saluare /per gratiam ⸴ per dominum.   [fo. 129v.

Post communionem.

Domine adiutor et protector noster adiuua [nos] et
refloreat caro nostra uigore pudiciti'alis † sanctimonię noui-

tate ereptamque de manu tartari in resurrectionis gaudio
iubeas presentari :' per dominum.

PRO PLUUIA POSTULANDA.

[*Oremus*].

5 Deus in quo uiuimus et mouemur et sumus pluuiam nobis
tribue congruentem ut presentibus subsidiis sufficienter adiuti
sempiterna fiducialius appetamus per.

Secreta.

Oblatis domine placare muneribus et oportunum nobis
10 tribue pluuię sufficientis auxilium.

Post communionem.

Quesumus omnipotens deus tuere nos tua sancta sumentes
et ab omnibus propitiatus absolue peccatis terramque
aridiam † aquis fluenti celestis dignanter infunde :' per domi-
15 num.

CONTRA PLUUIAM.

· [*Oremus*].

Deus qui ministerio aquarum salutis nostrę nobis [sacra-
menta] sanxisti exaudi orationem populi tui· et iube terrores
20 inundatio† cessare pluuiarum flagellumque huius /eli- [fo. 130r.
menti ad effectum tui conuerte misterii· ut qui se regener-
antibus aquis gaudent esse renatos gaudeant his castigantibus
esse correctos :' per dominum.

Secreta.

25 Deus qui fidelium precibus flecteris et humilium confessione
placaris conuersis ad te propitiare supplicibus et quos fecisti
iram intelligere castigantibus † fac misericordiam sentire
parcentis· per.

Post [*communionem*].

30 Deus qui nos omnium rerum tibi seruiente natura per ipsos
motus æris ad cultum tue maiestatis instruis tranquillitatem
nobis misericordię tue remotis largire terroribus· ut cuius
iram expauimus clementiam sentiamus :' per.

PRO SERENITATE ERIS.

[*Oremus*].

35

Ad te nos domine clamantes exaudi et ęris serenitatem
nobis tribue supplicantibus ut qui iuste pro peccatis nostris

affligimur misericordia tua perueniente † clementiam sen-
tiamus· p[er] dominum.

Secreta.

Perueniat † nos quesumus domine gratia /tua [fo. 130v.
5 semper et subsequatur· et has oblationes quas pro peccatis
nostris nomini tuo consecrandas offerimus benignus assume
ut per intercessionem sanctorum tuorum cunctis proficiant ad
salutem ⫽ per.

Post [communionem].

10 Plebs tua domine capiat sacrę benedictionis augmentum·
et copiosis beneficiorum tuorum subleuetur auxiliis que tantis
intercessionum deprecationibus adiuuatur ⫽ per dominum.

PRO ITER AGENTIBUS.

[Oremus].

15 Adesto domine supplicationibus nostris et uiam famulorum
tuorum in salutis tuę prosperitate dispone ut in[ter] omnes
[uiæ] et uitę huius uarietates tuo semper protegantur auxilio ⫽
per dominum.

Post Secreta.

20 Propitiare domine supplicationibus nostris et has oblationes
quos † tibi offerimus pro famulis tuis benignus assume ut uiam
illorum et procedente † gratia tua dirigas· et subsequente
comitari digneris· ut de actu atque incolumitate eorum
secundum misericordię tuę presidia gaudeamus ⫽ per.

25 *[Post communionem].*

Deus infinitę misericordię et maiestati[s] /immense [fo. 131r.
quem nec spatia locorum nec interualla temporum ab his quos
tueris abiungunt· adesto famulis tuis in te ubique confidentibus
et per quam itueri † sunt uiam dux eis et comes esse dignare
30 nichil illis aduersitatis noceat· nichil difficultatis obsistat
cuncta eis salubria cuncta sint prospera et sub ope dextera †
tuę quicquid iusto expetierint desiderio celeri consequantur
effectu ⫽ per dominum.

PRO INFIRMIS.

35 *[Oremus].*

Omnipotens sempiterne deus salus ęterna credentium
exaudi nos orantes pro famulis tui[s] pro quibus misericordię

l. 19. The word *Post* is erased.
l. 21. The third letter of 'quos' is expuncted, and a written above the line in
a late hand.

tuę imploramus auxilium· ut reddita sibi sanitate gratiarum
actionem tibi in ecclesia tua reficiant † :' per.

Secreta.

Deus cuius nutibus uitę nostræ momenta decurrunt suscipe
5 preces et hostias famulorum tuorum· pro quibus misericordiam
tuam egrotantibus imploramus ut de quorum periculo metui-
mus deorum † salute lętemur per :' dominum.

Post [communionem].

Deus infirmitatis humanę singulare presidium auxilii tui
10 super infirmos

[AD POSCENDA SUFFRAGIA OMNIUM SANCTORUM].

[Oremus].

/Concede quesumus omnipotens deus ut intercessio [fo. 131v.
nos sanctę genitricis marię sanctarumque omnium celestium
15 uirtutum et beatorum patriarcarum· profetarum· apostolorum
martirum confessorum atque uirginum et omnium electorum
tuorum ubique letificet ut dum eorum merita recolimus
patrocinia sentiemus†· per dominum.

Secreta.

20 Oblatis quesumus domine placare muneribus et intercedente
dei genitrice maria· cum omnibus sanctis tuis· a cunctis nos
defende periculis· per dominum.

Post communionem.

Sumpsimus domine sanctæ marie et omnium sanctorum
25 tuorum merita recolentes sacramenta celestia· presta quesumus·
ut quod temporaliter agimus eorum precibus adiuti ęternis
gaudis consequamur :' per.

M[ISA]· COMMUNIS.

[Oremus].

30 Omnipotens sempiterne deus· qui uiuorum dominaris simul
et mortuorum omniumque misereris quos tuos fide et opere
futuros esse prenoscis· te suppliciter exoramus· ut pro quibus
effundere preces decreuimus /quosque uel presens [fo. 132r.
adhuc seculum in carne retinet· uel futurum iam exutos
35 corpore [suscepit] pietatis tuæ clementia delictorum suorum

---

l. 10. The postcommon is left incomplete in the MS.
l. 35. In the right margin is written 'suscepit' in a late hand.

omnium ueniam· et gaudia consequi mereantur eterna ꝛ́ per
dominum.

Secreta.

Deus cui soli cognitus est numerus electorum in superna
5 felicitate locandus tribue quesumus ut uniuersorum quos in
oratione commendatos suscepimus uel omnium fidelium
nomina beatę predistinationis liber ascripta retine[a]t ꝛ́ per
dominum.

Post communionem.

10 Purificent nos quesumus omnipotens et misericors deus
sacramenta que sumpsimus· et presta ut hoc tuum sacra-
mentum· non sit nobis reatus ad penam sed intercessio
salutaris ad ueniam· sit oblutio † scelerum sit fortitudo
fragilium· sit contra omnia mundi pericula firmamentum
15 sit uiuorum atque mortuorum fidelium remissio omnium
delictorum ꝛ́ per dominum.

MISA PRO OMNIBUS FIDELIBUS DEFUNCTIS.

/Requiem eternam dona eis domine et lux perpetua [fo. 132v.
luceat eis.
20 Ps. Te decet ymnus deus in sion et tibi reddetur uoltum † in
hierusalem. Exaudi· orationem.[1]
Requiem.

[Oremus].

Inclina domine aurem tuam ad preces nostras quibus
25 misericordiam tuam supplices deprecamur ut animas famulorum famularumque tuarum quas de hoc seculo migrare
iusisti in pacis ac lucis regione constituas et sanctorum
tuorum iubeas esse consortes ꝛ́ per dominum.

Lectio libri apocolipsis † iohannis· a.

30 In diebus illis ꝛ́ audiui uocem de celo dicentem . . . .
opera enim illorum sequuntur illos.[2]

Ad tesolonicenses.

Fratres, noluimus autem uos ignorare de dormientibus ꝛ́ . .
/ . . itaque consolamini inuice[m] ꝛ́ in uerbis istis.[3] [fo. 133r.

35 ### Lectio libri machabeorum.

In diebus illis ꝛ́ uir fortissimis † iuda[s] collatione facta .
. . pro defu[n]ctis exorare ꝛ́ ut a peccatis soluantur.[4]

---

[1] Ps. lxiv. 2, 3 a.   [2] Apoc. xiv. 13.
[3] 1 Thess. iv. 13-18.   [4] 2 Mac. xii. 43-46.

[Lectio libri iob].

Scio quod redemptor meus uiuit ʒ et in nouissimo die . .
/ . . reposita est hẹc spes mea in sinu meo.¹   [fo. 133v.

[Gradale].

5· Requiem eternam dona eis domine et lux perpetua luceat eis.
[*V.*] Absolue domine animas eorum ab omni uinculo delictorum.

[Tractus].

De profundis clamaui ad te domine domine exaudi uocem
10 meam.
[*V.*]   Fiant aures tuæ intendentes in orationem serui tui.
[*V.*]   Si iniquitates obseruaberis domine domine quis sustinebit.
[*V.*]   Quia apud te propitiatio est et propter legem tuam
sustinuit † te domine.²

15   *Secundum iohannem.*

In illo tempore ʒ dixit martha ad ihesum. domine ʒ si fuisses
híc ʒ . . . . christus filius dei uiui ʒ qui in hunc mundum
uenisti.³

               Secundum iohannem.

20   In illo tempore ʒ dixit ihesus turbis iudeorum. ego [sum]
/panis uiuus ʒ . . . . et ego resuscitabo eum ʒ in [fo. 134r.
nouissimo die.⁴

               Secundum iohannem.

In illo tempore ʒ dixit ihesus discipulis suis et turbis
25 iudeorum. omne quod dedit michi pater ad me ueniet ʒ . .
/ . . et ego resuscitabo eum ʒ in nouissimo die.⁵ [fo. 134v.

               Secundum iohannem.

In illo ʒ dixit ihesus discipulis suis. et turbis iudeorum
sicut pater . . . . sed transeat a morte ad uitam.⁶

30   *[Offerenda].*

Domine ihesu christe rex gloriæ libera animas omnium fidelium
defunctorum de manu inferni et de profundo lacu libera eos †
de ore leonis ne obsorueat eas tartarus ne cadent et † obscura
sed signifer sanctus michael representet eas in lucem sanctam.
35   Quam olim abrahẹ promisisti et semini eius.
[*V.*] Hostias et preces tibi domine offerimus.
Tu suscipe pro animabus illis aquarum † hodie memoriam agimus
fac eas domine de morte transire ad uitam· quam olim.
[*V.*] Hanc lucem /redde illis fons bonitatis lucis auctor [fo. 135r.
40 uerẹ patris unigenite· quia †.

¹ Job. xix. 25-27.   ² Ps. cxxix. 1-4 a.   ³ Joh. xi. 21-27.
⁴ Joh. vi. 51-55.   ⁵ Joh. vi. 37-40.   ⁶ Joh. v. 21-24.

[*V.*] Uenturus in mundum daturus uniuersis premia pro meritis presta lucem in celis˙ quam.

[*V.*] Redemptor animarum christe uniuersorum † mitte archangelum sanctum michaelem ut illi † dignetur eis † eripere de
5 rigirenibus † tenebrosum † et perducat eas in sinum abrachę et in lucem sempiternam.

[*V.*] Requiem eternam dona eis domine et lux perpetua, luceat eis.

Domine ihesu.

10   *Secreta.*

Animas famulorum tuorum ab omnibus uitiis humana †
condicionis quesumus domine hec obsoluat † oblatio que totius mundi tulit immolata peccatum ʿ per dominum.

                  [*Communio*].

15   Lux eterna luceat eis domine cum sanctis tuis in ęternum quia pius eis †.

[*V.*] Requiem eternam [dona eis] domine et lux perpetua luceat eis˙ cum sanctis.

[*V.*] Pro quorum memoria corpus christi sumitur dona eis
20 domine requiem sempiternam˙ et lux perpetua luceat eis.

[*V.*] Pro quorum memoria sanguis christi bibitur˙ dona eis domine requiem sempiternam.

              Post [*communionem*].

Annue nobis domine˙ ut per hoc sanctum sacrificium quod
25 sumpsimus animæ famulorum tuorum remisionem quam optauerunt mereantur percipere delictorum˙ per dominum.

          [PRO EPISCOPO DEFUNCTO].

                  [*Oremus*].

/Deus qui inter apostolicos sacerdotes famulos tuos [fo. 135v.
30 pontificali fecisti dignitate censeri presta quesumus˙ ut quorum uicem gerebant ad horam in terris eorum perpetuo consortio letentur in celis ʿ per dominum.

                  Secreta.

Suscipe quesumus domine pro animabus famulorum tuorum
35 pontificum quas offerimus hostias ut quibus pontificale donasti misterium dones et premium per.

              Post [*communionem*].

Propitiare domine supplicationibus nostris et animas famulorum tuorum pontificum in regione uiuorum ęternis gaudiis
40 iubeas sociari ʿ per dominum.

PRO SACERDOTE DEFUNCTO.

[*Oremus*].

Deus cuius misericordie non est numerus suscipe pro animabus famulorum tuorum sacerdotum preces nostras· et
5 lucis eis letitięque regionem in sanctorum tuorum societate concede ꞉ per dominum.

Secreta.

Quesumus domine ut oblationem quam tibi offerimus pro animabus famulorum tuorum sacerdotum placatus accipias·
10 ut quos tuis altaribus seruire tribuisti ad beatorum pertinere iubeas consortia

*   *   *   *

APPENDIX.

COLLATION OF THE SCRIPTURE LESSONS WITH THE TEXT OF
THE CLEMENTINE VULGATE (VERCELLONE'S EDITION, ROME, 1861).

IN the following collation variants marked with (‡) are supported by the Codex Amiatinus.   In the Gospels an asterisk has been prefixed to readings which are supported by one or more manuscripts of the group DELQRr_1r_2 (Wordsworth's notation) or by the Book of Mulling, against all other manuscripts of which collations are given in the Oxford Vulgate. These may usually be regarded as distinctively Irish readings.   For the MSS. DELR the collations of Wordsworth and White have been used. For the rest recourse has been had to the originals in the Library of Trinity College, Dublin.   Mere variations of spelling have not been recorded, but it has not been thought well in all cases to leave unnoticed what seem to be clerical errors.   Occasionally (as at Matt. xxvii. 38) they are survivals of true variants of the Irish type.

Gen. i. p. 33.

3. et dixit . . . fiat *om.*   4. diuissit (*sic*) + ‡deus 8. unus *pro* secundus   9. aqua . . . apariat (*sic*) + terra . . . ardia ‡factumque 12. ‡afferentem *pro* facientem   13. ‡factumque   16. ‡magna luminaria . . . et *pri. om.* . . . praeesset *sec.* + ne   18. preesset . . diuident   20. aqua . . . anima . . . et + et   21. perduxerant   26. faciemus . . . uniuersaque creatura *pro* uniuersaeque terrae 27. deus *om.*   28. illis + et . . . eos *pro* eam   30. in *om.* . . . hn̄t (= habent) *pro* habeant   31. ‡fecit.

ii. 1, 2.
p. 33.

1. terre . . . omnes   2. omni *pro* uniuerso . . . quod *om.*

Exod. xii. 1–11.
p. 29.

4. sunt *pro* ut . . . coniunctus . . . ‡eius *pro* suae . . . possint   5. enim *pro* autem . . . agniculus *pro* anniculus   6. seruabis . . . quartum decimum . . . uesperum 7. et *pro* ac . . . ut̃rque posteam . . . insuper luminaribus   8. agni *pro* igni 9. assum tantum . . . *fin.* + et os eius non confringetis   10. ‡ex eo quicquam 11. et *pri. om.* . . . ‡fesstinantes (*corr. e* fesstimantes *ut uid.*) . . . non enim est *pro* est enim.

Exod. xiv. 24–31.   24. noster *pro* super . . . interficit (=*Am*.*)
    p. 33.   25. fugiemus . . . pro eis pugant (*sic*)
                      26. equies   27. occurrerunt *om*.
                      28. suæ *pro* sunt . . . coopᵘerunt . . . equietes
                      29. ambulauerunt *pro* perrexerunt   30. ‡illo
                      31. lituri *pro* littus . . . magnum . . . quod *pro*
                      quam . . . dominus *om*.

xv. 1a. p. 33.   1. moysi . . . et *sec. om*.

Job xix. 25–27.   25. ‡resurturus (*sic : Am*. resurrecturus)
    p. 93.   26. deum + saluatorem.

Ps. lxxxviii. 14.   *Vide* p. 11.

Prov. x. 28–32.   29. uiæ   31. paʳturit.
    p. 65.

xi. 3, 6,   9. decepit   10. exaltabitur   11. *init.* +
  8–11a.   in.
  p. 65.

Sir. xv. 1–6.   1. dominum   2. obuiauit . . et quasi *usque fin.*
    p. 5.   *uers. om*.   3. illum *pri.* + dominus
                   5. et *pri. om*. . . . aperuit . . . implebit eum *pro*
                   adimp. illum + dominus . . . induit eum *pro*
                   uestiet illum   6. eum *pro* illum *pri*.

xxiv.   11. his *om*. A   16. partes AB   18. *init.* +
  11b–13,   et A . . . exalta A   19. *init.* + et A
  15–20.   20. di (= dei) *pro* dedi *pri*. A . . . sanitatem
  p. 64 (A);   *pro* suauitatem A.
xxiv. 14–16.
  p. 79 (B).

xxiv.   23. fructus *corr. e* fructum   25. ‡uitæ *pro* uiæ
  23–31.   28. ‡generatione   30. audiunt (*corr. e*
  p. 66.   audit *sec. m*.) . . . confundentur (*corr. e* con-
               fundetur *sec. m*.)   31. *init.* + et

Isai. iv. p. 34.   1. apprehendit . . . operimus . . . ·iii· *pro* modo
                     2. in *sec. om*.   3. sanctus + sanctus . . .
                     uocabus   4. si *om*. . . . sordem
                     5. creauit   6. turbidine

vii. 10–15.   14. concipiet + in utero
  p. 54.

xii. 3–5; xxv.   *Vide* p. 11.
  1 ; xxv.ii.
  5; xxxv. 1,
  2b ; xli.
  18a.

Isai. xlix. 1–3, 2. quasi *pro* sicut 3 est *pro* es 5. et *pri.*
  5a, 6b, 7b. + hec 6. ‡ecce *om.* 7. *uerb. ras.*
  p. 57. *inter* adorabunt *et* dominum (propter *ut uid.*) . .
  dominum + ‡deum' tuum . . . quia fidelis est *om.*

li. 11; lii. 13. *Vide* p. 11.

liv. 17b. = *Vulg.*
  p. 34.

lv. 1–11a. 1. uenientes *pro* uenite 2. in *sec. om.* . . . in
  p. 34. crassitudine *om.* 3. ‡fidelis 4. ac *om.*
  5. gentibus *pro* gentem . . . ‡non cognouerunt te
  . . . qui *pro* quia 7. dominum *pro* deum
  . . . cognoscendum *pro* ignosc. 9. quam
  pro quia 11. egredetur

lx. 1–6. 5. ‡afflues + et 6. operiat . . . differentes
  p. 10.

lxi. 10, 11. 10. gaudeo *pro* gaudebo . . . ‡exultauit' animæ . . .
  p. 63. uestimento . . . lętitiæ *pro* iustitiæ 11. sicut
  pro sic

lxii. 5. p. 63. 5. deus *om.*

Jer. i. 4–10. 6. dixit *pro* dixi 7. dicere + quia . . . que
  p. 56. *pro* quaecumque 8. e(;o tecum
  9. ecce *ras.*

Osee vi. 1–6. 1. suæ . . . me + dicentes 2. quam *pro* quia
  p. 28. . . . et *pri. om.* . . . saluabit *pro* sanabit
  3. nos *pri. om.* . . . tertio 4. tibi faciam
  pro. fac. tibi *pri.* . . . et quasi ros mane *om.*
  5. dolui . . . profetis (*sic*) + et . . . iudicia +
  mea uel 6. dei *om.*

Joel. ii. 12–19. 12. hæc *pro* nunc ergo . . . dominus + deus . . in
  p. 17. *ter. et quart. om.* 13. multum misericors *pro*
  multae misericordiae . . . malitiam
  14. ignoscat + deus . . . nostro *pro* uestro
  17. altare + et . . . ut + non 19. et *ter.*
  om. . . . replebimini + in

Mal. iii. 1–4. 1. preparauit . . . templum + sanctum
  p. 51. 3. purgauit . . . flauit *pro* colabit (*Am.* conflabit)
  4. placebunt

2 Mach. xii. 43. collatione facta . . offere (*sic*) + ea ibi . . .
  43–46. sacrificium *om.* . . . iuste *pro* bene
  p. 92. 44. ceciderunt 45. considerauit enim *pro* et
  quia considerabat . . . quod *om.* . . . dormita-
  tionem

Matt. i. 1–16.   2. *abraam (*sic*) + autem   3. ‡esrom (*bis*)
     p. 66.   6. salmonem . . . salmonem (em *ras.*)
                     7. asam   8. ozam   9. *iozias . . .
                     ioathas *pro* ioatham *sec.*   10. mansen *pro*
                     manassen   11. *iochoniam . . . transi-
                     migratione   12. iechonias (e *corr. e* o)

ii. 1–12.   1. iudæ   2. *uenimus + cum muneribus
     p. 10.   11. percidentes   12. somne *pro* somnis ne
                     . . . reuersi *om.*

ii. 13–18.   13. in *pri. om.*   15. per *om.*   16. eius *om.*
     p. 6.   18. plorans *pro* ploratus . . . ululatus *corr.*
                     e uu(.)latus

ii. 19–23.   19. ‡apparuit angelus domini   20. uade *corr. e*
     p. 9.   ualde   21. *accipit   22 ‡illuc *pro*
                     illo   23. habitabit . . . uocatur *pro*
                     uocabitur

iii. 13–17.   13. iordanes   14. ego + autem   17. hec
     p. 11.   *pro* hic . . . complacuit

iv. 1–11.   1. est + ihesus   2. *essurit   5. ‡supra
     p. 19.   9. procedens *pro* cadens   10. ei *om.*

iv. 18–22.   = *Vulg.*
     p. 46.

vi. 16–21.   16. quia *om.*·   19. *thesauro (= Q*) *pro*
     p. 18.   thesauros

ix. 9–13.   = *Vulg.*
     p. 68.

xiv. 22–33.   22. ‡iussit *pro* compulit . . . discipulos + suos
     p. 62.
                     23. uespere *usque ad fin. om.*   25 ·iiii· *pro*
                     quarta   28. ‡uenire ad te   29. aqua
                     30. ualidum (*corr. e* ualium) + uenientem ad se

xv. 21–28.   21. inde *om.* . . . + dominus *ante* ihesus
     p. 20.

xvi. 13–19.   15. me *om.*   17. reuelabit
     p. 60.

xviii. 1–10.   7. mundum . . ‡ab *pro* a   8. est tibi
     p. 69.   9. est tibi

xix. 27–29.   27. relinquimus A . . . *ergo *om.* B   28. ait
     p. 47 (A),   *pro* dixit A . . . eis B   29. *aut *pro* uel B
     p. 61 (B).   . . . uxores *pro* sorores B

Matt. xx. 1–16.   2. cum facta   4. ‡illis dixit   7. ‡meam
  p. 13.   *om.*   8. procurauit *pro* procuratori
                    9. acceperant   10. et *sec. om.*
                    12. portamus   13. uini (i *pri. exp.*)
                    14. nouissima   15. ante *(ut uid.) pro* an (te
                    ras.)

xx. 17–19.   17. discipulos + suos.
  p. 79.

xxiii. 34–39.   34. illis *pro* eis   35. ut ueniat super uos
  p. 4.   omnis *om.* . . . *abiel* . . . iusti *om.*
                    37. quotiens

xxvi. p. 25.   2. *fiat   4. ut *pro* et *sec.*   5. isto *pro* festo
                  (*marg.* festo)   6. esset autem iesus
                  7. albastrum (*sic*) habens ungenti (*marg.* pissici)
                  10. illi *pro* illis . . . ‡huic *om.* (*marg.* huic) . .
                  . . . ‡enim *om.*   11. habebitis *pro* habetis
                  sec.   13. quid *pro* quod . . . *fecit +
                  narrabitur . . . memoria   14. dicitur . . .
                  scariothis   16. querebant . . . tradet .
                  17. uis + ut   18. ad *om.* . . . prope *om.*
                  (*add. m. rec. sup. l.*)   20. ‡suis *om.*
                  22. domine *pro* dicere (mine *del., marg.* dicere)
                  24. *lit. ras. post* homini   31. *dixit
                  35. etsi *pro* etiamsi   37. esse *corr. e* esset
                  39. pusillum + et . . . procecidit . . . sic *pro*
                  sicut *pri.* . . . tu + uis   40. *ait . . .
                  una hora *om.*   41. promutus *pro* promptus
                  42. orauit + eundem sermonem   44. iterum
                  illis   45. *eis *pro* illis . . . appropinquabit
                  46. appropinquabit   47. ‡ipso *pro* eo *pri.*
                  . . . *uerb. ras. post* duodecim (uenit *ut uid.*)
                  48. *eis . . . quicunque *pro* quemc.
                  50. ‡quod *pro* quid . . . *uenisti + fac
                  51. erat . . . manum *om.* . . . fareseorum *pro*
                  sacerdotum   53. nunc *pro* non . . . meum
                  om. . . . m̅ (= me) *pro* m̅ (= modo)
                  55. *eram *pro* sedebam . . . et *sec. om.*
                  56. ‡implerentur . . . fugientes
                  57. *conuenerunt   62. *principis . . . *te
                  om.   63. principis . . . dei + uiui
                  67. scolophis . . . cederunt   68. profeta
                  72. cum iuramento *om.*   73. eloquia *pro*
                  loquella   75. foras + et

xxvii. p. 25.   3. *tradidit eum . . . ductus *om.*   7. inito *om.*
                  8. *init.* + et . . . acheldemach   10. illos
                  11. stetit *corr. e* stetis   12. cum *om.*
                  15. consuerat . . . ‡dimittere pro populo (*Am.*

dim. pop.)   16. *insigne (*sic*) uinctum
17. congregati *autem   18. quidem *pro* quod
. . . eum *om.*   19. ‡illum *pro* eum *pri.*
. . . paradisum *pro* passa sum   20. seniores
+ populi . . . persuaserunt + pro
22. *dixit . . . illis *om.*   23. *pilatus *pro*
praeses   24. si *pro* sed . . . manus +
suas . . . huius iusti   26. *uero *pro* autem
27. *suscipientes *om.* . . . ‡pretorio . . . ad
eum *om.* . . . *uniuersum chortem
28. exeuntes   29. flectentes . . . et *sec.*
om. . . . arundentem . . . ‡ei *om.*
34. cum felle *usque ad fin. om.*
35. diuisserunt (*sic*) *pri.* + sibi . . . *adimpler-
etur . . . per + ieremiam   37. ihesus +
nazenus (*sic*)   38. *unum (*bis*)
39. blasph (. .) abant (*ras. inter* h *et* a)
40. uæ *pro* uah . . destruit . . . troduo . . .
redificat . . . descende + nunc   41. *eum
pro cum . . . scribentes *pro* scribis·
42. nunc *om.*   43. *liberet + eum (*Am.*
nunc + eum) . . . ‡eum *om.* . . . enim *usque
ad* id (*v.* 44) *om.*   45. facta
46. exclamauit uoce magna ihesus . . . hely
hely lauat zaphnai   48. acepit
52. sanctorum corpora . . . dormierunt
62. pharasei (ra *sup. ras. p. m.*)
64. custodi (ri *add. sup. l.*) . . . tertiam . . .
discipuli eius ueniant   65. illi *pro* illis
66. inuenerunt *pro* munierunt

xxviii. 1–7.   2. *terrimotus . . . sedebit   3. *init.* + et
p. 35.   . . . *uestimenta   4. eius *om.* . . .
               custodies . . . ut *pro* uelut   7. precedet
               . . . galeam (e *corr. e* i) . . . *sicut *pro* ecce *sec.*
               . . . *predixit

Marc. vi. 17–29.   17. misit herodes . . unxit *pro* uinxit . . . carcerem
p. 65.   20. istum *pro* iustum   21. turbinis *pro*
               tribunis   22. herodiades   25. cum
               pro cumque   26. ‡recumbentes . . .
               contristari   28. pulla *pro* puella

xvi. 1–7.   2. momentum *pro* monum.   6. *ras. post*
p. 37.   surrexit   7. ‡et *om.* (*add. m. rec. sup. l.*)
               . . . precedet

xvi. 14–20.   14. illis *ras.* . . . ·xi· + discipulis . . . illis *add. m.*
p. 40.   *rec. sup. l. post* apparuit . . . apparuit + ihesus
               . . . ‡illorum *pro* eorum . . . *cordis + eorum
               . . . ‡his *pro* iis   15. eis + ihesus

17. iacent (*marg.* ‡eicient *m. rec.*)   18. eis
corr. e ‡eos . . . ‡egrotos   20. profecti
corr. e perf. . . . cooperantes (s *ras.*)

Luc. i. 5–17.   5. iudæ . . . uia *pro* uice . . . abia *ras.*   6. ambo
p. 57.   iusti . . . credentes (*corr. e* incredentes) *pro*
incedentes   8. fungeretur + zacharias
13. uocabit (*sic*) corr. *e* uocabitur (*Am.* uocabis)
16. conuertit

i. 26–38a.   32. *sui *pro* eius . . . iacob in *corr.* (*p.m.*) *e* in
p. 54.   35. obumbrauit   36. cognota . . . ‡est
sextus   37. apud *om.*

i. 57–68.   57. est *om.*   58. *ras. post* uicini *ut uid.* (? *eius)
p. 58.   . . . congratulabuntur   62. inueniebant
pro innuebant   65. diuulgabuntur
66. potuerunt (*corr. e* postuerunt) *pro* posuerunt
67. illius *pro* eius . . . ‡impletus

ii. 21. p. 7.   = *Vulg.*

ii. 22–33.   22. marie *pro* eius . . . ihesum *pro* illum
p. 52.   23. masculum   26. ‡ab *pro* a

ii. 33–40a.   33. ioseph *pro* pater eius . . . et *sec.* + maria . . .
p. 8.   *mater + ihesu   34. ihesu *pro* eius . . . et
tert. om. . . . ‡in *sec. om.* . . in *tert. om.*
37. *uidua + erat . . octoginti   38. et
pri. om. . . . expectant . . . ‡hierusalem *pro*
israel   40. confortabatur + in spiritu

ii. 42–52.   42. esset + ihesus . . . constitudinem *pro* consue-
p. 12.   tudinem   44. diei + unius   46. *eum
pro illum   50. et *om.* . . . ‡illos *pro* eos
51. hec (*sic*) + conferens

viii. 4–15.   4. ‡conueniret . . . ihesum *pro* eum   5. cedit
p. 14.   *pro* cecidit   7. cedit   10. autem *om.*
12. uiam + sunt . . . *audiunt + uerbum dei
13. *petram + hi sunt . . . quia *pro* qui *tert.*
14. ‡spinis . . . suffocant

x. 38–42.   = *Vulg.*
p. 64.

xi. 5–13.   5. decet *pro* dicet . . . mihi *om.*   6. et *om.*
p. 56.   8. ‡ille si   9. dico *om.* . . . accipietis *pro*
dabitur uobis   12. *scopionem
13. uester *om.*

xi. 14–28.   14. *turbae *om.* A   18. ipse *pro* ipsum A . . .
p. 21. (A);   ‡ipsius *pro* eius A . . . ‡eicere (*sic*) me A
xi. 27, 28.   19. belzebul   21. sint *pro* sunt A
p. 63 (B),   22. ‡illo *pro* eo A . . . aufert A   24. ·iii·
p. 80 (C).   *pro* meam A   25. eum *pro* eam A

26. ‡*init.* + et A . . . habitent A . . . ‡sunt *pro*
fiunt A   27. loqueretur ihesus ad turbas
pro haec diceret BC . . . uocem + suam A . . .
quaedam *om.* A . . . fecisti *pro* suxisti A
28. qui imma *pro* quinimmo A . . . et *om.* C

Luc. xviii. 31–43.   31. ˙xii˙ + *discipulos' suos secreto . . . consuma·
    p. 16.   buntur   33. ‡die tertia   34. erat autem
                    pro et erat   36. autem *pro* hoc   41. uis
                    + ut   42. at *pro* et

Joh. i. 5–14.   8. non *om.* (*add. sup. l. m. rec.*)   9. quae +
    p. 3.   et   14. gratia

iii. 1–15.   3. dicit . . . uobis *pro* tibi . . ‡natus *pro* ren.
    p. 43.   4. iterum *pro* iterato . . . ‡nasci *pro* renasci
                    5. *ihesus + et dixit . . . et spiritu ‡sancto *om.*
                    8. ‡non scis *pro* nescis   9. autem *pro* haec
                    11. *accipistis   12. creditis *pro* credetis
                    13. de celo discendit (*sic*)   15. ‡ipso *pro*
                    ipsum

v. 21–24.   22. ‡iudicium omne   24. *transeat . . . ad *pro*
    p. 93.   in *sec.*

vi. 1–14.   2. *faciebant   5. ‡dicit . . . admanducent
    p. 23.   10. dicit   13. ‡manducauerunt
                    14. ‡iesus *om.*

vi. 37–40.   37. dedit   40. ‡enim *pro* autem
    p. 93.

vi. 51–55.   51. sum *om.*   53. hoc *pro* hic . . . carnem
    p. 93.   suam dare nobis   54. filium
                    55. *carnem meam

viii. 46–59.   46. ‡arguit . . . ‡uobis *sec. om.* . . . . ‡quare + uos
    p. 24.   47. ‡est ex deo   52. propheta
                    54. *ergo *pro* ego . . . ‡noster *pro* uester
                    56. *exaltauit . . . ‡meum + et
                    59. ieicerent

xi. 21–27.   21. in *pro* non   25. dicit . . . et *om.* . . . .
    p. 93.   etsiamsi

xii. 31–36a.   31. huius *om.*   33. quia (i *ras.*) *pro* qua *ut uid.*
    p. 67.   34. audimus . . . hominis *pri.* + et
                    35. respondit ei *pro* dixit ergo eis . . . ‡tenebre
                    (*sic*) uos

xiii. 1–15.   1. eius hora   2. et *om.* . . . . iam + se . . .
    p. 27.   iudæ *pro* in cor . . . simonis *om.* . . . . scariothis
                    3. *ei *om.* . . . . exiuit a deo a deo (a deo *pri. ras.*)

5. misit   7. ‡dicit   8. mecum patrem
(*sic*)   9. et *pri*. *om.*   10. totus mundus
11. quiscam   14. magister et dominus
15. et *om.*

Joh. xiv. 15–21.   15. diligeritis   17. *nescit *pro* nec scit
    p. 41.   19. *iam me

xiv. 23–31a.   23. diligit *pro* diliget   24. meus est
    p. 42.   27. quomodo + hic   28. diligeritis . . .
pater *om.*   30. huius mundi
31. mundus + quia ego diligo *ras.* . . . *quia +
ego

xv. 1–11.   2. purgauit   7. fiet + in   11. et *pro* ut
    p. 70.

xv. 26, 27.   26. uobis *p.m. sup. ras. ut uid.* . . . perhibit
    p. 77.

xvi. 1–4.   1. ut *om.* (r_1 ne *pro* ut non)   2. ueniet . . .
    p. 77.   interfecit . . . se obsequium

xvii. 1–11a.   1. celum (*sic*) + ihesus   5. habui + apud te
    p. 39.   7. michi (*sic*) dedisti

xvii.   11. quo *pro* quos . . . sicut *om.*   12. ‡his *pro*
11b–26.   eis *sec.*   14. ‡odio eos   15. et *pro* a
    p. 72.   (*Am.* ex)   19. ego pro eis . . . et *sec. om.*
20. his *pro* eis *pri.* . . . et *om.*   21. *et *pro*
ut *tert.* . . . ‡mundus credat   24. ‡ego sum

xviii. p. 29.   2. quam *pro* quia   3. *igitur *pro* ergo . . .
chohorentem . . . laterinis *pro* lanternis
4. eum + et . . . procedit . . . ‡dicit
7. ‡eos interrogauit   8. dixit *pro* dixi
9. quam *pro* quia   10. *ras. post* habens
11. non + uis   12. tribuni   13. *eum
om. . . . autem *pro* enim   14. quam *pro* quia
16. alius discipulus   17. dixit (*bis*) . . .
ergo *om.*   18. stabunt . . . petrus cum eis
(et *tert. om.*)   19. de *pri. om.*
20. *ego *sec. om.*   21. ‡sum *pro* sim . . .
illis *pro* ipsis   23. cur *pro* quid
24. amas *pro* annas   25. simon *om.*
26. *dixit . . . ‡ei *om.* . . . cognotus . . .
nonne *corr.* (*m. rec.*) *e* (·)nne   28. ad caifan
pro a caipha   29. exiit . . . quam *corr. e*
quicam *ut uid.*   30. tradisemus
31. dixit *om.* . . . eis *om.*   34. ‡*init.* + et
. . . ‡tibi dixerunt   35. rependit *pro*
respondit   36. hoc *pro* hinc   37. tu es

‡ . . . ego rex sum . . . ‡meam uocem
38. exiit . . . nullam + nullam *ras.*
40. ‡ergo *om.*

Joh. xix. p. 29.   1. *fin.* + eum   4. ‡ergo *om.* . . . pilatus *om.*
 xix. 25–27.   (=r_1?) . . . et *om.* . . . ei *pro* eis . . . ecce +
 p. 80 (A).   ego . . . in eo causam inuenio   5. ‡exiit
                    . . . ‡spineam coronam . . . dixit
                    6. clamauerunt   7. iudei (*sic*) + et dixerunt
                    9. *est + in . . . iterum et (?) *ras.*   10. *ei
                    ergo   11. esset data (*Am.* esset datum)
                    13. ihesum foras . . . lithostratos ebrice
                    14. quassi (*sic*) hora   15. habens *pro* habemus
                    16. illis ihesum *pro* eis illum . . . ergo *pro*
                    autem   17. exiit . . . *locum *pro* eum . . .
                    locus   18. ‡eum crucifixerunt
                    19. *pilatus et titulum   20. ‡legerunt
                    iudeorum . . . erat *ciuitati (*sic*) . . . *erat
                    autem *pro* et erat   21. regem *pro* rex *pri.*
                    23. ihesum *pro* eum   24. ‡impleatur
                    25. clepa   26. ergo uidisset (*ita* A)
                    27. suam   28. ‡quia + iam . . . scripta
                    pro scriptura . . . ‡dicit   29. plenum possitum
                    (*sic*) erat acceto (*sic*)   33. mortuum iam
                    34. latus lancea . . . eius *om.* . . . exiit
                    38. per *pro* post . . . occulte . . . et *pri. sup.*
                    lin.   39. et *pri. om.*   40. ‡eum *pro*
                    illud . . . est mos   41. est + ihesus . . .
                    fuerat *pro* erat   42. quam *pro* quia

 xx. 24–31.   24. de *pro* ex   25. uidero + non *ras.* . . . in
 p. 38.   *pri. om.* . . . figuram   29. ‡dicit . . .
                    ‡thoma *om.* . . . . . *qui + me   31. christus
                    est . . . meo *pro* eius

 xxi. 15–19a.   15. *dixit   16. at *pro* ait   17. ‡dicit *pro*
 p. 59.   dixit *sec. et tert.* . . . ‡scis *pro* nosti . . . scis *sec.*
                    + domine

 xxi. 19b–24.   19. *dixit *pro* dicit + ihesus . . . petro *pro* ei
 p. 5.   20. pecusus domini *pro* pectus eius
                    21. hinc *pro* hunc . . . ‡dicit   22. sicut
                    pro sic . . . quidem *pro* quid   23. quod *pro*
                    quia . . . ille non moritur *usque ad* discipulus
                    (*v.* 24) *om.*

Act. i. 1–11.   3. suam pasionem (*sic*) . . . xl· dies   5. bapti-
 p. 40.   zabimini + in   7. eis + ihesus
                    8. accipetis (e *corr.* e i *ut uid.*)   9. hoc *pro*
                    haec . . . est + in celum   11. et *om.* . . . .
                    quid + hoc . . . ueniat . . . eundem *pro* euntem

Act. ii. 1–11. p. 42.	1. omnes + discipuli 2. replebit . . . erant + apostoli 4. linguis + magnalia dei . . . illis eloqui 7. mirabantur + adinuicem 9. parthei . . . ‡mesopot. + et 11. cèrte *pro* cretes
iii. 1–10. p. 58.	5. intenebat . . . qui *pro* aliquid 6. do tibi 7. et protinus *om.* 9. eum omnis populus 10. eum *pro* illum . . . ‡quoniam *pro* quod *pri.* . . . repleti
iv. 32–35. p. 39.	32. ‡possidebant . . . esse suum dicebant (*sic*) . . . omnia illis 34. aut *om.* (*add. sup. l. m. rec.*) 35. diuidebantur . . . cunque *pro* cuique
vi. 8–10. p. 4.	= *Vulg.*
vii. 54–60a. p. 4.	55. esset + stefanus . . . dei *sec. om.* 56. dex- tris + uirtutis 58. iecientes
ix. 1–22. p. 47.	2. in *om.* 5. ihesus + nazarenus 6. illum *pro* eum . . . ‡ibi *om.* 9. ‡ibi *om.* . . . manducabit 11. ‡illum *pro* eum . . . ‡et *sec. om.* . . domum *pro* domo *m. recentiss.* 12. uidet 13. ‡sanctis tuis fecerit 14. habet hic . . . sacerdote/ tum (te *ras.*) . . . tuum *om.* (*add. in marg. m. recentiss.*) 15. dominus ad eum . . . michi (*sic*) est 17. introibit . . . qui *om.* 20. continuo + ingresus (*sic*) paulus . . . sinagoga
xii. 1–11. p. 59.	4. tradiditque 5. sine *om.* 6. *lit. ras.* *post* d *in* custodes . . . custodiebant + in (*ut uid.*) *ras.* 7. et *sec. om.* . . . . caternę *pro* catenae 8. tuas + tuas 9. ‡estimabat 10. discessit *corr. e* dissessit
xix. 1–8. p. 41.	1. et *pro* ut . . . quosdam *om.* 6. ‡manum 8. autem + paulus
Rom. x. 10–18· p. 46.	12. est *om.* 16. autem *pro* enim 18. si *pro* sed
xi. 33–36. p. 77.	33. diuitiarum + et scripturarum 34. domini *om* 36. secula + seculorum
xii. 1–5. p. 12.	1. ut *om.* 2. bona *om.* 3. gratiam + dei 4. habent *om.* 5. ita multi unum *om.* . . . . sum *pro* sumus
1 Cor. v. 7, 8. p. 36.	= *Vulg*

1 Cor. ix. 24–27.   24. ‡hi *pro* ii   25. omnes enim   26. in *om.*
p. 13.

   x. 1–4.   1. autem *pro* enim
p. 13.

   xi. 20–32.   21. autem *om.*   23. et *om.* . . . dominus +
p. 26.   noster (= *Am. corr.*) . . . ihesus + christus
24. ‡accipite et manducate *om.*   25. est
calix noui testamenti . . . facite *om.*
26. bibetis calicem   27. ‡hunc *om.* . . .
et *pro* uel . . . bibit   29. et bibit *pri. om.*
30. et firmi *pro* infirmi . . . imbecilles *corr. e*
imbecillis   32. autem *om.*

   xiii. p. 15.   2. ‡si *sec. om.* . . . habeam *pro* habuero *tert.*
6. ‡iniquitatem   8. *init.* + caritas diligit
. . . ‡excedit   13. ‡his *pro* horum

2 Cor. vi. 1–10.   1. hortamur (*sic*) + uos   5. in laboribus *om.*
p. 19.

   xi. 19–33.   20. sustinentes . . . extollit (*sic*) + *litt. ras.* (? ur)
p. 14.   23. sunt + et ego   28. soliticudo (*sic ut uid.*)
corr. e solituudo   30. sicut *pro* si
31. deus + autem . . . ‡scit qui est benedictus
in secula

   xii. 1–9.   2. nescio *pri. om.*   3. nescio *om.*   4. liquet
p. 14.   *pro* licebat   5. gloriabor *sec. om.*
6. autem + ne quis *ras.* . . . audit aliquid
8. rogauit (t *ras.*)

   xiii. 13.   13. sit + semper   .
p. 77.

Gal. i. 11–20.   11. facio uobis . . . a me *om.*   12. enim *om.*
p. 60.   15. complacuit . . . ‡ de *pro* ex   20. non
corr. e nomen

   ii. 6b–10.   6. qui *pro* mihi . . . aliquid esse   7. et *pro*
p. 62.   e . . . ‡et *om.*   8. aplantu *pro* apostolatum
9. esse *om.*   10. id *pro* hoc

   iv. 1–7.   4. natum *pro* factum *pri.*   5. filiorum + dei
p. 8.   6. filii *pri.* + dei . . . ‡nostra *pro* uestra

   iv. 22–31.   24. dictam . . . montem   27. quia + et . . .
p. 22.   multi *om.*   29. ‡is *om.*

   v. 10–12.   10. de *pro* in *pri.*   11. ergo *om.*   12. abscidant
p. 43.

   vi. 12–14.   12. ‡enim *om.*   14. iesu *om.*
p. 43.   .

Eph. iv. 7–13.   8. dona *om.*   10. adimpleret
p. 68.

v. 1–9.   2. et *sec. om.* . . . nos *om.*   5. autem *pro* enim
p. 21.   9. enim *om.*

Phil. ii. 5–11.   6. rapina AB   8. factus + est pro nobis C
p. 25 (A),   9. ‡illum exaltauit AB   11. noster *pro*
p. 67 (B);   iesus C
ii. 8b–11.
p. 78 (C).

Col. iii. 1–4.   3. ‡abscondita est . . . celo *pro* deo   4. uita
p. 35.   *om. (add. sup. l. m. recentiss.)*

1 Thess. iv. 1–7.   1. ‡uos oporteat   4. ‡suum uas
. p. 20.

iv. 13–18.   15. aduentu   17. qui *pri. om.*
p. 92.

Tit. ii. 11a.   = *Vulg.*
p. 7.

iii. 4a.   4. apparuit benignitas *pro* cum autem benignitas et
p. 9.   humanitas apparuit

Heb. ix. 11–15.   14. ‡emundauit   15. meditabor *pro* mediator
p. 24.   . . . remsionem *(sic) pro* redemptionem . . .
earundem (earun *sup. ras. ut uid.) pro* carum
. . . pu(.)ricationum *(m. recentiss.* priuarica-
tionum *ut uid.)* . . . testamenta (to *sup. l. m.
recentiss.)*

Jac. v. 16–20.   19. fratres mei *om.* . . . quis + autem . . . conuertit
p. 55.   20. amore *pro* a morte . . . operit

1 Pet. i. 1–7.   2. sanctificatione . . . obedientia . . . aspersione
p. 53.   3. ‡magnam misericordiam suam   5. ut *pro*
in *pri.* . . . tempore + in   6. tribulationibus
pro tentationibus   7. fidei multo uestræ . . .
‡pretiossior *(sic)* + sit . . . gratiam *pro* gloriam
. . . ‡treuelationem . . . christi + domini nostri

1 Joh. v. 4–10a.   5. est *pri.* + autem . . . ihesus + christus
p. 38.   7. sanctus *om.* . . . hi *om.*   8. et tres *om.*
. . . et *sec. om.* . . . et ‡hi *om.*   9. ‡quia
pro quoniam *sec.*

Apoc. i. 1–5.   1. significauit deus quæ oportet fieri cito loquens *pro*
p. 69.   apocalypsis *usque ad* mittens   2. christo *(sic)*
+ in his   3. ‡et *pri.* + qui
4. conspectui *ut uid. (lit. ult. ras.)*   5. ‡ab
pro a *pri.* . . . est *om.* . . . regem

Apoc. v. 6–12.   6. et ecce *om.*   8. fiolas (*sic*) + et
     p. 70.   9. domine + deus   10. ‡regnabunt
                     12. uoce magna dicentium . . . *fin.* + in secula
seculorum

     vii. 1–12.   1. ‡flaret (*sic*) + ‡uentus   2. magna *om.*
     p. 71.   4. signati *om.*   6. neptalim   7. ischar
                    9. denumerare . . . lingis (*sic*) et populis
                    10. saulus *pro* salus (*ras. sequ. ut uid.*)
                    11. in circuitu *om.* . . . et *tert. om.*   12. amen
om. (*bis*) . . . et sapientia *om.* . . . ‡actio + et

     xiv. 1–5.   1. et ecce *om.* . . . super montem sion agnum
     p. 6.   stantem . . . quadraginti   2. uocem *sec. om.*
                    3. sedem + dei   4. hi *sec.* + sunt ‡qui
                    5. ‡ipsorum *pro* eorum . . . inuentum est . . .
‡enim *om.*

     xiv. 13.   = *Vulg.*
     p. 92.

NOTES AND INDICES.

SYMBOLS AND ABBREVIATIONS USED IN THE NOTES AND INDICES.

A = *The Missal of St. Augustine's Abbey, Canterbury* . . . *edited from a manuscript in the library of Corpus Christi College, Cambridge,* by Martin Rule, M.A., Cambridge, 1896. A¹ is sometimes used for the earlier writing of the manuscript, where it differs from the later text (A²).

C = *The Manuscript Irish Missal belonging to the President and Fellows of Corpus Christi College, Oxford,* edited with introduction and notes by F. E. Warren, B.D., London, 1879.

D = *Missale Drummondiense. The Ancient Irish Missal in the possession of the Baroness Willoughby de Eresby, Drummond Castle, Perthshire,* edited by the late Rev. G. H. Forbes, Burntisland, 1882.

E = The Rosslyn Missal as here printed.

G = *The Gelasian Sacramentary. Liber Sacramentorum Romanae Ecclesiae,* edited with introduction, &c., by H. A. Wilson, M.A., Oxford, 1894.

Γ = The Gregorian Sacramentary in *Liturgia Romana Vetus,* ed. L. A. Muratori, Venetiis, 1748, t. ii.

Γᵃ = The Gregorian Antiphonary as printed in the Benedictine edition of the Works of St. Gregory, t. iii, and in P.

H = *Missale ad usum percelebris ecclesiæ Herfordensis,* ed. W. G. Henderson, Leeds, 1874.

J = *The Missal of Robert of Jumièges,* edited by H. A. Wilson, M.A. (Henry Bradshaw Society, vol. xi), London, 1896.

L = *Sacramentarium Leonianum, edited with introduction, &c.,* by C. L. Feltoe, B.D. Cambridge, 1896.

Λ = *The Leofric Missal* . . . *edited with introduction and notes,* by F. E. Warren, B.D., F.S.A., Oxford, 1883. (Only the earliest portion of this Missal is cited in the collations of the text of the collects.)

M = *Liber Sacramentorum S. Gregorii Papae ex editione D. H. Menardi,* in the Benedictine edition of the Works of St. Gregory the Great, t. iii. (Venetiis, 1744).

P = *Liturgicon Ecclesiae Latinae,* ed. J. Pamelius, Coloniae Agrippinae, 1571, t. ii.

R = *Missale Romanum nouiter impressum, &c.* 'Impressum Venetijs per. D. Bernardinum Stagninum. Anno A natiuitate M.D.xviij. octauo idus Februarij.'

S = *Missale ad usum insignis et præclaræ ecclesiæ Sarum labore ac studio* F. H. Dickinson, A.M., Burntisland, 1861–1883.

Σ = The Stowe Missal (Royal Irish Academy MS.). The numbers following this symbol when enclosed in round brackets refer to the pages of the edition by the Rev. B. MacCarthy, D.D., in *Transactions of the Royal Irish Academy,* vol. xxvii, Dublin, 1877–1886 : otherwise to the edition by the Rev. F. E. Warren, B.D., in *The Liturgy and Ritual of the Celtic Church,* Oxford, 1881. The former edition has been used for the collation of the Canon.

W = *Missale ad usum Ecclesie Westmonasteriensis nunc primum typis mandatum curante* J. W. Legg (Henry Bradshaw Society, vols. i, v, xii), London, 1891–1897.

Y = *Missale ad usum insignis Ecclesiæ Eboracensis*, ed. W. G. Henderson (Surtees Society, vols. lix, lx), 1874.

Z = *Vetus Missale Romanum Monasticum Lateranense*, ed. Emmanuel de Azevedo, Romae, 1754.

ant. = antiphona.	int. = introitus.
ap. = apostolus, -i, &c.	m. = martyr, -ris, &c.
b. = beatus, -i, &c.	mis. = misericors.
c. = christus.	nr. = noster.
com. = communio.	o. = omnipotens.
d. = deus.	off. = offertorium.
dns., dni., &c. = dominus, -i, &c.	ps. = psalmus.
ep. = epistola.	q. = quaesumus.
eu. = euangelium.	s. = sempiterne.
gr. = gradale.	tr. = tractus.
j. = ihesus, -u, &c.	

TEMPORALE.

NATIVITAS DOMINI.

p. 3. l. 3. The manuscript begins in the middle of the Gospel (Joh. i. 1–14) for the third mass of Christmas Day. The earlier part of the Temporale probably filled a single gathering of four or five sheets, supposing that it contained the same masses as the corresponding part of C. But reasons have been given in the Introduction, p. xii, for believing that this was not the first quire of the manuscript in its original state.

l. 4. gratia] Read *gratiae*.

l. 5. offerenda] This rather than *offertorium* is the correct expansion of *off.* The word is only once written in full (p. 36, l. 1), and in that instance this is the form used. The same word is used for the offertory by Remigius of Auxerre in his *Expositio Missae* (quoted by Le Brun, *Explication*, vol. ii. p. 281, ed. 1777): 'Deinde sequitur offerenda, quae inde hoc nomen accepit, quod tunc populus sua munera offerat. Sequuntur versus a vertendo, dicte, quod in offerendis reuertantur, dum offerenda repetitur.' So also Mabillon's *Ordo* i. Appendix, cap. 10: 'Non cantent offerenda'; *Ordo* xi. cap. 20: 'Primicerius cum schola cantant offerenda'; cf. capp. 40, 43; *Ordo* xii. cap. 31. *Micrologus*, cap. 10 (Hittorp, *De Divinis Catholicae Ecclesiae Officiis ac Ministeriis*, Coloniae, 1568, p. 440): 'Finito euangelio statim est offerendum, dum et offerenda canitur'; cap. 11 : 'Romanus tamen ordo nullam orationem instituit post offerendam ante secretam.' Lanfranc, quoted by Martène, *De Mon. Rit.* III. xv. 22 (col. 413)[1]: 'In hac consuetudine concordant omnes fere principales monachorum ecclesiae, quae nostro tempore majoris authoritatis sunt, sicut et in eo quod offerenda et Agnus Dei et communio ad hanc Missam non dicuntur.' Durandus, *Rationale* IV. xxvii. 7 : 'Dicitur etiam offertorium, quia dum offerenda cantatur sacerdos accipit oblationes.' And so we find it in the Ambrosian Liturgy (Daniel, *Codex Liturgicus*, Lipsiae 1847, fasc. i. p. 72 ; Duchesne, *Origines du Culte Chrétien*, Paris, 1898, p. 196), the Book of Evesham, Λ, p. 98, note, and the Sarum Consuetudinary.

---

[1] The reference is to *De Antiquis Ecclesiae Ritibus Libri . . collecti atque exornati* a R. P. Domno E. Martene . . . editio secunda. . . . Antuerpiae, 1736–1738; the fourth volume of which is his *De Monachorum Ritibus.*

See also Radulphus de Rivo, *De Canonum Observantia,* prop. 23 (Hittorp, p. 574b). Amalarius uses the word, but with a different meaning, applying it to the portion of the mass extending from *Dominus uobiscum* to the end of the secret ; *De Eccl. Off.* iii. 19 (Hittorp, p. 188 *sq.*). Compare also Du Cange *s.v.*

l. 6. This is the offertory in CHARSWY, but in all these the verses (ll. 9–14) are omitted. In Iᵃ we find three verses : ll. 9–11 forming the major part of the first, and l. 12 sq. the third, between which is intercalated a second, *Misericordia et ueritas,* while *Firmetur* is omitted. Single verses are occasionally added to the offertory in late English Missals (e.g. SW), but they seem to have been generally disused since the custom of making the oblations at this part of the service was abandoned. Durandus, *Rationale,* IV. xxvii. 4 ; Bona, *Rerum Liturg.* II. viii. 3 (*Opera,* Paris, 1678, t. iii. p. 559) ; Frere, *Graduale Sarisburiense,* London, 1895, p. xxxiii.

l. 8. Read *iustitia.*

l. 10. Read *potestati, autem.* Compare Introduction, p. xxiv.

Secret. ACΓHJΛMPRSWYZ.

l. 16. oblata + tibi C.

l. 17. nosque] nos quoque WZ + per haec JΛ. maculis + clementer S.

l. 19. ut supra] Referring of course to one of the preceding Christmas masses, now lost.

l. 22. The scribe in no case gives this title in full. It is therefore impossible to determine with certainty whether he would have written *postcommunio* or *post communionem.* In most instances the spacing seems to favour the latter, and it has accordingly been printed throughout.

l. 25. Read *uiuit.*

Postcommon. ACΓHJLΛMPRSWYZ (G collect).

l. 23 quesumus *om.* GL. omnipotens] mis. GL.

l. 24 mundi *om.* G. nobis *om.* G. generationis] regenerationis P.

l. 25 qui tecum u.] per GL.

l. 26. *Alia ad horas diei*] This collect is found in several of the older Sacramentaries and Missals in a position corresponding to that which it occupies here, under various titles. Γ has it after the postcommon, and P after the super populum, as the first of 'Aliae orationes de natali dni.' In Λ it is headed 'ad populum,' in J simply 'alia.' On the other hand M has it with the title 'Ad matutinum' after the postcommon of the first Christmas mass (*in vig. dni. in nocte*), while in G it is one of the collects of the second mass (*mane prima*). The heading seems to imply that in E it was intended to be used (as apparently also in M) instead of the Mass Collect at the Divine Office. In this respect the usage in our missal differs from that of all the later English books.

Alia ad horas diei. (GΓJΛMP)

l. 27. nos + o. et G.

l. 28. ostende] infunde G. per eundem ΓJΛP. qui tecum M.

NATALE S. STEPHANI.

p. 4. l. 1. enair] An Irish name for January.

l. 6. The MS. has ' oᷓ.' This is the regular contraction of the scribe for 'oremus,' while ' orā ' represents 'oratio.' The word is written in full in many places, e.g. p. 10, l. 6.

l. 8. et *om.*

Collect. G (Γ 'alia oratio' after postc. ΛMP 'alia' after postc. JZ ad uesperas W in octauis L for Aug. 3).
l. 7.   sempiterne] aeterne G.
l. 8.   beati] sancti GL.   stephani + martyris Z.
l. 9.   existat] assistat G.   etiam *om.* P.
l. 10. exorauit] supplicauit GL + per GΓLM.
Epistle. Inflection marks are placed above the following words : *Title* apostolorum ; vi. 8 magna ; 9 cum ; 10 loquebatur ; vii. 56 et ait, uirtutis ; 57 unanimiter ; 58 uocabatur ; 60 hoc.

l. 25.   The offertory in Γ²ΛY is *In uirtute* : ACHRSW agree with E.
l. 31.   Read *innocuos.*

Secret. ACΓHJΛMPRSYZ. (D for Several Martyrs W for SS. Marcus and Marcellianus).
l. 29. + q. *post* suscipe ΛΛ *post* dne. S. pro + beati C + sancti HSY. commemoratione protom. stefani] tuorum com. (uenera-cione W) sanctorum ADΓJΛMPRWZ. protom.] m. CS + tui HSY.
l. 30. sicut] quod AΓJPZ quia Λ. illos ADΓJΛMPRWZ. pasio gloriosa effecit innocentem] passio gloriosos efficit et inno-centes Λ p. gloriosos efficit (effecit R) AR passio gloriosum reddidit C passio fecit (efficit Y) gloriosum (gloriosos P) HPSY fecit p. gloriosos Z passio gloriosos DΓJMW. sic] ita DRSW *om.* AΓHJΛPYZ.
l. 31. innocuos] acceptos W.

p. 5.
Postcommon. ACΓHJΛMPRSYZ (G 'per dominicis diebus' W for S. Agatha).
l. 2.   sumpta] suscepta C. intercedente . . . tuo *om.* G.
l. 3.   protom.] m. CΓJMPRZ (W). nos *om.* (*exc.* W).
l. 8.   per] *om.*, with all except Γ.
Alternative Collect. ACΓHJΛMPRSWYZ.
l. 6.   dne. q. Λ. imitari *om.*† J.
l. 7.   eius natalitia. celebramus] colimus Z.
l. 8.   suis *om.*   exorare *om.*† C. per† *om.* (*exc.* Γ).

NATIVITAS S. IOHANNIS EVANGELISTAE.

l. 9.   enair] See note on p. 4, l. 1.
l. 10. eum] Read *eius.*
l. 12. This office psalm appears to be found here in CEΛ lone among English missals. The rest have *Iocunditatem.* It is Gregorian.
Collect. ACΓHJLΛMPRSWYZ.
l. 14.   tuam + q. HSY. ut + apostolicis L.
l. 15.   iohannis + apostoli tui (*om.* AC) et ACHRSYZ.
l. 16.   sempiterna] quae de tua fidelibus retributione promisit L.
Epistle. Inflection marks over *Title* sapientiae ; v. 4 proxi-mos ; v. 5 induit.
l. 25.   est *sec.*] Read *eius.*
l. 29.   Read *offerenda.*
ll. 32, 33. Read *sollennitate, patrocinio.*
Secret. ACΓHJΛMPRSYZ (D 'in com. SS. Martini &c.' W for S. Agatha).
l. 32.   + q. *post* dne. Y *post* munera HS *ante* commemoratione D. munera (+ q. HS) dne. AΓHJMS. nostra *om.* in] inter† C. eius] b. agathe . . . w. tibi *om.* DHY. sollennitate] com-memoratione D.

l. 33. confidimus patrocinio] patrocinio credimus Z.

p. 6. **Postcommon.** ACΓHJAMPRSYZ (L for SS. Xystus &c. W for St. Agnes).

l. 6. supplices. deprecamur] exoramus ALSWZ.

l. 7. commemoratione] ueneracione W. percipimus H.

l. 10. This prayer appears in Z as the collect of the first mass for St. John's Day. Dr. Wickham Legg points out that it is also used as the postc. on the same day in Rouen MS. 10,048 : but in saying that it is an alternative for the postcommon in E he seems to have overlooked the word *oremus* in the heading. Except in Z and here I have not met with it as a mass collect. It is very common as the postcommon for the Vig. of St. Matthew (see W p. 1593).

l. 11. tribuat] Read *tribue.*

Alternative Collect. Z (ΓAMP ad uesperos AHJRWY postc. for Vig. of St. Matthew).

l. 10. euangelistae et ap. tui A.   ap. tui et *om.* ΓJAMPRZ. et euangelistae tui W.   + q. *ante* dne.

l. 11. nobis + delictorum HY.

NATALE SS. INNOCENTIUM.

l. 13. enair] See note on p. 4, l. 1.

l. 14. ap paul'] This appears to be intended to mark the Roman station, which is noted in ΓP and the Rheinau MS. of the Gelasian Sacramentary as 'ad sanctum Paulum.' The stations are given twice elsewhere in E (p. 14, l. 10 ; p. 15, l. 16), and occasionally in the older English missals, *e.g.* for Christmas Day in J and frequently in A. Our scribe seems not to have understood these indications, and he appears to have copied the one before us incorrectly. We should perhaps emend [*statio ad*] *apostolum paulum* : or, since *ap̄* elsewhere in the MS. always represents *apud, apud* [*sanctum*] *paulum.*

l. 16. ei *om.*

Collect. ACGΓHJAMPRSWYZ.

l. 22. per] qui cum HS.

Epistle. Inflection marks over v. 1 frontibus ; v. 2 tonitrui, cithitharis ; v. 3 sunt ; v. 4 quocunque ; v. 5 est, tronum.

l. 31. The scribe has omitted *Alleluia.*

l. 32. This verse is peculiar to E : see W p. 1452.

Gospel. Inflection mark over v. 18 consolari (l. 37).

p. 7. l. 5. Read *conciliet.*

Secret. ACΓHJLAPRYZ (M for St. Sylvester).

l. 4. tuorum + innocentium HY. dne. nobis RZ. nobis + q. H.

l. 5. nostra + tibi AY.

Postcommon. ACΓHJLAMPRSWYZ (G for Several Saints).

l. 11. dona] uota A. quae percepimus C.
sanctorum + tuorum HY. innocentium *om.* (*exc.* S).

l. 12. q. *post* uitae HASY *ante* uitae rell.

l. 13. tribuant† C. subsidium] praesidium GL.

OCTAVAE NATALIS DOMINI.

l. 14. The title of this mass is unusual. It combines that of the earlier books (*Octauae natalis dni.* ΓΓJAMPRZ) with that of the later missals (*In circumcisione dni.* AHSWY). It is thus a 'conflate' heading, and the mark of the conflation remains in the fact that the date *Kl̄ Ianuarii* is in the middle instead of at the beginning of the title.

l. 19.   This office psalm is found also in Γ^a(P)RSY.   HW have *Multi-plicabitur*, while C has no mass for this day.

l. 23.   Read *commercio reparati*.

    Collect.   ΛGHJΛMPSWY (Z alia after postc. of third Christmas mass).

    l. 22.   fac + quoque Z.   q. nos GΛMP.   q. *om.* Z.   eius *om.* W.

    l. 23.   qui tecum] per GJΛZ.

l. 25.   The epistle is not given in full, having appeared already in the first mass of Christmas Day.

l. 27.   The full text of the grail had no doubt been given in the third .Christmas mass.

l. 29.   E here agrees with Γ^a(P)HLY against ARSW (*Multifarie*).

l. 32.   Read *conciperetur*.

l. 34.   ut supra] Referring to the third mass for Christmas Day (p. 3, l. 6).

p. 8.   l. 2.   This secret, which is very rarely found here in English books, is a survival from the ancient commemoration of St. Mary on this day : as is also the alternative postcommon.

    Secret.   ΓPRZ (A de S. Maria &c. CHSWY for lxx^{ma} D for One Martyr G in nat. consecrationis presbyteri JA dominica i post nat. dni. &c. L 'prope pasca' M for S. Joh. ante port. lat.).

    l. 2.   q. *om.* GL.   dne. *post* muneribus D.

    l. 3.   nos *om.*† G.   et *sec.* + per intercessionem b. dei genetricis mariae A (*not so* p. 75) + intercedente b. N. m. tuo D.

    l. 4 dnm.] eundem A.

    Postcommon.   ΛGHJΛMPSWYZ.

    l. 8.   dne.] o. d. HY *om.* Z.   quod] quae Z + nati S. nostri saluatoris A.   nostri] mundi W *om.* S.

    l. 9.   sollennitate] festiuitate W.   percipimus GZ.   perpetuam Z.   redemptionis] saluationis HSWY.   conferant Z.

l. 13.   Read *uirguine*.

    Alternative postcommon.   Γ(L)PRΣZ(ACD de S. Maria HΛSWY for Monday after xl² &c. JM for St. Stephen (Aug. 3) &c.)

    l. 12.   dne. *om.* LΣ.   intercedente . . . uirguine *om.* ΓHLΛPS ΣWY(*semel*) interc. b. dei genetrice maria ACDRY(*semel*)Z interced. b. stephano . . . JM.

    l. 13.   caelestibus remediis Z.   remedii faciat] gaudii tribuat LΣ.

    l. 14.   consortes] participes Σ.

DOMINICA I POST NATALE DOMINI.

l. 15.   This mass appears with different titles in many missals and sacramentaries.   It is as here for the Sunday within the octave in AMPRZ, for the Sunday after the octave in ΓJΛW, for the sixth day after Christmas, whether Sunday or not, in S, for the sixth day, if a Sunday, in H.   On the other hand a different mass, with the same title, is found in Γ(col. 158)JΛ.   Y, in the mass for the Sunday within the octave, agrees with the latter group in the collects (except the postcommon), otherwise with the former.   See further Dr. Legg's note (W p. 1454).   This mass for the Sunday within the octave might more naturally have come before that for the Circumcision, but anomalies in the order of masses occur elsewhere in E, and in W the converse misplacement is found, the Sunday after the octave coming before the octave.   Moreover the order in AZ agrees with that of E.

l. 19. Read *indutus.*

l. 22. Read *mereamur.*

Collect. AΓHJΛMPRSWZ.

l. 22. ut + et z.

l. 23 qui tecum] per AΓJΛPRW.

Epistle. Inflection marks over *Title* ad, galatas ; v. 2 tempus ; v. 3 seruientes ; v. 6 abba.

l. 32. Read $\bar{V}$, *indutus* [*est*], *indutus* (or *induit, induit*).

l. 35. All the other missals in which I have observed this gospel (HRSWYZ) add at the end the remainder of v. 40 *et gratia dei erat in illo.*

p. 9. l. 3. We should probably read $\bar{V}$. *Dominus r*[*egnauit*]. The exemplar appears to have now and then used *ū* (not as our scribe *ʋ*) as the equivalent of $\bar{V}$, and the copyist has several times mistaken this symbol for *ú* (= *ut*). See p. 27, l. 1 ; p. 34, l. 6 : compare D p. 10, l. 15. Confusion might easily occur between *dm̃* (= *deum*) and *dñs* (= *dominus*) in an Irish hand. Thus at p. 77, l. 20 possibly *dominum* is a mis-reading of *deum.* More to the point is p. 52, l. 9, where E has correctly *deum,* while C (p. 149) has *dñi.* If we have succeeded in restoring the reading of the exemplar, the blunders of E point to its having been an Irish MS. In any case this verse is peculiar, it would seem, to E. ΓᵃHRSY have no verse, while W has *Lux fulgebit.* C is without the mass.

l. 6. Read *gratiam* for *gratia in.* See p. 26, l. 8.

Secret. AΓHJΛMRZ (PY for xlᵉ and Sabb. iv. temp. Sept. SW for St. Richard).

l. 5. dne.] o. d. R.

l. 6. nobis + pie R.

For full collation see on p. 26, l. 7 sqq., where R gives a different text, and where E reads *oblatum munus* and omits *beatæ.*

l. 9. Read *tolle.*

Postcommon. SW.

l. 12. sacrificio + q. S.

l. 13. absumptae] assumptae S.

VIGILIA EPIPHANIAE.

l. 15. non] The Irish equivalent of *nonae,* more usually written *noin.*

enair] See note on p. 4, l. 1.

epīs] Read *epif* = *epifaniae.*

l. 16. The full text of introit and psalm had been given in the second Christmas mass. Γᵃ has here as office, *Dns. dixit ad me filius,* E being in agreement with AHΛSWY.

Collect. AGHJΛMPSWYZ.

l. 19. tenebrast G. peruenire A.

l. 22. The first word should have been printed *K*[*arissi*]*me.* The full text had been given in the second Christmas mass. It will be observed that the grail, offertory and common are omitted, and catch-words are not given (as in the office and epistle) to guide us. It is natural to suppose that these choir parts were intended to be supplied from the immediately preceding mass for the Sunday after Christmas. And this conjecture is supported by other evidence in the case of the offertory and common. In HRSWY the common is repeated from the corresponding mass ; and so also is the offertory in all of these except H. The grail presents more difficulty. The

majority of English Missals use on this day the same grail as at the
second Christmas mass ; and no book cited by Dr. Legg (W p. 1455)
repeats that of the Sunday after Christmas.   But on the other hand
R and some MSS. of Γᵃ take all their choir portions from that mass :
and we may perhaps assume that in this case E follows Roman
rather than Anglican usage.

l. 27.   Read *eum.*

Secret.   AGHJΛMPSWYZ.

l. 27.   eum] ei P illum W illi M cum† J.   praesentibus illum
(illi M) immolemus MW.   praesentibus immolemus (-mur
P)AGHJΛPSYZ.

l. 28.   et + eum W.   sumamur† P.   quem] quae MP.   festiui-
tatis] sollemnitatis.

l. 29.   dnm. n.] per GJΛMZ qui tecum PW.

l. 31.   The postcommon in AP and the Arbuthnott missal, found also
in Γ among 'aliae orationes' after the postc. of Epiphany, agrees
with this down to 'accende,' but the remainder is entirely different.

Postcommon.   GJΛMYZ.

l. 33.   famulante *om.* J.   manifeste Z.   natiuitatis J.   et *om.*
JYZ.

l. 34.   semper reueletur Y.

p. 10.   EPIPHANIA DOMINI.

Collect.   ACΓHJΛMPRSWYZ.

Epistle.   Inflection marks over v. 2 caligo ; v. 3 ortus ; v. 4
latere ; v. 5 uenerit ; v. 6 madian, domino.

Gospel.   Inflection mark over v. 12 uiam (l. 23).

l. 26.   Read *offerent, arabum.*

l. 32 sq.   Read *eisdem, immolatur, christus.*

Secret.   ACΓHJΛMPRSWYZ.

l. 30.   dne. q. z.   intuere propitius C.

l. 31. iam non HY.   myrrham† JS.   quod + de ΓΛ.

l. 32.   eisdem] eis dne.† z.   i.c.] per dnm. ΓJΛPRZ. + dns. nr.
ACHMSY.

Communicantes.   ACGΓHJΛPRSWY.

l. 35.   coaeternus] sempiternus G.   nostrae carnis G + natus G.

l. 36.   uisibiliter] magis de longinquo uenientibus uisibilis et G.
apparuit + sed.

p. 11.   l. 2.   *d. = dominum.*

Postcommon.   ACΓHJΛMPRSWYZ.

l. 4.   dne. d. nr.] o. d. ACΓ (*but see col.* 78) HΛMPRSWY.
nr. *om.* J.   quae] quod AHWY.

l. 5.   purificatae mentis intelligentia] purificatis mentibus indulgentiam Z.

                              OCTAVAE EPIPHANIAE.

l. 7.   Read *epifaniae.*

l. 8.   See p. 10, l. 3.

Collect.   AHJΛMPRSWYZ (G for Epiphany Γ among 'aliae
orationes' after postc. of Epiphany).

l. 10.   cuius + filius A.

l. 11.   foras G.

l. 12.   per] qui tecum AHMRSWYZ.

l. 18.   The manuscript has a note of interrogation after *exultent* (the
penultimate letter of this word has been enclosed within square
brackets in error).

l. 20. lætitia] Vulg. *laude.*

l. 25. Read *dicetis.*

> **Epistle.** Inflection marks over uerum (l. 15), redemptus (l. 20), fontes (l. 22), nomen (l. 26), dicit (l. 28).

l. 30 sqq. See p. 10, l. 15 sqq.

l. 31. Read *illuminare* for *et lluminare.* The letter *i* has been mistaken for the sign 7 (= *et*), which is very common in Irish MSS. Or possibly the scribe, by a slip of the pen, has written 7 for *i.* See Plate I. l. 6.

l. 35. The parts of the mass following the gospel—viz. the offertory, secret, common and postcommon—are omitted. This may be accounted for either (1) by the carelessness of the scribe, or (2) on the supposition that the missing parts were intended to be supplied from the preceding mass (*cf.* above on p. 9, l. 22). Against the latter hypothesis is (*a*) the unlikelihood that there would be a special collect, epistle, and gospel for the octave, without a special secret and postcommon ; (*β*) the fact that there seems to be no other example of the secret and postc. of Epiphany being used for the octave ; and (*γ*) the further fact that the scribe has elsewhere left masses incomplete : see pp. 78, 91. If we have really here a blunder of the scribe it is unlikely that the missal should have been in use for any considerable time without at least the catch-words of the missing collects being supplied by a corrector. This is one of several indications that the book was little, if at all, used at the altar.

p. 12.   DOMINICA PRIMA EPIPHANIAE.

l. 1. Read *epifaniae,* as p. 11, l. 7. This seems the most natural emendation, the substitution of *a* for *ae* being frequent, though it yields what is apparently a unique title for this mass. Dr. Legg (W p. 1456) is probably right in taking it as equivalent to *Dominica i post Epiphaniam* (with AΓ (col. 159) JARZ) rather than *Dominica i post oct. Epiph.* (HSWY). Against this the position of the mass *after* the octave is no argument ; for the same order obtains in A : see also above on p. 8, l. 15. It is not impossible that the order in such cases may indicate the actual practice, the title being copied from an earlier book and therefore being misleading. If we have rightly understood the title of the present mass, it would seem that in it the word 'epiphania' is applied rather to the season beginning with Epiphany than to the day itself. A similar use of 'Ascensio' is found in Z, where the Sunday after Ascension is called *Dominica prima Ascensionis.* And in like manner Septuagesima seems to be a season in A, which has for the Conversion of St. Paul '*in lxxª. Tract.* Tu es uas.'

l. 5. This psalm (lxv. 1, 2) is found also in Γ^w and some St. Gall MSS. (Frere, *Graduale Sarisburiense,* Index.) More commonly (HRSY) we have here Ps. xcix. 2, *Jubilate deo omnis terra seruite.* There is no mass in C.

l. 7. Read *uota.*

> **Collect.** AΓHJAMRSWYZ.
>
> l. 7. populi + tui J.
>
> l. 9. uiderunt HSY.
>
> **Epistle.** Inflection marks over *Title* ad ; v. 2 et *tert.* ; v. 5 sum, alterius.

l. 17. Read ℣. The verse here intended may be either Ps. xcix. 2, or Ps. lxv. 1, 2 ; more probably the former, which is found in Γⁿ as well as in the English missals.

Secret. AΓHJΛMRSWYZ (P for lx^nª).
l. 25. tibi *om.* P.   nos + q. HSY.
Postcommon. SW.

DOMINICA IN SEPTUAGESIMA.

p. 13. l. 5. Read *Ps.*
Collect. ACΓHJΛPRSWYZ (G Sabbato iv temp. Decemb. M
super populum).
l. 7.   q. *om.* P.   dne.] deus G.
l. 8 sq.   pro &c.] pietatis tuae uisitatione consolemur G.
l. 9.   misericorditer *om.* Λ.
Epistle. Inflection marks over v. 24 comprehendatis ; v. 25
omnibus ; v. 27 reprobus ; v. 2 in *tert.*
l. 23. Read *sustinui.*
Gospel. Inflection marks over v. 8 cum ; v. 16 uocati (l. 28).
Secret. ACΓHJΛPRSWYZ (DGLM see above on p. 8, l. 1 sqq.)
For collation, see above p. 118. E here omits *nostris* after
muneribus.
p. 14. **Postcommon.** ACΓHJΛMPRSWYZ (G ad populum of Saturday
after 1ma).
l. 6.   fidelibus tuis GZ.   d.] dne. G *om.* Z.   per tua dona] perpetuis donis A perpetua (+ dne. Z) dona GZ perpetuo dono Λ.
firmentur] formentur Λ.   et *om.* CGΓ.
l. 7.   requirant] te quaerant G.

DOMINICA IN SEXAGESIMA.

l. 9. Read *lx^a.*
l. 10. see note on p. 6, l. 14.
l. 14. usque tuum] indicating the addition to the office of the words
propter nomen tuum, which are not found in AΓ^aHRSWY. C has no
mass.
Collect. AΓHJΛMPRSWYZ (C for One Confessor Bishop).
l. 17. actione confidimus] uirtute subsistimus C.
l. 18. omnia aduersa CS.   doctoris gentium protectione] intercessione . . . (*post* ut) C.
Epistle. Inflection marks over *Title* ad ; v. 19 sapientes ;
v. 20 uos *sec.* ; v. 21 hac ; v. 22 et *pri. sec. tert.* ; v. 23 et ;
v. 24 minus ; v. 25 naufragium ; v. 26 periculis *quart.*, falsis ;
v. 27 uigiliis, nuditate ; v. 31 non ; v. 33 manus ; v. 1 expedit,
reuelationes ; v. 4 homini ; v. 9 dixit.
l. 31. In the reading *electi,* E is supported by AΓ^aRY against HSW
(*dilecti*). See Legg (W p. 1458).
Gospel. Inflection mark over v. 15 afferunt (l. 34).
p. 15. **Secret.** AΓHJΛPRYZ (MSW see above on p. 12, l. 25).
For collation, see above.
l. 12. Read *reficis.*
Postcommon. AΓHJΛPRSWYZ (GM pro quacunque tribulatione).
l. 12. o. *om.* G.
l. 13. sacramentis + et G.   etiam *om.* GM.
l. 14. deseruire concedas] informes GM.

DOMINICA IN QUINQUAGESIMA.

l. 16. The missing words are supplied from the Rheinau and S.
Gallen Sacramentaries (G p. 325), ΓP &c. See note on p. 6, l. 14.

Collect. AΓHJΛMPRSWYZ.

l. 23. peccatorum + nostrorum R. nos *om.* S *post* peccatorum HY.

Epistle. Inflection marks over *Title* ad ; v. 1 cimbalum ; v. 2 nichil ; v. 7 omnia *quart.* ; v. 8 nunquam, distruetur ; v. 10 parte ; v. 11 cogitabam, erant ; v. 12 facie ; v. 13 autem *sec.* (l. 27).

l. 32. The reading *iacob et ioseph* is rare : see W p. 1458.

p. 16. l. 1. The words *et non ipsi nos* after *nos* pri. (AΓ*(P)HRSWY) have been omitted by homoeoteleuton, and the symbol ℣, which in most missals precedes *ipse* sec., has also fallen out. Apparently in the exemplar *Nos* sec. was the beginning of a fresh ℣.

Secret. AΓHJΛMPRSWYZ (D Vig. of Several Martyrs).

l. 10. haec *om.* D. q. dne. DHRSY.

l. 11. et + ad DΓHJRSYZ. sacrificium celebrandum] uenturam festiuitatem sanctorum m. tuorum 'n' celebrandam D.

Postcommon. AΓHJΛRSWYZ (MP for St. Vincent, &c.)

l. 17. *init.* + da P.

l. 18. percepimus + intercedente b. uincentio m. tuo MP.

BENEDICTIO CINERUM.

l. 19. There is considerable variation between the different books in the service for the Blessing of the Ashes. E throughout closely follows S, only departing from it by the insertion of two psalms, and in the final collect. C gives a shorter office all the parts of which are found in S. That in H is identical with C except that the final collect is omitted.

l. 25. Read *niniuitarum.*

l. 26. eos qui omnes] Read *omnes qui eos.*

First collect. SWY.

l. 23. sancti✠ficare.

l. 24. nostra delicta WY.

l. 25. more nineuitarum ferre constituisti S.

l. 26. inuocationem + sancti S.

l. 29. sic + eorum. inchoare sancta ieiunia S. sancta *om.* Y.

l. 31. accipere] percipere W.

At the conclusion of the first collect the ashes are sprinkled with holy water in S.

l. 33 sqq. This second prayer of benediction is found in many books, and is the only one in C at this place.

l. 33. Read *non.* The confusion between ī (= *in*) and n̄ (= *non*) is frequent. Both abbreviations are common in Irish MSS.

p. 17. l. 1. Read *imponi* : the substitution of *e* for *i* being not unusual. *Impon*[*er*]*e* is a tempting emendation, but this reading appears to be unsupported by MS. authority.

p. 16. Second Collect. CHRSWY.

l. 33. non + uis W. desideras sed penitentiam C. peccatoris C.

l. 34. humanae conditionis C.

l. 35. perferendae] praeferendae CHSY proferendae RW. promerendae *om.* C.

p. 17. l. 1. decreuimus HS. benedi✠cere] benedicere C + et sancti✠ficare C (*om.* ✠) S. pro tua bonitate bene✠dicere Y.

l. 2. pro *om.* C. pietate] bonitate HY. dignare R. nos + in W. cineres SY + esse CHRY + esse monuisti S.

l. 3. cognouimus] cognoscimus CHRSWY.

l. 4. peccatorum + omnium.

l. 6.   This rubric is found *verbatim* in C.   See below on p. 32, l. 4.

l. 7.   This form (both in C and E, as in four of the ordines given by Martène *De Ant. Eccl. Rit.* vol. iii. col. 140 sqq.) is a combination of two which are found apart in other missals (HSY : RW).   We have already seen a similar conflation in the title of the mass for Jan. 1 (p. 7, l. 14).

   Memento. CHRSWY.

    l. 7.   homo *om.* W.   cinis . . . reuerteris *pri. om.* RW.

    puluis . . . reuerteris *sec. om.* HSY.

    l. 8.   *fin.* + in nomine patris &c. S.

l. 10.   This antiphon appears in RW at an earlier part of the service (in W without psalm).   In HSY, as in E, it is sung with the psalm *Saluum me fac* during the distribution of ashes.   In C the same ant. and psalm come before *Memento*, without any rubric indicating when they were to be said.   It is natural to infer that they were intended to be used in the same way.   In RW the ant. during the distribution is *Immutemur* (see l. 19), R adding also *Iuxta uestibulum* (l. 15), with psalm or responsory differing from those given here ll. 18, 22.

l. 15 sqq.   These two antiphons are omitted in C and the printed editions of Y.   They are said (without psalms) during the procession in H and some MSS. of Y (Henderson p. 46 note, p. 47).   One of them (*Immutemur*) in W, and both in R, are connected with the distribution. At Evesham the antiphon *Immutemur* was sung 'cum interpollatione uersuum psalmi *Deus misereatur nostri*'; and according to the Bodleian MS. Rawl. c. 425 the psalm *Deus misereatur* was to be used during the procession 'si opus fuerit' (W col. 555 note).

l. 15 sq.   Read *plorabunt . . . et dicent* with HY (MSS.) and the Vulgate ; or *plorabant . . . dicentes* with RS.

l. 15.   Read *leuitae.*

l. 17.   Read *ad te : ate* not, however, being a scribe's error, but an orthographical solecism not uncommon to Irish MSS.

   Second Antiphon. HRS.

    l. 15.   plorabunt H.

    l. 16.   et dicent] dicentes RS.

    l. 17.   dissipes] despicias H.   clamantium] canentium R.

l. 18.   S has no psalm here.

   Third Antiphon. HRS.

    l. 19.   cilicio] ieiunio H.

l. 22.   This psalm is not given here in S.

l. 24.   E seems to be unique in placing this collect here.   It is usually the mass collect.

   Collect. (ACГHJAMPRSWZ as mass collect G in ieiunio mensis septimi.)

    l. 24.   praesta + q. CGHMS.

     IN CAPITE IEIUNII AD MISSAM.

   Collect.   JY (CRS final collect of blessing of ashes ГAP collecta ad s. anastasiam GL in ieiunio quarti mensis M ad collectam Z first collect of blessing of ashes.)

    l. 33.   + q. *post* nobis SY *post* dne. CA.   christiane + sic S.

   Epistle.   Inflection marks over *Title* iohelis ; v. 16 sanctificate, sugentes, talamo.

p. 18. l.   2.   Read *anima mea.*

   Gospel.   Inflection mark over v. 21 tuus (l. 17).

   Secret.   ACGГHJAMPRSWYZ.

    l. 23.   dne. q. HAMPSY.

l. 24. quibus + ipsius (*exc.* W). ieiunii] sacramenti (*exc.* SW) + uenturum C (?) G.
Postcommon. ACΓHJΛMPRSWYZ (G for Saturday after xlⁱ).
l. 30. praebeant + tua G.
l. 31. et *pri. om.* PR.
Super populum. AΓHJΛMPRSWYZ (L mense Iulio).
l. 34. se] te† Γ. intende *om.*† L.
l. 35. nutriantur] muniantur L.

DOMINICA IN QUADRAGESIMA.

p. 19. l. 3. Read *longitudine.*
Collect. ACΓHJΛMPRSWYZ.
l. 6. quadragesimae AΓPW.
l. 8. operibus] moribus P. exsequamur J.
Epistle. Inflection marks over v. 1 recipiatis ; v. 2 adiuui, dies ; v. 7 uirtute ; v. 8 bonam.
l. 15. Read *unquam.*
l. 21. All the printed missals (ACHΛRSWY) and Γᵃ add the remainder of the Psalm (except vv. 8-10). Probably the omission is accidental in E.
l. 29. The concluding words *non timebis,* &c., seem peculiar to E, if we except Γᵃ, which has for the first verse of the offertory *Dicet dno. susceptor meus es, non timebis,* &c. In the other books examined *Scuto,* &c., is not marked as a ℣.
Secret. ACGΓHJΛMPRSWYZ.
l. 32. sacrificium + dne. G. sollennitatis C.
l. 34. uoluntatibus† Z. temperemur GHJPRSV.
l. 36. Read *dominus.*
p. 20. l. 3. Read *misterii.*
Postcommon. ACΓHJΛMPRSWYZ.
l. 3. in misterii] ministerii† C.

DOMINICA II IN QUADRAGESIMA.

l. 5. Read *Dominica secunda,* in accordance with the usage of the MS. elsewhere, though *dominicus* has much support from other books.
l. 7. Read *unquam.*
l. 12. Read *interius.*
Collect. AΓHJΛMPRSWY.
l. 13. et *om.* JRSW.
Epistle. Inflection marks over *Title* tesolonicenses ; v. 1 abundetis.
l. 18. The latter part of the mass, including a portion of the epistle, being absent from R through the loss of a leaf, I have used for the purpose of collation another pre-Pian edition, *Missale Romanum impensis Lucantonii de giunta* Venetiis 1506. V Id. Jan., which I designate as R'.
l. 19. It will be observed that there is no grail. Γᵘw in like manner have two tracts and no grail. Ps. xxiv. 17 sq., here given as the tract, is in the vast majority of English books the grail. S and the Sherborne missal include the first half of v. 17, beginning *Tribulationes cordis,* and mark a ℣ before *uide* (l. 20) : so R'. But the greater number begin, as ΓᵐE, with *De necessitatibus* (see Dr. Legg's note, W p. 1461, in which, however, there is an error with regard to our manuscript). C is without the mass.
l. 21. Read *meum.*

l. 22 sq. *Ad te . . . inimici mei* is a $\mathbb{V}$ in ΓᵃHY. This addition to the grail is not found in R's.

l. 23 sqq. *Etenim*, &c., appears also in Γᵐ, where it is marked as a separate $\mathbb{V}$. I have not found it elsewhere.

l. 34. Read *ecclesiae tuae.*

Secret. GHMPSW (L in ieiunio mensis decimi).

l. 35. in *om.*† P.

p. 21. l. 3. adorabo] The usual reading is *ad te orabo.*

Postcommon. SW.

DOMINICA III IN QUADRAGESIMA.

l. 11. This is part of the office in ΑΓᵃHRSWY. Probably *Ps.* has been inserted by a clerical error.

Collect. ΑΓHJΛMPRSWYZ.

Epistle. Inflection marks over *Title* ad ; v. 3 decet ; v. 8 lux, ambulate ; v. 9 bonitate (l. 20).

l. 29. Most books (AHΛSWY and Γᵐ, but not R) insert $\mathbb{V}$ before *ita.*

Gospel. Inflection mark over v. 28 dei (l. 34).

p. 22. **Secret.** MPSW (G Friday after xlᵐᵃ L in nat. innocentium).

l. 6. dne. q. L. ·famulorum + tuorum W.

l. 7. tua] tuis GL.

l 10. Read *nidum.*

l. 11. Probably a $\mathbb{V}$ was marked before *Altaria* in the exemplar, which the scribe has omitted.

l. 14 sq. Either *dignanter* or *propitius* is superfluous.

Postcommon. ΑΓHJΛMPRSWYZ (G as secret for Monday after xlⁱ).

l. 14. a *om.* GΓJΛMP. nos + q. GPRZ. dignanter *om.*

l. 15. propitiatus. tantis (tantit R) mysteriis GR. participes] consortes G.

DOMINICA IV IN QUADRAGESIMA.

l. 20. Read *uberibus.*

Collect. ΑΓHJΛMPRSWYZ.

l. 23. ex *om.* P.

Epistle. Inflection marks over *Title* ad ; v. 22 unum *sec.* ; v. 23 natus, repromissionem ; v. 24 alligoriam, est ; v. 26 mater ; v. 27 habet.

p. 23. **Secret.** SW (L orationes ieiunii mensis septimi).

l. 12. nobis *om.* L. diuinis] tuis L.

l. 13. sacris] eorum L.

Postcommon. , ΑΓHJΛMPRSWYZ.

l. 20. q. *om.* ΑΓJΛMP.

l. 21. incessanter. semper fideli ΓΛMZ.

l. 22. semper *om.* Y.

DOMINICA V IN PASSIONE DOMINI.

l. 27. This office psalm seems peculiar to E. ΓᵃHΛRSWY have *Emitte lucem* : in A the psalm is not given. C has no mass. •

Collect. ΑΓHJΛMPRSWYZ.

Epistle. Inflection marks over *Title* ad ; v. 11 creationis ; v. 12 redemptione ; also over ihesu (p. 24, l. 1).

p. 24. l. 9 sqq. The $\mathbb{V}$s are differently placed in HΛRSWY and Γᵃ.

Secret. HSW.

l. 23. o. d.

l. 25.   per dnm.] qui tecum.
Postcommon. AΓHJΛMPRSWYZ (L among July masses).
l. 31.   nobis + q. HSY.
l. 32.   praesidiis] subsidiis HPRY.

DOMINICA PALMARUM.

p. 25.   **Collect.** ACGΓHJΛMPRSWYZ.
l. 7.   o. s. *om.* G.
l. 8.   nostrum + et G.
l. 9.   et *sec. om.* P.
l. 10.   ipsius] eius G.   documentum G.   eius *om. (exc.* CG).
l. 11.   consortium z.   per eundem] qui tecum uiuit M.
c. dni. nostri qui uiuit . . . per G.
Epistle.   Inflection mark over *Title* ad.

l. 16.   Read *manum*.

l. 20.   Read *uidens*.   Most missals do not mark *Quia,* &c., as a
verse.

l. 21.   There can be little doubt that the scribe has blundered here.
Deus deus meus is the beginning of the tract in CΓ^mHARSWY, and
apparently in almost all other English books. For ℣ we should therefore read *Tractus*. And if this correction be accepted we may, with
the authorities just mentioned, supply after *usque* the words *populo
qui nascetur quem fecit dns.*, making the tract Ps. xxi. 2–9, 18*b*, 19, 22,
24, 32, as in S.

l. 22 sqq.   There is a paragraph in all missals (marked in E by a
large ornamental initial) at *Altera autem die,* the beginning of the
Gospel. But the break at *Et hymno dicto* is rare. It is found also
in C.

It will be observed that this passion is lettered in such a way
as to suggest that it was intended to be recited by three persons. This
fact may perhaps give some help in determining the date of the
missal, since the custom of reciting the passion in this manner seems
not to have been ancient. It should be noticed that the lettering
does not appear in the passion according to St. John in the Good
Friday service. And in this respect E agrees with its contemporary
C. In the latter the Palm Sunday passion is given at full length and
lettered, but in the case of the Wednesday and Friday passions the
text is not transcribed, and they were clearly supposed to be read
from a book of the Gospels. Thus in both missals the Palm Sunday
passion alone was to be divided between three ministers. The
elaborate singing of the Passion would quite naturally at first be
confined to this day,[1] and so we may have here an indication that
both the Corpus and Rosslyn Missals belong to a period when the
custom referred to had not fully established itself in the Irish Church.
Unfortunately, however, data are not at present available for fixing
the date when the practice had its beginning. In Rome it would
seem not to have had place before the fifteenth century, since
Mabillon's *Ordo* xv (end of fourteenth century) directs that the
passion is to be said by a single Cardinal deacon. In some French
Churches it was not in vogue till the seventeenth or eighteenth

---

[1] So it would seem to have been at Rome : Catalani, *Rituale Romanum*, Patavii,
1760, vol. ii, p. 188 (§ viii): 'Forte seculo xv inualuit mos ut Passio a tribus diceretur
in solemni missa *huius diei.*'

century.[1] Elsewhere it arose much earlier. In the Bobbio Missal
in the Ambrosian Library (D. 84. inf.), which belongs to the tenth
century, the words of our Lord are indicated by a mark in the
margin, just as we find in two early printed Sarum missals (4° Venice,
1494, folio Rouen, 1497) His words marked with a cross. The
evidence of Durandus (*Rationale*, VI. lxviii. 6) proves that the custom
goes back to the thirteenth century. In England the evidence of
manuscript Sarum Missals shows that it was prevalent at the
beginning of the fifteenth century ; but whether it may be traced to
an earlier date I do not know.

The letters used to indicate the different parts in E are unusual—
t, c, s. The two latter are found in Roman books both modern and
pre-Pian, in which the sayings of Christ are indicated by a cross.
It seems probable that the scribe of E mistook the cross, in the
manuscript from which he copied the symbols, for a T, and that from
this error has arisen his use of that letter for the words of Christ,
which I believe is without parallel. He may very well have found
✠ *c s* in an English book. In Dickinson's reprint of the Sarum
Missal the letters are *b m a* (for the explanation of which see the
rubric in col. 264); but in the early printed editions ✠ *c s* are not
uncommonly used,[2] while in MSS. of the fifteenth century they
appear to be the rule. In C we have *i c s*, the first of which clearly
stands for *ihesus*. See further Gavanti, *Thesaurus Sacrorum Rituum*,
iv. 7. 18 ; Catalani, *Rituale Romanum*, ix. 5. 7, 8 (second edition,
Patavii typis seminarii, 1760, vol. ii. p. 187 sq).

[Since writing the above my attention has been directed by Mr. Dewick
to a Utrecht Missal printed at Leyden in 1514 in which the letters of the
passions are *t m a*, explained in the following rubric : 'Est notandum quod
vbicunque habetur *m* . . . mediocriter cantari debet. vbi autem *a* alte . sed
vbi *t* tacite.' This seems to suggest that at Utrecht the passion was sung
by one person with varying tones, rather than by three persons. This is
consistent with the words of Durandus above referred to, 'Cantus uerborum
Christi dulcius moderantur (*v.l.* modulantur) . . . euangelistae . . . uerba in
tono euangelii proferentur (*v.l.* -untur). Verba uero impiissimorum Iudae-
orum clamose et cum asperitate uocis'; and possibly also with the lettering
of E. Further, it may be plausibly conjectured that the *t* of E is not a
mistake of the scribe, but, as in the Utrecht book, equivalent to *tacite* ; *c* and
s representing respectively *clare* and *sonoriter*. The word *sonoriter* is used
in a somewhat similar manner in the Dublin manuscript Pontifical B. 3. 6.]

p. 26.   **Secret.** AΓHJΛMPRYZ (SW for St. Richard).
               l. 7.   dne.] mis. d. SW. ut + intercedente . . . SW.
                       munus oblatum.
               l. 8.   deuotionis] bene uiuendi SW. effectum + beatae
                       AΓHJΛMRYZ + nobis P. effectum perhennitatis] gloriam
                       sempiternam SW + post hanc uitam W.
         l. 14.   Read *misterii.*
               Postcommon. AΓHJΛPRYZ (MSW Friday after xl^{ma}).
               l. 15. purgentur] curentur A. impleantur ΓΛM.

[1] De Moléon, *Voyages Liturgiques de France, ou Recherches faites en diverses Villes
du Royaume*, pp. 63, 96, 302, 418 (8vo. ed. Paris, 1757). Martène (*De Mon. Rit.*,
III, xii. 21, xiv. 21, coll. 346, 391) speaks of the passion as read by a single
deacon.
[2] So in Paris, 1503; Rouen, 1514; Paris(?), 1519 (?); Rouen, 1521 ; London, 1557
—all in the Gough room of the Bodleian Library. Also in Paris, 1504, in Trinity
College Library, Dublin (FF. ee. 13).

MISSA IN CENA DOMINI.

ll. 18, 20. Read *resurrectio, ps.*

l. 20. Γᵃ has *Cantate dno.* ; but E is in agreement with CHARSWY.

l. 24. Read *sua.*

l. 25. Read *utrisque.*

l. 26. Read *ablato.*

Collect. ACΓHJAMPRSWYZ (G for Good Friday).

l. 22. proditor *om.* ACGΓAMPZ. reatus + sui.

l. 23. nobis + tuae.

l. 24. affectum W. in *om.* G. sua passione P. ihesus *om.* G.

l. 25. utrisque intulit.

l. 32. Read *obediens.*

p. 27. l. 1. ut] Read ℣. See above, on p. 9, l. 3.

l. 5. In W the Gospel is much longer, including vv. 16-32.

l. 12. *hec* is probably an error for *hoc.* The latter (written *h̄*) would easily be mistaken for the former (*h̄*) in an Irish MS.

Secret. ACΓHJAMPRSWYZ.

l. 10. aeterne *om.* JMP.

l. 12. commemorationem AMSWZ. hec] hoc.

l. 13. traditione] die Z. c. + filius tuus RWZ.

l. 15. I have not found this *Communicantes* elsewhere.

l. 19 sq. Read *et cunctae familiae.*

Hanc igitur. AGΓHJAMPRSWYZ.

l. 19. et *om.*† W. seruitutis . . . tuae] famulorum famularumque tuarum G. sed . . . tuae *om.* Z.

l. 20. offerunt G.

l. 22. sui *om.* W. ut *om.* G.

l. 23. accipias + et tua pietate &c. G.

l. 24 sq. In the manuscript *qui pridie* follows *accipias* without any indication that it belongs to a later part of the Canon. It is difficult to believe that if the book had been much used at the altar this error of the scribe would not have been marked in some way, so that the priest might be prevented from omitting the clause *Hanc igitur.* Compare above, note on p. 11, l. 35.

l. 24. Read *quam, nostra.* The symbols for *quam* and *quia* in Irish MSS. are sometimes scarcely distinguishable.

Qui pridie. AΓHJAMPRSWYZ.

l. 24. omniumque] omnium JMP. pateretur *ante* pro S.

l. 25. + hoc est *ante* hodie. hodie] hodierna die W.

Common. CHRSWY.

l. 28. quae] quid.

l. 29. enim *om.* ita uos HY. *fin.* + ℣ Surgit autem W.

l. 32. Read *tempore.*

Postcommon. ACΓHJAMPRSWYZ (GL orationes mensis decimi).

l. 31. refecti] repleti Z. d. nr. *om.* GL.

l. 32. ut *om.* L. quod] quae Z. mortalitatis nostrae A + cultu HR.

l. 33. tuae immortalitatis R.

l. 35. The office of vespers here given agrees exactly with that in S (Dickinson, col. 304 ; Procter and Wordsworth fasc. i. col. dcclxxxiv) H (p. 87) Y (Henderson, p. 98 ; Lawley, vol. i. col. 384) and the Aberdeen Breviary (vol. ii. part ii. f. 111r.)

p. 28. l. 4. omnibus] Read *hominibus.*

l. 6. Read *mihi.* *m̄* has been confused with *m̄.*

l. 12. euangelium] The correct reading is probably *Ant. ad euan-*

gelium (cf. C p. 135). The antiphon which follows is that which is found in HSY and the Aberdeen Breviary in the corresponding place for *Magnificat:* and it is doubtless this canticle which is here indicated by the word *euangelium.* So Y p. 109, '*In euangelio antiphona* Iesus autem, &c. *Ps.* Magnificat.' Cf. Mabillon's *Ordo* i. Appendix, cap. 12 sqq.; Duchesne, *Origines du Culte Chrétien*, 2nd ed. pp. 304, 456.

hec] An error for *autem*: the Irish symbol *h̄* having been read *h̆*.

l. 15. The repetition of the postcommon is explained by the rubrics of S (coll. 304, 308). Vespers are said immediately after the common, and for the vesper collect is substituted the postcommon of the mass, followed by *Ite, missa est*: 'Et sic missa et vesperae simul finiantur.' In HY no postcommon is given, and *Refecti* at vespers is headed '*oratio.*'

FERIA VI IN PARASCEVE.

l. 16. Read *viᵃ, parasciue.*

l. 18. ut supra] Referring to the mass for the previous day, p. 26, l. 22. This prayer is found before the first lesson in CGAPW, and apparently in A. This is its place probably also in Z, where immediately after the super populum of Maundy Thursday we have *Deus a quo*, headed *oratio*: Then *Feria sexta in Parasceue. Oratio. D. qui peccati.* The title *Feria sexta in Parasceue* has apparently been misplaced. In HJRSY there is no collect before the first lesson, *Deus a quo* being used before the second. In a Roman Pontifical printed at Venice ('per spectabilem virum dominum Lucamantonium de giunta florentinum') Sept. 15, 1520, the same two collects that we have here are given, but in inverted order. In the collation below this book is indicated by the symbol R".

First Lesson. Inflection mark over v. 3 cognoscamus.

l. 22. gradale] Usually entitled *Tractus* (CHJRSWY): but in A *Responsorium*, in M *Canticum.*

l. 23. Read *tua.*

l. 25. Read *appropinquauerint.*

ll. 27, 29. Read ℣. The indication of a verse (ṽ) has evidently been misread as s̄ (= *sed*): s and v when carelessly written being easily confused in the Irish script.

l. 31. Read ℣. *operuit.*

p. 29. l. 1. Read *passione soluisti.* Here again v of the exemplar is read *s*.

l. 2. Read *naturae. Terreni* is not an error for *terrenae*, though we have the authority of P and the Rheinau MS. of the Gelasian Sacramentary for the latter reading. The collect is plainly founded on 1 Cor. xv. 49, 'Sicut portauimus imaginem terreni, portemus et imaginem caelestis.' The words should therefore be rendered: 'that as by necessity of nature we have borne the image of the earthy, so by sanctification of grace we may bear the image of the heavenly.'

p. 28.   **Collect.** ACGAPWZ (M after 3rd lesson in sabbato sancto R" before 1st lesson).

l. 34. omne genus R". filii *om.* CGAMPR". tui *om.* CR". dni. nostri i. c. R". dni. + dei W. dni. nostri *om.* Z.

p. 29.   l. 1. da] dona ACGW + q. Z. confirmes R"Z. eiusdem facti] eidem facti CGMW eidem facto AR" eadem facta Z + et Z.

l. 2. sicut] ut qui R". terrenae creaturae P terrenique parentis nature R". naturae necessitate *om.* Z.

l. 3. ita + et P. imaginem + unigeniti filii tui dni. nostri i. c. A.

l. 4.   i. c. dni. nostri qui tecum] per ACWZ eiusdem unigeniti filii dni. nostri i.c. qui tecum R". i.c. dni. nostri *om.* AP. ihesu *om.* GM.

Second Lesson. Inflection mark over v. 8 lactucis.

l. 8.   gradale]   See above on p. 28, l. 22.
l. 14.   Read *iniquis* : in the exemplar, no doubt, written *ii*.
l. 19.   Read *meae.*
l. 20.   Read *meae obumbrasti.*
l. 22.   Read *ne.*
l. 27 sqq.   This passion is not lettered. From which we may perhaps infer that it was not intended to be sung, like that appointed for Palm Sunday, by three cantors. So also C, which for Palm Sunday gives the text of the passion in full, with the letters indicating the division between the cantors, here and at the Wednesday of Holy Week has merely a direction that the passion is to be read, without any text. See above, note on p. 25, l. 22.
l. 29.   Read *quia* : cf. above on p. 27, l. 24.

Orationes in Parasceue. ACGΓHJΛMPRSWYZ.

l. 32.   Read *dilectissimi.*

First Bidding.
l. 32.   nobis+inprimis GHJSY.
l. 33.   pacificare + adunare GRYZ.   et custodire *om.* W.   toto orbe] per uniuersum orbem G.
l. 34.   terrarum orbe Γ.
l. 35.   tranquillam et quietam G.   deum] dnm. P + et W.

First Collect.
l. 39.   custodi + q. s.

p. 30.   l. 1.   tua *om.* ΓΛPR.   orbe + terrarum W.
l. 2.   dnm.] eundem.

Second Bidding.
l. 3.   'n'] *om.* Y + et pro antistite nostro 'n' G.   et dns. nr.] o. G.
l. 4.   eum] eos G.   ordine GHRSYZ (*hiat* W).   saluos G.
l. 5.   et incolumes G.

Second Collect.
l. 8.   cuius + aeterno GΛ.
l. 9.   electos G + a te G.
l. 10.   antistites G.   talibus G te Γ.
l. 11.   auctoribus sub tantos pontifices G.
l. 13.   Read *presbyteris diaconibus.*
l. 15.   Read *confessoribus.*

Third Bidding.
l. 13.   oremus + et.   episcopis + et R.   presbyteris + et W.   diaconibus + et R.
l. 18.   Read *sanctificatur.*
l. 20.   Read *seruiatur.*

Third Collect.
l. 18.   sanctificatur] multiplicatur C.
l. 20.   tibi gradibus (*exc.* G) *om.* G.   fidelitur *om.* Γ.

Fourth Bidding.
l. 21.   christianissimo. imperatore] rege HMS + uel rege G.   'n' *om.* AΓΛWY.   et dns. nr.] o. G.
l. 22.   subditas + illi (illis G).   nationes + et faciat sapere ea quae recta sunt atque contra inimicos catholicae et apostolicae ecclesiae triumphum largiatur uictoriae CWY.
l. 26.   Read *potestates.*

Fourth Collect.

l. 25. in cuius . . . regnorum] qui regnis omnibus aeterna potestate dominaris G.

l. 26. omnia] omnium JRSWZ *om.* A. respice + propitius G. ad *om.* Y.

l. 27. christianorum] christianum AAWY romanum ΓPRZ romanum siue (romanorum atque M) francorum GM anglorum J. quae] qui CW. uirtute] feritate.

l. 28. dexterae tuae potentia G.

l. 32. Read *inueniantur.*

Fifth Bidding.

l. 29. ut + et M. ac] et.

l. 31. misericordiae + suae RS.

l. 32. + digni *post* ipsi AHSY *post* peccatorum GW. et ipsi *om.* G.

Fifth Collect.

p. 31.   l. 2. dnm.] eundem R.

l. 4. mundum· ut cunctis] Read *ut cunctis mundum.*

Sixth Bidding.

l. 4. d. pater o. *om.*

l. 5. depellat] repellat CHY.

Seventh Bidding.

l. 13. et *sec.*] atque M. et *tert.*] ac ΓAMW.

l. 14. i.c. *om.* AGΓAMPRYZ. uniuersis *om.* C.

l. 15. ecclesiam *om.* A. et] atque.

l. 19. Read *diabolica.*

Seventh Collect.

l. 18. omnes saluas G + homines HS.

l. 19. respice ad animas.

l. 20. prauitate deposita] peruersitate depulsa G.

l. 21. unitatem] firmitatem G.

Eighth Bidding.

l. 23. cognoscant G.

l. 24. c.i. GΓP.

l. 25. So most medieval books. But G 'Annuntiat diaconus ut supra.' Similarly also the Sherborne Missal. The Durham Missal omits the rubric, thus apparently agreeing with E (see Dr. Legg, W p. 1470 : where S is wrongly cited as in agreement with Durham).

Eighth Collect.

l. 26. iudaicam *om.* Z.

l. 28. quas + tibi G. agnita] cognita G. ueritate tua (*om.* luce) Z.

l. 29. est c. W. est *om.*† C.

l. 30. Read *paganis.*

Ninth Bidding.

l. 31. de] a GΓJAMPRWZ. ut] et GΓJAMPW.

l. 32. deum + uiuum et (*exc.* G). c. + deum et (*exc.* A).

l. 33. d. cum sancto spiritu Z d. in unitate spiritus sancti G. cum spiritu sancto *om.* C.

l. 34. amen] This seems quite out of place here, and might be regarded as a scribe's error, due to the fact that *amen* usually elsewhere follows the words *in saecula saeculorum.* But it is found here in CYZ and the Cod. Ottob. of Γ. On the other hand R is express : 'et non respondetur. *Amen.*'

p. 32. l. 2. Read *ecclesiae tuae sanctae.*

Ninth Collect.

p. 31.   l. 36.   uis *om.* AGΓΛMPRZ.

p. 32.   l. 3.   dnm.] eundem P.

l. 4.   The resemblance between the rubrics of E and C is very striking. They are often verbally identical when, in other books, even though the same sense is expressed, it is couched in different terms. It is a reasonable inference that they were derived from a common source ; and, if this be so, the rubrics of the one may be taken as giving the practice supposed in the other, even when there is no expressed direction. An illustration is afforded by the present rubric, which is identical with that in C, except that the latter reads *sustentatur* for *sustineatur.* Cf. above on p. 17, l. 6, and below on p. 48, l. 24 sqq.

5.   acolitis]   So we find in M, Mabillon's *Ordo* i., Hittorp (p. 66), Λ (p. 62), and in service books of the Churches of Noyon, Châlons en Champagne, St. Germain des Prés, Corbie, and Montecassino, cited by Martène, *De Ant. Eccl. Rit.* IV. xxiii. 27 (t. iii. coll. 372, 379, 382), *De Mon. Rit.* III. xiv. 25, 26 (col. 392 sq.), ' Post orationes praeparatur crux ante altare . . . sustentata hinc et inde a duobus *acolythis.*'   Similarly a Poitiers book, Martène, *De Ant. Eccl. Rit. l.c.* (iii. col. 375).   I have not noticed elsewhere, except in C, the direction that the Cross is to be supported by acolytes.   R has simply *ministris,* S *presbyteri de superiori gradu,* V *vicarii,* H *presbyteri.*

cantantibus hos uersus]   The manner of singing this part of the service (ll. 7-24) seems to be nearly identical in the two Irish Missals and in the uses of Hereford, Salisbury, and York.   The antiphons are sung by the two who support the cross, *Agios* by two others (deacons in SY), and *Sanctus* by the choir.   In R the arrangement is different : ' Duo fratres ex parte hebdomadarii cantant . . . ℣. *Popule meus* usque *Agyos otheos* ℣. *Popule meus* . . *mihi.* ℣. *Quia* . . . *tuo.* Chorus ex parte hebdomadarii cantant *Agyos otheos.* Alius chorus respondet *Sanctus deus* . . . . Postea duo fratres de secundo choro cantant ℣. *Quia eduxi* . . . . et chori respondent alternatim *Agios* . . . *Sanctus.* Ita tamen quod primus chorus semper reincipit *Agyos.* Deinde duo fratres de primo choro cantant ℣. *Quid ultra* . . . Item chori alternatim respondent *Agyos. Sanctus* ut dictum est.'   In HSY (and so apparently E) the uncovering of the cross follows, in R it precedes, the singing of the antiphons.

l. 6.   episcopus]   The bishop, it will be noticed, takes the chief place ; which points to the fact that our missal belonged to a cathedral church. capa]   During the lessons he had been vested in a chasuble (RS &c.).

First Antiphon. CHRSY.

l. 8.   quit C.

l. 10.   Read *alii.*   ' Duo diaconi de secunda forma . . . ad gradum chori ad altare conuersi ' S : ' duo diaconi . . . in medio chori ante ostium occidentale chori ' Y : ' alii duo . . . . stantes in medio chori ' H.   C is again similar to E : ' Quibus respondendum sit *a duobus aliis paratis* qui sic dicunt.'

l. 12.   Read *dicat.* Cf. C : ' Deinde subsequatur chorus et dicat flectendo genua.'

l. 14.   C is again identical with E.

Second Antiphon. CHRSY.

l. 15.   annis. uestimenta . . . atrita *om.*

l. 16.   + et *ante* manna. quoque *om.*

l. 17.   introduxi + te CR. optimam] bonam S. parasti . . . tuo *om.* R.

l. 18.   preui] cantores C (so H).   The reference is to the ' duo parati ' previously mentioned (l. 10).

l. 19.   duo primi] i.e. the two who hold the cross (ll. 5, 14).
l. 22.   Read *potasti.*
   Third Antiphon.   CHRSY.
   l. 21.   uinea mea f. decora S.   fructu decoram] speciosissimam
      HR.   satis] nimis (*exc.* C).
   l. 22.   mixto cum felle *om.* CR cum felle mixto H.   siti mea C.
   l. 23.   preforastit C.   saluatori tuo CHR.
l. 24.   C inserts here an address to the people followed by a rubric,
which appears to be in part a misplaced repetition with slight variation
of that given above l. 4 sq. (' Post host orationes (*sic*) expletas preparatur crux ante altare . . . sustentata huict et inde a duobus diaconibus', &c.).   Then follow antiphons and psalms during the adoration
of the priest, and finally the hymn *Crux fidelis*, as here (l. 26).
l. 31.   Here we may suppose, as in C, took place the adoration of the
clergy and people.
l. 32.   A rubric has clearly been omitted here.   It may be supplied
from C : ' salutata uero cruce et reposita in loco suo discendit pontifex
aut sacerdos ante altare et dicit oremus. preceptis salutaribus moniti.
Pater noster sed libera.   Sumit de sancto et ponit in calicem nihil
dicens.'   Compare Hittorp, p. 66 (*recte* 68), M.   There is no mention
of the *Confiteor* and other prayers directed to be said here in HSY.   See
Martène, *De Ant. Eccl. Rit.* IV. xxiii. 23 (t. iii. col. 366) : ' Veteres
nihil praeter orationem Dominicam et *Libera nos* dicebant.'
l. 34.   This is the postcommon for the preceding day.   I know of no
other authority for saying it at this place on Good Friday.   In GMPR
there is no postcommon.   In HY *Refectibus uitalibus* comes at the end
of Vespers, and in S, in the same place, *Respice q. dne.* : but here there
is a separate collect for Vespers (p. 33, l. 7).
l. 34.   HSY and the Aberdeen Breviary have the same psalms and
antiphons for Vespers on Good Friday as on Maundy Thursday.   And
this was the usual rule.   In E, however, there is a variation.   The five
psalms are sung under a single antiphon *Calicem salutaris*, instead of
having (p. 27, l. 34 sqq.) a separate antiphon for each psalm.   The
closest parallel which I can cite is the direction of a Strasbourg
Ordinary of A.D. 1364 that the vesper psalms on Good Friday shall
be sung without antiphons (Martène, *De Ant. Eccl. Rit.* t. iii. col. 395).
p. 33.   l. 4.   S and the Aberdeen Breviary have the same antiphon for
Magnificat as on Maundy Thursday : *Cenantibus autem.* HY have
Ihesus autem cum accepisset (the two first words omitted in H).
l. 7.   This collect is not found here in any other missal with which
I am acquainted.   Two collects occur elsewhere in E, both of which
begin with these words, and either of which may therefore be here
intended—that for the Exaltation of the Cross, p. 67, l. 16, and that for
the Mass de S. Cruce, p. 78, l. 30.   The latter, as being the more
frequently used of the two, is probably the one here referred to :
though it may be noted that the former (with some variations) is
found between the adoration and the mass of the pre-sanctified in a
Lyons MS. of the thirteenth century, and in a sixteenth century printed
missal of the same Church (Martène, *De Ant. Eccl. Rit.* IV. xxiii., t. iii.
col. 384 sq.).   But it must be remarked that in all previous instances
where the parts of masses are indicated by cues the full text had
appeared in an *earlier* part of the book.   Not improbably therefore the
Missa de S. Cruce came before that now under consideration.   If so
the arrangement of our missal resembled that of C, the Votive Masses
preceding the Temporale.   Other indications pointing to the same
conclusion will be noticed hereafter.

VIGILIA PASCHAE.

l. 10. On the lessons, see W. pp. 1414, 1470.

hic induit se casula] The form of this rubric and the absence of the title in the MS. appear to indicate that in the exemplar this was not the beginning of the service. The 'benedictio cerei' probably preceded the lessons, as in C. There is no rubric here in C, but Y (p. 111) has the direction 'Sequitur benedictio Cerei Paschalis . . . *Prælato capato interim in sede sua residente*'; and later on, when the lessons are about to begin, ' Prælatus interim Casula in reuestiario indutus' &c., which agrees with, and explains, the rubric before us. Compare the Sarum Consuetudinary (ed. Frere, 1898, p. 151)

l. 15. Read *mirabilius*.
l. 16. Read *peccati*.
    First Collect. ACΓHJAMPRSWYZ.
    l. 15. hominem creasti HY.
    l. 16. nobis + q. AΓHJAPRSYZ. oblectamina A.
    l. 17. resistere J. eterna gaudia R.
l. 22. gradale] *tractus* in ACHJRSWY : *canticum* in GΓAMP.
l. 31. Read *uni*.
l. 32. Read *dextrae*.
l. 33. Read *regenerationis*.
    Second Collect. ACGΓ (col. 148) HJARSWY.
    l. 30. miracula] mirabilia R.
    l. 31. egyptiaca HRSY.
    l. 32. potentiam SY. in] ad S. in salutem id H.
    l. 33. praesta + q. HSY.
    l. 34. ut + et GΓHJASWY.
p. 34. l. 2. Read *apprehendent*.
l. 4. See above on p. 33, l. 22.
l. 5. Read *dilecto*.
l. 6. Read Ɏ, and compare above on p. 9, l. 3.
circumdedit *sec.*] read *circumfodit*.
l. 8. Read *torcular, uinea*.
l. 12. Read *utriusque*.
l. 13. Read *misericordias*.
    Third Collect. ACGΓHJAMPRSYZ (W for Whitsun eve).
    l. 11. paschale sacramentum] praesentem festiuitatem W.
    l. 12. imbuisti] instruis AΓMPRWZ.
    l. 13. misericordiam tuam AΓHAMPRWYZ. munerum *om.* M.
    Fourth Collect. ACΓHJAMPRSYZ (W for Whitsun eve).
    l. 20. semper] per P. uocationem P.
l. 23. gradale] *tractus* in ACHJMRSWY ; *canticum* in A.
l. 25. Read *ad te*. This is not an error of the scribe : see above on p. 17, l. 17.
l. 27. Read *faciem*.
l. 32. *fonte* is read also by Z.
    Fifth Collect. CΓHJMPSYZ.
    l. 31. paschalia festa Z.
    l. 33. per *om.* HY.
l. 34. post est] The MS. reads *p̄t* followed by the symbol for *est* (see Plate II. l. 6 from end). The former usually signifies *potest* : but is once (p. 27, l. 27) used for *post*. The letter *e* with a subscribed *a* might be confused with the symbol for *est* (cf. D p. 7, l. 13 from end, *est s* for *es*). Hence we may conjecture with probability that the exemplar read *postea*.

redeunte in uestiarium] The priest here exchanges his chasuble for a cope : see S col. 348, Y p. 120.

procedat ad fontes] Both C and E omit the Blessing of the Font ; but this rubric evidently implies it. It was probably in the exemplar. The rubric is omitted in C.

l. 36. subiectam letaniam] In S the litany after the Blessing of the the Font is metrical : but CRWY have here litanies similar to that in E.

l. 37. The litanies in CRWY begin with *Kyrie eleison, Christe eleison,* which may have been accidentally omitted here. But, on the other hand, the litany at the beginning of the Stowe Missal (MacCarthy, p. 192) begins with *Christe audi nos* thrice repeated : followed, however, by *Kyrie eleison.*

l. 38. Read *dei.*

p. 35. l. 4. Read *sancte, stephane* (or *zephane*).

l. 6. Read *gregori.* For Sylvester and Gregory C has Martin and Patrick.

l. 7 sq. After *S. Benedicte* C inserts *S. Maria Magdalena, S. Felicitas.* It also omits *S. Agatha,* reverses the order of *S. Petronilla* and *S. Margareta,* and adds *S. Brigida.*

l. 8. Read *sancta.*

l. 19 sqq. The greater part of this rubric is omitted in C.

l. 19. duo cantores] Apparently those who had sung the litany : see W col. 589 sq.

l. 23. We should probably read *pulsentur* (sc. *campanae*) : cf. S col. 353, H p. 112, Y p. 124, R f. 131v, &c.

l. 25. Read *dominicae.*

l. 27. Read *renouati.*

l. 29. *per* is misplaced. It should follow *seruitutem.*

Collect. ACGΓHJAMPRSWYZ.

l. 26. illustrasti C. nouam HY. progeniem HY.

l. 28. tuam] tibi.

Epistle. Inflection mark over *Title* ad.

l. 32. *Alleluia* is written in the same hand as the epistle, not in the smaller script used for the choir portions. This may be explained as implying the manner of singing the Alleluia enjoined in R : ' Finita epistola sacerdos qui cantat missam incipit *Alleluia,* et totum decantat ter exaltando uocem gradatim : et chorus post quamlibet uicem in eadem uoce repetit illud idem. Postea uersus *Confitemini* . . . Cantatur communiter uel sicut cantor disposuerit,' &c. Compare Martène, *De Monachorum Ritibus,* III. xv. 22 (t. iv. col. 412). Somewhat similar directions appear in S and Y, but for the celebrant we have in S 'duo clerici de secunda forma,' and in Y 'duo uicarii.'

l. 33. Read ℣ with CRSWY.

p. 36. l. 5. Read *misteriis.*

l. 6. Read *proficiant.*

Secret. ACGΓJAPRSWYZ (DHM for the day).

l. 4. q. dne. AHSZ. q. *om.* G.

l. 5. initiata ADGΓJMRZ.

l. 7. Read *hac.* At p. 45, l. 2, *et* is omitted.

Communicantes. ACDGΓHJAMPRSWYZ.

l. 8. sacratissimum HY.

l. 10. semper] semperque R *om.* A.

l. 11. dei et dni. nostri + i.

l. 14. Read *quam.*

Hanc igitur. ACDGΓHJLAMPRSWYZ.

l. 13. seruitutis . . . tuae *om.* L.

l. 14.   quoque *om.* C (*semel*) L.
l. 15.   ex aqua ct spiritu sancto *post* quos L.
l. 16.   omnium *om.* D (*semel*) *post* peccatorum D (*semel*).   peccatorum + ut inuenires eos in c. i. dno. nostro G.   dne. *om.*
L.   ut *om.* GL.

Postcommon.   ACΓHJΛPRSWYZ (DM for day G ' pro caritate ').
l. 18.   spiritum + in W.
l. 19.   sacramentis paschalibus] uno caelesti panc G.
tua] una G.

IN DIE PASCHAE.

l. 24 sq.   CDHRSWY have but one *alleluia* after *tuam*, and two after
tua.

Collect.   ACDΓHJΛMPRSWYZ.
l. 30.   eundem *om.* J.

Epistle.   Inflection mark over v. 7 estis.

p. 37. l. 6.   This $\bar{V}$ is omitted in HRS.   In the printed edd. of V it is
marked 'ad uesperas.'   It is found as here in CDΓΛWY (MSS.).
l. 13 sq.   These two lines are omitted in CDHRSWY.   They are found,
however, in Γ, where they are the verses of the offertory, $\bar{V}$ being
inserted before *notus, et factus,* and *ibi ;* and *alleluia* after *eius* pri.
(l. 13), *sion* and *aeternis.*   Λ has the first two verses.   See above on
p. 3, l. 6.
l. 15.   This secret is, in this position, apparently peculiar to E among
the more modern uses.   See Dr. Legg's note in W p. 1472.
l. 16.   *in* is possibly an error for *et*, which appears in the closely
similar secret in G p. 88.   The mistake would be natural if the
exemplar were in an Irish hand.   See above on p. 11, l. 31.

Secret.   G(AΓJΛMPRSWY for Thursday after Easter.)
l. 16.   suscipe + q. AΓJΛMPRSWZ.   propitius *post* tuorum
(*exc.* G).   dne. propitius G.   famulorum] populorum (*exc.* GW).
in *om.* (*exc.* Y).
l. 18.   consequamur W.

Postcommon.   ACDΓHJΛMPRSWYZ.
For collations see notes on p. 36, l. 18 sqq.

DOMINICA IN ALBIS.

l. 26.   This title for Low Sunday appears in CE alone of the printed
editions of early missals which I have examined.   ΓP have *Dominica
post albas,* Λ *Dominica i post Pascha,* the remainder *Octaua (Octauae)
Paschae.*
The mass itself in S and other books is for the following week.   See
W p. 1474.

Collect.   ACΓHJΛMPRSWY.
l. 31.   festa paschalia CW.

p. 38. l. 5.   Read *induit* (or *indutus*), *se uirtute.*   The word *seruitute* does
not occur in the psalm referred to (xcii).
This grail is peculiar to E (see W 1475).   C also differs from all the
books collated by Dr. Legg in its second $\bar{V}$; but agrees with AHSWY
and others in its first $\bar{V}$.   The grail in Γ also differs from all
those given in Dr. Legg's note : *Et cibauit illos,* with *All.* un-
determined.
l. 9.   The gospel in ACHRSWYZ is longer, including vv. 19–23.
l. 13 sqq.   The second *alleluia* and all following it is omitted in
AHRSWY (*hiat* C).   This addition is however found in Γ (only the
catch-words *Angelus dni.* being given in this place, the full text in the

mass for the previous Monday), in which it stands as the verses of the offertory. The second *alleluia* (l. 13) is there omitted, ℣ is inserted before *euntes* and *ihesus*, and *alleluia* added at the end. The words *dixit* pri. and *sicut dixit* in l. 15 are omitted. They should have been marked with an obelus (†) in the text. Compare above on p. 3, l. 6.

Secret. AΓHJΛMPRSWYZ (G for Saturday after Easter).

l. 18. dne. q. Z.

l. 19. prestetesti] contulisti AS. perpetuae AWZ.

l. 22. Read *manum.* The other books add one (AΓᴿᵃ(M)) or two (Γᵃ(P)HRSWY) *alleluias* at the end of the common.

l. 26. Read *reparationis.*

Postcommon. AΓHJΛMPRSYZ (W for Sabb. iv temp. advent.)

l. 27. facias esse A.

VIGILIA ASCENSIONIS.

l. 29. Other books add two (RS) or three (AHWY) *alleluias* at the end of the office. Not so however Γᵃ.

Collect. AHΛMSWYZ (GL for the day).

l. 32. q.] nobis Z. d.] pater (*exc.* LΛ).

l. 33. quo + unigenitus filius tuus dns. nr. S + filius tuus H. sollennitatis hodiernę] uenturae solemnitatis S sollemnitatis uenturae HYZ sollemnitate hodierna Λ. auctor + caelum Z.

p. 39. l. 3. Read *cuique.*

Epistle. Inflection mark over *Title* apostolorum.

l. 5. This grail is peculiar to E (W p. 1476). It forms part of the grail in Σ 229 (199). C is wanting at this place.

l. 12. This is the offertory in HΛSY, where, however, all following *alleluia* (l. 14) is omitted. Γᵃ approaches closely to E, making *Cumque intuerentur* the verse of the offertory, with the words added at the end *qui et dixerunt Sic ueniet quemadmodum uidistis eum ascendentem in caelum alleluia.* These words may have been omitted in E (by accident or design), having appeared already, l. 13 sq. C is wanting here. Compare above on p. 3, l. 6.

Secret. AHJΛMSWYZ (G for the day).

l. 17. quam preuenimus *om.* AGJZ.

l. 18. + nunc *ante* ascensione (*exc.* ΛW) *ante* preuenimus Λ.

l. 19. sacrosanctis commerciis SW.

l. 20. per] qui tecum AHSY.

Postcommon. AHJΛMSWYZ (ΓP Wednesday after Easter 'ad s. andream' GL for day).

l. 26. dne. q. M. dne.] o. d. ΓP. per . . . sumpsimus *om.* ΓLP. sacramenta] sacra AGJM sancta HYZ.

l. 27. tendant Z + christianae ΓLP. nostrae *om.* ΓP.

l. 28. est] sit Γ. i. c. dns. nr.] *om.* M per GΓL. i. c. + filius tuus HPYZ.

ASCENSIO DOMINI.

l. 33. The other books (DIΓᴿHRSWY) have three *alleluias.*

l. 34. The psalm in AHRSWY &c. is *Cumque intuerentur.* DΛ agree with E, as do also Γᵃ, and some tenth and eleventh century continental MSS. (Frere, *Grad. Sarisbur.* Index), against the vast majority. C is wanting.

p. 40. **Collect.** ADΓHJΛMPRSWYZ.

l. 5. dnm.] eundem (*exc.* D).

l. 8. Read *ueniet.*
l. 9. Read *euntem.*
    Epistle. Inflection marks over *Title* apostolorum ; v. 7 potestate.
l. 11. Almost all English missals agree in having *Ascendit* for the first $\mathbb{V}$ as here. But in giving *Dns. in sina* for the second $\mathbb{V}$ E, agreeing with R, has little support from English books : so however A. W has it as the fourth $\mathbb{V}$. The second $\mathbb{V}$ in DHSY is *Ascendens*, to which D adds a third, *Non uos relinquam.* Γ^{a} has 'Ad Resp. *Ascendit deus in iubilo.* $\mathbb{V}$ *Psallite deo.* All. $\mathbb{V}$ *Ascendit*' ; with the alternative, All. $\mathbb{V}$. *Dns. in sina.*
l. 19 sqq. This addition to the offertory appears to be peculiar to E among the more modern missals, C being mutilated here. It is found as the verses of the offertory in Γ^{n}, $\mathbb{V}$ being inserted before *quoniam* (l. 19) and *subiecit* (l. 21).
    Secret. ADΓHJAMPRSWYZ.
    l. 24. ut + et HY.
    l. 25. aeternam perueniamus D. permaneamus† J.
    Communicantes. ADGΓHJLAMPRSWYZ.
    l. 27. i. c. *om.* (*exc.* HSWY). nr. i. c. HSWY. filius tuus. unitum GL.
    l. 28. nostrae fragilitatis A. fragilitatis . . substantiam] hominem nostrae substantiae GL. dexteram DHV.
    l. 29. collocauit + sed.
l. 32. DΓ^{n}HRSWY add *alleluia* at the end of the common.
l. 35. Read *sumenda*, in spite of the reading of L (see below).
    Postcommon. ADΓHJLAMPRSWY.
    l. 34. nobis *om.* A. q. *om.* LW. sumenda] celebrando L. suscepimus L.

VIGILIA PENTECOSTES.

p. 41. l. 2. The words *ad misam* without any further title seem to imply that the exemplar contained the lessons for the Vigil. Compare C ; where after the lessons we have the heading *ad missam* as here. But we note in J pp. 117, 221, similarly laconic titles which will not admit of an analogous explanation.
l. 7. Read *tuae.*
l. 8. Omit *et.*
    Collect. ACΓHJAMPRSWYZ.
    l. 8. illustratione] illuminatione A.
    Epistle. Inflection marks over *Title* apostolorum ; v. 2 dixitque ; v. 4 in *sec.* ; v. 8 suadens (?).
l. 15. *Laudate dnm.* is the tract in the other books, including C. That it is here included in the grail is probably a scribal error. Cf. above on p. 25, l. 21.
    Gospel. Inflection mark over v. 21 manifestabo (l. 19).
    Secret. AΓHJAPRYZ (CDMSW for the day).
    For collation see below on p. 43, l. 2, where we have *q. dne.* for *dne. q.*
    Communicantes. ACDGΓHJLAMPRSWYZ.
    l. 27. diem sacratissimum (*exc.* L). diem pent. sacratissimum L. celebrantes penticostes D. pentecosten GJ (*semel*) LAP *om.* Γ. celebrantes] praeuenientes (on the Vigil only) AGHAMPWY.
    l. 28. sanctus] *om.* W (*semel*) + adueniens Z. apostolis *om:* AΓ (*semel*). apostolis . . . apparuit] apostolos plebemque

credentium praesentia suae maiestatis impleuit GLAMW (not so on the day AMW). innumeris] in innumeris A in igneis HM (on day) SY in uariis J.

Hanc igitur. ACDGΓHJLAMPRSWY.

For collation see above on p. 36, l. 13.

p. 42.   **Postcommon.** AΓHJAPRYZ (CDMSW for the day G ad uesperas infra octauas).

l. 7. intima aspersione] ubertate G.

DOMINICA PENTECOSTES.

l. 11. The psalm in AR, the $\overline{V}$ in C, and the first of the two psalms in W is *Omnium est enim.* The psalm in Γᵃ is Ps. lxvii. HSW (second psalm) Y give Ps. lxvii. 2, D Ps. lxvii. 29b (*Confirma*), while E has both these verses. CA (*Exsurgat d.*) are ambiguous, but probably agree with H &c.

Collect. ACDΓHJAMPRSWYZ.

l. 14. sancti spiritus.

Epistle. Inflection marks over *Title* apostolorum ; v. 1 eodem ; v. 9 mesopotamiam.

l. 23. This verse seems peculiar to EA among later books (W p. 1480). DR have *Ueni sancte spiritus*, HY *Paracletus spiritus*, W both of these, while CS give *Spiritus sanctus procedens.* Γᵃ, as printed, has only one versus alleluiaticus, but manuscripts cited by the Benedictine editors have two, identical with those in E.

Gospel. Marks are found over some words in this gospel which do not occur elsewhere in the missal, viz : ⌣⌣ over v. 23 diligit *pri.*, ad eum ; v. 24 qui non, audistis ; v. 25 hec ; v. 26 pater ; v. 27 pacem *pri.* ; v. 28 ego, diligeritis : and ⌐ over v. 24 meus ; v. 27 uobis *pri.*

p. 42. l. 26. It is observed in the footnote that the rubricator has omitted to supply titles on f. 73, and the three following leaves. This may be accounted for as the result of pure accident. This explanation however is scarcely satisfactory in view of the fact that the leaves in question form a complete gathering. If it be rejected it may be suggested either (1) that the writing of this gathering was not completed when the remainder of the manuscript was rubricated, or (2) that it was intended to cancel these leaves and that in consequence of this the rubricator passed over them. In favour of (1) is the fact, the probability of which will presently appear, that the major part of the contents of this gathering was inserted as an after-thought : in favour of (2) certain mistakes in the prefaces which will be mentioned below. On either hypothesis the MS. was left unfinished—a confirmation of the supposition that it was used but little, if at all, at the altar. Indeed the fact that the titles of the prefaces were not added till a date considerably later than that of the writing of the missal, and then (in one case) erroneously, points to the same conclusion significantly enough.

l. 31 sqq. This occurs in Γᵃ as the verses of the offertory, with the exception of *Ibi beniamini usque excessu,* which is clearly an additional verse. $\overline{V}$ is inserted in Γᵃ before *in ecclesiis* (l. 32) and *regna* (l. 33). In CDHARSWY all after l. 30 is reiected. Compare above on p. 3, l. 6.

l. 32. Read *dno. deo.*

l. 33. Read *regna terrae.*

p. 43.   **Secret.** ACDΓHJAMPRSWYZ.

l. 2. dne. q. CDΓJAMPS.

l. 3. illustratione sancti spiritus M.

l. 4. This clause of the Canon is not exactly the same for the Vigil and the day in AMW &c., and even here we must at least substitute *diem* for *noctem.*

l. 9. CDΓᵐHRSWY add a second *alleluia.*

Postcommon. ACDΓHJAMPRSWYZ (G ad uesperas infra octauas). For collation see above on p. 42. l. 6, where (as at p. 87, l. 14) *sancti spiritus* is read for *spiritus sancti.*

l. 12. The absence of a special mass for Trinity Sunday is worthy of note. The festival was certainly observed in Ireland as early as A.D. 1305. It is mentioned in the letter of the nobles of Ireland to Pope John XXII, preserved in Bower's additions to the *Scotichronicon* of Fordun, as the occasion of a banquet to which in that year Peter Bermingham treacherously invited some of his kinsmen, whom he murdered after the repast (*J. de Fordun Scotichronicon . . . curâ* W. Goodall, Edinburgh, 1759, vol. ii. p. 263 ; King's *Primer of the History of the Holy Catholic Church in Ireland,* vol. iii. Dublin, 1851, p. 1127).

DE INVENTIONE S. CRUCIS.

l. 13. The position of this mass as a sort of appendix to the Temporale is peculiar. The simplest account of the matter appears to be the following. The mass was accidentally omitted from its proper place in the Sanctorale. Now in the gatherings assigned to the Sanctorale there were no vacant pages. It happened however that the small gathering of two sheets at the end of the Temporale was not completely filled. Two or three of its blank leaves were therefore utilized for the omitted mass. It will be observed that the grail, offertory and common all differ from those of C ; which suggests the possibility that this mass was not taken from the exemplar which supplied the remainder of the Sanctorale. See Introduction, p. xxix *sq.*

l. 15. Read *uita et.*

l. 21. Read *suffragia.*

Collect. ACGHJAMPRSWYZ.

l. 21. qui uiuis] per GJAZ.

Epistle. Inflection marks over v. 10 sapietis ; 11 quid (?) ; vi. 13 glorientur ; 14 est.

l. 26. There is much variety here among the different books. See W p. 1546 sq. (where, however, E is wrongly stated to be in exact agreement with C). EC agree against almost all others in having *Christus factus.* But they differ in the ℣, C being singular in giving *Nos autem,* while E with AR &c. has *Dulce lignum.* Γᵐ, as edited, has simply 'All. *Dicite in gentibus*' : but a ninth century MS. cited by the Benedictine editors has 'Resp. *Christus factus. ℣. Propter quod.* All. *Dicite in.* All. *Dns. reg. a ligno.*'

p. 44. l. 2. E here agrees with ΓᵐR against nearly all other authorities (W p. 1547) : C standing almost alone with *Ueniens uir splendidissimus.*

Secret. ACGHJAMPRSWYZ (Γ in tempore belli).

l. 6. sacrificium + nostrum HY. quod + tibi RSZ. placatus *om.* Γ.

l. 7. omnibus J. nos *om.* J. eruat RZ. bellorum. nequitiis J. per . . . insidias (l. 9) *om.* Γ.

l. 8. aerias potestates A. potestatis (*exc.* AΓRS) *om.* R. ereas et *om.* (*exc.* AS). aduersae CHJMPWYZ.

l. 9. nos *om.* AΓ. constituat (*exc.* W).

l. 11.   In the common E agrees with Iᵃ.\, but apparently differs from all other books (W p. 1547).   CHSY have *Per lignum serui,* W *redemptor mundi,* R *Per signum crucis.*

l. 14.   Read *recreati.*

Postcommon. ACGHJ.\MPRSWYZ.

l. 15.   nos *om. (exc.* AR) *post* maligno R.   ab + omni S.

l. 16.   arma GJAMPS.   filii tui armis iustitiae *om.* CW.

ante triumphare + pro salute mundi *(exc.* ACW) + mundum ACW.

l. 17.   per eundem] qui tecum MPS.

PRAEFATIONES.

l. 18.   On this collection of prefaces several remarks suggest themselves :—

(1) They are those sanctioned by the Council of Westminster, 1175 (see *Chronica Rogeri de Hoveden,* Rolls edn., ii. p. 76 ; Wilkins, *Concilia,* i. 478), except that there is no preface *de Apostolis,* and that the Trinity preface is omitted, being given elsewhere (p. 73, l. 16).

(2) They are not, as in CD, given with the masses to which they belong, but gathered together apart.   This is the more remarkable since the special clauses of the Canon *Communicantes,* &c., are always given in full with their masses, and not as in S, &c., with the prefaces.

(3) They are in an unusual position, not in immediate connexion with the Canon.

(4) The order in which they are arranged is incorrect, and would have been confusing if the book had been in actual use : those for Pentecost and Ascension being transposed, and the two belonging to the Sanctorale and Votive Masses being intruded into the middle of those connected with the great festivals of the Temporale.   The last four, in fact, appear to be in the reverse of their proper order.

(5) They were left without titles by the original scribe.

(6) In the masses to which they belong the cues are not (with one exception, p. 36, l. 7) given.   This seems unusual, though it has a parallel in the Lateran Missal edited by de Azevedo.

(7) In the one case in which the text, though ultimately derived from the same original, differs remarkably from that given in C (p. 45, l. 8), the more ancient English form is departed from in favour of that found in later books.   And, in like manner, in the Epiphany preface, E, agreeing with the majority, deserts C, while the latter has the support of AJ.

(8) In one case (p. 80, l. 22) a preface, identical with that which is similarly placed in D, is found in its proper position in the mass to which it belongs, no corresponding form appearing here.

From these facts certain inferences seem to follow with greater or less probability :—

1. That the book was not in use at the altar.   See (4), (5), (6), and compare (3).

2. That the collection of prefaces was added, subsequently to the writing of the main part of the missal, on the blank pages left in the final gathering of the Temporale.   This accounts for (3).   Compare above on p. 43, l. 13.

3. That in the exemplar from which E was copied the prefaces were

given with their respective 'masses, but were omitted by the scribe; the single one which remains·in situ, having escaped his vigilance. Cf. below on p. 73, l. 16. This would account for (6). It will also explain (4) and the omission mentioned under (1), if we suppose that the prefaces were not simply transcribed from a similar collection, but collected by the scribe himself from a book in which they were distributed through the masses on the older plan.

4. That the prefaces of the exemplar resembled those of D rather than those of C : see (8).

5. That the prefaces which replaced them were probably taken from a different and later source : see (7).

Christmas Preface. ACΓHJAMPRSWYZ.

l. 22. hunc + in AHRSWYZ. amorem AHRSWYZ.

Epiphany Preface. GΓHAMPRSWYZ (A Sunday after Epiphany J Octave and Sunday after Epiphany).

l. 27. quia] qui R.

l. 28. mortalitatis] carnis SW. apparuit . . . immortalitatis *om.*† G. in *om.* R. noua AΓJAPRYZ. immortalitatis + suae (*hiat* G).

l. 29. luce AΓJAPRYZ.

Lent Preface. ACDΓHJAMPRSWYZ.

p. 45. l. 2. It should be noted that the first words of this preface differ from the cue given at p. 36, l. 7, by the omission of 'et.' This confirms conclusion 5 above.

Easter Preface. ACDΓHAMPRSWYZ (GJ for Vigil).

l. 2. salutare + et ACHSWY. quidem + dne. PRZ. hac] hoc AY.

l. 3. cum] quo A.

l. 6. reparauit + propterea profusis paschalibus gaudiis &c. G.

l. 8. The rules for the use of this preface vary in the different books. In HRSWY it is assigned to all festivals and votive masses of our Lady except the Purification (and votive masses between Christmas and Purification, SW) ; in J to the votive masses and the Assumption ; in AΓAM to the Assumption only. C has it for the votive masses and the Purification, no preface being given in the masses for the Annunciation, Assumption and Nativity. E agrees with C, against the bulk of other authorities, in directing its use on the Purification ; but differs from it and most others in having a different preface for the votive masses : see p. 80, l. 22.

purificatione &c.] The word *ueneratione* is used on all occasions alike in ACΓJAM, *commemoratione* in R (except in the votive masses, for which it gives *veneratione*) Z. In other books the word is varied according to the day : H, however, giving *ueneratione* for the Annunciation as well as for the votive masses. In the important various readings recorded in the following collation at ll. 9, 10, it will be seen that E follows the later English group SWY against CΓJAM. It should here be remarked that the more modern form of the preface is found on the first page of C in an English hand (Warren's Introduction, p. 30), and that the older form has, in the votive mass in that MS. (Warren, p. 61), been corrected so as to bring it into conformity with the later. Thus we have proof that in at least one Irish monastery the later Preface of our Lady was introduced from England at a time perhaps not far distant from that at which E was written.

Preface of our Lady. ACΓHJAMRSWYZ.

l. 9. b. mariae semper uirguinis] sanctae dei genitricis uirginis mariae cuius assumptionis diem celebramus A sacrarum uirginum CΓJΛM. b. + et gloriosae SW. semper uirginis mariae SW.

l. 10. exultantibus animis *om.* RZ. laudare *(exc.* RZ) + benedicere *(exc.* H). praedicare + inter (intra C) quas intemerata dei genetrix uirgo maria ¹cuius assumptionis (purificationis C) diem celebramus¹ gloriosa effulsit CΓJΛM.

l. 12. huic *om.* ΓRZ. lumen aeternum mundo RZ. lumen + in C. aeternum lumen J *(semel).* effundit H.

l. 13. c. *om.* Z.

l. 16. Read *ut.*

Preface of the Holy Cross. ACHJΛRSWYZ.

l. 16. oriebatur] sortiebatur Λ.

l. 17. per lignum] in ligno *bis (exc.* AZ) in ligno . . . per lignum AZ. uicerat S.

Whitsunday Preface. ACΓHJLΛMPRSWYZ (G for Vigil).

l. 21. ascendit L.

l. 22. sanctum *om.* C. hodierna die *om.* GL.

l. 23. quapropter &c.] unde laetantes inter altaria tua dne. uirtutum hostias tibi laudis offerimus per c. dnm. quem laudant GL.

Ascension Preface. ADΓHΛMPRSWYZ (J for Vigil).

l. 30. cernentibus + eum D. eleuatus est D.

l. 31. suae *om.* H.

SANCTORALE.

IN DIE S. ANDREAE.

p. 46. l. 2. The title of this mass as it is written in the manuscript—*In die ad misam* —implies that in the exemplar it was preceded by a mass for the Vigil. We have thus an indication that E was copied from a fuller missal, from which only a selection of masses was made. Compare above on p. 33, l. 10; p. 41, l. 2, and below on p. 68, l. 14. This may perhaps help to explain the omission of the Invention of the Cross from the Sanctorale. See above on p. 43, l. 13.

l. 3. The full text of this office does not appear in the missal. And it seems not to occur in other books outside the Sanctorale and Common of Saints. St. Andrew's Day being the first festival in the former according to the arrangement of our Missal, it is not likely that it was intended that the remaining words should be supplied from another mass in it. The inference is plain that either E when perfect, or its exemplar, had a Common of Saints. And this conclusion is confirmed by the fact that *Mihi autem* is the office of One Apostle in both C and D.

Collect. AGΓHJLΛMPRSWY.

l. 5. supplices dne. M. supplices ΛM.

l. 6. b.] sanctus GL. apostolicus L.

l. 7. apud te sit pro nobis *(exc.* GLP) apud te pro nobis sit P sit pro nobis *(om.* apud te) G. pro nobis apud te *om.* L. inter- cessor] suffragator GL.

l. 12. The full text of the grail would doubtless have been found in the Common, though it does not occur therein in C or D. Cf. above on l. 3.

---

¹—¹ These words are omitted in the votive masses in J, and apparently also in C.

l. 13.   Γᵃ has here ℣ *Nimis honorati.*
l. 18.   I have not found this offertory here except in E and the MS. Missal of Kilcormic (T.C.D., MS. B. 3. 1).   ΓᵃARSWY have *Mihi autem,* H *In omnem terram.* C has no mass for this day.   It appears in the Common of One Apostle in CD.

   Secret.   AGΓHJAMPRSWY (D for One Confessor).
   l. 20.   andreae + apostoli tui AJR.
   l. 21.   precatio] praedicatio P.   sancta *om.* G.   ut + in R. exhibetur + eius RS.
l. 24.   The common is rare (see W p. 1613).   HRSWY have *Uenite post me* (no mass in C).   ΓᵃA agree with E.
l. 28.   Read *nobis.*

   Postcommon.   AΓHJLAMPRSWY.
   l. 27.   + apostoli tui *post* b.   L *post* andreae J.
   l. 28.   sanctis tuis HWY.   gloriam + ita.

CONVERSIO S. PAULI.

p. 47.   **Office.**   CHSW.
   l. 4.   celebrantes + in HS.   quo] quam C in quo HS qua W. presentem] per omnem C.
l. 6.   The psalm is identical with that in C, and is rarely found elsewhere.   HSW have *De illustratione,* RY *Dne. probasti,* A *De reliquo.* See W p. 1531.   Γᵃ makes no provision for this day.
l. 10.   Read *hodierna.*

   Collect.   ACHJAMPRSWYZ.
   l. 9.   apostoli] *om.* C + tui HAMPSWY.
   l. 10.   qui eius] cuius W.   hodierna die] hodie (*exc.* AR) *om.* R.
   l. 11.   conuersionem] conuersationem A.   coliimus] celebramus P.
l. 17.   In this grail C and E are in exact agreement and apparently differ more or less from all other books, among which there is here great variety: see W p. 1531.   Γᵃ does not provide for this mass. It was no doubt intended that the complete text should be sought in the Common.   It occurs in D for One Confessor: and so also, apparently, in the exemplar of C.
l. 22.   Read *uas.*
l. 26.   For *ad eum* ACRS have *ad deum*: HY *ad dnm.*   Probably the former of these is the reading intended here, the preposition being closely joined with its substantive and a single written for a double letter.
l. 32.   CE are in agreement in the offertory, with a few English missals: but almost all others (HARSWY &c.) have *Michi autem*: A *In omnem terram.*   See W p. 1532.   As to Γᵃ, see on l. 6.   This offertory does not appear in full in the missal.   But it is found in the Common of D for One Martyr and for the Vigil of One Confessor. Probably in E or its exemplar it was intended that the text should be sought for in the Common, now lost.   It does not occur in the Common of C.

   Secret.   ACHJAMPRSWYZ (L for SS. Peter and Paul).
   l. 34.   apostoli tui pauli] b. pauli apostoli tui S apostolorum tuorum L.   dne. precibus A.   + q. *post* precibus HSWY *post* dne. L (*semel*).
   l. 35.   tuo tibi grata A.   tuo grata AHJLMPRYZ.   sunt tuo W. fiant gratiora L.   eius *om.* (*exc.* A).
   l. 36.   supplicantis patrocinio W.   supplicantum L.
l. 38.   This common is given in full at p. 61, l. 19, and p. 69, l. 6, and occurs nowhere else.   But both these instances of its use must, both

in E and its exemplar, have followed the present. The words *ut supra* prove that it occurred in E or its exemplar either in a previous mass of the Sanctorale or in the Common of Saints. Now it is not found in HRSW or Y for any day between Nov. 30 and Jan. 25, and it does occur in DHRY in the Common of One Apostle (not so in CSW). We have here therefore an almost certain reference to the Common, and with it a proof that the Common preceded the Sanctorale.

p. 48.   **Postcommon.** CSW.
    l. 4.   semper facias S.
    l. 5.   gratulari] famulari W.

IN DIE SANCTAE BRIGIDAE.

l. 6.   This mass is identical (even in the scribe's blunder l. 17) with that for the same day in C, and the three collects are founded on English models. The following collects for St. Brigid's Day from the Breviary of Kilmoon (Trinity College, Dublin, MS. B. 1. 5) f. 117r a appear to be without exact English parallel. (1) *O. s. d. qui elegis infirma mundi ut forcia queque confundas: da nobis in festiuitate sancte brigide mentis et corporis ut ad te toto corde curramus et corpore tibi semper seruiamus. per.* The text is here evidently corrupt, a word having fallen out before *mentis.* This collect is found in a somewhat shorter form in the Gregorian Sacramentaries and the Roman missal for SS. Agnes and Euphemia, in the Common of One Virgin in D, and for S. Agnes in S, and one somewhat similar in the Leonine and Gelasian Sacramentaries for S. Cecilia. (2) *D. qui uirginitatis gloriam nascendo demonstrare uoluisti concede q. ut qui de brigide uirguinis tue† gloriosa celebramus sollempnia semper senciamus suffragia per.* Several others are printed by Colgan (*Trias Thaumaturga,* p. 599 sqq.).

    Collect. CHJW.
    l. 8.   terrarumque H.   et] atque H.
    l. 9.   deprecanti H.   tua (tuo J) succurre HJW.
    l. 10.   in *om.* J.   honorem W.   huius diei H.
    l. 11.   misericordia] gloria J.
l. 17.   Read *eius,* though *cuius* is supported by C.
    Secret. CHW.
    l. 16.   indefensam H.
    Postcommon. C (DJMY Common of One Virgin Martyr SW for St. Prisca AJ for St. Genouefa GP for St. Agnes).
    l. 20.   dne. q. S + et ADJMPSW.
    l. 21.   ueneranda] gloriosa P.

IN PURIFICATIONE S. MARIAE. BENEDICTIO CANDELARUM.

l. 23.   The service for the blessing of the candles in our missal very closely resembles one which was widely used in England—at least in the Province of Canterbury—in the twelfth century. It is here printed from four manuscript Pontificals, which, with one other belonging to the diocese of Winchester (Cambridge University Library Ee. 2. 3), form a group apart.[1] They are the following: a. Magdalen College, Oxford, MS. 226 (belonged to Hereford in fourteenth century); β. Cambridge University Library, MS. Ll. 2. 10 (Diocese of Ely); γ. Trinity College, Cambridge, MS. B. 11. 10. (Diocese of Ely); δ. Trinity College, Dublin, MS. B. 3. 6. (apparently

---

[1] Henderson's *York Pontifical* (Surtees Society, vol. 61), p. xxxi.

Diocese of Canterbury). The variants are given in the footnotes. I am indebted for the readings of the Cambridge manuscripts to Mr. Jenkinson and Dr. Sinker, and for those of the Magdalen College, Oxford, manuscript to Mr. Wilson.

BENEDICTIO CANDELARUM IN PURIFICATIONE SANCTAE MARIAE.

Benedic domine iesu christe hanc creaturam cerę . . .
alia oratio.[1] Domine sancte pater omnipotens ęterne deus qui omnia ex nichilo . . .
item benedictio. Omnipotens sempiterne deus qui hodierna die . . .
Tunc aspergantur[2] *aqua benedicta et thure adoleantur et illuminentur et interim canatur a clero antiphona.*
Lumen ad . . . israel.
Alia[3] *ant.* Nunc dimittis . . . salutare tuum.
Alia[3] *ant.* Puer iesus proficiebat . . . hominibus.[4]
Post hoc accipiant omnes singulos cereos de manu pontificis uel editui. et dicatur [5]*oratio haec.*[5]
Omnipotens sempiterne deus qui unigenitum tuum ante tempora . . .[6]
Hac oratione. expleta circumeant[7] *ęcclesiam cantando antiphonas ad diem pertinentes.*[8] *cum autem in*[9] *chorum redierint. dicta antiphona dicatur uersus.* Benedicta tu in mulieribus.
Kirrieleison .iii.[10] [11]Pater noster.[11] Post partum uirgo.
Oratio. Erudi[12] quesumus domine plebem . . .

The Winchester Pontifical referred to above has a service closely resembling this, but with rubrics which, though equivalent in meaning, are differently expressed. It adds a preface before the sprinkling and censing of the candles, *Uere dignum . . . fons et origo,* and a collect immediately after the distribution, while the antiphon *Puer iesus* is omitted. This service therefore was used very generally throughout the Province of Canterbury.

Now when we compare the service in the Canterbury, Hereford and Ely books with that of our missal we discover a marked resemblance between them. The rubrics, so far as they are common, are almost verbally identical; the same may be said of the prayers, as the collations given below prove; and there are in fact only the following instances of divergence :—

(1) The first rubric in E is absent from the English books, as are also the words *ante altare,* p. 50, l. 18.

(2) The two collects *Deus cuius unigenitus,* and *Immensam maiestatis* are also absent from the English Pontificals.

(3) For the antiphon *Puer iesus* (omitted at Winchester) there is substituted in E *Aue gratia plena.*

It is clear that the office in E is founded on that in use in England in the twelfth century. For the bearing of this fact on the history of our missal see the Introduction, p. xxii.

l. 24. This rubric is not found in the Pontificals of Canterbury, Ely and Hereford, and in directing that the candles shall be blessed at the altar of our Lady it contradicts the Winchester book, which

---

[1] *om.* γδ.
[2] *aspergatur* a, *n* being added after second *a* above the line in black ink.
[3] *om.* β.   [4] + euouœ γ.   [5]—[5] oratio a : haec oratio βγ.
[6] This collect and the preceding rubric are scored through with a dry point in *a.*
[7] + in† β.   [8] + ad processionem β.   [9] *om.* βγ.   [10] *om.* βγ.
[11]—[11] *oratio dominica* et ne nos inducas aβγ.   [12] Exaudi β (*e* erudi *ut uid.*).

enjoins, 'fiat processio ad altare crucifixi in quo candelae sunt bene-dicende.' Indeed it bears clear marks of being a later addition in its inconsistency with another rubric of our service, p. 51, l. 12, where the words 'cum in chorum redierint' plainly imply that the blessing had taken place at the High Altar. An almost verbally identical rubric is found in this place in C and in a Pontifical of Besançon cited by Martène, *De Antiquis Ecclesiae Ritibus*, IV. xv. 5. (*Ordo* ii.) tom. iii. col. 129, and assigned by him to the first half of the twelfth century. The service to which it is prefixed in the latter has no very close resemblance to that of our missal.

fratres] This word appears at first sight to imply that the service was intended for monastic use : and if so it is the only direct indica-tion in the manuscript that E is a monastic missal. But the inference is uncertain, for the word is also found in the Besançon Pontifical just mentioned. In this book the rubric seems to have had primary reference to collegiate churches—such as those of St. Stephen and St. John, which in the twelfth century were rival claimants for the possession of the Chair of the Archbishop of Besançon[1]—presided over by Dean and Canons. In this case the words *frater* might be used of any member of the corporation, clerical or lay : see Du Cange s.v.

a capitulo] That is, from the service at which the martyrologium was read in the Chapter House, and which usually followed Prime. See Procter and Dewick's *The Martiloge in Englysshe* (H.B.S. vol. iii.) pp. v. xxxii–xxxv. ; Maskell's *Monumenta Ritualia*, 2nd ed., 1882, vol. i. pp. clxx–clxxiv. ; Todd's *Obits and Martyrology of Christ Church* (Irish Archæological Society) pp. lxxxviii–xcii. The implied use of this service, and indeed the mere mention of the 'capitulum,' seems to indicate a monastic or Cathedral church. If in the Church for the use of which our missal was intended the service in capitulo followed Prime, the Blessing of the Candles must have taken place at a somewhat unusual time. Most commonly (HRW) it was after Tierce, at Salisbury in earlier centuries after Tierce (*Consuetudinary*, ed. Frere, 1898, p. 131 sq.), at a later date after Sext (S) at Evesham, 'post vi^{am} uel iii^{am}.' But one of Martène's ordines (*De Ant. Eccl. Rit.* IV. xv. *Ordo* vi. t. iii. col. 134), directs that the candles are to be blessed after Prime. On the other hand the service in capitulo was occasionally held after Tierce (Procter and Dewick, p. xxxii. ; Martène, *De Mon. Rit.* I. v. 2. (col. 52)).

ter] This is no doubt correct, as it is found in the Pontifical of Besançon : C has *tunc*.

l. 26. ueniendum] Before this word C and the Besançon MS. insert *et sic*.

ante altare sancte mariç] The practice here enjoined, of blessing he candles at the altar of St. Mary rather than at the high altar, seems to show that this service assumed the form which it has in our missal at a date considerably earlier than that of the manuscript in which it is preserved. It was in vogue about A.D. 1100—the date according to Martène of the Pontifical mentioned in the preceding notes—at Besançon : and apparently also at Tours, for the Besançon Pontifical was 'ad usum ecclesiae Turonensis accommodatum' (Martène, *De Ant. Eccl. Rit.* t. i. Syllabus). It has place also in a service book of the Church of Châlons sur Saone, to which Martène assigns no date (*ib.* IV. xv. *Ordo* vii. t. iii. col. 135). Martène mentions.

---

[1] *Gallia Christiana*, vol. xv., 1860, Instrumenta, cols. 19, 21.

it as an ancient custom of the Benedictines, *De Ant. Monachorum Rit.* (III. vii. 16, col. 300): 'In *antiquioribus* Ordinis nostri monasteriis in alio oratorio extra propriam ecclesiam, aut saltem in aliquo sacello, quo processionaliter pergebatur, cerei consecrabantur. . . . Einsid-lenses, aliique Germanorum ↓monachi, Cluniacenses, Corbeienses, Divionenses, uti et Tullenses S. Apri, in oratorio B. Mariae.' In England we have possibly an example of the same practice at the beginning of the eleventh century in J (see below, note on p. 50, l. 19), which is a Benedictine book : it certainly survived in the Benedictine monastery at Evesham as late as the beginning of the fourteenth century (H. A. Wilson, *Officium Ecclesiasticum Abbatum secundum usum Eveshamensis Monasterii.* Henry Bradshaw Society, vol. vi., p. xv., col. 57, p. 190 sq.). Mr. Wilson conjectures that it may have been introduced there towards the end of the twelfth century from Cluni.

l. 27. diacono] C and the Besançon Pontifical read *decano* : and this must give the correct sense. But we cannot be certain that *diacono* is a scribe's error ; for in the Terrier of Down and Connor (A.D. 1615) we find the entry, 'Ecclesia Parochialis of Ballee. The Prior of Down had it always, and he was *Deacon*, as the Bishop was Abbot.'[1] Com-pare also the variation between the Customary and Consuetudinary of Sarum, Frere's edition (1898), p. 7.

l. 30. In the collations of this and the following collects it has not been thought necessary to note the varying positions of the crosses in the different books.

l. 32. Read *repellendas*.

l. 37. Read *inquietare*.

 First Collect. CSZ αβγδ.

 l. 30. cerei S. supplicationibus nostris z.

 l. 31. crucis + tuẹ δ.

 l. 32. ut] et z.

 l. 33. generi] usui CS. sanctae *om.* z.

 l. 34. in *om.* CS.

 l. 35. apposita S.

 l. 37. inquietare + uel illudere z.

 l. 38. seruientibus dno. z + proinde supplices te &c. z. qui cum &c.] benedico te cera in nomine &c. z.

p. 49. l. 6. Read *sanitatem*.

 l. 9. Read *deuote*.

 Second Collect. CRSZ αβγδ.

 l. 2. dne. . . . deus] ⊕ . . . exorantes clementer exaudire dignare z.

 l. 3. per opera] operâ z.

 l. 4. cereorum S *om.* z. uenire RSZ.

 l. 7. animarum + praeparatas S.

 l. 8. sanctissimi] sancti S. tui sanctissimi nominis RZ. sanctẹ] b. R.

 l. 9. semper uirginis] genetricis filii tui z. festa hodie deuote celebramus z. et] ac z.

 l. 10. tuorum *om.* z.

 l. 11. et] ut SZ. honorifice *sup. ras.* δ.

 l. 12. portare desiderat RS portant z. laudando exultare] cantando laudare (-dant z) RZ.

 l. 13. uocem z. et propitius] propitiusque z.

---

[1] Quoted by Reeves, *Antiquities of Down, Connor and Dromore*, p. 42.

l. 14. sis *om.*† β. ad te clamantibus z.

l. 15. tecum + et cum spiritu sancto s. regnat in unitate] gloriatur d. per omnia &c. s.

Third Collect. RSZ αβγδ (W after the sprinkling).

l. 18. tuum + in R.

l. 19. presentasti] praesentari uoluisti sw. tuam supplices deprecamur clementiam] te suppliciter deprecamur z. ut + omnes z. has candelas quas] hos cereos (+ tuos z) quos swz.

l. 20. tui famuli] famuli tui sδ fideles tui z. in tui nominis] omni z. magnificenciam w.

l. 21. accensos swz.

l. 22. sanctificare + atque lumine supernae benedictionis accendere. eas] eos sz nos w.

l. 23. offerendo *om.* z. tue *om.* w. dulcissimae tuae s. caritatis] claritatis sz ueritatis w.

l. 24. sanctae z.

l. 28. Read *a parentibus.* This seems almost certainly correct, though *apparentibus* is not absolutely impossible, and appears in H, the only other missal in which I have found this prayer. Compare the similar collect (J.\R, Hittorp, p. 23) : 'Dne. i. c. qui hodierna die in nostrae (nostra J) carnis (*om.*J) substantia inter homines apparens *a parentibus* in templo es praesentatus,' &c.

Fourth Collect H.

l. 30. quoadusque.

l. 31. meruit c. uidere.

l. 33. templo caelesti. perfrui uisione.

p. 50.

l. 1. ea gestauerint] ex eis acceperint + tutelam.

l. 2. medelam *om.* + atque eorum habitacula &c. *ante* per.

l. 6. Read *substantia.*

l. 7. Read *beati.*

l. 11. Read *illuminati.*

l. 12. Read *sanctam.*

Fifth Collect. (W after sprinkling).

l. 4. immense.

l. 7. representari.

l. 10. sinceritate] securitate.

l. 11. illuminati] exubera.

l. 12. exhibere ualeamus placentem.

l. 13. Read *ture.*

l. 13-p. 51, l. 11. This part of the office may be compared with that of the Ordo Romanus of Hittorp (p. 23), which throughout bears no little resemblance to ours. ' *Tunc adspergantur aqua benedicta, et thure adoleantur et illuminentur et interim canatur a clero antiphona* Hodie beata virgo Maria puerum Iesum. *Post haec accipiunt omnes singulos cereos de manu pontificis vel editui et dicit sacerdos hanc orationem.* O. s. d. qui unigenitum . . . *Oratione hac expleta . . . . clerus circuit ecclesiam et inchoat schola primam Antiphonam* Ave gratia . . *Alia.* Adorna thalamum . . *Alia.* Responsum accepit.'

l. 16. *Alia ant.*] We might perhaps rather have expected *Ps.*, as in the majority of books in which *Nunc dimittis* occurs in this office. But the four Pontificals the text of which is given above are unanimous with regard to the title *antiphona :* and with them agrees the Book of Evesham (col. 60).

l. 18. *Ante altare*] This rubrical direction seems peculiar to E.

It appears to relate to the following anthem, which in most other books, as in Hittorp, is the first of the *processional* antiphons. The words *ante altare* are probably a warning, which would be needed by persons accustomed to the use of the office from which ours is revised, that *Aue gratia* was to be sung, not during the procession, but at the altar where the candles had been blessed, before the procession began.

l. 19. *Aue gratia*, as just observed, is the first processional anthem in most books. Some give a more precise direction. Thus in Λ (the eleventh century portion) it is to be sung 'ad stationem sancte marie' : in the Sydney Sussex MS. of Y 'in egressu de choro usque ad altare beatae mariae,' the antiphon *Adorna thalamum* following 'in statione ante altare beatae mariae.' This gives the reason for the substitution of *Aue gratia* for *Puer iesus* in E. The benediction took place, not as in the English Pontificals at the High Altar, but at the Lady Altar. If therefore this anthem was to be used in the customary way it must be said before, not after, the procession set out : *ante altare*, not *ad processionem*. It may be remarked that a similar transposition of *Aue gratia* takes place in J. It is not impossible that this missal also supposes the benediction to take place at the altar of Saint Mary.

l. 21.   Read *ulnas*.

l. 23.   Read *accipiant*.

l. 24.   editui] So in Hittorp's Ordo quoted above. In J (p. 159) the candles are distributed by the edituus. And similarly in the Bodleian MS. Rawl. c. 425 (W col. 624), 'distribuantur cerei *per secretarium*' ; and in the Book of Evesham (col. 60), 'Secretarii uero distribuant singulis fratribus singulos cereos.' This was in fact the usual rule among the Benedictines : see Martène, *De Ant. Mon. Rit.* III. vii. 21 (col. 303).

Sixth Collect.   αβγδ (S after the sprinkling).

l. 28.   repellendas s.

l. 32.   dnm.] eundem.

l. 33.   The superfluous *in* is found also in β.

l. 34.   antiphonas] The abbreviation is unusual : *anthãs.*

The words *ad processionem* are absent from the English Pontificals (except β), from which circumstance we may infer that they are not to be connected with *pertinentes*. Though written by our scribe continuously with what precedes they were probably in his exemplar the heading of the antiphons which follow. Their absence from the Pontificals, in which the text of these antiphons is not given, is thus easily accounted for.

p. 51. ll. 1–11.   No doubt the 'antiphonae ad diem pertinentes' of the Pontificals were the two here given, preceded by *Aue gratia.*

l. 4.   non uero] Read *nouo* : written doubtless in the exemplar *noũ*, which the scribe mistook for *nõ ũ.*

l. 9.   Read *templum.*

l. 15.   'Collecta ad s. adrianum' in ΓΛP ; 'ad collectam' in M.

Seventh Collect.   ΓΓΛΜΡΥΖ αβγδ (R before the procession).

l. 16.   'erudi] èxaudi CRYZ β *sec. m.*   q. + o. P.

l. 17.   intercedente . . . maria *om.* (*exc.* αβγδ).

l. 18.   semperque βγδ. lucem R.

PURIFICATIO S. MARIAE AD MISSAM.

l. 20.   non] See on p. 9, l. 15.

l. 26.   Read *maiestatem.*

Collect. ACΓHJΛMPRSWYZ.

l. 26. suppliciter J.

l. 27. tuus filius P. filius *om.* CW. nostrae carnis cum P.

l. 28. nostra J. in templo est.

l. 29. faciat Z. tibi purificatis HY. dnm.] eundem.

p. 52. l. 2 sq. These two lines, which probably in the exemplar were a distinct ℣, are omitted in CΓᵃHΛRSWY, and are apparently peculiar to E (see W p. 1534).

l. 4 sq. This ℣ is found in C and a few English missals. ΓᵃHSWY have *Adorabo ad templum,* Λ *Aue maria,* R *Senex puerum,* followed by ℣ *Post partum* (see l. 9).

l. 7. This is the tract in CHY and other English missals : but RSW have *Nunc dimittis,* and Γᵃ *Diffusa est gratia.*

l. 21. Read *claritatis.*

Secret. CSW.

l. 19. dne.] o d. s. hodierna + die s.

l. 20. consecrantur + sic.

l. 27. Read *auctorem.*

Postcommon. C (S de S. Maria Christmas to Candlemas).

l. 26. da + q. s. nobis *om.* S. eius + nos S.

praesenti festiuitate] continua intercessione S.

l. 28. per] dnm. nostrum &c. (*om.* per) S.

CATHEDRA S. PETRI.

l. 29. marta] The Irish name for the month of March.

This mass is identical with that assigned in G to 29th June, under the title ' In natali S. Petri proprie.'

l. 30 sq. This office and psalm do not appear in full in the missal. They are found, however, in the Mass for One Confessor in CD, as in other books ; another indication that E originally possessed a Common of Saints.

Collect. AGHJΛMPRSΣWYZ (Γ for St. Peter ' ad uesperos ').

l. 33. b. *om.* Γ. apostolo tuo (*om.* ΓJ) petro GΓJMP.

l. 34. animas *om.* ΓP.

l. 35. concede . . . auxilio] suscipe propitius preces nostras et intercessione eius q. dne. auxilium ut Σ. concede + propitius SW.

l. 36. qui uiuis] per AGΓJΛΣ.

p. 53. l. 6. Almost all other books agree as to the grail with E, against Γᵃ.

l. 10. The title *Tractus* is here supplied on the authority of AHRSWY. But it may be remarked that Γᵃ has for the grail *Jurauit. Tu es* &c. (ll. 11-16), and gives no tract.

l. 14. Read *ligaueris.*

l. 18. require] This gospel is given in full p. 60, l. 4, and it is conceivable that the reference which the scribe has unfortunately omitted was to that place. But the passage occurs in S in the Mass of One Apostle : it seems therefore more probable that the text was to be taken from the Common of Saints, which, as we have already seen, preceded the Sanctorale, though it does not occur in the Common of either C or D.

l. 20. The offertory in AΛSW is *Constitues eos,* in ΓᵃY *Ueritas mea.* HR agree with E. C is without the mass.

Secret. AGHJΛMPRSWYZ (Γ for St. Paul L for SS. Peter and Paul ?).

l. 24. q. dne. preces (*exc.* ΛW) dne. q. preces W. q. dne. (*ante* beati) Λ. munera] hostias (*exc.* SW).

l. 25. petri apostoli tui (*om.* GAMP) (*exc.* ΓLW).   b. apostoli tui petri] apostolica ΓL.   illius] illorum ΓL.
l. 26. prosit] proficiat J.

Postcommon. AGHJAMPRSWYZ.

l. 30. nos *om.* HY.   + q. *post* nos AW *post* dne. HSY.
oblatum munus Z.   oblatum] sumptum S.   in *om.* HY.
l. 31. mirabilem te P.
l. 32. tuae sumamus (susenciamus† W) (*exc.* P).   indulgentiae tuae P.

ANNUNCIATIO S. MARIAE.

l. 34. Γᵃʀ have as office and psalm *Vultum, Eructauit*; almost all other books agreeing with E in the office, and most of them in the psalm.
l. 35. *et iustitia . . . eum* would seem to be the psalm, as in most books; though in both W and E it is written as if it were part of the office.

p. 54.   **Collect.** ACHJRSWYZ (D de S. Maria ΓAMP collect before mass).

l. 2. de *om.* ΓJA in MP.   mariae *om.* ΓA.
l. 3. annuntiante M.   uoluisti] uouisti† R.
l. 4. dei genetricem RSW.

l. 9. Read *gradale*.
l. 10 sqq. Apparently (as in CHSWV, &c.), ll. 14-21 are the tract, though written here as if they formed part of the grail. If so the grail is ll. 10-13; which do duty as the grail also in C, and apparently not elsewhere (see W p. 1540). Γᵃʀʀ have *Diffusa est*.
l. 12. Read *occursus*.
l. 14 sqq. This is the tract also in CH. In SW ll. 16–18 are omitted, and in V l. 16. Γᵃ has no tract.
l. 25. Read *offerenda*.

Secret. ACΓHJARSWYZ (MP as postc. D missa in commemoratione incarnationis &c.).

l. 29. q. *om.* ΓAMP.   dne q. J.
l. 30. uerum *om.* D.   hominem + firmiter S.
l. 31. eius] eiusdem DRS.   resurrectionis] incarnationis S incarnationis . . . et aduentus spiritus sancti D.
l. 32. mereamur peruenire (*exc.* C).   laetitiam *om.*† C.   per] qui tecum HY.

p. 55.   **Postcommon.** ACΓHJARSWYZ (D de S. Maria MP among 'aliae orationes' at the end of the mass).

l. 2. q. *om.* AΓJAPR.
l. 3. tui *om.* W.
l. 4. crucem + perque mariam uirginem dei genitricem D.
l. 5. per dnm.] per eundem (*exc.* M) qui tecum &c. M.

IN DIE S. PATRICII.

l. 6. The mass for St. Patrick's Day should have preceded the last. Possibly its misplacement may be accounted for by its being taken from a different source from the remainder of the missal. It is found, with one or two slight variations in the collect, in C. And the Missal of Kilcormic (Trinity College, Dublin, MS. B. 3. 1), which was written in 1458 for the Carmelite Priory of Kilcormic (now Frankford, in King's County), by Dermot O'Flanagan, a brother of the Priory of Loughrea, County Galway, gives a recension of it which may be printed here.

Officium. Gaudeamus omnes.

Oratio.

Omnipotens sempiterne deus qui beatum patricium ybernensium elegisti apostolum tuum presta quesumus : ut cuius doctrina fidem sumpsimus eius intercessione in bonis actibus roboremur per.
Epistola. Ecce sacerdos.
Gradale. Domine preuenisti. *V.* Uitam petiit. Alleluia *V.* Iustus germinabit.[1] *vel Tractus.* Beatus uir qui.
Sequencia. Dei per patricium. . . .
Euangelium. Uigilate quia nescitis.
Off. Ueritas mea.

Secreta.

Hostias tibi domine in honore quesumus sancti patricii offerimus deuote accipias : ut nos a penali gehenna iudicii liberemur per.
Communio. Fidelis seruus.

Post communionem.

Omnipotentem deum uniuersitatis auctorem deprecamur ut sumptum sacrificium per beatum patricium fiat nobis remedium sempiternum per.

l. 10. scotorum] This was the name applied to the Irish, and to them alone, for many centuries. The cognate term ' Scotia' was first used of that portion of the modern Scotland which is bounded on the south by the rivers Forth and Clyde, early in the eleventh century, the word 'Scoti' having been applied to its inhabitants somewhat earlier (Skene, *Celtic Scotland*, i. 398). But long after that date the island now known as Ireland continued to be called indifferently 'Hibernia' and 'Scotia.' See the letter from Stephen White to Colgan, published in the *Proceedings of the Royal Irish Academy*, vol. viii. p. 34 ; Ussher, *Works*, vol. vi. p. 283 sq. An early use of Scotia applied to North Britain will be found above, p. xxii note 1 ; and on the other hand an interesting example of the late period to which the name Scotland continued to be used for Ireland may be seen in the *Martiloge* of Richard Whytford, printed in 1526, where under Feb. 1 and Mar. 17 we have ' in Scotlonde the feest of saynt Brigide,' 'in scotlonde the feest of saynt Patrike bysshop and confessour that fyrst preched there Christes fayth' (Procter and Dewick's edition, H.B.S. vol. iii. pp. 19, 42).
l. 11. ut hibernenses . . . efficeret] It is difficult to believe that we have this collect in its original form. It seems unlikely that the people to whom St. Patrick preached should be described in two successive clauses by the different names of ' Scoti' and 'Hibernenses gentes.' Moreover the words between *elegisti* and *tribue* are a mere amplification of *scotorum apostolum.* We may suspect that they are a later explanatory addition, made after the word ' Scoti' had come to be used for the inhabitants of North Britain as well as for those of Ireland : that is about the eleventh or twelfth century. Compare the words of a scribe employed by Marianus Scotus, penned (for the benefit of foreign readers) on June 28, 1072 : 'Et scripsi hunc librum pro caritate tibi et Scotis omnibus *id est Hibernensibus*, quia sum ipse Hibernensis' (MacCarthy, *The Codex Palatino-Vaticanus*

[1] MS. g'.

No. 830. R. I. A. Todd Lecture Series, 1892, p. 15).[1] Our suspicion is confirmed when we turn to the Breviary of Kilmoon (Trinity College, Dublin, MS. B. I. 5), which, at f. 122 r a, has the following collect for St. Patrick's Day :

Deus qui beatum patricium hybernie apostolum tua prouidencia elegisti tribue nobis quesumus. eius intercessionibus ut ad ea quae recta sunt quam tocius festinemus per.

This omits, it will be seen, the suspected clause, and proclaims its comparatively late date only by the substitution of *hybernie* for *scotorum.* It is the link which connects the collect of our book in its original form with the more divergent recension in the Kilcormic missal printed above. Yet another example of the collect with the word *scotorum* and the explanatory insertion is given by Colgan (*Trias Thaumaturga*, p. 193) from an ancient Breviary of Armagh. It varies from our text as follows :

l. 9. sanctum] beatum.
l. 11. ad lumen . . . reduceret et *om.*
l. 12. lauacra. dei excelsi efficeres.
l. 13. piis *om.* ut *post* quesumus.

It may be added that the inserted clause recalls, though perhaps not very vividly, various phrases in Jocelin's *Life of St. Patrick*, and may with some likelihood be referred to him as its author. The contrast between the darkness of heathen error and the light of Christianity is very frequent. See e.g. §§ 51, 55, 62, 153; and note especially § 40 'Populus ergo gentium illarum qui sedebat in tenebris jam videns lumen magnum acclamando gratiarum actiones summae luci . . . Patriciumque praeconem perennis lucis magnificabat' : § 41 'ad discernendam lucem verae fidei a tenebris idololatriae' : § 48 'Ipse vero S. Patricium sicut angelum pacis et lucis . . suscepit . . . credidit et per lauacrum regenerationis . . . christo incorporari meruit : § 63 'Ne, tali lucerna extincta, populus Hiberniae iterum in tenebris ambularet.' All these expressions are of course reminiscences of Isai. ix. 1, which usually served as the text of Irish homilies on St. Patrick. But similar phrases are found also in the *Vita Kentegerni*, where there is perhaps less opportunity for using them, and where they cannot have been due to any such obvious suggestion. Thus cap. i (I quote from Forbes' edition, *Historians of Scotland*, vol. v. p. 162) 'Quomodo candor lucis eterne, sol iustitie, . . . radiis sue cognitionis et dilectionis mundum illuminauerit . . . suos inducens in omnem plenitudinem ueritatis efficatius', &c. Cap. iv (p. 169) 'Lauacro regenerationis et renouationis illos perfudit.' Cap. 24 (p. 203) 'Sedenti namque in tenebris exterioribus uerus lucifer cordi illius illuxit ; et lux exterior ad tempus adempta de tenebrosis, et umbra mortis, illum educens in lucem ueritatis induxit. Interius igitur illustratus . . . ut . . . fontem salutis ipsum ablueret, cepit deuote deprecari,' and the remainder of the chapter. See also chapters ix (p. 178), xxvii (p. 208), xxxii (p. 218),

---

[1] St. Bernard's *Vita S. Malachiae* (written A.D. 1149) supplies an instructive illustration of the ambiguity of 'Scotia' and its cognates nearly a century later. Ireland is usually named 'Hibernia' (cf. Ep. 374); once 'ulterior Scotia' (§ 72) : 'Scotia' is regularly used for North Britain, and the 'Scoti' are its inhabitants, being once contrasted with the 'Hiberni' (§ 8). But once, in the mouth of an Irishman, 'Scoti' is used in its older meaning (§ 61), while the meaning which Bernard attached to the phrase 'opus Scoticum' (§ 14), probably copied from the notes of his Irish correspondent Congan, is uncertain.

xxxiv (p. 219), xxxv (p. 222), xxxix (p. 229). Jocelin uses ' Scoti ' for
the inhabitants of modern Scotland. Thus, *Vita Kent.* cap. xxvii
(p. 209), St. Kentigern preaches to the Picts and Scots, while a few
pages later we are told (cap. xxix. p. 213) that Rederech was baptized
by the disciples of St. Patrick ' in Hibernia.'

Another collect for St. Patrick's Day is found in two inedited Irish
Breviaries, which stand side by side in the library of Trinity College,
Dublin (B. 1. 3, 4), and which belonged respectively to the Church of
Clondalkin and to that of St. John the Evangelist, Dublin. It runs thus :
*Deus qui beatum patricium hybernie apostolum signis multimodis decor-
atum ad celestem gloriam transtulisti presta quesumus ut eius meritis
et precibus adiuti eterne beatitudinis premia consequamur per.* This
collect reappears in an office of St. Patrick printed at Paris in 1622
(Colgan, *Trias Thaumaturga*, p. 189), and, with two slight variations
in the text, in another printed at Rheims in 1612 (*ib.* p. 196, *recte* 195).
Besides these two main groups of collects for St. Patrick's Day we
find three others having nothing in common with any of those here
printed, or with each other, which Colgan (*ib.* p. 194 sqq.) reprinted from offices published respectively at Venice in 1522 (Roman
Breviary), at Brussels in 1622, and at Rome in 1635.

     Collect. C.

     l. 11. uerum dei lumen.

     l. 14. sunt *om.*

l. 17. Mr. Warren has aptly cited[1] in illustration of the closing words
of the secret the Irish notion of the function assigned to St. Patrick
in the Day of Judgement. This traditional belief seems to assume
two forms. According to one the saint was to be the judge of the
Irish. Thus to the words of St. Sechnall's hymn,[2] 'cum apostolis
regnabit sanctus super Israel,' the glossator appends the note, ''i'
regnabit Patricius super Scotos in die iudicii,' quoting Matt. xix.
28, in which the apostles are described as sitting on thrones *judging*
the tribes of Israel. So, according to Muirchu Maccu Mactheni's
notes in the Book of Armagh,[3] it was granted to St. Patrick 'ut
Hibernenses omnes in die iudicii a te iudicentur,' language which is
echoed by the homilists.[4] The other form of the tradition makes
Patrick the defender of the Irish on Doomsday. Thus the Prayer of
Ninine :[5]

    We pray to Patrick, chief apostle,
       who hath saved us to Doom's day
    From judgement by the malevolence
       of dark demons—

the gloss on which supplies a very close parallel to our secret : ' i.e.
who will save us, i.e. who will effect our deliverance.' This probably
gives the meaning of Fiacc's ' Around thee in the Day of the Judgement men of Ireland will go to Doom '[6] : and to this latter form of the
belief about St. Patrick, rather than to the former, allusion appears to
be made in the text. The *Second Vision of Adamnan*[7] combines both

[1] *Liturgy and Ritual*, p. 271, C p. 150.
[2] *Liber Hymnorum* (ed. Bernard and Atkinson), i. 12.
[3] Stokes, *Tripartite Life*, pp. 296.
[4] *Trip. Life* (ed. Stokes), pp. 30, 258, 260, 477, 486.
[5] *Liber Hymnorum*, ii. 36, 187.
[6] *Liber Hymnorum*, ii. 33, 34 (ll. 36, 52).
[7] *Revue Celtique*, xii. 425.

views of the Saint's office : ' It is Patrick who will be their judge and their advocate on Doomsday.'

The variant of the Kilcormic Missal—*penali gehenna* for *timore*—is curious.

Secret. C.

l. 19. The unusual form of the postcommon, in which God is not directly addressed, will be noticed. Compare the metrical collect following the hymn *Alto et ineffabili* in the Irish *Liber Hymnorum* (i. 157).

Postcommon. C.

MISSA IN LETANIA MAIORE.

l. 22. From its position in the missal it appears that this mass was intended to be used on St. Mark's Day : and for this day it is appointed in ΓΡΖ. But, on the other hand, the majority of later books assign it to one or more of the Rogation Days. Thus in AHΛMSWY it is the mass for Rogation Monday ; in W, and in HY with a change of lessons, also for Rogation Tuesday. In the modern Roman missal the same mass serves for all three Rogation Days and for St. Mark's Day, while in R it comes between the mass for the 5th Sunday after Easter and that for the Vigil of Ascension with the heading *In Letaniis maioribus*.[1] And with this usage the *title* in E agrees. It seems clear that in the exemplar it was a Rogation Day mass, and that it was transferred to its present place, without altering the title, in accordance with the principle expressed in the rubric in R : 'Officium misse de letaniis ante vigiliam ascensionis positum : fiat eo tempore quo fit in terris in quibus fratres morantur.' The converse transposition has been made in J, where it appears as the mass for the Monday before Ascension Day, but with the title *vii. Kal. Mai. Laetania Maiore.* Thus the position in the missal, rather than the title, in both E and J, indicates the usage. Compare above on p. 12, l. 1.

Collect. ΑΓΗJΛMPRSWYZ.

l. 29. contra + aduersa.

Epistle. Inflection mark over *Title* iacobi.

p. 56. l. 7. adexteram] For *ad dexteram*.
saluum] Read *saluam*.

l. 10. Read *prauitatis*.

Secret. ΑΓΗJΛPRSWYZ (GM Sabb. in ieiunio mensis septimi).

l. 10. munera] hostia GM. dne. q GJMPSW. prauitatis] iniquitatis GM.

---

[1] Mr. Warren supposes that the nine excised leaves of C, intervening between the present f. 117 and f. ·118, contained, *inter alia*, masses for the Rogation Days. Though this conjecture is probably correct, it cannot be regarded as certain ; for, besides the nine here referred to, six leaves have been removed from the MS. by excision, and in each of these cases the excision took place at an early stage of the scribe's work and has left no lacuna. It is quite possible that this may be true also of some of the nine excised after f. 117. The following indication of the arrangement of the gatherings of C, which I owe to the kindness of Mr. Plummer, the Librarian of Corpus Christi College, Oxford, will supplement what Mr. Warren has written (C p. 20 sq.) :

i (i. 1, probably blank, lost), ii, iii, iv[12], v[14] (v. 3 and v. 11 excised) vi[10] (vi. 2 and vi. 8 excised), vii, viii, ix[12], x[14] (x. 5 and x. 9 excised), xi (xi. 3–11 excised), xii, xiii, xiv, xv, [xvi], [xvii], [xviii][12], [xix][3] (xix. 1 lost), [xx][6].

Possibly the final leaf of the manuscript has been lost. If so, it was probably the conjugate of xix. 1, and thus what we have called gatherings xix, xx are the remains of a single composite gathering of 12. The stitching of these two folds is modern.

l. 11.   absoluat GM.   tuae + nobis (*exc.* P).   conciliet GM.
Postcommon.   AΓHJΛMPRSWYZ.
l. 18.   tua dona ΓΛ.   tribulatione + nostra W.   percepimus
AΓHΛPSYZ.

VIGILIA S. IOHANNIS BAPTISTAE.

l. 21.   Read *zacharia.*   C also has *zacharias.*
l. 25.   CW have the psalm *Apparuit autem.*   ΓᵃHΛRSY agree with the
text.
l. 28.   Read *incedat.*
Colleot.   ACΓHJΛMPRSWYZ.
l. 28.   iohannis + christi S.
l. 29.   per] dnm. nostrum i. c. &c. AΓHMPRSWYZ.
p. 57. l. 11.   Read *per.*
Secret.   AΓHJΛMPRWY(Z for the first mass of the day).
l. 10.   munera + q. HY.
l. 11.   nostrorum *om.* Z.
l. 17.   Read *poscat.*
Postcommon.   ACΓHJΛMPRSWY (G as collect L for the day
z ' ad uesperas ').
l. 16.   q. *om.* (*exc.* HV).
l. 17.   et + per sanctum corpus et sanguinem filii tui W.
l. 18.   fore] fauere GΓLMZ fieri P.   i. c. dnm. nostrum] dnm.
nostrum i. c. filium tuum HRY dnm. nostrum PZ dnm. nostrum
i. c. AΓJAS per GLΛM.

IN DIE S. IOHANNIS BAPTISTAE.

l. 24.   This psalm is found in CE and in no other book cited by Dr.
Legg (W p. 1559) ΓᵃΛRSY have *Bonum est confiteri,* HW *Audite
insulae.*
l. 27.   Read *spiritualium.*
Colleot.   ACGΓHJLΛMPRSWYZ.
l. 26.   honorabilem + nobis.   iohannis + baptistae J.
l. 27.   da + populis tuis.
l. 29.   ęterne] et pacis GL.
p. 58. l. 1 sq.   In R these two verses are replaced by *Tu puer propheta*
and *Ne timeas zacharia,* in ΓᵃΛ by *Beatus uir.*   C has *alleluia* at the
end of l. 1 : probably omitted here by an error of the scribe.
l. 2.   This verse is common to C and E, but is found in no other book
cited by Dr. Legg (W p. 1559.)
Secret.   ACGΓHJLΛMPRSWYZ.
l. 11.   tua + nos JS.   dne. *om.* Λ.   illius] sancti ioannis G +
nobis per haec opem adesse poscentes et M.
l. 12.   uenerantes] celebrantes (*exc.* CSW).   et opem . . .
deprecantes *om.* (*exc.* CSW).
l. 15.   monstrauit + praesentem S.   i. c. &c.] dnm. nostrum
i. c. (+ filium tuum HRYZ) ΓHJΛMPRYZ i. c. dnm. nostrum
AC per L.
l. 19.   Read *ecclesia.*
Postcommon.   ACGΓHJΛMPRSWYZ.
l. 20.   auctorem + per GJ.
l. 21.   dnm. nostrum *om.* CW.

VIGILIA SS, PETRI ET PAULI.

l. 22.   Sanctorum . . .   Pauli] *Sancti Petri* ΓJ.
l. 28.   This psalm is found in CE alone of the books collated by Dr.
Legg (W p. 1560).   ΓᵃHΛRSWY have *Caeli enarrant.*

Collect. ACGHMPSWZ.

l. 30.   nos CSW.   ap. beatorum GM.   ap. *om.* P.   tuorum *om.* CGMP.

l. 31.   natalitia gloriosa (*exc.* C).   preuenire] praeire (*exc.* CS).

l. 32.   et *pri. om.* P.   beneficiis praeueniri.

p. 59. l. 1.   Read *terrae.*

l. 9.   Read *offerenda.*

Secret. AΓHJAPRY (D commemoratio de apostolis).

l. 13.   populi] apostoli HY.   dne. q. DΓHJPY.

l. 17.   This common is found also in CΓᵃA and in only one other book cited by Dr. Legg (W p. 1560).   *Simon iohannis* is that usually given.

19.   ab elimento].   Read *alimento* as p. 60, l. 18.

Postcommon. AΓJAPRYZ (CHMSW for day G for Annun. B.V.M.)   For collations see below on p. 60, l. 18 sq.

NATALE SS. PETRI ET PAULI.

l. 21.   *Natale S. Petri ap.* ΓAP.

l. 24.   The same psalm is found in CHS and a few other English books : also in R.   W prefixes (from v. 10) *Et exeuntes processerunt* &c., while ΓᵃAY have *Dne. probasti.*

Collect. ACGΓHJLAMPRSWYZ.

l. 26.   hodiernam] hunc GL.   diem + b. GL.   tuorum *om.* GL.

l. 27.   martyriis H martyrist Y.   tuae] *om.* L + toto terrarum orbe diffusae GL.   in . . . preceptum] semper magisterio gubernari GL.

l. 28.   sumpsit religionis GL.

p. 60. l. 1 sq.   This verse is common to CES, but no other examples of its use are given in W p. 1561.   ΓᵃHAR have *Tu es petrus,* W *Tu es pastor,* Y *Non uos me.*

Secret. ACΓHJLAMPRSWYZ.

l. 11.   q. dne. A.   q. *om.* (*exc.* CA).   sacrandas] consecrandas HY.

l. 12.   apostolica] sanctorum ap. tuorum petri et pauli Z.   et *om.* AΓJLAMPRWZ.

l. 13.   tribuis ΓJLAP.

l. 16.   Read *amo te* : *t* having been mistaken for *c̄.*   This common is found also in CΓᵃA and very rarely elsewhere (see W p. 1561).   The majority of books have *Tu es petrus.*

Postcommon. ACΓHJAMPRSWY (G for Annunc. B.V.M.)

l. 18.   satiasti + q. s.   appostolicis intercessionibus] b. (sanctorum p. 228) ap. tuorum petri et pauli intercessionibus z intercedente b. . . . maria G.

l. 19.   omni + nos Y (not so on Vigil) GH + q. G + propitius Z (*semel*).

NATALE S. PAULI.

l. 23.   This psalm seems to be peculiar to E (W p. 1561), C wanting this mass.   ΓᵃARSY have *Dne. probasti,* H *De reliquo reposita,* W *Non solum autem michi.*

Collect. AGΓHJAMPRSWYZ.

l. 26.   gentium + in Z.   apostoli + tui HJSWYZ.

l. 27.   natalia J.

l. 28.   patrociniotJR.

l. 29.   Read *galatas.*

Epistle. Inflection mark over *Title* ad.

l. 31. E agrees with HR, against SWY, in omitting vv. 21–24.

p. 61. l. 6. In this ℣ E agrees with HSWY. Iᵃᴧ have *Gaudete iusti.*

l. 17. Read *nostrum perueniat.*

Secret. SW (L for SS. Peter and Paul).

l. 15. oblatio L. uotiua L. deferentes] defertur L deferimus S. precamur] deprecantes S deprecamur W. ut + pariter L.

l. 17. perueniat] proueniat LW.

l. 24. Read *percipiat.*

Postcommon. SW.

l. 22. tua + et S.

l. 23. apostoli + tui S.

OCTAVAE SS. PETRI ET PAULI.

l. 26. non] See on p. 9, l. 15.

l. 28. This office appears to be peculiar to E. Iᵐʜᴧʀswy have *Sapientiam sanctorum.* All these books except ᴧ seem to agree with E in having the psalm *Exsultate.* ᴧ has the office *Caeli enarrant.* The mass is wanting in C.

Collect. AGᴦʜJᴧMPRSWYZ (C de petro et paulo).

l. 32. b. *om.* G. petrum + apostolum GHJRSY.

l. 34. pelago G. exaudi . . . et *om.* G.

l. 35. concede + propitius G. eternitatis gloriam] aeternam trinitatis gratiam G.

l. 36. per] qui uiuis AHRSY.

p. 62. l. 2. This epistle is somewhat unusual. It is found in W.

Epistle. Inflection mark over *Title* ad.

l. 5. *Constitues* is very rare here (see W p. 1564). It is found in H for the second, and Y for the third day within the octave, but with a different ℣. Iᵃ, with most English books, has *Iustorum animae* There is no mass for the octave in C.

l. 6. This is the ℣ in most books. Iᵃᴧ have *Sancti tui.*

Verse. HSWY.

l. 6. et duo *om.* W.

l. 14. The offertory seems peculiar to E, C wanting the mass. In H it is for the second, and in Y for the third day within the octave.

Secret. LSW.

l. 16. altissime + d. S. tibique] tibi ; quae et S et tibi L.

l. 17. eorum fieri W. concede *post* honore L.

l. 20. The common appears to be peculiar to E (C has no mass) : it belongs to the fourth day within the octave in H and to the second in Y. [ut] uen[ia]tis] This should have been printed *uentis*†. It is apparently a corruption of *ut eatis*, the former word having been written in the exemplar *ú*. The confusion of *a* with *n* is easy in Irish MSS. Compare above, p. 25, l. 20. Or possibly we should emend [*ut*] *uen*[*ia*]*tis.*

Postcommon. SW.

l. 23. sacramenta + caelestia S. ap. + tuis petro et paulo SW.

VIGILIA ASSUMPTIONIS S. MARIAE.

l. 28. Apparently the scribe began to write the psalm, but, in error, after its opening word (or words) copied again the end of the office. He then commenced the psalm afresh, not perceiving his mistake. This appears to be the psalm given in almost all English books, if we may assume that *Et gaudium* in the Durham and Whitby missals

(W p. 1580) is a mere variant, following more closely the text of Sedulius, as we have *Et gaudia* in D p. 7. But S has *Benedicta tu, Eructauit,* and W adds a second psalm *Quia concupiuit.* C (see p. 60) agrees with E. Γᵃ does not provide for this mass.

ll. 29, 30. Read *honore, es.*

l. 32. Read *aulam.*

p. 63. l. 2. *te* (i.e. *tecum*) is certainly wrong, though read by Γ.

    Collect. ACΓHJΛMPRSWYZ.

    l. 1. iocundos + nos Z. facias R. suae faciat HY. festiuitati] commemorationi Z.

    l. 2. qui &c.] per Z.

l. 3. Probably this should be expanded *r[equire] i[n] co[m]me[moratione] d[um] respo[nsorio]*: the meaning being that the following lesson, of which the cue only is given here, and its responsory are to be found in the commemorative mass of the B.V.M., p. 79, l. 35. So in C we have 'Ab initio et ante secula *ut supra.* Gradale *ut supra,*' the reference again being to the commemorative mass (C p. 60). And similarly in the Missal of Kilcormic (T.C.D. MS. B. 3. 1), 'Ab initio et ante saecula et caetera sicut in commemoracione.' We have thus an indication that the Votive Masses originally preceded the Sanctorale. Compare above on p. 47, l. 38.

l. 7 sqq. This alternative lesson, with its grail, appears to be peculiar in this place to E. They are found, however, in W, and the lesson with a different grail in S, in the Common of One Virgin not Martyr.

l. 18. The full text is given, p. 80, l. 16, where we have *es* for *est.* Here again we note that the votive masses probably preceded the Sanctorale.

    Secret. ACΓHJΛMPRSWY (Z on the day 'ad uesperas').

    l. 20. munera nostra] magna est ΓJMPZ. dne. + q. AS.

    l. 21. commendet *om.* ΓJMPZ.

    l. 22. pro *om.*† C. fiducialiter apud te HY.

    l. 23. per] dnm. nostrum Z.

l. 25. For the text see p. 80, l. 28, and compare above on ll. 3, 18. This common appears to be found here in CE only (W p. 1581). It is the common for the day in Y and the Sherborne Missal (W p. 1582).

    Postcommon. CΓHJΛMPRSWY (Z 'ad uesperas').

    l. 27. concede + q. HΛSYZ. mis.] o. Z. d. + per tanti misterii dulcedinem W.

    l. 28. et uirguinis] *om. (exc.* CSW) + mariae S.

    l. 29. eiusdem C.

ASSUMPTIO S. MARIAE.

l. 32. This title should be omitted.

l. 33. This is the usual office : but Γᵃ has *Vultum tuum.*

l. 34. Read *gaudent.*

    Office. ACHRSWY.

    l. 34. sancte] *om. (exc.* R) b. R.

p. 64. l. 1. For the psalm ΓᵃΛRSY have *Eructauit.* E agrees with CHW and the Sherborne Missal (W p. 1581).

l. 6. Read *nexibus.*

    Collect. ACHJSWYZ (ΓΛMP before the mass collect).

    l. 4. huius + est ΓMP. opem conferat sempiternam *om.* MP.

    l. 5. sempiternam] salutarem HZ.

    l. 6. nec + tamen. nexibus mortis Γ.

    l. 7. tuum *om.* M. de se *om.* Γ.

ROSSLYN.   **M**

l. 9. per octauas] A special collect throughout the octave appears to be unusual. HW have this collect on the octave day only.

l. 12. Read *tribuis.*

> **Collect during octave.** (A Postc. of Vigil Γ for S. Maria ad martyres J ad uesp. M alia after postc. of Vigil P for Vigil ad uesp. HW in octaua).
>
> l. 10. concede + nobis A. b. mariae semper uirguinis] eorum Γ.
>
> l. 11. nos *post* d. HW *post* cuius JMP *post* ʼquorum *et ante* gaudia Γ *om.* A. eterna *om.* H. cuius] quorum Γ.
>
> l. 12. ueneranda assumptione] uirtute Γ.

l. 23 sq. In HSY this verse is said during the octave, not on the day. CW and a few other books agree with E (see W p. 1581). In R it is said without the previous ℣ on the day, reading *gaudet exercitus angelorum* for *gaudent* &c. Γᵃ has *Specie tua,* also omitting *Hodie.*

l. 24. Read *benedicunt.* CHSWY have *benedicunt* (-*ant* C) dnm.

> **Gospel.** Inflection mark over v. 38 et (?).

l. 30. There appears to be no English missal which has this offertory for the Assumption (see W p. 1581). C agrees with E. In R it appears as the offertory for the Vigil, and in S as a ℣ of the offertory for the Vigil. In Γᵃ we have here *Offerentur regi.*

> **Offertory.** C (RS for Vigil).
>
> l. 30. dnm.] omnium R. mundi *om.* R.
>
> **Secret.** CSW.
>
> l. 33. dne. + q. S. efficiat + b. S.
>
> l. 35. te + iugiter S.

l. 38. This common is found here in CES and apparently in no other English missal (W p. 1582). HRWY have it for the Vigil. Γᵃ has here *Dilexisti iustitiam.*

p. 65.

> **Postcommon.** ACΓHJΛMPRSWYZ.
>
> l. 4. cunctis *om.* ΛΓHJΛMPY. eius intercessionibus *om.* C. intercessione R.

DECOLLATIO S. IOHANNIS BAPTISTAE.

l. 7 sqq. This office and psalm are rare. They are found here in CEW and one other English book (see W p. 1586). Γᵃ has *In uirtute tua, Vitam petiit.*

l. 8. Read *discipulis.*

> **Collect.** ACGHJMPRSWYZ.
>
> l. 13. baptistae + praecursoris Z. m. + tui.
>
> l. 14. festiuitas] solemnitas Z. augmentum] effectum (*exc.* SW) + et nos ad gaudia aeterna faciat peruenire Z.
>
> **Epistle.** Inflection mark over *Title* sapientiæ.

l. 19 sqq. ll. 19–22 are found in CWY and the Abingdon Missal only. Of these W (? Abingdon : see W 1586) does not contain ll. 23, 24. Apparently therefore CY alone agree with E throughout. Γᵃ has *Dne. praeuenisti, B. uir.*

l. 21. Read *fratre suo uiuenti.*

l. 29. This offertory is found in CEW and one or two other English books, but not in ΓᵃHΛSY or R.

l. 34. Read *passione.*

> **Secret.** ACGHJΛMPRSWYZ.
>
> l. 33. munera + quae P. tibi *om.* C. dne. + quae HY. iohannis baptistae (+ et SY) m. tui SWY. m. tui *om.* A. tui *om.* G.
>
> l. 34. deferimus] offerimus H. quia . . . perpetuus *om.* P. quia] qui (*exc.* JPR). est + in W.

l. 35. q. . . . salutem *om.* G.AZ. q. *post* tibi (l. 33) R.

p. 66. l. 2. The common, it would seem, is found here in CEW and one other English book only (see W p. 1586). ΓᵃHSY &c. have *Magna est gloria,* Λ *Mirabilis,* R *Posuisti.*

l. 7. precibus] MS. *prĩbus,* which should have been expanded *patribus* in the text. This reading is found also in three printed editions of S, viz. Rouen fo. 1492, London fo. 1504, London fo. 1557.

    Postcommon. ACGHJMPRSWYZ.

    l. 5. + q. *post* nobis A *post* dne. S. baptizae *om.* AGJMZ. utrunque] utraque W beata P.

    l. 6. et *om.* GHJPY. sumpsimus + et A.

    l. 7. patribus nostris] *om.* (*exc.* CS) precibus nostris CS. significata] sanctificata HY digne M. in *om.* M. potius &c.] salutaria sentiamus M.

NATIVITAS S. MARIAE.

l. 9. Read *mariae.*

l. 10. Γᵃ has the office *Vultum tuum.*

l. 12. Read *angeli.*

    Office. CHSWY.

    l. 11. sanctę *om.* (*exc.* C).

l. 13. Read *ex . . . dauid.* The exemplar must have had *d̄d̄,* which if written in an Irish hand might easily be confused with *d̄o* (= *deo*), especially if the horizontal stroke were omitted. This psalm is not very common here. It is found in HW, the Sherborne Missal (see W p. 1589), and apparently also in C. Γⁿ, with ΛSV, has *Eructauit cor meum.*

l. 15. Read *miserator.*

    Collect. ACHJSWYZ (ΓΛP before the mass collect M ad processionem).

    l. 16. sanctae *om.* (*exc.* C).

    l. 17. intercessionibus + complacatus ΓJΛPZ + complacati Y.

    l. 18. dnm.] eundem.

    Epistle. Inflection mark over *Title* sapientiæ.

l. 22 sqq. The full text of l. 22 sq. is given at p. 80, l. 2 sqq., an indication that the votive masses preceded the Sanctorale. ll. 22, 23 are found in CR and some other missals, two only of which are English ; also in the missal of Kilcormic. The majority have the ℣ which appears here, l. 24 sq. (see W p. 1589). Not so, however, ΓᵃΛR.

l. 30. This offertory occurs here in CΛY and one other English missal, and as an alternative in R. Γᵃ has *Offerentur.*

    Secret. ACΓHJΛMPRSWY.

    l. 32. nobis dne. S.

    l. 33. integritatem matris SW.

    l. 34. eius + uotiuis W.

p. 67.   l. 1. tibi] sibi (*exc.* AMS) sibimet S. faciat + esse S. i. c. &c.] per eundem HY qui tecum ATJΛMP.

l. 4. The same common is found in CV and the Sherborne Missal : apparently not elsewhere (see W p. 1589). See above on p. 63, l. 25.

    Postcommon. ACΓHJΛMPRSWYZ (G Tuesday after xl¹ L mense decembri).

    l. 6. annue uotiua] hodiernae annua cum deuotione Z.

    l. 7. ut *ante* et *pri.* (l. 8) M. intercedente . . . uirguine *om.* (*exc.* CMSWZ). maria semper uirguine] et gloriosa semperque uirgine dei genetrice maria z semper uirgine maria M.

l. 8.   et *pri. om.* GΓΛ.   nobis uitae ΓHJΛMPSYZ.   praebeant remedia A remedio perueniant G.   aeterna HY.

EXALTATIO S. CRUCIS.

l. 10.   Read *exaltatio.*

l. 11 sqq.   The office is that of C and four other English missals ; the psalm is found in CE only.   Most books have the office *Nos autem gloriari* and psalm *D. misereatur* (W p. 1591).   Iᵃ has *Nos autem, Dns. regnauit.*

Collect.   CΓJMPSYZ (Λ as ad populum de s. cruce).

l. 16.   filii *om.* ΓJΛMPZ.   i. c. *om.* M.

l. 18.   uiuificam + eius M.

l. 19.   adueniunt.   eundem] dnm. Γ.

l. 21.   The epistle for this day varies considerably in the different English books : see W p. 1591.   That which is here given is found elsewhere in C only ; but it differs from that of R and one or two others, only by including vv. 5–7.

l. 24 sq.   The full text is given, p. 26, l. 32, and p. 43, l. 27.

l. 26 sqq.   There is much variation in these verses.   R has *Dulce lignum, Nos autem gloriari* ; HSWY *Dulce lignum,* Iᵃ *Dicite in gentibus.*   The two verses are found as here in CE only, from which the St. Albans Missal differs by the omission of the first (see W p. 1591).

l. 34.   In the offertory E is in agreement with most books : but IᵃΛ have *Dextera dni.*

Offertory.   CHRSWY (AD de s. cruce).

l. 34.   signum] lignum HY (but 'signum' for the Invention).

l. 36.   tibi *om.* R.

l. 37.   alleluia *om.* S.   alleluia alleluia D.

p. 68.   Secret.   ACGJΛMPSWY.

l. 2.   deuotas + in hoc festo S.

l. 3.   precedat] comitetur ΛP.   per + protoplastum P.   adam] euam S.

l. 4.   paradisi ligno MY.   ligno P.   temeraria Y.   rursum] sursum† C crucis Y.

l. 7.   CE share this common with W and the Abingdon Missal, but most English missals have *Per lignum serui* (W p. 1591) ; IᵃΛ and the Sherborne Missal, *Nos autem.*

Common.   CW.

l. 7.   nos ab omni W.

l. 8.   qui] quia C.

Postcommon.   ACHΛMPSW (ΓRZ as secret).

l. 10.   et sanguine *om.* CΓΛPW.   saginati et sanguine S.   sanginandi RZ.

l. 11.   quem + sanctae A.

l. 12.   d.] + nr. (*exc.* A) *om.* A.   sicut . . . ita] per haec sancta quae sumpsimus Λ.   sicut] sicuti Γ + eius misterium W + illud RZ + hanc HS.   perenniter RZ perenni CW.   gloria &c.] beneficio perfruamur CW.   gloriae AΓHMPRZ.

l. 13.   salutaris ΓPRZ salutis Λ.   affectu S.   eundem] dnm. M.

IN DIE S. MATTHAEI.

l. 14.   The title as given in the MS. implies that the exemplar had a mass for the Vigil.   Compare above on p. 46, l. 2.

l. 15. This office and psalm appear to be assigned to St. Matthew's Day in EY only. C has no mass. Iᵃ has *Os iusti, Noli aemulari.*

    Collect. AHJAMPRSWYZ (Γ for St. John Ev. ad fontes).

        l. 19. matthei ap. tui (*om.* W) et euangelistae AHSWY matthei euangelistae JAM euangelistae matthei (iohannis Γ) ΓPRZ. + q. *ante* dne. A *post* dne. P.

l. 25 sq. This grail does not occur elsewhere in E. But it is the grail for One Martyr in both C (Vigil) and D, and for One Confessor in C. Compare above on p. 46, l. 3. Y has this grail and ℣ for St. Matthew: ΓᵃAR have the same grail, but with a different ℣ : s has the ℣ but not the grail.

l. 34. This offertory in found here in Y. ΓᵃARS have *Posuisti dne.*

p. 69.   **Secret.** AHJAMPRSWYZ (GL for St. John Evang.).

        l. 2. supplicationibus + nostris† J. apostolicis *om.* HS. mathei] iohannis GL. ap. tui (*om.* W) et euangelistae SW. et ap. tui *om.* (*exc.* SW).

        l. 3. ecclesiae tuae dne. GJLP.

l. 6. This is the common also in W. Most other books (including Iᵃ) differ. C has no mass.

    Postcommon. SW.

        l. 10. tui + et euangelistae.

        l. 12. quod + praedicauit et S.

FESTIVITAS S. MICHAELIS ARCHANGELI.

l. 13. ocťa] Evidently the month October (*a* for *o*). This mass is often entitled *Dedicatio basilicae* (*om.* R) *S. Michaelis* (*om.* Γ) *archangeli* (*angeli* Γ *om.* MP) : so DΓJAMPR. z has *Inventio basilicae S. Michaelis,* a different mass serving for the Dedication ; AHSWY agree more or less closely with E : while in C the title of the mass is identical with that in our book. L has *Prid. Kl. Oct. Ñ basilicae angeli in Salaria.*

l. 16. uirtutes] MS. uiℙ. The word is written in full l. 26. c here reads *uirtutes,* DHRSWY *uirtute.*

    Collect. ACDΓHJAMPRSWYZ.

        l. 20. qui + in Y (not so ii. 166, Missa de angelis) H.

        l. 21. ut + a ΓSZ.

        l. 22. his + in terra (etiam in terra J). nostra uita ΓJAMP.

l. 30. D has *Concussum est mare* : and this is one of the verses in R. Iᵃ has *Laudate dnm., Confitebor tibi.*

p. 70. l. 4. DW add the ℣ *In conspectu,* thus agreeing with one MS. of Iᵃ cited in M. The other MSS. of Iᵃ have ' Off. *In conspectu.* ℣ *Confitebor.* ℣ *Confiteantur.*'

    Secret, CGLPSWZ.

        l. 6. tui populi Z. dne. q. GLPZ.

        l. 7. sed] acceptum efficitur id Z. archangeli] angeli Z. michael L + omniumque b. spirituum S.

        l. 8. tibi *post* quod (l. 6) S *post* non (l. 7) Z *om.* GLP. sit gratum] gratum maiestati tuae reddatur Z.

l. 14. Read *prosequimur.*

    Postcommon. ACDΓHJLAMPRSWYZ (G as collect).

        l. 13. michaelis archangeli tui D. tui *om.* GL. michael L. intercessione] interuentione GLS.

        l. 14. dne. te L. precamur L. quod] quos GΓHJLAMPWY + in D. ore] honore GΓHJLAMPSWY. consequimur C

VIGILIA OMNIUM SANCTORUM.

l. 16. naūi] This seems to be an accidental repetition of the name of the month, in its Irish form and with *a* for *o* (cf. above p. 69, l. 13), *nauimbir*.

l. 17 sq. C seems to have no office, but the psalm as here, *Iusti epulentur* (without title). The office in Γᵃ (most MSS.) is *Iudicant sancti*.

l. 17. Read *quoniam*.

l. 18. dest] = *deest*, *e* being written for *ee* as not uncommonly elsewhere.

l. 19. The insertion of the title *Ps.* appears to be an error. *Diuites* is part of the office.

l. 21. This appears to be the psalm also in C. HASWY, with the same office, have *Benedicam dnm.* Γᵃ (most MSS.) has *Exultate iusti*.

> **Collect.** ACHJAMPRSWYZ (G missa plurimorum sanctorum L in a July mass).
>
> l. 24. gratiam] misericordiam PZ. et] ut† JW + sanctorum tuorum S.
>
> l. 25. preuenimus] celebramus GL. sollennia] certamina GL.
>
> l. 26. professione] profectione PZ promissione R. lętitiam] *om.†* C uictoriam GL.

l. 34. Read *iohannem*. This gospel is unusual, but it is found in Y; where, however, vv. 8–11 are omitted.

p. 71. l. 2. This is the offertory in CR and Γᵃ. HASWY have *Laetamini in dno*. The full text is not given in our Missal, but it is found in the Common of Several Apostles (Vigil), Martyrs and Confessors in D.

> **Secret.** ACHJAMPRSWYZ.
>
> l. 4. d. *om.* CHSWYZ. da *om.* AR.
>
> l. 5. ad *om.†* P. tuorum *om.* P.
>
> l. 6. precatione.

l. 9. This is the common also in CA. HRS have *Iustorum animae*, W *Beati mundo*, Y *Ego sum uitis*, Γᵃ *Dico autem uobis amicis*.

l. 12. Read *obtata* with CHJMRYZ. In AP however we find *oblata* in E.

> **Postcommon.** ACHJAMPRSWYZ.
>
> l. 12. optatae celebritatis ASW.

IN DIE OMNIUM SANCTORUM.

> **Office.** CHRSWY.
>
> l. 17. omnium sanctorum (*exc.* CR).

l. 23. Read *propitiationis*.

> **Collect.** ACHJAMPRSWYZ (G 'orationes ad uesperum' after S. Paul's Day L mense Iunio).
>
> l. 21. sanctorum] apostolorum GL + tuorum ARWZ.
>
> l. 22. tribuis HJY. celebritate] sollemnitate HV.
>
> l. 23. desideratam] celeriter G celerem L. nobis *om.* L.
>
> l. 24. intercessoribus ACGLRSWZ.

l. 26. This lesson is common to CE and the Sherborne Missal (W p. 1605). With the omission of the first verse it appears also in HRSWY.

l. 31. *quoniam* is superfluous, having crept in from the line above.

l. 33. This verse seems peculiar to CE. In a folio Paris Missal of 1543, cited by Dr. Legg (W p. 1605) the grail is *Gloriosus, Dextera*: and so Γᵃ for the Vigil. The text of *Gloriosus* does not

appear in E, but it is found in the Common of Several Martyrs in D.
l. 34. *in* is superfluous. This verse is found in CHSWY and most other
books ; but R has *Venite ad me, Haec est uera fraternitas* ; ΓᵘΛ *Iusti
epulentur.*
l. 2. The gospel in CHRSWYZ is Matt. v. 1-12.

p. 72. l. 5 sq. Read *offerenda, plebi.*
l. 10. Read *pro.* P also has *per.*
Secret. ACHJΛMPRSWYZ (Γ for SS. Felicissimus and Agapitus,
&c.)
l. 10. cunctorum] tuorum ΓΛ + qui P. grati P. sunt ΛP.
iustorum] sanctorum CMSW.
Postcommon. ACHJΛMPRSWY.
l. 16. populis] *om.* Λ + per huius sacramenti participationem
SW.
l. 17. tuorum *om.* AHJΛMPY.

IN TERTIA ET IN SEXTA FERIA.

l. 19. The title of this mass is in H *Oratio generalis de omnibus
sanctis,* in S *Oratio generalis,* in C *Missa communis,* in W *Alia missa
generalis.* I have not found it elswhere. H alone agrees with E in
expressly connecting it with the commemoration of All Saints.
Bishop Forbes (*Arbuthnott Missal,* p. xxxix) reads the title in E, *In
ni. et in ni. fe.* This appears certainly incorrect, though the numerals
are somewhat indistinct. The position of the mass, combined with its
title, seems to indicate that it was used on the Tuesday and Friday after
Nov. 1 : or the third and sixth feria may possibly mean Nov. 3 and 6.
But whatever may be intended the expression is unusual. A parallel
is found in the *Annals of Ulster* under the date 1263 : 'Friar
Patrick O'Sgannaiḥ, Archbishop of Ard-macha, held a General
Chapter in Drochet-atha this year feria secunda, tertia et quarta post
festum omnium sanctorum.' On which Dr. MacCarthy remarks that
the entry proves that in the year referred to Nov. 1 fell on a Sunday,
and (this not having been the case in 1263) he emends the date
accordingly. The title of our mass shows that the inference is
precarious.
Collect. CHSW.
l. 21. sanctorum + tuorum (*exc.* W).
l. 22. semper protegat] saluet semper C. semper *om.* W.
protege HS. protegat + et cunctis coniunctis nobis oracione
uel confessione consanguinitate aut familiaritate et pro
quibus promisimus uel obnoxii sumus orare W. fidelibus]
omnibus.
l. 23. tuam *om.* HS.
l. 24. impugnationibus + sint (*exc.* C). tua opitulatione defensi
(*exc.* C).
l. 25. saluentur *om.* (*exc.* C). suorum omnium (*om.* W) *post*
mereantur CW *ante* peccatorum HS.
l. 26. accipere] percipere HS.
Secret. CHSW.
l. 28. oblationes nostras S. q. *om.* W. dne. *om.* C. propitius
HW.
l. 29. tuorum *om.* W.
l. 30. nostrorum *om.* W. delictorum] peccatorum SW⸤pecca-
minum H + et cunctis &c. (*ut sup.* l. 22) W. ac] et (*exc.* C).
l. 31. sancta *om.* (*exc.* C). libatio] oblatio HS. praesentis uitae
(*exc.* C.)

l. 32.   commoda] subsidia (*exc.* C).   futuri regni] futurae praemia aeterna (*exc.* C) + pręmia C.

Postcommon. HSW.

l. 34.   dne. *post* sacrificia S.   intercessionibus (*exc.* H).

l. 35.   sanctorum + tuorum (*exc.* W).   ad salutem proficiant (*exc.* H) + et cunctis &c. (*ut sup.* l. 22) W.

l. 36.   christianis omnibus uiuentibus atque defunctis (*exc.* H). christianis omnibus H.   fidelibus *om.* (*exc.* W).

p. 73.   CANON.

The following have been collated for the Canon : ACDGΓHJΛMPRSΣWYZ.

l. 2.   amen *om.* JY.

l. 3.   *om.* GΣ.

l. 4.   habeamus CD.

l. 5.   deo *om.* J.

Common Preface (not in A).

l. 6.   salutare + est Σ.   tibi + hic Σ.

l. 7.   pater *om.* Σ.

l. 12.   uti Σ.

l. 13.   dns. + d.   et + uniuersa Σ.

l. 15.   *fin.* + dne. exaudi orationem meam.   et clamor meus ad te ueniat Z.

l. 16.   It is somewhat surprising to find the Preface of the Holy Trinity, and it alone of the Prefaces, inserted after the Common Preface in the Ordinary of the Mass.   The most obvious explanation of this fact is that this Preface was so frequently used that it was inserted here for greater convenience.   But another (not inconsistent) hypothesis may be suggested, of which some confirmation will be found hereafter (see notes on p. 78, ll. 2 sqq., 23).   We find in the 'Missa Canonica'[1] of the Stowe missal (Σ 233(206)) the following arrangement of prefaces.   First there is the former part of the Common Preface.   Then follows a clause which cannot as it stands be satisfactorily construed—'Qui cum unigenito' &c.   It is clearly a somewhat divergent recension of the usual Trinity Preface. To this succeeds what may well be an Easter Preface—'Per quem salus,' which again can scarcely be connected with what immediately precedes it.   It is, in fact, identical with the opening words of the preface of the mass for the dead in C (p. 74), D (p. 34). This seems to be given as a sort of specimen Proper Preface, and it is followed, after an obscure rubric, by the remainder of the Common Preface.   It is at least possible that the corresponding portion of the exemplar of E, or of one of its ancestors, was arranged on a somewhat similar principle—that the Missa de Sancta Trinitate was in fact a sort of Missa Canonica, including the entire Ordinary and Canon, with the parts peculiar to the Trinity Mass inserted in their proper places.   When the missal was rearranged, these portions of the service would of course be taken out and placed apart as a separate mass, while the preface would be removed to the part of the book assigned to the Proper Prefaces.   We may suppose that the scribe (or editor) omitted to perform the latter portion of his task. And so the Trinity Preface remains in the Canon as a survival of the older arrangement of the book, just as the Preface de S. Maria is a witness to the fact that in the exemplar the Prefaces did not form a collection apart, but were distributed through the masses. See above on p. 44, l. 18.

If the hypothesis that the mass de S. Trinitate was a missa canonica be not accepted, the presence of the Trinity Preface in the Canon appears to imply that in the Church to which our missal belonged it was in frequent if not weekly use. Such was the practice directed in the fourteenth century in the St. Alban's Missal (W p. 1504), and the writer of the Micrologus (cap. lx) speaks of the ' prefationem de Sancta Trinitate quam in diebus dominicis frequentamus.

But if it be held as probable that, as we have suggested, the Trinity mass was the setting, so to speak, of the Ordinary and Canon, the question may be asked : Why was it chosen for this purpose, rather than any of the other masses? One or other of two answers may be given. Either (1) this mass was in more constant use than the others ; or (2) its position in the missal naturally led to its selection as the missa canonica. It was probably in the exemplar, as in our MS., the first in the series of Votive Masses ; and, if we are right in our view that the Votive Masses originally preceded the Temporale (see above, p. xiii), it is not unlikely that it was actually the first mass in the book. If then the Canon was to be incorporated with any mass this is the one in which it would naturally be inserted. Both causes may perhaps have conspired to produce the connexion of the Canon with the Mass of the Holy Trinity. See further above in the Introduction, p. xviii.

l. 20. differentia discretione] This reading can scarcely be defended, though it is supported by GJ (p. 241). The obvious emendation is *differentiae discretione*, which is read by ΓJ(*semel*)Λ(*semel*)MV, seeing that the confusion of *a* with *ae* is very frequent in our manuscript. The corrector however (see footnote) appears to have thought that *discretione* was the word to be altered. On that supposition we should read *differentia discretionis* with ACDHΛ(*semel*)PRSWZ.

Trinity Preface.

l. 16. filio *om.* Σ. sancto spiritu GΓΛ(*semel*).

l. 17. d. es unus Σ + et immortalis d. incorruptibilis . . . Σ. unus es dns. *om.* Σ. in *om.* Σ. singulariter Σ.

l. 18. in *om.* Σ. trinitatis Λ(*semel*)Σ. quod enim *usque fin.*] te credimus . . . . Σ.

l. 20. differentiae ΓJ(*semel*)Λ(*semel*)MY. discretionis ACDHΛ (*semel*)PRSWZ. ut] et D. in *om.* Λ(*semel*).

l. 21. sempiternae P. deitatis] diuinitatis Z. et in personis proprietas *om.* Z.

l. 23. quem &c.] per D. quam AJMRSWYZ. atque &c.] adorant dominationes tremunt &c. Γ. archangeli + omnesque uirtutes caelorum quem Z. quoque ac] et Z.

l. 24. clamare iugiter W. iugiter *om.* HRSYZ. clamare] *om.* C + quottidie R.

Te igitur. Some missals do not place the crosses as E. Thus J has them before *benedicas, haec* (l. 31) and *haec* pri. (l. 32) ; C omits the second in l. 32, and ΓMΣ have none. On the other hand G has five—those marked here, and two others, over *benedicas* (l. 31) and *illibata* respectively.

l. 29. *init.* + oremus Z.

l. 30. supplices + te Σ. et] ac AHPRSYZ.

l. 31. uti] ut R.

l. 33. tua sancta ecclesia Σ. sancta *om.* P.

l. 34. adunare] et unare Σ.

l. 35. cum + beatissimo DΓΛPΣ. papa nostro] *om.* Λ. + episcopo sedis apostolicae Σ. 'n' *pri.*] *post* tuo Σ + (. . .) Aˡ. et antistite nostro 'n'] *om.* ΓMΣ. 'n' *sec.*] *om.* AD + episcopo G. + et rege nostro 'n' (*om.* AP) *post* 'n' *pri.* JM *post* 'n' *sec.* AHPSY (*hiat* W). et *sec.* . . . cultoribus (l. 36) *om.* GΓ.

l. 36. catholicę et *om.* Σ. cultoribus + et abbate 'n' episcopo Σ. **Memento.**

l. 37. memento + etiam Σ. famulorum + tuorum (*om.* A) 'n' ΛΣ. tuarum + 'n' ACJΛMRSWYZ.

p. 74.   l. 1. circumstantium] circumadstantium AGΓJΛMPΣWZ+atque omnium fidelium christianorum Aˡ(?)DY.

l. 2. pro . . . uel *om.* CGΓMΣ.

l. 4. suarum + pro stratu seniorum &c. Σ (208 sq.). tibique Aˡ(?)ΓHPSYZ.

l. 5. uero et uiuo G.

Communicantes.

l. 7. semperque GRSZ. genetricis + eiusdem J.

l. 9. ac] et C.

l. 10. petri + et GRΣ. thomae + et Σ.

l. 11. simonis + et (*exc.* D). taddei + mathiae D. cleti] ancleti Σ.

l. 13. damiani + martini grigorii augustini hironimi benedicti patricii necnon et illorum martyrum confessorum uirguinum quorum hodie in conspectu gloriae tuae celebratur triumphus D + georgii benedicti martini gregorii J + dionysii rustici et eleutherii G + hilarii martini augustini gregorii hieronymi benedicti GM + (. . . .) Aˡ.

l. 15. eundem *om.* GΓΛMP.

l. 16. *fin.* + amen DHRSWYZ.

Hanc igitur.

l. 18. tuae + quam tibi &c. Σ. suscipias Σ + eumque atque omnem populum ab idolorum cultura eripias &c. Σ. dies quoque Σ.

l. 20. eripias Σ.

l. 21. c. *om.* Σ. *fin.* + amen DHRSWYZ.

Quam oblationem. The following are the variations in the disposition of the crosses: CGΓ have none, Σ only the first, M omits the first three, P the last, and J both those in l. 24.

l. 22. tu] te Σ. d. + o. SY. q. *post* d. Aˡ.

l. 24. digneris ut] dignareque Σ.

l. 25. dei *om.* ACDHPRSΣWYZ. nostri *om.* J.

l. 37.   Read *facietis.*

Qui pridie. The crosses are omitted in CGΓJΣ.

l. 27. suas + et AˡHΛPRSWYZ. oculis + suis Σ. in] ad Σ. celum + et Σ.

l. 28. agens] *om.*† C egit Σ.

l. 29. benedixit + ac AˡHYZ. deditque HPRSYZ.

l. 30. enim *om.* AΓ.

l. 31. postquam AˀZ. est *om.* Σ. accepit Σ.

l. 33. deditque RSY.

l. 34. eo] hoc AˡDΣ. calix + sancti Σ.

l. 36. remissionet† G.

¹ Ebner, *Quellen und Forschungen zur geschichte . . . des Missale Romanum.* Iter Italicum, pp. 303, 367.

l. 37.　memoriam mei H.　facietis + passionem meam praedi-
cabitis &c. Σ².

l. 45.　Read *dignatus.*

Unde et memores.　CGΓΣ have no crosses ; J omits the two
last, D and the printed edd. of H the last.

l. 37.　memores + sumus DGΓJMΣ.

l. 38.　serui tui PRΣW.　eiusdem *om.* Λ²CGΓHΛMRΣWZ.

l. 39.　dni. *om.* CM.　dei *om.* RΣZ.　nostri + tam (*exc.* CD).

l. 40.　caelis G.

l. 44.　aspicere dignare Σ.

l. 45.　sicut HSY.

p. 75.　l.　2.　obtulit tibi H.

Supplices te.　All the crosses are omitted in CGΓJΣ, the last in
ΛΛMPZ.

l.　4.　rogamus + et petimus Σ.　hec *om.*† Σ.　perferri *om.*† C.
sancti *om.* CGΓM.

l.　5.　tui *om.* Z.　sublimi altari tuo Σ.　conspectum P.

l.　6.　ut] et Z.　hac altaris participatione] hoc altari sanctifica-
tionis Σ.

l.　8.　celesti *om.* Σ.　per &c.] *om.* Σ.　eundem] *om.* GΓJMPZ +
i. Y.

l.　9.　*fin.* + amen DGHSYZ.

l.　9.　J here inserts a paragraph beginning *Memento mei.*

l. 11.　For ·n· JPΣ have *nomina,* C ·n· *et illorum.* Neither of
these can be considered a true variant, the former being
probably merely the expansion of ·n·¹, the latter a misreading
of *ill. et ill.,* and thus simply an equivalent of ·n·.

Memento etiam : omitted in G.

l. 10.　dne. + animarum S.　famulorum . . tuarum] et eorum
JPΣ.　famulorum + tuorum D.

l. 11.　·n· *om.* D.

l. 12.　pacis + *ill.*† J + cum omnibus &c. Σ (215-218).
dne.] *om.* CΓΣW *post* omnibus Λ.　et] ut Z.

l. 13.　ut *om.* CZ.

l. 14.　per &c. *om.* CΣ.　per + eundem ADHΛMRSWYZ.
c. + filium tuum Γ.　*fin.* + amen DHRSWYZ.

l. 22.　We should probably read *meriti,* with the bulk of MSS. But
Σ has *aestimatis meritis sed uenia,* which may possibly be the reading
intended here. It will be remembered that *uenia* might easily be
written *uenię* by our scribe. The St. Amand *Ordo* agrees exactly with
E (Duchesne, *Origines du Culte Chrétien,* 2nd ed. 1898, p. 449). In the
Vatican MS. of G we have *non stimamur*† *meritis,* and in Cod. Vat.
4770 *non estimamur* † *meritis* (Ebner, *Quellen und Forschungen,*
p. 424). And it may be noted that the final letters of *estimator* are
in the St. Gall MS. of the Gelasian Sacramentary written over an
erasure (G p. 239).

Nobis quoque.

l. 16.　et societatem] societatis G.

l. 17.　dignare Σ.　sanctis tuis C.　et] ac Λ.　martiribus + cum
petro paulo patricio Σ.

l. 18.　mathia barnaba ignatio *om.* Z.

l. 19.　felicitate *om.* C *post* cecilia (l. 20) Σ.　perpetua *om.* C.
agatha lucia *post* anastasia Σ.　agne] agna CDΣ agnete
ΛΓHRSWYZ.

¹ See Σ (215) with Dr. MacCarthy's note, and P p. 182 note.

l. 20.   anastasia + eufemia A¹ + eugenia brigita D + aethel-
drythae geretrudis J.

l. 21.   cum *om.* R.   consortia Σ.

l. 22.   aestimatis meritis Σ.   meriti . . . largitor *om.*† D.
uenia Σ ueniam† G.

l. 23.   *fin.* + amen HY.

Per quem haec omnia. CGГ have no crosses : JΛΣ omit the
last three. Additional crosses are placed in Σ at *creas* (l. 24) ;
in HRSYZ at *patri* (l. 26) and *spiritus* (l 27).

l. 28.   amen *om.* ΣY.

Praeceptis salutaribus.

l. 28.   oremus] oratio D *om.* Σ.   preceptis . . moniti] diuino
magisterio edocti Σ.

l. 35.   amen *om.* CGГHΛMR.

Libera nos.

l. 36.   q. *om.* Σ.   omni malo praeterito praesenti et futuro Σ.

l. 37.   et *sec. om.* Г.   intercedentibus Σ + pro nobis DGHΣYZ.
beata . . . maria et *om.* Σ.   et *tert. om.* R.   semper (*exc.* GSΣ).

l. 38.   et *om.* Z.   b.] sanctis G.

l. 39.   et *om.* Z.   atque *om.* ΣZ.   andrea] patricio Σ + necnon
et b. stephano protom. tuo M + necnon et b. Cyriaco m. tuo
et sancto martino confessore tuo P.   cum omnibus sanctis
om. GГΣ.   cum] et ΛMR.   sanctis + tuis J.

l. 40.   pacem + tuam DΣ.   in *om.* M.

l. 41.   peccatis G.   liberi semper G.

l. 42.   per + eundem ACDHRSWY.

l. 44.   per . . . amen *om.* M.   amen *om.* Y.

Pax domini. No crosses in ACDGГHJΛMPΣW : additional
crosses at *semper* and *uobiscum* in RSYZ.

l. 45.   pax + et caritas Σ.   dni. + nostri i. c. et communicatio
sanctorum omnium Σ.

l. 46.   Neither *Agnus,* nor any of the prayers following, is given
in GΣ. The *Agnus,* without the succeeding prayers, is found in ГΛMP.

p. 76.   l. 2.   *Agnus* and the prayers on this page are found also with some
omissions and inversions of order in ACDHJRSWYZ. The differences
in their arrangement are exhibited in the subjoined table, which takes
no account of prayers in some of these books which have not place
in E.

EY.	AJ.	C.	D.	H.	R.	S.	W.	Z.
Agnus	*Agnus*	*Agnus*	*Agnus*	*Agnus*	*Haec*	*Agnus*	*Agnus*	—
Haec sacro-sancta	*Haec*	*Haec*	*Dne. sancte*	*Haec*	*Agnus*	*Haec*	*Haec*	*Haec*
Dne. sancte pater	*Dne. sancte*	—	*Haec*	*Dne. sancte*	—	*Dne. sancte*	*Dne. sancte*	—
Perceptio	—	—	*Perceptio*	—	*Dne. i. c.*	*Dne. i. c.*	—	*Perceptio*
Dne. i. c.	*Dne. i. c.*	*Dne. i. c.*	—	*Dne. i. c.*	*Perceptio*	*Perceptio*	*Dne. i. c.*	*Dne. i. c.*
Placeat tibi	—	*Placeat*	*Placeat*	*Placeat*	*Placeat*	*Placeat*	*Placeat*	*Placeat*

Haec sacrosancta. ACDHJRSWYZ. SW have a cross at *sacro-sancta* (l. 2).

l. 2. hec sacrosancta *om.* RZ. commixtio + et (*om.* Z) conse-cratio RZ.

l. 3. sit] fiat (*ante* commixtio (l. 2) RZ) + mihi (nobis Y)et HJWY. omnibus] mihi omnibusque S. omnibus sumentibus] accipientibus nobis R nobis accipientibus Z. salus . . . corporis et *om.* RZ.

l. 4. et]atque A. ad] in R. et ad . . . salutaris *om.* C. ad . . . eternam] uita aeterna Z. promerendam . . . salutaris *om.* RZ. eternam promerendam] capessendam aeternam DJW aeternam capessendam Y + et capescendam HS + sit J.

l. 5. *fin.* + per &c. DHSY + amen JRWZ.

Domine sancte pater. ADHJSWY.

l. 6. michi] nobis Y. hoc] *om.* D + sacrosanctum HJS.

l. 7. filii tui dni. (+ dei Y) nostri i. c. (*exc.* DH). dni. nostri i. c. *om.* H. ita] tam W + digne HJSW.

l. 8. assumere A. merear (mereamur JY) per hoc (hec W) (*exc.* D). omnium *om.* Y.

l. 9. meorum] nostrorum JY. de *om.* (*exc.* J). tuo *om.* A. spiritu sancto A. repleri + et (atque W) ab aeterna damna-tione liberari et in die iudicii cum sanctis et electis tuis in perpetua requie collocari AW + et pacem tuam habere S. quia &c.] per eundem A.

l. 10. d. + solus JSW. et preter te non est alius *om.* D. alius + nisi tu solus Y. cuius regnum &c.] qui uiuis &c. Y.

l. 11. gloriosum *om.* HJW. + sine fine *ante* permanet HJSW. amen *om.* Y.

Perceptio corporis. DRSYZ.

l. 12. perceptio *om.* S. et sanguinis *om.* RZ. c. + sacramen-tum S.

l. 13. quam] quod S. ego *om.* (*exc.* R). + licet *ante* indignus S. peccator *om.* sumere presumo] accipio S. michi pro-ueniat] proueniat mihi Z sit mihi S mihi ueniat Y.

l. 14. in] ad Y. in iudicium] iudicio S. et]nec ad Y. condem-nationi S. sed + pro (*exc.* S). prosit pietate S.

l. 15. michi ad &c.] corporis mei et animae saluti amen S. ad purgationem peccatorum et *om.* RYZ. mentis] animae Y.

l. 16. corporis + et ad medelam percipiendam R.

Domine ihesu christe. ACHJRSWYZ.

l. 18. sancto spiritu C. uiuificasti] saluasti C.

l. 19. me + quaeso SW. sacrum] sacrosanctum AHJSYZ. et + hunc S. a cunctis] ab omnibus HRYZ (?).

l. 20. et *pri.* + ab HJSW. meis *post* iniquitatibus AHJRSW.

l. 21. semper *om.* ACY *hiat* Z. oboedire] inherere R *hiat* Z. preceptis] mandatis HJRSWZ. in perpetuum *om.* JR.

l. 22. + permittas *post* separari JRSY *post* perpetuum (l. 21) H. + saluator mundi *ante* qui uiuis S. qui uiuis] amen J.

Placeat tibi. CDHRSWYZ.

l. 23. dne. d. *om.* (*exc.* D). sancta trinitas *om.* D. trinitas + d. W. + sanctum *ante* obsequium D.

l. 24. ut + hoc CHSWY.

l. 25. maiestatis *om.*† W. tibi . . . obtuli (l. 26) *om.*z. tibi] *om.* C + sit (*exc.* CZ). acceptabileque† C. michique *om.* C. et] in† W.

l. 26. propitiabile te miserante z + meritis et intercessionibus &c. z.

l. 27. qui uiuis &c.] per c. dnm. nostrum amen R *om.* CZ.

MISSAE VOTIVAE.

DE S. TRINITATE.

l. 2. In M this is the mass for the Octave of Pentecost.
Office and Psalm. ACDHRSWY.

l. 3. trinitas + atque.
Collect. ACDΓHJΛMPRSWYZ.

l. 7. dedisti + nobis JY.

l. 9. maiestatis + tuae D.

l. 10. semper *om.* Γ.

l. 11. qui uiuis &c.] per dnm. DΓJΛMPRWZ in qua uiuis &c. CHY.

l. 13. This is the usual epistle in this mass. But CRW include v. 11
(not v. 12) as well as v. 13.

l. 17. This epistle appears along with the last in HYS.

l. 19. The grail in ACDΓ*ᵃ*HARSWY begins *Benedictus es dne. qui
intueris abyssos et sedes super cherubin.* Probably these words have
been accidentally omitted here : which would account for the heading
℣ instead of *Gradale.* The resemblance of the words *Benedictus* and
Benedicite, over which the scribe stumbles in l. 22, would suffice to
explain the error.

l. 20. In this ℣ E agrees with CΓᵃ. ADHSY have *Benedicite deum
caeli quia fecit*, RW *Benedictus es in firmamento.*

l. 22. Read *Benedictus.* E here follows DΓᵃHRSWY : while C,
agreeing with A, has *Libera nos.* S adds another ℣ *Laudate pueri.*

l. 24. This may represent a ℣ in the exemplar which the scribe began
to copy, but changed his mind.

Gospel. Inflection mark over v. 4 reminiscamini (l. 27).

Offertory. ACDHRSWY.

l. 30. benedictus + sit.

l. 31. alleluia *om. (exc.* S *in tempore paschali).*

p. 78. l. 1. silenter] The direction that *Suscipe s. Trinitas* should be said
silently seems to be unusual. It is found, however, in Montecassino
Cod. 127 (xi. 5), a manuscript of the eleventh or twelfth century
(Ebner, *Quellen und Forschungen zur Geschichte und Kuntsgeschichte
des Missale Romanum* Iter Italicum, p. 310) : ‘Sacerdos . . .
secrete dicat hanc orationem, *Suscipe*,’ &c.

l. 2 sqq. We have here a portion of the ordinary of the mass. This
seems to confirm the conclusion already reached (above p. 168) that
the mass for the Holy Trinity in E was a missa canonica, embodying
the ordinary and canon.[1] Our scribe has written this mass very
carelessly (see below on l. 23), and may well be supposed to have
forgotten to omit portions which, in the rearrangement of the book
(see above, p. 168), ought to have been struck out. His error, if such
it was, has preserved to us the only portion of an Anglo-Irish Ordinary
now remaining, with the exception of *In spiritu humilitatis*, left in the
Missa pro defunctis in D (p. 34). The form of *Suscipe* given here is

---

[1] It may be observed that the collect following the hymn *Sēn dé* in the Irish *Liber
Hymnorum* (ed. Bernard and Atkinson, vol. i. p. 30), is made up of phrases from
Suscipe s. Trinitas and the secret of this mass.

longer than those of HSY, and differs much from them in other respects. The form, so far as I have noticed, which approaches most closely to ours is that given in Λ (p. 9). With this and with R it is collated below. Almost identical with Λ is the form given in Martène, *De Eccl. Rit.* I. iv. 12. t. i. col. 509, from an ordo edited by Flaccus Illyricus, which Martène believed to have been in use at Salzburg.

l. 6. The omission of the name of St. John Baptist is worthy of note. Le Brun says (*Explication*, Pt. iii. art. ix. note 41) that St. John is not named in the Micrologus, nor in any missal before the twelfth century. This statement cannot indeed be accepted without reserve (see Paciaudi, *De Cultu S. Johannis Baptistae*, Rome, 1755₁ p. 138): but the absence of the clause containing the name may indicate an early date for the text of E at this place.

l. 7. Read *placuerunt*.

et] This word is, of course, superfluous. But in a very large number of instances a clause is introduced at this point, beginning with *et*, and apparently intended to adapt the general form for use on special occasions not otherwise provided for (see below in the collation). When the missal was revised and rearranged, this clause, if it were specially appropriate to the Trinity Mass, would quite naturally be marked for omission. It is not impossible that the scribe, by an oversight, allowed the first word to stand, while passing over the remainder.

Suscipe Sancta Trinitas. ΛR.

l. 2. offerimus R. in] ob R.

l. 3. incarnationis natiuitatis *om.* R.

l. 4. atque] et R *om.* Λ. i. c. dni. nostri R.

l. 5. honore ΛR. beatissime . . . christi et *om.* Λ. beatae R. uirginis marie] mariae semper uirginis R. genitricis . . . christi *om.* R.

l. 6. + et b. ioannis baptiste et sanctorum ap. petri et pauli et istorum *ante* et omnium R. tuorum . . . mundi et *om.* R.

l. 7. et † + eorum quorum hodie festiuitas celebratur et quorum hic nomina et reliquiae habentur Λ.

l. 8. omnibusque fidelibus christianis *om.* ΛR.

l. 9. ut] et R. omnes *om.* R.

l. 10. qui in trinitate &c.] per &c. R *om.* Λ.

l. 12. deinde] E here follows the Roman rather than the English usage. In HSY *Orate* does not immediately follow *Suscipe*.

l. 17. These verses, or some of them, were not uncommonly used as a response to *Orate*. See Rome Bibl. Angelica Cod. D. 7. 3 (Ebner, *Quellen und Forschungen*, Iter Italicum, p. 135), Milan Bibl. Ambros. Cod. H. 255. inf. (*ib.* p. 306), Amalarius *De Eccl. Off.* iii. 19 (Hittorp, p. 192*b*), Ps-Alcuin *De Div. Off.* (Hittorp, p. 82*b*), Durandus, *Rationale*, IV. xxxii. 3, the York Missal (Y i. 171 sq.) and the usage of the Carmelites as reported by Le Brun (*Explication . . . des Prières et des Cérémonies de la Messe*, Liège, 1777, t. i. p. 372).

Secret. ACDΓHJΛMPRSWYZ.

l. 19. dne. *om.* Y. d. nr. *om.* AC. nr. *om.* DΓHPSWZ. + trinitas sancta *ante* per HSY. per . . . uirtutem et *om. (exc.* HΛY) *post claus. sequ.* (et *ante* per) HY.

l. 20. et . . . inuocationem *om.* ΛM. sancti nominis AHJRSWY. sancti *om.* CDΓPZ.

l. 21. cooperante sancto spiritu *om. (exc.* HMSY). spiritu sancto HMSY.

l. 22.   per &c.] qui uiuis &c. HSW qui in trinitate perfecta &c. V per CDJΛPZ *om.* Γ.   eundem *om.* AR.

l. 23.   The concluding portion of the mass has been omitted.   Compare above on p. 11, l. 35 and below on p. 91, l. 10.   This blunder of the scribe is readily accounted for, in the present instance, on the supposition that in the exemplar the Trinity Mass was a missa canonica. For in that case several pages, containing the Canon, would intervene between the secret and the common.   See above on p. 73, l. 16 ; p. 78, l. 2.

DE S. CRUCE.

l. 24.   feria vi] so CHJΛPSW.   Bishop Forbes (*Arbuthnott Missal,* p. xxxix) here incorrectly reads *feria iii,* as does also Mr. Warren in C.
l. 26 sq.   Read *uita, liberati, saluati.*
Office. ACDHRSWY.
l. 26.   salus + et D.   quem] quam DW.   et *sec. om.*   saluati et liberati.
l. 27.   sumus + per W.
Collect. ACDHJΛPRSWY.
l. 30.   dni. nostri i. c. *om.* ΛPR.   i. c. *om.* A.
l. 31.   sanctificari ΛPW.
l. 32.   q.] propitius D.
l. 33.   ubique *om.* C.   per + eundem ACHRSWY.

p. 79.   l. 5.   We have this ℣ in DHRSWY : not in AC.   AR add a ℣ : *Dicite in gentibus* : C has ℣ *Nos autem* : D combines these two, giving *Nos autem, Dicite in gentibus.*   Thus in this grail E differs from DR, still more from AC, and agrees with HSWY.   Γᵃ has no provision for this mass.
l. 5.   Read *dulcia* : though D has *dulce.*
℣. DHRSWY.
l. 5.   ferens] pondus† D.
l. 6.   portare] sustinere.   dnm.] deum D.
l. 7.   Read *matheum.*
Gospel.   Inflection mark over v. 19 die (l. 9).
Offertory. ACDHRSWY.
For collations see on p. 67, l. 34.
Secret. ACDHJΛPRSWY.
l. 15.   nos q. dne. ab omnibus R.   q. dne. AS.   q. *om.* JΛP. mundet] purget (*exc.* AD).
l. 16.   + immolata *post* crucis HRSWY *post* etiam C.   offensa DJΛP offensas HSV offensum C.
l. 17.   per + eundem HY.
Common. ACDHSWY.
l. 19.   liberati + sumus.
l. 20.   redemit + nos.   alleluia *sec.om.* (*exc.* D).   *fin.* + alleluia D.
Postcommon. ACDJΛPRSY.
l. 22.   nobis *om.* J.   + q. *ante* dne. AJ.   quos + in D.
l. 23.   fecisti (*post* honore P) DJP.   eius] tuis Λ.   presidiis Λ.

DE S. MARIA.

l. 24.   in sabbato] So JP : compare *Micrologus,* cap. 60, and S col. 759*, where five reasons are given why 'Sabbato celebratur de beata Virgine.'   But Γ (col. 388) has *feria tertia.*   In S the mass of the B.V.M. is said daily (col. 761*).

ab octauis] There are in E four masses de S. Maria, the period during which each is to be used being indicated in its title, viz. : (1) p. 79, l. 24 *ab octauis* ; (2) p. 80, l. 35 *in aduentu dni.* ; (3) p. 81, l. 14 *de natiuitate dni. usque ad purificationem* ; (4) p. 82, l. 30 *in resurrectione usque ascensionem iocl.* Now (2) and (3) account for the interval between the beginning of Advent and Feb. 2. The meaning of (4) is not so clear : but it seems likely that *iocl* is an error for [*et*] *ī ocl*, i.e. *et in octauis* [*eiusdem*] ; or for 7 [*per*] *ocl* (see above on p. 11, l. 31), i.e. *et per octauas* [*eiusdem*]. If so this mass is intended for use from Easter to the Octave of Ascension. It seems clear that 'octave' most probably refers to the same festival in (1) as in (4). Thus (1) will mean 'from the Octave of Ascension (to Advent).' Our four masses therefore are for (1) Octave of Ascension to Advent ; (2) Advent ; (3) Christmas to Candlemas ; and (4) Eastertide. Now if we turn to R we find the last three of these, the first with a slight variation to be noticed immediately, and a fifth which is obviously needed to complete the series, viz., from Candlemas to Easter. How are we to account for the absence of a mass for the last of these periods in E ? Most probably by supposing that it was accidentally omitted by the scribe. This part of the missal is extremely confused in its arrangement, as we shall have to notice hereafter, and bears tokens of a bungling attempt to alter the order of the masses. Nothing is more likely than that in the process of changing the sequence a mass should be omitted. Or possibly (1) served for the earlier period as well as for that with which its title connects it. But, however this may be, it suffices to say that similar lacunae occur in other books, as, for example, Y. It remains to observe that the mass for the time preceding Advent is entitled in R 'a penthecoste usque ad aduentum,' not as here 'ab octauis [ascensionis].' The difference is trifling, affecting at the most only the mass for the Vigil of Pentecost. But indeed it is possible that E contemplates no mass of St. Mary on that day. In the case of the Missa de S. Cruce, which was said weekly, a long list of circumstances is given in S (col. 748*) which would entail its omission. And where the Mass of the B.V.M. was used only once a week, it is not improbable that it was similarly superseded on certain great days, of which Whitsun Eve might well be one. If there was no Missa de S. Maria on Whitsun Eve, the directions in R and E are equivalent.

The mass which corresponds to the present in its contents is variously headed. It is *Missa de S. Maria* without addition in ACΓJΛP, while in R the addition is given *a penthecoste usque ad aduentum*, in S *a purificatione usque ad aduentum dni.*, in W *a festo purificationis usque ad pascha et a festo s. Trinitatis usque ad aduentum dni.*, in Y *a festo purificationis ad caput ieiunii et a festo*, &c. (as W), in H *post purificationem.* D has no title.

l. 25. Read *puerpera.*

l. 27. This is the psalm in CD (*et gaudia*) HY. A has *Quia concupiuit*, S *Benedicta tu*, W both of these latter, R *Virgo dei genitrix*. Γᴺ is without the mass.

Collect. ACDΓHJΛPRSWY.

l. 30. nobis famulis tuis ΛP.

l. 31. salute] sanitate ACDHJRY prosperitate ΓΛP.
gloriosa] gloriosae ac CD.

l. 33. futura] aeterna HRSWY.

Epistle. Inflection marks over *Title* sapientiae ; v. 15 potestas.

p. 80. l. 6. For Mondays only in S. D adds two, and W one verse after l. 7. ACHRV agree exactly with E. No mass in Γⁿ.

l. 8. Read *iohannem.*

l. 9. *Stabant iuxta crucem* occurs in W as an alternative gospel in this mass, as here. HRSWY direct its use at Eastertide.

First Gospel. Inflection mark over v. 27 hora (l. 10).

Offertory. ACDHRSWY.

l. 16. felix + nanque (*exc.* C) + ualde C (*om.* nanque D 7 + nanque C 164). es *om.* C *post* sacra D (p. 7).

l. 17. d.] dns. AC. nr. *om.* W. *fin.* + alleluia alleluia D + alleluia AHS ('extra lxx usque ad pascha') Y.

l. 19. Read *beatae.*

Secret. ACDΓHPRSWY (J in another mass de S. Maria).

l. 19. dei . . . mariȩ] mariae semper uirginis AΓJPRS. semper HY.

l. 21. nobis *om.* C. *fin.* + et pacem CHRSWY + et iram tue indignacionis quam iuste meremur propiciatus auerte W.

l. 22 sqq. See above on p. 44, l. 18.

Preface. AD.

l. 25. concedas sempiterna A. concedet D.

l. 28. Read *tuo.* C reads *domina* for *domino* : and so we have it p. 67, l. 4. So also Y ii. p. 83. I have not found this common here elsewhere, except in C.

Postcommon. ACDΓHJPRSWY.

l. 31. beatissimae J. beatȩ . . . mariȩ] b. mariae semper uirginis AR eius ΓPS.

l. 32. nos patrociniis HJY. nos *post* q. (l. 31) A.

l. 33. cuius + sanctissima A.

l. 34. dnm. &c.] eundem HWY.

DE S. MARIA.

l. 35. in aduentu dni.] *ab aduentu dni.* C : *ab aduentu usque ad natiui-latem* R : *infra aduentum . . . nisi in festo conceptionis* S : *in aduentu* HY : *per totum aduentum usque ad festum natalis dni.* W.

Collect. CDHRSWY (AJZ for Annunciation AMP collecta for Annunciation).

For collations see on p. 54, l. 2.

p. 81. **Secret.** ACDJΛ (S for trans. of St. Martin HY for St. Egidius).

l. 4. semper *om.* C.

l. 5. in . . . sancta *om.* S. eius ueneratio (*om.* in) ADHY. sancta *om.* CJΛ.

l. 6. maiestati tuae S.

Postcommon. ACD (G for Assumption).

l. 8. satiati] sacrati C. q. *om.*† G. nos *om.*† G.

l. 9. protectione + ubique Λ.

l. 10. sancta + uirgine Λ.

l. 12. per &c.] qui tecum AC per eundem D.

DE S. MARIA.

l. 14. *Ab octauis epiphaniae usque ad purificationem* Y : *A die cir-cumcisionis usque ad purificationem* H : *In natali dni.* A : CDRSW as here.

l. 18. Read *praemia.*

Collect. ACDHRSWY (G for Assumption JA for Sunday after Christmas ΓMP for January 1).

l. 17. qui + spe G.

l. 18. humano . . . praemia *om.*† C. prestitisti] praetulisti J.

l. 19. per] ext Λ.

l. 20. uitae + nostrae G. per *om.* (*exc.* G).

Secret. CDSW.

l. 25. substantiam *post* eiusdem (l. 24) CS. praesenti hoc C.

l. 26. dnm.] eundem CS.

l. 29. Read *auctorem.*

Postcommon. S (C for Purification).

 For collation see on p. 52, l. 26, where the text in E differs from that given here.

DE RESURRECTIONE.

l. 32. The scribe in error wrote here the title of the next mass. He subsequently altered it (see footnote) to *De resurrectione usque ascensionem,* which agrees with D, *De resurrectione.* D is the only other missal in which I have found this mass. It is evidently out of place here, intruded into the series of missae de S. Cruce and de S. Maria. Probably a rearrangement had been attempted of the Votive Masses, and the difference in order of the masses in E and its exemplar was the cause of the error in the rubrication. Bishop Forbes (*Arbuthnott Missal*, p. xxxix) omits the title of this mass.

p. 82. l. 1. *nostra*] This word is an error of the scribe for *noster.* It should have been marked with an obelus.

p. 81. Collect. D(ΓΛMP orationes paschales G orationes paschales uespertinales).

l. 36. in *om.* D.

p. 82. l. 1. nostra† *om.* D. baptismo regenerari fecisti D.

l. 2. b. immortalitate facias D. dnm.] eundem ΓΛMP.

l. 3. See footnote. I am unable to offer any satisfactory explanation of this line. The latter part should probably be expanded *in resurrectione (usque) as(censionem).* The fact that these words occur in the title of the next mass suggests that we have here a second fruitless attempt of the scribe to insert it in its proper place (see above on p. 81, l. 32). But the two first letters cannot represent *de sancta cruce,* and there were no letters before those which now remain legible.

l. 7. Read *id.* The symbol for *est* (pl. II. l. 6 from end) is confused with the letter *d.*

 Secret. D (ΓJΛMP orationes paschales G as collect for Wednesday after Easter).

l. 5. unigenitum tuum *om.* (*exc.* D). unigenitum + filium D.

l. 6. ut] et M.

l. 7. nos] quos G. quod] quo P.

l. 8. reconciliatur† G + et DP. quod] quo P.

l. 9. i. c. + filius tuus (*exc.* DG).

Postcommon. D(ΓΛP orationes paschales).

l. 12. actionibus] actibus DP rationibus ΓΛ. deponentes + in P.

l. 14. i. c. &c.] per eundem ΓΛP.

DE S. CRUCE.

l. 15. Incorrectly read by Bishop Forbes (*Arbuthnott Missal*, p. xxxix) *De S. Maria ad resurrectionem*. This mass, like the last, appears to be misplaced. It would naturally have followed the Missa de S. Cruce on p. 78. The scribe may have thought it fitting that the three masses for the Easter season should be brought together. They are together also in D, but in a different order. The corresponding mass in most books is that for the Wednesday before Easter. In some the collects are also used in a missa de S. Cruce.

Collect. ACDΓHJAMPRSWYZ.

l. 19. uoluisti] fecisti PZ. repelleres D. potestates Z.

l. 20. resurrectionis + eius DS. gratiam] gloriam DHY.

l. 21. dnm.] eundem.

Secret. AΓHJAPRYZ (SW for Thursday after xl⁴ GM for Tuesday after xl⁴ L mense septembri).

l. 23. nos + o. et Y (*semel*).

l. 24. gratae (*exc.* HYZ). sint A. pia + 'sacra' L. deferentis M.

Postcommon. ACDΓHJAMPRSWYZ.

l. 27. d. + intelligentiam spiritalem Z. temporalem + in cruce D.

l. 28. uitam + te HMRY (*semel*) Z.

l. 29. dedise] uenisse A.

DE S. MARIA.

l. 31. ioc͠i] Probably an error for *et* [*per*] *octauas* : so p. 11, l. 31 the symbol 7 (= *et*) is confused with the letter *i*.

Colleot. D.

l. 35. fieri participes.

p. 83.   Seoret. (D for missa in commemoratione incarnationis &c. dni. ACΓHJARSWYZ for Annunciation &c. MP among aliae orationes after postcommon of Annunciation.)

For collations see on p. 54, l. 29, where *q.* is inserted after *nostris* (l. 2).

l. 8.   Read *nostris*.

Postcommon. D (ACΓHJARSWYZ for Annunciation MP among aliae orationes after postc. of Annunciation).

For collations see on p. 55, l. 2.

DE OMNIBUS APOSTOLIS.

Colleot. D (J for St. Alban).

l. 14. et mis. *om.* J. d. + ut† J. b. . . ap. (l. 15)] sanctum albanum &c. J.

l. 15. celesti] martyrii J.

l. 16. praesta q. *ante* o. (l. 14) J.

l. 17. frequentamus obsecrando] passionis agimus J.

l. 18. ita *om.* J. iugiter *om.* J.

l. 22.   Read *andreae.*

l. 24.   *suppliciter offerimus* is superfluous.

Seoret. D (AΓ for SS. Abdon and Sennen G for Ember Saturday in September J for St. Alban HY for SS. Tiburtius &c.).

l. 21. salutaris *om.* AGΓHY. dne. q. G. quam . . . offerimus (l. 24) *om.* G. quae† D. sanctorum . . . ap. (l. 23)] sancti albani &c. J.

l. 22. apostolorum *om.* AΓHY. petri . . . commemoratione] natalitiis AΓHY.

l. 23. commemorationis† D. tuę maiestati *om.* AΓHY. suppliciter] recensentes AΓHY.

l. 24. ligamina] uincula AGΓHY. prauitatis] iniquitatis G.

l. 25. karismata] dona AGΓHY.

l. 26. tribuat] conciliet AGΓHY.

Postcommon. D (J for St. Alban).

l. 28. quos] nos D.

l. 29. ap. *om.* J. petri . . . ap. *om.* J.

l. 31. satiati D. indulgentiam + nos J.

IN COMMEMORATIONE SS. PETRI ET PAULI.

l. 33. The masses with similar headings in ACRWY differ from this in all their collects.

Collect. D (L mense aprili in dedicatione).

l. 35. b. . . . pauli] b. petri ap. L. tuorum *om.* D.

l. 36. gloriosam . . . perfecisti] facis esse gloriosam L. + praesta L.

l. 37. ut et DL. doctrina semper ipsius L. muniamur] foueamur L.

p. 84. l. 2. Read *uota populi*. The origin of the present reading is plain. The exemplar must have had *uota uota plī* : taking the letter *a* with the third instead of the second word and omitting *o*, the scribe wrote *uota ut aplī*, as in the text.

l. 3. Read *confidentem, hostiae* : the interchange of *d* and *t* and of *a* and *ae*, is frequent in Irish MSS.

Secret. D.

l. 7. Read *participare*.

Postcommon. D (G as ad populum for Tuesday after xlˡ P as vesper collect for Wednesday after xlˡ).

l. 6. protege] respice GP. dne. + propitius ad GP.

l. 7. participare] proficere GP. apostolica intercessione *om.* GP.

DE SANCTIS QUI IN ECCLESIA REQUIESCUNT.

l. 9. Read *in ecclesia*. This mass appears, with some variety in the text of the collects, in many missals. The wording of the title is not uniform, but it seems in almost all cases to imply either that the saint or saints commemorated were buried in the Church, or that relics of them were preserved there. The title of our mass is apparently almost decisive that the Church for which E was written claimed to be the actual place of burial of the saints mentioned in the collects. The wording of the collects themselves does not indeed support this conclusion, and the use of *reliquię* in l. 12, without the alternative *corpora*, may seem to tell against it. But A was certainly used in the resting place of St. Augustine (Rule's edition, p. xi sq.), and *reliquiae* is found in it without *corpora* in all the collects. And *reliquiae* seems to be frequently applied to the *bodies* of the three Irish Patrons. See, for example, the Office for their translation as quoted by Colgan, *Trias*, p. 618, and compare the Annals at A.D. 1293.

l. 12. patricii 'n'] I am not aware that any parallel can be cited for this form of expression, and it certainly needs explanation. I mention first two suggestions which have been made to me, and which seem worth recording. 1. That it is a corruption of *patrocinium*. This would be possible, with a careless scribe like ours, if the exemplar had *patroctiū* : but *patrocinium* seems to be a reading entirely without support from other missals, and very improbable. 2. That it should be expanded *patricii nostri.* But (1) the scribe did not so understand it, for *n* with a point *before* as well as after it is nowhere used for *nostri*; and (2) though examples of *Patricius noster* in Irish literature may be forthcoming, it is not a phrase which might be expected to occur in a mass collect. I believe the most likely supposition to be the following : 3. That in the exemplar *patricii* did not occur in the text of the prayer, but was written in the margin opposite ·*n*·. The scribe transferred it to the text, but in doing so, instead of putting the word in place of ·*n*·, wrote it before this letter. We have here in short a conflate reading—by no means the only one in our MS. This hypothesis is borne out by the fact that the collect reads better without the name than with it: in fact, omitting *patricii*, it is almost identical in text with CD. And it is further supported by the absence of the name from the secret and postcommon.

The two foregoing notes appear to establish a probability that the Church to which our missal belonged claimed to be the burial-place of St. Patrick. But here an objection to this view must be considered. The title is inconsistent with the text of the prayers, the former implying the possession of the body of the saint, while the latter is quite appropriate if mere relics were preserved in the Church. Is it not possible, then, that the scribe simply copied the title without making the alteration in it which was required to adapt it to the collects over which it was placed? He has certainly been guilty of a similar blunder elsewhere (p. 55, l. 22). That he has been equally remiss here must be admitted to be a possibility : but it seems an improbable supposition, for the following reasons : (1) It involves the assumption that the scribe transcribed the title and the collects from different MSS. Otherwise the same incongruity between heading and prayers must have existed in his exemplar. Either in it, then, or in one of its ancestors, a definite title must have been substituted for one that was indefinite, without the corresponding changes being made in the prayers—a fact very difficult to account for in the case of a scribe less stupid than ours. (2) A more likely theory of the origin of the phenomena may easily be suggested. Let us suppose that the exemplar of E had a mass (as in C) headed *De sanctis presentis ecclesie,* with the words *corpora uel reliquiae* in all the collects. On its margin notes would be written, with the view of adapting the mass to the special circumstances of the church where St. Patrick was buried. Thus opposite the title would appear *qui in ecclesia requiescunt* : while opposite the collect would be the name *patricii, corpora uel* being marked for deletion. These latter notes would of course be intended to apply to all the prayers, though actually written opposite the first only. It would be quite in keeping with all we know of the scribe of E to suppose that a bungling attempt to incorporate the marginalia with the text produced the mass as it now stands. By some such hypothesis we must account for the conflate title for the mass of January 1 (p. 7, l. 14 ; see note) and for the reading *dignanter propitius,* p. 22, l. 14.

For the bearing of this mass on the history of the missal, see the Introduction, p. xiv *sqq.*

Collect. ACDJPZ (Y for Feast of Relics).

l. 11. q. *om.* P. nobis] *post* propitiare Y + indignis D.

l. 12. sanctorum . . . ·n·] sancti augustini confessoris tui

atque pontificis A huius sancti 'n' m. tui Z horum m. tuorum P.
sanctorum + confessorum CD. patricii *om.* CDJY. 'n' *om.*J.
+ necnon *ante* et A. 'n' et eorum *om.* Y. et eorum . . .
ecclesia *om.* J. et eorum . . . reliquiae] qui PZ. eorum]
ceterorum (*om.* A) omnium sanctorum ACD. quorum + corpora uel CD.

l. 13. hac] praesenti (*exc.* J). continentur] requiescunt (-scit
Z) CDPYZ. eorum] eius Z. piis intercessionibus ADY.

l. 14. semper *om.* P. protegamur] muniamur C.

Secret. ACDJPZ (W for trans. of St. Aldhelm, Y for St. John of
Beverley and Feast of Relics).

l. 16. clementia] pietas WY (*semel*) ecclesia† P. dne. q. (*exc.*
CY). q. *om.* Y (*semel*). dne.] d. Y (*semel*) *om.* C.

l. 17. munus oblatum] hanc oblacionem W. et] quod A.
b. . . . ecclesia] sancti aldelmi . . . pontificis W sancti confessoris tui iohannis episcopi Y (*semel*) praesent.um sanctorum Y
(*semel*) sanctorum tuorum J huius sancti m. 'n' tu i Z horum
b. m. tuorum P.   b. . . . tuorum] sancti augustini confessoris tui atque pontificis necnon et ceterorum omnium
sanctorum A horum sanctorum tuorum 'n' atque eorum D.

l. 18. tuorum + et omnium sanctorum C.   quorum . . . re-
liquiẹ]qui D. corpora uel *om.* A. requiescunt] continentur A.

l. 19. ecclesia + sacras A. orationes] orationem P. emundet]
emundent† C absoluet Y (*semel*).

l. 22. Read *pro.*

Postcommon. ACDJPZ (W for St. Taurinus Y for Feast of
Relics).

l. 22. misteria] *om.* C + dne. Z. pro . . . ueneratione] in
honore sancti confessoris tui taurini atque pontificis W pro
ueneratione sanctorum tuorum J. sanctorum . . . ecclesia]
sancti augustini &c. (*ut sup.*) A huius sancti 'n' m. tui Z
sanctorum m. tuorum P praesentium sanctorum Y.

l. 23. 'n' et 'n' *om.* C. et 'n'] atque eorum D. + et omnium
sanctorum *ante* quorum C. quorum . . . ecclesia] in
praesenti aecclesia quiescentium D.

l. 25. dne. q. A. dne. *om.* YZ. mereamur + habere Z
peccatorum] delictorum W *om.* C.

l. 26. gratie] gloriae Z *om.*† C.

PRO EPISCOPO.

l. 27. This mass is entitled *pro abbate* in AW, *pro antistite* in Y.

l. 32. Read *piissimo.*

Collect. AHJSWY.

l. 29. 'n' *om.* (*exc.* W) *post* nostro W. episcopo] abbati AW
antistiti HY.

l. 30. exempla J.

l. 34. Read *suscipe.*

Secret. ASWY.

l. 34. placatus suscipe S placatus admitte Y.

l. 35. episcopum] abbatem AW. episcopum nostrum *om.* Y.
'n' *om.* S *post* tuum W. gregemque . . . commisum] commissumque sibi gregem A *om.* Y.

l. 36. benignus *om.* Y. ubique + hic Y.

p. 85. **Postcommon.** ASWY.

l. 2. dne. ç̧ommunio W.

l. 3. episcopum] abbatem AW antistitem Y. ·n· *om.* AS *post* tuum Y. et commissum S. commissumque . . . gregem *om.* Y.

l. 4. + tua semper *ante* benigna Y. benigna + q. S: conserua] custodi Y.

PRO EPISCOPO.

l. 5. *Pro papa* HRSY, *Pro episcopis et sibi commisis* D, *Pro pastore* W, *Pro pontifice* Z. The mass here is really for an archbishop, as the text of the prayers shows. Compare above, Introduction, p. xvi.

Collect. CDHRSWYZ.

l. 7. fidelium omnium HY. tuum + ·n· (*exc.* CD) + et HY.

l. 8. archiepiscopum] *om.* (*exc.* Z) pontificem nostrum Z. pastorem quem HY. pastorem *om.* CDW.

l. 9. et *pri. om.* (*exc.* CD). exemplo + eis HY.

l. 10. commisso] credito (*exc.* CD.)

Secret. CDHRSWY.

D uses plural for singular.

l. 13. q. *om.* HY.

l. 14. archiepiscopum nostrum *om.* ·n· *om.* CD. pastorem ecclesiae tuae R pastorem populo tuo HSWY.

l. 15. esse HSY.

l. 20. Read *saluet.*

Postcommon. CDHRSWY.

l. 17. q. *om.* W. dne.] dni.† C + diuini (*exc.* CD).

l. 18. archiepiscopum nostrum *om.* ·n· *om.* D.

l. 19. pastorem ecclesiae tuae esse (preesse W *om.* HY) uoluisti (*exc.* CD). commisso sibi (*om.* HY) grege HRSY.

l. 20. sibi *om.* HWY. ac] et (*exc.* CD).

PRO REGE.

l. 25. Read *decenter.*

l. 26. Read *ad te* : cf. above on p. 17, l. 17.

Collect. ACΓHJAMRSY.

l. 23. rex nr. *om.* ΓAM. ·n· *om.* CHJRY *post* tuus A.

l. 24. qui + a Γ. tua miseratione] tuo nutu C. suscepit.

l. 25. omnium *om.* C. accipiat W.

l. 26. uoraginem] monstra (*exc.* ACS). euitare HY. et hostes superare *om.* ΓAMR. hostem AHJY.

l. 27. uita et ueritas HY.

l. 29. Read *suscipe, tue.*

Secret. CDG (A pro rege et regina populoque christiano ΓA in another missa pro regibus HS pro rege et regina JW pro rege et regina liberisque (uel filiis J) eorum R pro imperatore).

Variants in AHJSW, which are obviously due to the different purposes for which the mass is used in these books, are not recorded.

l. 29. + q. *post* suscipe S *post* dne. H. tue + quas S.

l. 30. ·n· *om.* (*exc.* GΓJ) *post* nostri J. regis nostri *om.* GΓAR. te *om.* (*exc.* C). supplicantis (-tes AHJS) *om.* D *ante* ut antiqua (l. 31) AHJSW. in *om.* ADGHJSW.

l. 31. populorum + quas (*om.* S) tuae maiestati offerimus HS. ut *ante* antiqua AHJSW. operare] te operante AHJSW.

l. 32. pacis *om.* AHJSW. christianorum ADHJSW romana G. libertas christiana C.

p. 86. l. 2. Read *sacramenti*.
    Postcommon. ACΓHJΛMRSWY.
    l. 2. salutaris . . . perceptio] communio salutaris ΛC oratio
    salutaris ΓJM oblatio salutaris HΛRY. perceptio *om*.† W.
    l. 3. tuum + regem nostrum ACHJSWY. 'n' *om*. CHJRY.
    ab *om*.† R. omnibus + q. HSY. et *om*. R.
    l. 4. obtineant† C. post *om*.† J.

PRO AMICIS CARNALIBUS.

l. 7. *Pro deuotis amicis* RZ (*marg.*), *Pro familiaribus* ACΓHJΛMWY,
Pro familiam† D, *Pro anniuersario* Z (*text*): without title in S (col.
741*).
    Collect. ACDΓHJΛMRSWYZ.
    l. 9. in] sancti. tuorum + cordibus (*exc.* HY) + corda HY.
    l. 10. infudisti ΓHJΛMRYZ. famulis + tuis DHY. et famula-
    bus] + 'n' D *om*. M. tuis] *om*. D + 'n' Λ + fratribus et
    sororibus nostris CS.
    l. 12. sunt placita C.
    Secret. ACDΓHJΛMRSWYZ.
    l. 15. q. *om*. Λ. dne. + d. ΓΛM. et famulabus *om*. ΓM. tuis
    + 'n' ΛΛ.
    l. 16. maiestati + et praesta S.
    l. 17. sacrificia *om*. (*exc.* C). benedictionis] beatitudinis ΓJΛ.
    l. 18. gloriam eterne felicitatis] aeterne beatitudinis gloriam Z.
    felicitatis] beatitudinis DΓHJΛMRYZ.
    Postcommon. ACDΓHJΛMRSWYZ.
    l. 20. haec + salutaria.
    l. 21. quorum + quarumque AHJRSWY.

PRO SEIPSO.

    Collect. DHRSW.
    l. 27. quesso] propitius R.
    l. 28. meorum + mihi. peccatorum] delictorum R. merear
    ministrare D merear famulari R.
    Secret. ΓHJΛMSWZ (R in another missa pro se ipso).
    l. 32. offerre ΛZ. indignus R.
    l. 33. meis manibus Z. ut et MWZ.
    l. 34. quo] quod S quatenus R atque J. per *om*. Z.
    l. 35. mysterii SHZ. exhibitione Z. peccatorum + meorum Λ.
    Postcommon. HRSW.
    l. 39. per huius . . . misterium (p. 87, l. 2) *om*. R. filii tui dni.
    nostri i. c. HS.

p. 87.   l. 3. et . . . percipere *om*. R.

MISSA S. SPIRITUS.

l. 5. The collects of this mass are, as in most books, identical with
those for Whitsunday, except that in the first of them *hodierna die* is
omitted. For collations see above on p. 42 sq.
l. 8. Read *spiritu*.

PRO EMUNDATIONE CARNIS.

l. 16. The title of this mass varies. C has *Missa spiritus sancti*,
Γ *Missa de spiritu sancto*, and similarly W has the three collects as
alternatives in the *Missa de sancto spiritu*. DHSZ have *Ad inuocandam*

(*poscendam* DZ) *gratiam spiritus sancti*, P *De gratia sancti spiritus postulanda*, Λ *De cordis enundatione per spiritum sanctum postulanda*, Y *Ad postulandam gratiam.*

Collect. CDΓHΛPSWY.

l. 19. quem *om.* DΓΛ.

Secret. CDΓHΛPSWY.

l. 23. oblatio + q. HY. d.] *om.* C + q. S. ut] et ΓW.

l. 24. digna + in nobis D. habitatio efficiatur S.

l. 26. Read *offerentes.*

Postcommon. CDΓHΛPSWYZ.

l. 26. tibi offerentes] sumentes CΓHWYZ. nobis] *om.* W nos Z + q. CΓHSWY.

l. 27. dne.] o. Γ. d.] *om.* SZ + nr. D. + per gratiam sancti spiritus *ante* purificatis HSY. + q. *ante* purificatis Z. sepius *om.* C. celebrare] frequentare CHWY.

PRO PACE.

l. 33. Read *hostium.*

Collect. ACDGΓHJΛMRSWY.

l. 31. desideria + et G.

l. 32. tuis *om.* D. non potest dare M (*semel*).

l. 33. nostra *om.* G.

p. 88. l. 1. Read either *dicatae* with almost all MSS., or *dicatas* with D.

p. 87. **Secret.** ACDGΓHJΛMRSWY.

l. 36. concuti] noceri G.

p. 88. l. 1. dignare + et M. precibus et hostiis G. dicatae (*exc.* D) dicatas D + tibi (*ante* dicatas D). plebis+tuae D.

l. 2. pax + a GR. christianorum] romanos G.

l. 6. Read *supplices.*

Postcommon. ACDGΓHJΛMRSWY.

l. 7. ut] att C. in *om.* G. fidimus GM (*semel*).

PRO PETITIONE LACRIMARUM.

l. 9. *Pro lacrymis deuotionis* Y.

l. 12. Read *aquae.*

Collect. CDΓHJΛPRSY.

l. 11. o. + et RS. mitissime] clementissime CD mis. S.

l. 12. aquae uiuentis Λ.

l. 14. remissionemque + peccatorum R + eorum S. accipere mereamur S.

l. 18. Read *produc.*

l. 20. Probably we should read *ualeamus* with CS : but it is possible that *ualeant* is correct and *extingere* an error for *extingui*, which is found in most missals.

Secret. CDΓHJPRSY.

l. 17. hanc + igitur ΓJ. tuam *om.* quam . . . deus]q. dne. d. quam tuae maiestati (pietati C maiestati tuae Γ) (*exc.* HSY) quam tuae maiestati dne. HSY + supplices D. peccatis + nostris.

l. 18. q. *om.* respice propitius RS.

l. 19. nostris + copiosa HSY.

l. 20. ualeamus CS possint HY. extingui (*exc.* CS).

l. 24. Read *nostrorum.*

Postcommon. CPR (J as super populum).

l. 22. spiritus sancti R. dne. d. cordibus nostris.

l. 23.   nos + a R.   efficiat lacrimarum (*exc.* R).
l. 24.   atque + ad† C.
l. 25.   te largiente indulgentiae (*exc.* C).

PRO TEMPTATIONE CARNIS.

L 26.   This mass has the first person singular throughout, for the plural, in A.

Collect. ACΓHJAPRSWY.
l. 28.   corda nostra HY.
l. 29.   casto] caste et ΓJP.   corpore] corde J.   mundo *om.* ΓJAP.   corde] corpore CJ mente A.

l. 32.   Read *sacrificare.*
l. 33.   Read *absoluta.*

Secret. ACΓHJPRSWY.
l. 32.   dne. + igne sancti spiritus CS.   et *om.* (*exc.* JS).
l. 33.   libertate + ac munda mente S.   possimus + et C.   retribue . . . tribuisti *om.* HY.
l. 34.   saluare dignatus es ARW.

l. 38.   Read *pudicitiae uel*, with C.   The usual symbol for *uel* in Irish MSS. (†) is not unlike that for final *-lis* (l′).

Postcommon. ACHJAPRSWYZ.
l. 37.   dne.] d.HJY + d.S.   nr. et protector CHY.   nr. + q. P.   adiuua nos et *om.* JAP.   nos + per uirtutem sancti spiritus tua sancta sumentes HSY.   et *sec.*] ut AHSY.
l. 38.   nostra + uel C + et J.   uel] et (*exc.* C).   nouitatis W.

p. 89.   l. 1.   in *om.* J.   resurrectionis gaudio] resurrectione iustorum aeternis gaudiis A.   gaudium CARW.
l. 2.   iubeas + me A.

PRO PLUVIA POSTULANDA.

Collect. ACΓHJLAMRSWY.
l. 5.   et *pri. om.*

Secret. AGΓHJAMRSWY.
l. 9.   oblatis + q. RW.   tribue nobis G.

l. 12.   This postcommon is made up of two, the first of which is found in GΓAM, beginning *Tuere* and ending with *peccatis* (l. 13); the other in ΓJMR, running thus: *Da nobis q. dne.* (*dne. q.* ΓM) *pluuiam salutarem et aridam terrae faciem fluentis caelestibus dignanter infunde per.*   Only the first of these is included in the collations.   The two are combined as here in AW.

l. 14.   Read *aridam.*

Postcommon. AGΓAMW.
l. 12.   q. . . . . nos] tuere nos dne. q. (q. dne. AMW).
l. 13.   propitius GΓAM.   terramque . . . infunde *om.* GΓAM.

CONTRA PLUVIAM.

l. 16.   I have not found this mass elsewhere.   But the collect occurs as an alia for the postcommon in Gerbert, *Monumenta Veteris Liturgiae Alemannicae*, Typis San-blasianis, 1777, I. p. 303, and as a collect in the Liber Sacramentorum of Grimoldus (P p. 449), in addition to the places mentioned below.   The postcommon also occurs as a collect in Grimoldus (P p. 450).   The mass here serves the same purpose as that which follows, and these two are the only pair of alternative masses in the book (unless we are to except p. 87, ll. 5, 16).   The moist climate of Ireland suggests an explanation of the fact that there are two masses for fair weather. It is perhaps worthy of remark that there is no mass for rain in CD.

l. 20.   Read *inundationis*, or (with MP Gerb. &c.) *inundantium.*

> **Collect.** (MP one of two prayers for fair weather, headed in M *ad poscendam serenitatem*, in P *quando multum pluit*).
>
> l. 18.   *init.* + dne.   ministerio] in mysterio P in ministerio M. nostrae] tuae.
> l. 20.   inundantium.
> l. 21.   se *post* aquis P.   regenerationis P.
> l. 22.   esse *om.*   castigationibus P.

l. 25.   This is the second of three collects in a mass in G *ad poscendam serenitatem*, of which the third is the postcommon of this, and the first the collect of the next, mass.

l. 27.   Read *castigantis.*

> **Secret.** (G).
>
> **Postcommon.** (G as above Γ as collect of mass 'ad repellendam tempestatem' M 'oratio ad repellendam tempestatem').
>
> l. 30.   nos *om.*   seruientium naturam.
> l. 31.   instruis] instituis.

PRO SERENITATE AERIS.

p. 90. l. 1.   Read *praeueniente.*

p. 89.

> **Collect.** ACDGΓHJAMRSWY.
>
> l. 36.   clamantes + clementer A.
> l. 37.   iuste *post* nostris DGΓJAMW.

p. 90. l. 4.   Read *preueniat.*

> **Secret.** ACDGΓHJAMR (S for SS. Marcus and Marcellianus).
>
> l. 4.   dne. q. AH.   tua gratia M.
> l. 5.   semper *om.* H.
> l. 6.   offerimus] deferimus GΓHJAMR.   benignus *om.* H.
> l. 7.   intercessionem + omnium D.   cunctis + nobis DGΓJAMR proficiat S.   ad salutem *om.* D.
>
> **Postcommon.** ACDGΓHJAM (S for St. Richard).
>
> l. 10.   dne. + per haec sancta quae sumpsimus S.
> l. 11.   et + intercessione . . . S.   tuorum + semper S.   subleuemur S.   que . . . adiuuatur *om.* S.
> l. 12.   intercessionem† G intercessorum ACDH.

PRO ITER AGENTIBUS.

l. 13.   *Orationes ad proficiscendum in itinere* G.   The singular is used instead of the plural throughout in AM, and in the collect and secret in GJ.

> **Collect.** ACDGΓHJAMRSWY.
>
> l. 15.   uiam + et actus HY.
> l. 16.   tuorum + 'n' ADGΓAM.
> l. 17.   uiae et *om.* G.   et] ac D uel J.   huius *post* omnes HJY. protegamur CAW protegatur† Γ.

l. 21.   Read *quas.*

l. 22.   Read *precedente.*

> **Secret.** ACDGΓHJAMRSWY.
>
> l. 20.   propitiare + q. MS.   dne. *post* nostris R.   oblationes has M.
> l. 21.   tuis + 'n' ADGΓAMW.   ut] et DΓ. ˙
> l. 22.   illis D.   et *pri.*] + actus HY *om.* DJ.

l. 23. comitare GΓJR (*semel*). atque] ac D. eorum] illorum Λ
om.† G.

l. 24. praesidium D.

l. 29. Read *ituri*.

l. 31. Read *dexterae*. '

Postcommon. ACGΓM (J as collect 'pro fratribus in uia diri-
gendis' S as collect after mass).

l. 28. disiungunt M. tuis] *om.* C + 'n' AΓM. fidentibus GΓJM.

l. 29. et + praes taut S. per + omnem (*exc.* Λ). ituri] acturi G.
eis *om.* J. digneris S.

l. 30. nichil *pri.* . . . effectu (l. 33) *om.* AC. illis] eis S.

l. 31. eis] *om.* J + sint S. sint + et S. et] ut GS.

l. 32. iuste S. expetierunt G petierint S expetiemur J. celeri
+ et prospero S. consequamur J.

PRO INFIRMIS.

l. 34. The singular number is used in AHJSY throughout.

p. 91. l. 2. Read *referant*.

p. 90. **Collect.** AGΓHJΛMRSWY.

l. 37. orantes *om.* pro *pri.* + infirmis R.
tuis + 'n' (*exc.* R). pro *sec. om.* M.

p. 91. l. 2. tibi in ecclesia tua referant (conferant J) actionem
(actiones JR).

l. 7. Read *de eorum*.

Secret. AGΓHJΛMRSWY.

l. 4. d. + sub GMR. nutibus] uiribus W. suscipe + propitius A.

l. 5. tuorum] famularumque tuarum GΓΛ + 'n' HJSWY
misericordiae tuae MS.

l. 6. aegrotantibus *om.* S *post* quibus (l. 5) HMY. imploramus
+ auxilium MS. periculis M.

Postcommon. AGΓHJΛMRSWY.

l. 10. The postcommon is left incomplete (at the end of a page)
in the MS. Compare p. 11, l. 35, and p. 78, l. 23.

AD POSCENDA SUFFRAGIA OMNIUM SANCTORUM.

l. 11. This title is taken from D. The running title is that found
in ASWY. ΓR have the same title as D except that they omit *omnium* ;
and similarly Z *Missa omnium sanctorum.* H has *Oratio dicenda de
omnibus sanctis in dominicis et in festis ix lectionum*, J *In honore
omnium sanctorum*, Λ *Ad suffragia sanctorum postulanda*, C *Missa
communis.*

l. 18. Read *sentiamus*.

Collect. ACDΓHJΛRSWY.

l. 13. o. + et mis. H.

l. 14. nos *post* tuorum (l. 17) HS. sanctę + dei. genitricis
+ semperque uirginis HY. sanctorumque DΓJΛR. celestium . . . profetarum *om.* DΓJΛR.

l. 15. beatorum] sanctorum Y. apostolorum + euangelis-
tarum SY.

l. 16. martirum + et Γ. atque uirginum *om.* Γ. atque] ac Λ
et J *om.* D.

l. 17. tuorum] *om.* C. ut] et Γ.

l. 18. dnm.] eundem ASY.

Secret. ACDΓHJΛRSWY.

l. 20.   q. *om.* (*exc.* ACW). dne. q. CW. intercedente . . .
cum] intercedentibus DΓJΛR. intercedente + b. ACHSWY
+ et gloriosa semperque uirgine S.
l. 21.   genitrice + semperque uirgine HY.
l. 22.   dnm.] eundem AWY.
Postcommon.   ACDΓHJΛRSΣWY (L mense Aprili).
l. 24.   sanctae marie et *om.* DΓJLΛΣ. omnium *om.* Σ sanctae]
b. HRSWY + dei genetricis HSY + semper uirginis SY.
mariae + semper uirginis RW. omnium *om.* ΓJLΛ.
l. 25.   tuorum *om.* C. merita] memoriam HRS commemora-
cionem W sollemnia DΓJLΛΣ. recolentes] facientes WY celebrantes DΓJLΛΣ. caelestia sacramenta LΣ. praesta q.]
quorum suffragiis q. largiaris L.
l. 26.   agimus] gerimus. eorum . . . adiuti *om.* DΓJLΛRΣ.

MISSA COMMUNIS.

l. 28.   The title of this mass takes many forms, but they are generally
equivalent to that of JW, *Pro uiuis atque defunctis.* In HS it is
simply *Oratio generalis* : in C *Missa communis.* In D it has no title.
Collect.   ACDΓHJΛPRSWY.
l. 31.   misereris *om.* P.
l. 32.   supplices RW. exoramus] exoro ΓP imploramus J.
l. 33.   decreui ΓP. adhuc uel praesens J.
l. 34.   saeculum adhuc CDPRSW.
l. 35.   suscepit + intercedentibus omnibus sanctis tuis R.

p. 92.   l. 1.   omnium *post* clementia (p. 91, l. 35) CDRSW *om.* ΓHJPY.
et gaudia *om.* ΓPR. consequi mereantur] consequantur ΓPR.
mereatur† W. eterna *om.* ΓPR.
Secret.   ACDΓHJΛPRSWY.
l. 4.   superna] eterna W.
l. 5.   locandorum P. quaeso ΓP. ut + intercedentibus omnibus
sanctis tuis R.
l. 6.   suscepi ΓP. uel] et CDHRWY siue S. nomina omnium
fidelium R. fidelium + uiuorum atque mortuorum CDHWY.
l. 7.   scripta A.
l. 13.   Read *ablutio.*
Postcommon.   ACDΓHJΛRWY.
l. 10.   purificet AJR. o. et mis. d. *om.* C. et mis. *om.* A.
l. 11.   sacramentum quod A. et + intercedentibus omnibus
sanctis R. hoc tuum sacramentum *om.* A. tuum] tui mysterii
Γ corporis tui W.
l. 13.   ad ueniam] adueniat† C. ablutio] remissio J. sit *sec.*]
om. Λ + defensio et ereptio de manibus omnium inimicorum
nostrorum sit D.
l. 14.   omnia *om.* CΓHJΛY.
l. 15.   fidelium *om.* ΓJ. omnium remissio D.
l. 16.   delictorum] peccatorum AHJΛY. per &c.] qui uiuis W.

PRO OMNIBUS FIDELIBUS DEFUNCTIS.

l. 17.   Most of the parts of this mass are found in S. In the main E
follows the missa pro trigintalibus of S.
Collect.   ACGΓHJΛPRSWY.
Expressed in the singular number in ΓJΛPRWY.
l. 24.   inclina + q. G. aures tuas G. nostras + pro G.
l. 25.   deprecamur] exoramus G.

l. 26. famularumque tuarum] tuorum (*exc.* GHS) + 'n' ΛΓJΛΡW. quas . . . iusisti *om.* G. quas] quem Λ (*semel*).

l. 27. in *om.*† C.

l. 28. tuorum *om.* G.

l. 29 sqq. The first three of these epistles are found in CHRSWY, with some diversity as to the occasions of their use. The books mentioned agree in giving also one or more epistles taken from I Cor. xv, CR having vv. 51–57, WSY vv. 20–23, while H has both these passages.

Second Epistle. Inflection mark over *Title* tesolonicenses.

l. 36. Read *fortissimus.*

p. 93. l. 2. I have not found this lesson elsewhere in the mass for the dead. But at Salisbury (Procter and Wordsworth, *Sarum Breviary*, vol. ii. col. 274), Aberdeen (*Aberdeen Breviary*, vol. ii, pt. i. f. 83 v.), York and Hereford (*York Manual*, Surtees Society, vol. lxiii. pp. 68, 123*) it was the responsory to the first lesson at matins in the office of the dead.

l. 6. This is the ℣ in ACDWY. IᵃHS have *Animae eorum*, R *In memoria aeterna.*

l. 9. There is no tract in Iᵃ.

l. 14. Read *sustinui.*

l. 15 sqq. A has the same four Gospels as E : CR have likewise four, but replace our fourth by Joh. v. 24 (R 25)–29 : HW have five, adding to the four here given (of the second of which H omits the last verse) Joh. v. 24–29 : while to these five S (which again omits the last verse of the second) and Y add a sixth, Joh. vi. 53 sq.

l. 31. Iᵃ has a different offertory : *Erue dne. animas.* ℣. *Tuam d. piissime.*

l. 32. Read *eas.*

l. 33. Read *in* : the scribe having mistaken 7 for ī. Compare above on p. 11, l. 31.

l. 36. ℣ is inserted here on the authority of AR. The rubric for the use of *Hostias* is in Y 'Sacerdos ad altare incipiat,' in C 'Sacerdos se inclinat et dicit,' in S 'Post ablutionem manuum incipiat sacerdos . . . in medio altaris,' in W 'Faciendo oblacionem sacerdos super corporalia cum calice et patena dicat,' and in H 'Sacerdos . . calicem eleuans deuote dicat.'

l. 37. Read *quarum. Tu suscipe* is assigned to the choir in CHS.

l. 39 sqq. From *Hanc lucem* to *dne. ihesu* (p. 94, l. 9) I have not found elsewhere.

l. 40. Read *quam.* The symbols for *quam* and *quia* are easily confused in Irish manuscripts.

Offertory. ACDHRSWY.

l. 32. manu] paenis R. lacus D.

l. 33. absorbeat (*exc.* CD) absorueat C obsorbeat D. obscurum R obscuris A + tenebrarum loca HSWY.

l. 36. dne. + laudis R.

l. 37. agimus] facimus DR.

l. 39. hanc . . . ihesu (p. 94, l. 9) *om.*

p. 94. l. 3. Read *uniuersarum.*

l. 4. Read *ille, eas.*

l. 5. Read *regionibus tenebrosis.*

l. 11. Read *humanae.*

l. 12. Read *absoluat.*

Secret. ACHSW (J in another missa pro defuncto).

Expressed in the singular in JW.

l. 11. tuorum] famularumque tuarum HS + 'n' AW + dne. J. uitiis] *om.*† C + et peccatis JW. conditionis humanae HJS.

l. 12. q. dnc. *ante* ab (l. 11) HS. quae + etiam HS.
l. 16. Read *es.*
l. 19 sqq. *Pro quorum* is a separate common in S for use 'in omnibu missis pro corpore praesenti et in omnibus anniuersariis et trigintalibus et in die animarum et quando ultimo fit seruitium mortuorum ante pascha,' ll. 15-18 serving for all other occasions. In C it is the common, ll. 15-18 being omitted. In AHRWY it is entirely omitted. In D the common is *Ego sum resurrectio.*

Postcommon. ACΓHJΛPSWY.

Expressed in the singular in JΛPWY.

l. 24. nobis + q. H. ut *om.* C *post* sumpsimus (l. 25) HS. per . . . sumpsimus *om.* AΓJΛPWY. sanctum *om.* HS.

l. 25. tuorum] famularumque tuarum HS + famularumque tuarum C + 'n' AΓJΛPW. quam + semper (*exc.* CHW).

l. 26. mereantur *om.*† C. accipere Λ (*semel*). delictorum] peccatorum (*exc.* ACS).

PRO EPISCOPO DEFUNCTO.

l. 27 sqq. The interchange of *sacerdos, episcopus, pontifex* and their cognates, in the different authorities in these two masses, is very remarkable. It is no doubt a survival of the ancient use of *sacerdos* as the equivalent of bishop. Thus in the present mass *sacerdos* would seem throughout to be a very early, if not the earliest reading, being changed to *episcopus* or *pontifex* when *sacerdos* became limited to the second order. The mass *pro sacerdote defuncto* appears to have been originally for a deceased bishop, and, in consequence of this change in the signification of the word *sacerdos*, to have been assigned in later books to priests. The reading *episcopi* in G at p. 95, l. 4, should be noticed in this connexion. See Bishop Dowden's monograph, *Observations and conjectures on the Kirkmadrine Epitaphs*, in the *Proc. of the Soc. of Ant. of Scotland*, vol. xxxii, p. 247 sqq.

l. 27. In GJΛZ the heading is *Pro defuncto sacerdote*, in R *Pro defunctis episcopis seu sacerdotibus.* The title here supplied is in the singular, in accordance with the analogy afforded by the next mass. The singular number is used in the collects in AGJLΛMWY.

Collect. ACDGHJLΛMRSWY.

l. 29. qui *om.*† G. tuos + 'n' (*exc.* HRSY).

l. 30. pontificali] *om.* JL sacerdotali AM + seu sacerdotali R. dignitate (*om.* J) censeri fecisti JY. dignitate *om.* JL. censeri] uigere AGLMR + pontificem L. quorum . . . terris (l. 31) *om.* GLMR.

l. 31. gerebant] regebat† J. ad horam gerebant (gessit Λ) CHΛS. ad horam *om.* Y. eorum + quoque GΛMR + et G. perpetuo *om.* Λ perpetua L. consortio . . . caelis] aggregentur consortio GMR quoque sede potiatur L.

Secret. ACDGJLΛMRWY.

l. 34. q. *om.* AW. dne. q. CLMR. famuli + et G. tuorum] *ante* quas (l. 35) G + et Λ.

l. 35. pontificum] sacerdotum (-tis) AGJΛMW episcoporum DLY + seu sacerdotum R + tui Λ. + 'n' *post* tuorum (l. 34) ALM *ante* quas GΛW. quas] preces nostras pro quibus D. quas offerimus *om.* L. hostias offerimus D. hostias *ante* pro (l. 34) L. ut *om.* D. quibus + in hoc seculo R. pontificale cui M. pontificale] sacerdotale AJ + seu sacerdotale R.

l. 36. misterium] ministerium ΛW meritum (*ante* donasti Λ) DGJLΛMRY + in celesti regno R. donasti J. dones et

praemium] sanctorum tuorum iubeas coniungi consortio R.
premium] meritum ACW.

l. 37. The postcommon is headed *Ad complendum pro sacerdote* in Z.

Postcommon. ACDGJAWYZ.

l. 38. dne. + q. D. et] ut CZ + per haec sacrosancta mysteria DW.

l. 39. famulorum + et Λ. + ˙n˙ *post* tuorum ACDGW *ante* in ΛZ. tui *ante* ˙n˙ in Λ. pontificum] sacerdotum (-tis) AJΛZ episcopi GY. uiuorum regione GJΛ. iubeas (iube C) gaudiis AC.

PRO SACERDOTE DEFUNCTO.

p. 95. l. 1. Between this and the preceding mass C has a ' Missa pro abbate defuncto.'

The singular number is used throughout in GHMS.

Collect. CGHS (M as postcommon 'pro episcopo defuncto').

l. 4. tuorum + ˙n˙ GM. sacerdotum] episcopi G.

l. 5. letitięque + in C (*lapsu*) G. regione G. in *om.* C. societatem G.

Secret. CHS.

l. 8. dne. + d. nr. (*exc.* C).

l. 10. ut] et (*exc.* C). pertinere] peruenire (*exc.* C).

l. 11. The secret is left unfinished at the end of the last page of the gathering. It seems most likely that this gathering was followed by another, now lost, which contained the remainder of the present mass, and probably other masses for the dead. But this cannot be regarded as quite certain : other masses have been left incomplete by the scribe. See p. 11, l. 35 ; p. 78, l. 23 ; p. 91, l. 10.

INDEX OF LITURGICAL FORMS.

O 2

---

[1] Two different collects.

---

[1] MS. ' Domine ne *et cā* ' : which seems to mean the seven penitential psalms (*cf.* C p. 100), however the abbreviation is to be expanded (? = *et caetera*).

[1] Two different collects.

---

[1] Different collects.

¹ Two (or possibly three) different collects.

¹ After 'dixit' follows 'ihesus,' 'dominus,' or 'dominus ihesus.'

[1] See p. 197, note.

---

[1] A different lesson from the two others.

ROSSLYN.   P

Exsultabunt sancti in gloria   ...   .*gr.* C 173 ; D 55 ; E 70 :
                                off. C 173 ; D 47, 60, 72 ; E 71

Exsultate
    deo adiutorio ...   .   *int.-ps.* C 137 ; E 37
    iusti in dno.   ...   . *int.-ps.* C 174, 184 ; D 55 ; E 61, 71
                           gr. D 58 : *com.* C 175, 185 ; D 61 ; E 72)
Exsultatio diuina pietas   ...   .   Σ 246 (228)
Exsultet iam angelica turba   ...   .   C 126
Exsurgat d. et dissipentur   ...   ...   *int.-ps.* C 58, 143 ; E 42 : *ps.* C 81
Exsurge
    dne. non praeualeat ...   .*gr.* E 21
    quare obdormis   ...   .*int.* E 14
Exsurgens princeps sacerdotum ...   .*ep.* D 43

Fac nos *q. dne. (dne. q.)*
    b. uirginum tuarum continuis   ...   .   D 81
    his muneribus offerendis   ...   .   C 103 ; E 18
Facta est contentio inter ...   .*eu.* D 44
Factum est cum
    apollo esset corinthi   ...   .*ep.* E 41 (C 141)
    loqueretur i. ad turbas   ...   ...   *eu.* C 60, 164 ; D 8 ; E 63, 80
Factum est
    in uigilia matutina   ...   .   *lesson* C 130 ; E 33
    uerbum dni. ad me dicens priusquam   ...   ...   *ep.* C 154 ; E 56
Factus est repente de caelo   ...   .   *com.* C 144 ; D 16 ; E 43
Famulorum tuorum dne. munus   ...   .   D 69
Fecisti mirabilia dne. cum patribus   ...   .   Σ 226 (192)
Felix *nanque (om.* D 7 ; E 80: *ualde* C 61) *es sacra (est sacra* E 63 : *sacra* C 61 :
           sacra es D 7) uirgo *gr.* D 7 : *off.* C 61, 164 ; D 8 ; E 63, 80
Fiat
    commixtio *et (om.)* consecratio : *see* Haec sacrosancta commixtio
    dne. misericordia tua...   ...   .   ℣ Σ 241 (219) *bis*
Fideles
    tui d. *per tua dona (perpetuo don? : perpetuis donis) firmentur (formentur)*
                                            C 100 ; E 14
    tuos dne. benignus intende ...   .   C 115
Fidelibus tuis *dne.* (*d.*) perpetua : *see* Fideles tui
Fidelis seruus et prudens quem ...   .   *com.* C 186 ; D 68 ; E 154
Fidelium d. omnium conditor   ...   .   C 80
Fili
    dei fecisti mirabilia ...   .   Σ 226 (192)
    quid fecisti nobis sic ...   :   ...   .   *com.* E 12
Fortitudo mea et laudatio...   ...   .   ℣ Σ 225, 229 (199)
Fuit
    homo missus a deo ...   .   *gr.* C 155, 156 ; E 57, 58
    in diebus herodis   ...   .   *eu.* C 155 ; E 57
Fulgebunt iusti et tanquam   ...   .   *gr.* E 6

Gaude maria uirgo cunctas   ...   .   *tr.* C 149 ; E 52
Gaudeamus omnes in dno.   ...   ...*int.* C 147, 165, 168, 174, 191 ; D 73 ;
                                         E 63, 66, 71, 154
Gaudens gaudeo in dno. ...   .*ep.* E 63
Gaudete
    iusti in dno.   ...   ...   *gr.* D 58 : *com.* C 175, 185 ; D 61 ; E 72
                       (*int.-ps.* C 174, 184 ; D 55 ; E 61, 71)
    perfecti estote exhortamini ...   .   *ep.* C 56 (D 4 ; E 77)
Gauisi sunt discipuli uiso ...   .   *gr.* C 137
Gloria
    et honore coronasti eum   ...   *gr.* C 182 ; D 49 : *off.* C 155, 177, 181 ;
                                          D 42 ; E 57
    in excelsis deo   ...   .   E 35 ; Σ 227 (196)

----

[1] Two different collects.

---

[1] Different collects.

---

[1] Different collects.

ROSSLYN.   Q

[1] *See also* Dignum et iustum.

⊕[1] Et te in

  purificatione uel annunciatione[2] . . . mariae   C 61 ; E 45 (C 61, 150)
  sanctorum tuorum uirtute   ...   .   D 68
  ueneratione sacrarum uirginum   ...   ...   C 61, 150 (C 61 ; E 45)

Et te
  laudare mirabilem deum   ...   .   D 46
  quidem omni tempore   ...   ...   C 134, 136 ; E 36 (D 11 ; E 45)

Et tuam *immensam clementiam* (*misericordiam*)   ...   ...   D 42

Exorantes clementer exaudire dignare : *see* Dne. sancte pater o. aeterne d. qui
                                                                    omnia

Fons et origo   ...   .   E 147
Misericordiae dator et totius   ...   ...   D 56

Per quem
  maiestatem tuam   ...   C 53 ; D 19 ; E 73
  salus mundi   ...   C 74 ; D 34 ; Σ 233 (206)

Qui
  ad laudem nominis   ...   .   D 67
  ascendens super omnes   ...   ...   C 142, 144 ; E 45
  corporali ieiunio uitia...   ...   ...   C 103 ; D 31 ; E 44

Qui cum
  unigenito *filio* (*om.* Σ) tuo   ...   ...   C 57 ; D 5 ; E 73 ; Σ 233 (206)
  unigenitus tuus : *see* ⊕ Quia cum

Qui
  ecclesiam tuam in   ...   .   D 47
  foedere nuptiarum   ...   .   C 82
  glorificaris in tuorum...   ...   .   D 72
  humanum genus   ...   .   D 54
  (+ *in*) infirmitate uirtutem ...   .   D 78
  inuisibili potentia   ...   .   C 200
  nobis in christo   ...   .   D 39
  nos assiduis m. passionibus ...   .   D 60
  per filii tui uocationem   ...   .   D 48
  post resurrectionem ...   .   D 14 ; E 45
  sacramentum paschale (*sacramenta paschalia*)   ...   ...   D 16
  salutem humani generis   ...   .   C 60 ; D 6 ; E 45
  ut de hoste humani   ...   .   D 81

Quia
  cum unigenitus tuus   ...   ...   E 44
  dignum et iustum est ...   ...   C 127
  notam fecisti in populis   ...   C 98
  per incarnati uerbi   ...   C 88 ; E 44

Quoniam
  a te constantiam   ...   .   D 61
  sicut humanum genus : *see* ⊕ Et maiestatis omnipotentiam

  tuo dono actum est ut   ...   .   D 79

Te
  in tuorum apostolorum N.   ...   .   D 48
  quidem (+ *dne.*) omni tempore   ...   D 11 ; E 45 (C 134, 136 ; E 36)

Teque laudare mirabilem : *see* Et te laudare

Uere sanctus uere benedictus   ...   .   Σ 246 (228)
Ueritas mea et misericordia   ...   .   *off.* C 187 ; D 67 (E 154)
Uespere autem sabbati quae   ...   .   *eu.* C 134 ; E 35 : *ant.* C 135
Uias tuas dne. demonstra   ...   .   *int.-ps.* C 85
Uidens turbas i. ascendit ...   .   *eu.* C 175 ; D 59
Uideo caelos apertos   ...   .   *gr.* C 93 ; E 4 : *com.* C 93 ; E 4
Uiderunt omnes *fines* (*termini* E 8)   ...   ...   *gr.* C 91 ; E 7 : *com.* C 92 ; E 3, 8

---

[1] *See also* Dignum et iustum.
[2] *ueneratione* C : other books read *commemoratione.* The majority omit *purifica-tione uel.*

INDEX OF NAMES AND SUBJECTS.

LONDON :

HARRISON AND SONS, PRINTERS IN ORDINARY TO HER MAJESTY,

ST. MARTIN'S LANE.

HENRY BRADSHAW SOCIETY,

FOR EDITING RARE LITURGICAL TEXTS.

1891. I. MISSALE AD USUM ECCLESIÆ WESTMONASTERIENSIS, fasc. i. Edited by Dr. J. WICKHAM LEGG F.S.A. 8vo.
[Dec. 1891.]

III. THE MARTILOGE, 1526. Edited by the Rev. F. PROCTER M.A., and the Rev. E. S. DEWICK, M.A., F.S.A. 8vo.
[May, 1893.]

1892. II. THE MANNER OF THE CORONATION OF KING CHARLES THE FIRST, 1626. Edited by the Rev. CHR. WORDSWORTH, M.A. 8vo. [Dec. 1892.]

IV. THE BANGOR ANTIPHONARIUM. Edited by the Rev. F. E. WARREN, B.D., F.S.A. Part I. containing complete facsimile in collotype, with historical and palæographical introduction. **4to.** [Aug. 1893.]

1893. V. MISSALE AD USUM ECCLESIÆ WESTMONASTERIENSIS, fasc. ii. Edited by Dr. J. WICKHAM LEGG, F.S.A. 8vo.
[Aug. 1893.]

VI. OFFICIUM ECCLESIASTICUM ABBATUM SECUNDUM USUM EVESHAMENSIS MONASTERII. Edited by the Rev. H. A. WILSON, M.A. 8vo. [Aug. 1893.]

1894. VII. TRACTS OF CLEMENT MAYDESTONE, viz. DEFENSORIUM DIRECTORII and CREDE MICHI. Edited by the Rev. CHR. WORDSWORTH, M.A. 8vo. [Oct. 1894.]

VIII. THE WINCHESTER TROPER. Edited by the Rev. W. HOWARD FRERE, M.A. 8vo. [Nov. 1894.]

1895. IX. THE MARTYROLOGY OF GORMAN. Edited by WHITLEY STOKES, D.C.L., Foreign Associate of the Institute of France. 8vo. [July, 1895.]

X. THE BANGOR ANTIPHONARIUM, Part II. containing an amended text with liturgical introduction, and an appendix containing an edition of Harleian MS. 7653. Edited by the Rev. F. E. WARREN, B.D., F.S.A. **4to.** [Nov., 1895.]

1896. XI. THE MISSAL OF ROBERT OF JUMIÈGES, BISHOP OF LONDON, A.D. 1044–1051, AND ARCHBISHOP OF CANTERBURY IN A.D. 1051. Edited from a MS. in the Public Library at Rouen, by the Rev. H. A. WILSON, M.A. 8vo. [July, 1896.]

XII. MISSALE AD USUM ECCLESIÆ WESTMONASTERIENSIS, fasc. iii. Containing an appendix giving certain Offices from Westminster MSS. in the Bodleian Library and the British Museum, together with full indices, notes, and a liturgical introduction. Edited by Dr. J. WICKHAM LEGG, F.S.A. 8vo. [Nov. 1897.]

1897. XIII. THE IRISH LIBER HYMNORUM. Edited from MSS. in the Libraries of Trinity College, and the Franciscan Convent at Dublin by the Rev. JOHN H. BERNARD, D.D., and ROBERT ATKINSON, I.L.D. Vol. I., Text and Glossary.
XIV. Vol. II., Notes and Translations of the Irish Prefaces and Hymns. 8vo. [July, 1898.]

1898. XV. THE ROSSLYN MISSAL. An Irish manuscript in the Advocates' Library, Edinburgh. Edited by the Rev. H. J. LAWLOR, D.D. 8vo. [April, 1899.]

The following Works are in preparation :

THE CORONATION BOOK OF CHARLES V. OF FRANCE. Edited by the Rev. E. S. DEWICK, M.A., F.S.A., with reproductions in collotype of the miniatures which illustrate the ceremony. 4to. [In the Press.]

MISSALE ROMANUM, Milan, 1474. (The first printed edition of the Roman Missal.) Edited by the Rev. ROBERT LIPPE, LL.D. [In the Press.]

THREE ENGLISH CORONATION ORDERS : (1). The Coronation Order of William III. and Mary II. (2.) An Anglo-French version of the English Coronation Order. (3.) A Pre-Norman Coronation Order. Edited by Dr. J. WICKHAM LEGG, F.S.A. [In the Press.]

THE HEREFORD BREVIARY. Edited by the Rev. W. HOWARD FRERE, M.A. 8vo. [In the Press.]

ABBOT WARE'S CONSUETUDINARY OF WESTMINSTER. Edited by Sir E. MAUNDE THOMPSON, K.C.B., LL.D., D.C.L., F.S.A. 8vo. [In the Press.]

FACSIMILES OF HORÆ B.M.V., reproduced in collotype from English MSS. of the 11th Century. Edited by the Rev. E. S. DEWICK, M.A., F.S.A. 4to. [In the Press.]

THE PROCESSIONAL OF THE NUNS OF ST. MARY AT CHESTER. With English rubrics. Edited by Dr. J. WICKHAM LEGG, F.S.A.

[In the Press.]

CLEMENT MAYDESTONE'S DIRECTORIUM SACERDOTUM. Edited by (the late) Rev. Canon COOKE, M.A., and the Rev. CHRISTOPHER WORDSWORTH, M.A.

THE LITURGY OF ST. JAMES. Edited by the Rev. F. E. BRIGHT-MAN, M.A.

A MISCELLANEOUS VOLUME CONTAINING :

THE CANON OF THE MASS, AND ITS VARIANTS. Edited by the Rev. H. A. WILSON, M.A., and Dr. J. WICKHAM LEGG, F.S.A.

AN EDITION OF A BODLEIAN MS. (Wood MS. 17) Langforde's *Meditatyons for Goostly Exercyse in the tyme of the Masse.* Edited by Dr. J. WICKHAM LEGG, F.S.A.

A REPRINT OF *Instructio seu Alphabetum Sacerdotum.* Edited by Dr. J. WICKHAM LEGG, F.S.A.

Ordinarium Missæ. From an early 14th Century Sarum Missal formerly in the possession of the late Mr. WILLIAM MORRIS, F.S.A.

A MISCELLANEOUS VOLUME, containing facsimiles of early liturgical MSS., including an early copy of *Quicunque vult*, from an Irish MS. in the Ambrosian Library (O. 212, sup.). **4to.**

THE BENEDICTIONAL OF ROBERT OF JUMIÈGES. Edited by the Rev. H. A. WILSON, M.A.

April, 1899.

⁎ Persons wishing to join the Society are requested to communicate with the Hon. Secretary, the Rev. H. A. WILSON, Magdalen College, Oxford ; or with the Hon. Treasurer, the Rev. E. S. DEWICK, 26, Oxford Square, Hyde Park, London, W.

The books are issued to members in return for an annual subscription of one guinea, payable at the beginning of each year.